Crime Prevention Technologies and Applications for Advancing Criminal Investigation

Chang-Tsun Li
University of Warwick, UK

Anthony TS Ho
University of Surrey, UK

Managing Director:	Lindsay Johnston
Senior Editorial Director:	Heather A. Probst
Book Production Manager:	Sean Woznicki
Development Manager:	Joel Gamon
Acquisitions Editor:	Erika Gallagher
Typesetter:	Deanna Jo Zombro
Cover Design:	Nick Newcomer, Lisandro Gonzalez

Published in the United States of America by
Information Science Reference (an imprint of IGI Global)
701 E. Chocolate Avenue
Hershey PA 17033
Tel: 717-533-8845
Fax: 717-533-8661
E-mail: cust@igi-global.com
Web site: http://www.igi-global.com

Library of Congress Cataloging-in-Publication Data

Crime prevention technologies and applications for advancing criminal
investigation / Chang-Tsun Li and Anthony T.S. Ho, editors.
      p. cm.
  Includes bibliographical references and index.
  Summary: "This book addresses the use of electronic devices and software for
crime prevention, investigation, and the application of a broad spectrum of
sciences to answer questions of interest to the legal system"--Provided by
publisher.
  ISBN 978-1-4666-1758-2 (hbk.) -- ISBN 978-1-4666-1759-9 (ebook) -- ISBN 978-
1-4666-1760-5 (print & perpetual access) 1. Criminal investigation--
Technological innovations. 2. Crime prevention--Technological innovations. 3.
Law enforcement--Technological innovations. I. Li, Chang-Tsun. II. Ho,
Anthony T. S., 1958-
  HV8073.C6924 2012
  364.4028'4--dc23
                              2012002115

British Cataloguing in Publication Data
A Cataloguing in Publication record for this book is available from the British Library.

The views expressed in this book are those of the authors, but not necessarily of the publisher.

International Editorial Review Board

Table of Contents

Section 1
Multimedia Forensics Based on Intrinsic Data

Chapter 1

Roberto Caldelli, University of Florence, Italy
Irene Amerini, University of Florence, Italy
Francesco Picchioni, University of Florence, Italy

Chapter 2

Irene Amerini, University of Florence, Italy
Roberto Caldelli, University of Florence, Italy
Vito Cappellini, University of Florence, Italy
Francesco Picchioni, University of Florence, Italy
Alessandro Piva, University of Florence, Italy

Chapter 3

H. R. Chennamma, University of Mysore, India
Lalitha Rangarajan, University of Mysore, India

Section 2
Multimedia Security Based on Extrinsic Data

Chapter 4

Xi Zhao, University of Surrey, UK
Anthony T. S. Ho, University of Surrey, UK
Yun Q. Shi, New Jersey Institute of Technology, USA

Section 3
Applications of Cryptography in Digital Forensics

Section 4
Applications of Pattern Recognition and Signal Processing Techniques to Digital Forensics

Section 5
Digital Evidence

Detailed Table of Contents

Section 1
Multimedia Forensics Based on Intrinsic Data

Chapter 1
Roberto Caldelli, University of Florence, Italy
Irene Amerini, University of Florence, Italy
Francesco Picchioni, University of Florence, Italy

Digital images are generated by different sensors, understanding which kind of sensor has acquired a certain image could be crucial in many application scenarios where digital forensic techniques operate. In this paper a new methodology which permits to establish if a digital photo has been taken by a photo-camera or has been scanned by a scanner is presented. The specific geometrical features of the sensor pattern noise introduced by the sensor are investigated by resorting to a DFT (Discrete Fourier Transform) analysis and consequently the origin of the digital content is assessed. Experimental results are provided to witness the reliability of the proposed technique.

Chapter 2
Irene Amerini, University of Florence, Italy
Roberto Caldelli, University of Florence, Italy
Vito Cappellini, University of Florence, Italy
Francesco Picchioni, University of Florence, Italy
Alessandro Piva, University of Florence, Italy

Identification of the source that has generated a digital content is considered one of the main open issues in multimedia forensics community. The extraction of photo-response non-uniformity (PRNU) noise has been so far indicated as a mean to identify sensor fingerprint. Such a fingerprint can be estimated from multiple images taken by the same camera by means of a de-noising filtering operation. In this paper, the authors propose a novel method for estimating the PRNU noise in source camera identification. In particular, a MMSE digital filter in the un-decimated wavelet domain, based on a signal-dependent noise model, is introduced and compared with others commonly adopted for this purpose. A theoretical framework and experimental results are provided and discussed.

H. R. Chennamma, University of Mysore, India

Lalitha Rangarajan, University of Mysore, India

A digitally developed image is a viewable image (TIFF/JPG) produced by a camera's sensor data (raw image) using computer software tools. Such images might use different colour space, demosaicing algorithms or by different post processing parameter settings which are not the one coded in the source camera. In this regard, the most reliable method of source camera identification is linking the given image with the sensor of camera. In this paper, the authors propose a novel approach for camera identification based on sensor's readout noise. Readout noise is an important intrinsic characteristic of a digital imaging sensor (CCD or CMOS) and it cannot be removed. This paper quantitatively measures readout noise of the sensor from an image using the mean-standard deviation plot, while in order to evaluate the performance of the proposed approach, the authors tested against the images captured at two different exposure levels. Results show datasets containing 1200 images acquired from six different cameras of three different brands. The success of proposed method is corroborated through experiments.

Section 2
Multimedia Security Based on Extrinsic Data

Xi Zhao, University of Surrey, UK

Anthony T. S. Ho, University of Surrey, UK

Yun Q. Shi, New Jersey Institute of Technology, USA

In the past few years, semi-fragile watermarking has become increasingly important to verify the content of images and localise the tampered areas, while tolerating some non-malicious manipulations. In the literature, the majority of semi-fragile algorithms have applied a predetermined threshold to tolerate errors caused by JPEG compression. However, this predetermined threshold is typically fixed and cannot be easily adapted to different amounts of errors caused by unknown JPEG compression at different quality factors (QFs). In this paper, the authors analyse the relationship between QF and threshold, and propose the use of generalised Benford's Law as an image forensics technique for semi-fragile watermarking. The results show an overall average QF correct detection rate of approximately 99%, when 5%, 20% and 30% of the pixels are subjected to image content tampering and compression using different QFs (ranging from 95 to 65). In addition, the authors applied different image enhancement techniques to these test images. The proposed image forensics method can adaptively adjust the threshold for images based on the estimated QF, improving accuracy rates in authenticating and localising the tampered regions for semi-fragile watermarking.

Roland Kwitt, University of Salzburg, Austria

Peter Meerwald, University of Salzburg, Austria

Andreas Uhl, University of Salzburg, Austria

In this paper, the authors adapt two blind detector structures for additive spread-spectrum image watermarking to the host signal characteristics of the Dual-Tree Complex Wavelet Transform (DT-CWT) domain coefficients. The research is motivated by the superior perceptual characteristics of the DT-CWT and its active use in watermarking. To improve the numerous existing watermarking schemes in which the host signal is modeled by a Gaussian distribution, the authors show that the Generalized Gaussian nature of Dual-Tree detail subband statistics can be exploited for better detector performance. This paper finds that the Rao detector is more practical than the likelihood-ratio test for their detection problem. The authors experimentally investigate the robustness of the proposed detectors under JPEG and JPEG2000 attacks and assess the perceptual quality of the watermarked images. The results demonstrate that their alterations allow significantly better blind watermark detection performance in the DT-CWT domain than the widely used linear-correlation detector. As only the detection side has to be modified, the proposed methods can be easily adopted in existing DT-CWT watermarking schemes.

Chapter 6

Yaqing Niu, Communication University of China, China

Sridhar Krishnan, Ryerson University, Canada

Qin Zhang, Communication University of China, China

Perceptual Watermarking should take full advantage of the results from human visual system (HVS) studies. Just noticeable distortion (JND), which refers to the maximum distortion that the HVS does not perceive, gives a way to model the HVS accurately. An effective Spatio-Temporal JND model guided video watermarking scheme in DCT domain is proposed in this paper. The watermarking scheme is based on the design of an additional accurate JND visual model which incorporates spatial Contrast Sensitivity Function (CSF), temporal modulation factor, retinal velocity, luminance adaptation and contrast masking. The proposed watermarking scheme, where the JND model is fully used to determine scene-adaptive upper bounds on watermark insertion, allows providing the maximum strength transparent watermark. Experimental results confirm the improved performance of the Spatio-Temporal JND model. The authors' Spatio-Temporal JND model is capable of yielding higher injected-watermark energy without introducing noticeable distortion to the original video sequences and outperforms the relevant existing visual models. Simulation results show that the proposed Spatio-Temporal JND model guided video watermarking scheme is more robust than other algorithms based on the relevant existing perceptual models while retaining the watermark transparency.

Chapter 7

B. R. Matam, Aston University, UK

David Lowe, Aston University, UK

This paper addresses the security of a specific class of common watermarking methods based on Dither modulation-quantisation index modulation (DM-QIM) and focusing on watermark-only attacks (WOA). The vulnerabilities of and probable attacks on lattice structure based watermark embedding methods have been presented in the literature. DM-QIM is one of the best known lattice structure based watermarking techniques. In this paper, the authors discuss a watermark-only attack scenario (the attacker has access to a single watermarked content only). In the literature it is an assumption that DM-QIM methods are secure to WOA. However, the authors show that the DM-QIM based embedding method is vulnerable against a guided key guessing attack by exploiting subtle statistical regularities in the feature space embeddings for time series and images. Using a distribution-free algorithm, this paper presents an analysis of the attack and numerical results for multiple examples of image and time series data.

Section 3
Applications of Cryptography in Digital Forensics

Chapter 8

Niall McGrath, University College Dublin, Ireland
Pavel Gladyshev, University College Dublin, Ireland
Joe Carthy, University College Dublin, Ireland

When encrypted material is discovered during a digital investigation and the investigator cannot decrypt the material then he or she is faced with the problem of how to determine the evidential value of the material. This research is proposing a methodology titled *Cryptopometry*. *Cryptopometry* extracts probative value from the encrypted file of a hybrid cryptosystem. *Cryptopometry* also incorporates a technique for locating the original plaintext file. Since child pornography (KP) images and terrorist related information (TI) are transmitted in encrypted formats, the digital investigator must ask the question *Cui Bono?*—who benefits or who is the recipient? By following *Cryptopometry*, the scope of the digital investigation can be extended to reveal the intended recipient. The derivation of the term *Cryptopometry* is also described and explained.

Chapter 9

Qiming Li, Institute for Infocomm Research, Singapore
Sujoy Roy, Institute for Infocomm Research, Singapore

A robust hash function allows different parties to extract a consistent key from a common fuzzy source, e.g., an image gone through noisy channels, which can then be used to establish a cryptographic session key among the parties without the need for interactions. These functions are useful in various communication scenarios, where the security notions are different. The authors study these different security notions in this paper and focus on forgery attacks, where the objective of the attack is to compute the extracted key (hash value) of a given message. This paper will examine information-theoretical security against forgery under chosen message attacks. The authors prove that it is not possible due to the entropy of the hash value of a given message can be reduced arbitrarily when sufficient message/hash pairs have been observed. In this regard, the authors give a computationally secure scheme, where it is computationally infeasible to compute the hash value even when its entropy may not be high.

Chapter 10

Natthawut Samphaiboon, Asian Institute of Technology, Thailand
Matthew N. Dailey, Asian Institute of Technology, Thailand

Steganography, or communication through covert channels, is desirable when the mere existence of an encrypted message might cause suspicion or provide useful information to eavesdroppers. Text is effective for steganography due to its ubiquity; however, text communication channels do not necessarily provide sufficient redundancy for covert communication. In this paper, the authors propose a novel steganographic embedding scheme for Thai plain text documents that exploits redundancies in the way particular vowel, diacritical, and tonal symbols are composed in TIS-620, the standard Thai character set. This paper provides a Thai text stegosystem following a provably secure construction that guarantees covertness, privacy, and integrity of the hiddentext message under meaningful attacks against computational adversaries. In an experimental evaluation, the authors find that the message embedding scheme allows 203 bytes of embedded hiddentext message per 100KB of covertext on average, and that the document modifications are not readily noticed by observers. The stegosystem is thus a practical and effective secure system for covert communication over Thai plain text channels.

Section 4
Applications of Pattern Recognition and Signal Processing Techniques to Digital Forensics

Jin Liu, Huazhong University of Science and Technology, China

Hefei Ling, Huazhong University of Science and Technology, China

Fuhao Zou, Huazhong University of Science and Technology, China

Weiqi Yan, Queen's University Belfast, UK

Zhengding Lu, Huazhong University of Science and Technology, China

In this paper, the authors investigate the prospect of using multi-resolution histograms (MRH) in conjunction with digital image forensics, particularly in the detection of two kinds of copy-move manipulations, i.e., cloning and splicing. To the best of the authors' knowledge, this is the first work that uses the same feature in both cloning and splicing forensics. The experimental results show the simplicity and efficiency of using MRH for the purpose of clone detection and splicing detection.

Jonathan Weir, Queen's University Belfast, UK

Raymond Lau, Queen's University Belfast, UK

WeiQi Yan, Queen's University Belfast, UK

In this paper, the authors splice together an image which has been split up on a piece of paper by using duplication detection. The nearest pieces are connected using edge searching and matching and the pieces that have graphics or textures are matched using the edge shape and intersection between the two near pieces. Thus, the initial step is to mark the direction of each piece and put the pieces that have straight edges to the initial position to determine the profile of the whole image. The other image pieces are then fixed into the corresponding position by using the edge information, i.e., shape, residual trace and matching, after duplication or sub-duplication detection. In the following steps, the patches with different edge shapes are searched using edge duplication detection. With the reduction of rest pieces, the montage procedure will become easier and faster.

Kosta Haltis, University of Adelaide, Australia

Matthew Sorell, University of Adelaide, Australia

Russell Brinkworth, University of Adelaide, Australia

Biological vision systems are capable of discerning detail as well as detecting objects and motion in a wide range of highly variable lighting conditions that proves challenging to traditional cameras. In this paper, the authors describe the real-time implementation of a biological vision model using a high dynamic range video camera and a General Purpose Graphics Processing Unit. The effectiveness of this implementation is demonstrated in two surveillance applications: dynamic equalization of contrast for improved recognition of scene detail and the use of biologically-inspired motion processing for the detection of small or distant moving objects in a complex scene. A system based on this prototype could improve surveillance capability in any number of difficult situations.

Chapter 14

Moussadek Laadjel, Algerian National Centre for Research and Development, Algeria
Ahmed Bouridane, Northumbria University, UK
Fatih Kurugollu, Queen's University Belfast, UK
WeiQi Yan, Queen's University Belfast, UK

This paper introduces a new technique for palmprint recognition based on Fisher Linear Discriminant Analysis (FLDA) and Gabor filter bank. This method involves convolving a palmprint image with a bank of Gabor filters at different scales and rotations for robust palmprint features extraction. Once these features are extracted, FLDA is applied for dimensionality reduction and class separability. Since the palmprint features are derived from the principal lines, wrinkles and texture along the palm area. One should carefully consider this fact when selecting the appropriate palm region for the feature extraction process in order to enhance recognition accuracy. To address this problem, an improved region of interest (ROI) extraction algorithm is introduced. This algorithm allows for an efficient extraction of the whole palm area by ignoring all the undesirable parts, such as the fingers and background. Experiments have shown that the proposed method yields attractive performances as evidenced by an Equal Error Rate (EER) of 0.03%.

Section 5
Digital Evidence

Chapter 15

Gary Edmond, University of New South Wales, Australia

This article examines the standards governing the admission of new types of expert evidence. Based on the rules of evidence and procedure in Australia, it explains how judges have been largely uninterested in the reliability of expert opinion evidence. Focused on the use of CCTV images and covert sound recordings for the purposes of identification, but relevant to other forensic sciences, the article explains the need for interest in the reliability of incriminating expert opinion evidence. It also explains why many of the traditional trial safeguards may not be particularly useful for identifying or explaining problems and complexities with scientific and technical evidence. In closing, the article argues that those developing new types of evidence and new techniques, whether identification-based or derived from IT, camera or computer forensics, need to be able to explain why it is that the court can have confidence in any opinions expressed.

Chapter 16

Kevin Curran, University of Ulster, UK
Andrew Robinson, University of Ulster, UK
Stephen Peacocke, University of Ulster, UK
Sean Cassidy, University of Ulster, UK

During the past decade, technological advances in mobile phones and the development of smart phones have led to increased use and dependence on the mobile phone. The explosion of its use has led to problems such as fraud, criminal use and identity theft, which have led to the need for mobile phone forensic analysis. In this regard, the authors discuss mobile phone forensic analysis, what it means, who avails of it and the software tools used.

Cloud computing has been heralded as a new era in the evolution of information and communications technologies. ICT giants have invested heavily in developing technologies and mega server facilities, which allow end users to access web-based software applications and store their data off-site. Businesses using cloud computing services will benefit from reduced operating costs as they cut back on ICT infrastructure and personnel. Individuals will no longer need to buy and install software and will have universal access to their data through any internet-ready device. Yet, hidden amongst the host of benefits are inherent legal risks. The global nature of cloud computing raises questions about privacy, security, confidentiality and access to data. Current terms of use do not adequately address the multitude of legal issues unique to cloud computing. In the face of this legal uncertainty, end users should be educated about the risks involved in entering the cloud.

This paper concerns the use of in-depth analytical/conceptual techniques pertaining to the Artificial Intelligence domain to deal with narrative information (or "narratives") in the terrorism- and crime-related areas. More precisely, the authors supply details about NKRL (Narrative Knowledge Representation Language), a representation and querying/inferencing environment especially created for an advanced exploitation of all types of narrative information. This description will be integrated with concrete examples that illustrate the use of NKRL tools in two recent 'defence' applications, the first dealing with a corpus of "Southern Philippines terrorism" news stories used in an R&D European project, the second, carried out in collaboration with the French "Délégation Générale pour l'Armement" (DGA, Central Bureau for Armament), which handles news stories about Afghanistan's war.

Preface

The unprecedented development and convergence of information and communication technology (ICT), computational hardware, and multimedia techniques witnessed in the last decade have revolutionized how people exchange information, learn, work, interact with others and go about daily life at the personal level. At the organisational and global level, these techniques have enabled a wide range of services across national borders through e-commerce, e-business, and e-governance powered by the existing IT infrastructures and emerging cloud computing. This wave of ICT revolution has undoubtedly brought about enormous opportunities for the world economy and exciting possibilities for every sector of the modern societies. Willingly or reluctantly, directly or indirectly, we are all now immersed in a cyberspace, full of e-opportunities and e-possibilities, and permeated with rich multimedia and information. However, this type of close and strong interweaving also causes concerns and poses threats. When exploited with malign intentions, the same technologies provide means for doing harms at colossal scale. The £1.3 billion loss of the Swiss banking group, UBS, due to unauthorised trading by a rogue trader in its investment bank is just one of many typical examples. These concerns create anxiety and uncertainty about the reality of the information and business we deal with, the security the information infrastructures we are relying on today and our privacy. Due to the rise of digital crime and the acute need for methods of fighting these forms of criminal activities, there is an increasing awareness of the importance of digital forensics and investigation. As a result, the last decade has also seen the emergence of the new interdisciplinary research field of digital forensics and investigation, which aims at pooling expertise in various areas to combat the abuses of the ICT facilities and computer technologies.

The primary objective of this book is to provide a media for advancing research and the development of theory and practice of digital crime prevention and forensics. This book embraces a broad range of digital crime and forensics disciplines that use electronic devices and software for crime prevention and investigation, and addresses evidential issues. It encompasses a wide variety of aspects of the related subject areas and provides a scientifically and scholarly sound treatment of state-of-the-art techniques to students, researchers, academics, personnel of law enforcement, and IT/multimedia practitioners, who are interested or involved in the research, use, design, and development of techniques related to digital forensics and investigation. This book is divided into five main sections according to the thematic areas covered by the contributed chapters.

- Section 1. Multimedia Forensics Based on Intrinsic Data
- Section 2. Multimedia Security Based on Extrinsic Data
- Section 3. Applications of Cryptography in Digital Forensics

- Section 4. Applications of Pattern Recognition and Signal Processing Techniques to Multimedia Forensics and Security
- Section 5. Digital Evidence

It should be noted that these five parts are closely related. Such a division is only meant to provide a structural organisation of the book to smooth the flow of thoughts and to aid the readability, rather than proposing a taxonomy of the study of digital forensics.

Section 1. Multimedia Forensics Based on Intrinsic Data

This section of the book is concerned with the use of intrinsic data (i.e., information extracted from multimedia content) in multimedia forensic investigations such as source device identification, device linking, and content integrity verification. Usually the process of acquiring an image with an ordinary digital camera is as follows. The light from the scene enters a set of lenses and passes through an anti-aliasing filter before reaching a colour filter array (CFA) that is intended to admit one of the red (R), green (G) and blue (B) components of the light per pixel for the following semi-conductor sensor to convert the signal into electronic form. A de-mosaicing process is subsequently carried out to get the intensities of the other two colours for each pixel by interpolating the colour information within a neighbourhood. A sequence of image processing operations, such as colour correction, white balancing, Gamma correction, enhancing, JPEG compression, et cetera then take place before the photo is saved in the storage medium. The hardware or software used in each stage in the image acquisition process may leave unique traces in the content, which can lead to the identification of the imaging device. As such, to help with forensic investigations, researchers have proposed ways of identifying and linking source devices, classifying images and verifying the integrity of images based on the detection of existence or local inconsistencies of device attributes or data processing related characteristics, such as sensor pattern noise (SPN), camera response function, re-sampling artefacts, colour filter array (CFA) interpolation artefacts, JPEG compression, lens aberration, et cetera. Other device and image attributes such as binary similarity measures, image quality measures and higher order wavelet statistics have also been exploited to identify and classify source devices.

While many methods require that specific assumptions be satisfied, methods based on sensor pattern noise have drawn much attention due to the relaxation of the similar assumptions. Another advantage of sensor pattern noise is that it can identify not only camera models of the same make, but also individual cameras of the same model. The deterministic component of sensor pattern noise (SPN) is mainly caused by imperfections during the sensor manufacturing process and different sensitivity of pixels to light due to the inhomogeneity of silicon wafers. It is because of the inconsistency and the uniqueness of manufacturing imperfections and the variable sensitivity of each pixel to light that even sensors made from the same silicon wafer would possess uncorrelated pattern noise, which can be extracted from the images produced by the devices. This property makes sensor pattern noise a robust fingerprint for identifying and linking source devices and verifying the integrity of images. Another type of intrinsic data related to sensor is sensor readout noise. This section of the book covers the first three chapters, concerned with the use of sensor-based intrinsic data for multimedia forensic applications.

In chapter 1, *A DFT-Based Analysis to Discern between Camera and Scanned Images*, Caldelli *et al.* propose a novel approach to determining as to whether a digital image has been taken by a camera or has been scanned by a scanner. Such a technique exploits the specific geometrical features of the sensor pattern noise (SPN) left in the content by the sensor of the devices in both cases and analyse the frequency spectrum of the images to infer if periodical patterns exist. If periodicity exists in the frequency domain along the scanning direction, the image is deemed as having been taken by a scanner. Experimental results are presented to support the theoretical framework.

The sensor pattern noise and scene details coexist in the high-frequency band of images. Because the magnitudes of scene details tend to be many orders greater than those of the sensor patter noise, the estimated sensor pattern noise is actually highly contaminated by scene details. As such, a central part of sensor pattern noise estimation methodologies is the filter used to sift the high-frequency components. Chapter 2, *Estimate of PRNU Noise Based on Different Noise Models for Source Camera Identification*, presented by Amerini *et al.*, introduces another novel method for estimating sensor pattern noise as device fingerprint for source camera identification. The focus of this work is to study the characteristics of different filters involved in the analysis of sensor pattern noise. Based on the effective application of the MMSE filter in speckle and film-grain noise removal in coherent radiation imaging systems, the author propose to use a MMSE digital filter in the undecimated wavelet domain for estimating sensor pattern noise. They assume that the digital camera noise is dependent on the sensed signal when applying the MMSE filter. The proposed method is compared with the Mihcak filter - a signal-independent noise model. Their experimental results show that when the noise model matches the actual digital image acquisition process, the filter based on such a signal-dependent model (e.g., the MMSE filter) yields better performances if the parameters needed for the filtering operation are accurately estimated.

Chennamma and Rangarajan discussed *Source Camera Identification Based on Sensor Readout Noise* in chapter 3. Readout noise is a unique and intrinsic characteristic of a CCD or CMOS digital imaging sensor, which can be used in multimedia forensic applications by connecting the unique noise pattern to the source camera. First, the authors discuss the related work about source camera identification and describe the basic processing stages carried out inside a typical digital camera. Then they explain the origin of readout noise in digital cameras and how to measure it using the mean-standard deviation plot. Application of the proposed approach to the identification of source camera model based on readout noise is presented to validate their technique.

Section 2. Multimedia Security Based on Extrinsic Data

This section of the book is concerned with multimedia content protection and authentication through the embedding of extrinsic data. This set of techniques is about protecting the value of digital content or verifying the integrity and authenticity by embedding secret data in the host media and matching the hidden secret data against the original version at a later stage. Compared to cryptography, the use of extrinsic data for content protection is a relatively younger discipline. Digital watermarking is a typical example of content protection and authentication based on extrinsic data. It has been an active research area in the past 15 years. This set of digital watermarking techniques have found their applications in copyright protection (e.g., ownership identification, transaction tracking/traitor tracing and copy control), which is of great interest to the multimedia and movie industry. They are also applicable to content integrity verification and authentication, which is of high interest to the security sector, medical community, legal systems, et cetera. To ensure the security of these content protection schemes, the sophistication of countermeasures and attack models have to be in the mind of the developers of the protection schemes.

Semi-fragile and fragile digital watermarking has been widely employed for multimedia authentication and content integrity verification. The main difference between these two classes of watermarking schemes is that the former is made to be sensitive to only malicious manipulations of image content and to remain insensitive to incidental manipulations. These incidental manipulations include compression and mild signal processing operations due to transmission distortion. Because JPEG compression is the most common approach to saving storage and bandwidth, a substantial proportion of semi-fragile watermarking algorithms were designed to tolerate JPEG compression. However, watermarked images may be compressed with unknown JPEG Quality factors (QF). As a result, to be able to authenticate the watermarked images, a pre-determined threshold is set for most watermarking schemes to allow an anticipated QF bound. However, the predetermined threshold is usually rigidly fixed, making the schemes inadaptable to different levels of distortions caused by unknown QF set in the JPEG compression. In chapter 4, *Image Forensics Using Generalised Benford's Law for Improving Image Authentication Detection Rates in Semi-Fragile Watermarking*, Zhao *et al.* analyse the relationship between the QF and threshold, and propose to use the generalised Benford's Law to detect the unknown QF of the images before the scheme carries out watermark extraction. They observed an overall average QF correct detection rate of approximately 99% when 5%, 20%, and 30% of the image content are subjected to manipulation as well as compression using different QFs (ranging from 95 to 65). In addition, the authors also applied different image enhancement techniques (i.e., another form of incidental manipulation) to test images and observed that the QF correct detection rate can still be greater than 90%. The experiments described in this chapter indicate that their image forensic method can adaptively adjust the watermark detection threshold based on the estimated QF, making the proposed scheme more desirable in real-life applications.

While fragile and semi-fragile watermarking schemes (e.g., the schemes introduced in the previous chapter) are mainly intended for integrity verification and authentication, robust watermarking algorithms have been proposed for copyright protection through the embedding of an imperceptible, yet detectable watermark in digital multimedia content. Because the visual quality of the multimedia protected by robust watermarking should not be noticeably compromised by the embedding operation, human perception modelling has been an active research area in the digital watermarking community. The objective of the modelling is to strike a good balance between watermark imperceptibility and robustness. Transform domains such as the DCT or DWT facilitate decomposition of multimedia signals and allow adaptive selection of signal components for human perception modelling. Therefore, human perception modelling in the transform domains has been the mainstream approach. In chapter 5, *Blind Detection of Additive Spread-Spectrum Watermarking in the Dual-Tree Complex Wavelet Transform Domain*, Roland Kwitt *et al.* adapt two blind detector structures for additive spread-spectrum watermarking to the host media characteristics of the Dual-Tree Complex Wavelet Transform (DT-CWT) domain coefficients. The incentive of their research is the superior perceptual characteristics of the DT-CWT and its active use in watermarking. To improve the performance of the existing watermarking schemes in which the host media is modelled as a Gaussian distribution, the authors demonstrate that the Generalized Gaussian properties of Dual-Tree detail subband statistics can be exploited for better detector performance. They found that the Rao detector is has greater advantages over the likelihood-ratio test. They investigate the robustness of the proposed detectors under JPEG and JPEG2000 manipulations and evaluate the perceptual quality of the watermarked images. The results demonstrate that their DT-CWT domain approach significantly outperform the widely used linear-correlation detector. Because only the detection component of a complete watermarking scheme has to be modified to take the advantage of their findings, the proposed methods can be easily adopted in existing DT-CWT watermarking schemes.

Chapter 6 - *Spatio-Temporal Just Noticeable Distortion Model Guided Video Watermarking* - is also concerned with watermark imperceptibility. The authors, Yaqing Niu, Sridhar Krishnan, and Qin Zhang, address the imperceptibility issue surrounding spatio-temporal just noticeable distortion model guided video watermarking. They argue that perceptual watermarking should take full advantage of the outcomes from human visual system (HVS) researches. Just Noticeable Distortion (JND), which refers to the maximum distortion that the HVS cannot perceive, gives designer the reference for assuring watermark robustness without inflicting distortion noticeable to the HVS. The proposed watermarking scheme is based on a more accurate JND visual model which incorporates spatial Contrast Sensitivity Function (CSF), retinal velocity, luminance adaptation, temporal modulation factor, and contrast masking. The proposed watermarking scheme, in which a JND model is fully used to determine scene-adaptive upper bounds on watermark embedding, allows the user to provide the maximum strength transparent watermark.

Security of the watermark plays a central part in the design of feasible digital watermarking schemes because counter measures advance as the watermarking techniques evolve and can render new schemes useless if security gaps are left open. Chapter 7 - *Watermark-Only Security Attack on DM-QIM Watermarking: Vulnerability to Guided Key Guessing* - addresses the security of a specific class of common watermarking methods based on Dither Modulation-Quantisation Index Modulation (DM-QIM) with a focus on watermark-only attacks (WOA). DM-QIM is one of the well known lattice structure based watermarking techniques. The vulnerabilities of many lattice structure based watermark embedding schemes and possible attacks on these methods have been introduced in the literature. In this chapter, a watermark-only attack scenario (i.e., the attacker only has access to a single watermarked content) is discussed. In the literature, it is assumed that DM-QIM methods are secure against WOA. However, the authors of this chapter (Matam and Lowe) show that the DM-QIM based embedding schemes are vulnerable to a guided key guessing attack through the exploitation of subtle statistical regularities in the feature space embeddings for time series and images. Using a distribution-free algorithm, they conduct an analysis of the attack and present numerical results for multiple examples of image and time series data.

Section 3. Applications of Cryptography in Digital Forensics

Law enforcement agencies (LEA) quite often encounter encryption in their investigations to in the distribution of child pornography (KP) images and terrorist related information (TI). KP images in circulation are most likely to be encrypted so that the content can avoid being detected by watchful eyes and the anonymity of all involved parties can be preserved. Chapter 8 - *Cryptopometry as a Methodology for Investigating Encrypted Material* – is concerned with the identification of the PGP encrypted material. The authors of this chapter, Niall McGrath *et al.*, indicate that the use of PGP encryption is a major hurdle in the investigations into the distribution of child pornography images and terrorist related information. It is therefore important to enable digital forensic investigators to identify encrypted material, analyse it and finally extract valuable evidence or information from it. This chapter presents *Cryptopometry* - a methodology that facilitates the identification of the PGP encrypted material. A technique for identifying plaintext files that are encrypted is also presented. The incorporated search technique establishes correlation between the ciphertext file under investigation and the original plaintext file. A case study was carried out to validate the methodology. False positive rate is reported to be low.

A robust hash function allows involved parties to extract a consistent key from a common noisy data source (e.g., an image transmitted through a noisy channel), which can then be used to establish a cryptographic session key among the parties without having to transmit the key through a secure channel. This function is desirable in various communication applications, where the security notions are different. In chapter 9 - *Secure Robust Hash Functions and Their Applications in Non-interactive*

Communications - Li and Roy investigate these security notions and forgery attacks, where the objective of the attack is assumed to be the computation of the extracted key (i.e., the hash value) of a given message. They study information-theoretical and computational security against forgery under chosen message attacks and found that it is not possible to ensure information-theoretical security because it is not possible for the hash value in question to have conditional entropy that is not negligible, while keeping enough entropy for the secret key. They found that the entropy of the hash value of a given message can be reduced arbitrarily when sufficient message/hash pairs have been observed. However, they proposed a scheme that is computationally secure. With the scheme, it is computationally infeasible to compute the hash value even its entropy may not be high. They also analyze the collision resistance of robust hash functions in the scenario where the attacker attempts to manipulate messages to create a collision. They formulate a sufficient condition for a collision resistant robust hash function by using a pseudo-random transformation.

Steganography is the technique for covert communication. In Chapter 10, *Steganography in Thai Text*, Samphaiboon and Dailey propose text steganographic scheme with arbitrary documents written in the Thai language as cover media. Redundancies due to the way TIS-620 represents compound characters combining vowel, diacritical, and tonal symbols are exploited in the embedding process. The authors claim that their technique is applicable to any language whose Unicode character sets contain redundancies and the original covertext is not required at decoding side. The embedding capacity is as high as 203 bytes per 100 kilobytes, making the scheme practical for covert communication through text. Because the proposed embedding scheme hides secret data in plain text documents, it is robust against changes in font size and colour. The scheme is also proved to be robust against format changes, e.g., insertion of whitespace between words and line space adjustment. However, as the authors have reported, the scheme is not robust to insertion and deletion of SARA-AE, SARA-AM, and their replacements in the stegotext.

Section 4. Applications of Pattern Recognition and Signal Processing Techniques to Digital Forensics

Forensic investigators and law enforcement agencies quite often find themselves in the situations where evidence collection from electronic devices and scientific investigations into the implication of the evidence are required. This usually entails the use of signal processing and pattern recognition techniques either in the collection of evidence or in the analysis regarding the admissibility of evidence. Pattern recognition and digital signal processing have been in use by expert witnesses in forensic investigations for decades and their role is becoming increasingly important in law enforcement given the pace of the advances of electronic devices and ICT. Section 4 of this book deals with methods that harness these two sets of techniques for biometric applications and multimedia forensics.

Contributed by Liu *et al.*, chapter 11 - *Digital Image Forensics Using Multi-Resolution Histograms* - deals with the use of multi-resolution histograms (MRH) both in splicing detection and clone detection. The MRH of an image is employed to serve as the feature for describing the image and is then trained with a Support Vector Machine (SVM) to detect the splicing operations. With the MRH's simplicity and efficiency and the use of an SVM tool, the entire method is simple and highly efficient. Although the detection rate is only 65%, which did not really advance the state-of-the-art in splicing detection, the main contribution is the simplicity gain through the combination of MRH and SVM. To detect the clone operation within an image, the authors examine as to whether there are a number of similar block pairs with the same pair distance in an image or not. Again, MRHs are used as features of each image block.

Weir *et al.* present another splicing detection technique in chapter 12 - *Digital Image Splicing Using Edges*. The authors splice together an image that has been split up by using duplication detection. The nearest pieces are connected using edge searching and matching. For the pieces that have graphics or textures, the matching pieces are sought for using the edge shape and intersection between the two pieces. To start with, they mark the direction of each piece and put the pieces that have straight edges to the initial position to determine the profile of the whole image. The other pieces are then fixed into the corresponding position by using the edge information (shape, residual trace and matching) after duplication or sub-duplication detection. The patches with different edge shapes are searched for using edge duplication detection.

Taking inspiration from the biological vision system of insects, Haltis *et al.* implement a real-time biological vision model using a high dynamic range video camera and a General Purpose Graphics Processing Unit (GPGPU). The implementation of the proposed biologically-inspired vision system is based on the understanding that pixel-wise image processing could be computed in parallel using a parallel processing system designed for such graphics applications. The details are presented in chapter 13, *A Biologically Inspired Smart Camera for Use in Surveillance Applications*. The authors demonstrate the effectiveness of this photoreceptor-based processing in two surveillance applications: 1) dynamic equalization of contrast for improved recognition of scene detail and 2) the use of biologically-inspired motion processing for the detection of small or distant moving objects in a complex scene.

Chapter 14, *Palmprint Recognition Based on Subspace Analysis of Gabor Filter Bank*, by Laadjel *et al.*, presents a novel technique for palmprint recognition based on Fisher Linear Discriminant Analysis (FLDA) and Gabor ðreco bank. This approach involves the convolution of a palmprint image with a bank of Gabor ðlters at deferent scales and orientations for robust palmprint feature extraction. After the features are extracted, FLDA is applied to reduce feature dimension. In order to enhance the recognition accuracy, the authors suggest that, when selecting the appropriate palm region for extracting features, one should take into account the fact that palmprint features are derived from the principal lines, wrinkles and texture along the palm area. To tackle this problem, the authors proposed an improved region of interest (ROI) extraction algorithm, which allows for an efficient extraction of the whole palm area by ignoring all the undesirable areas, such as ðngers and background.

Section 5. Digital Evidence

Maintaining the chain-of-custody for evidence is of paramount importance in civil and criminal legal cases. To ensure the admissibility of evidence in the court of law, technical measures applied in the digital forensic investigation procedures are required to assure not only that evidence is not tampered with or manipulated due to their application, but that malicious attacks aiming at hiding or manipulating evidence are effectively detected. To serve these purposes, like physical world forensic investigation, digital forensic investigation usually has to follow three main steps:

1) *Event preservation* which entails, for example, the need for a bit-by-bit duplication of the volatile memory or file systems;
2) *Evidence search* which aims at collecting forensic information such as making timelines of system and file activities, device fingerprint (e.g., sensor pattern noise of digital cameras), keywords, contraband media, telecommunication data, steganography;

3) *Event Reconstruction* which is about interpreting the collected information /evidence in order to establish what have happened and who has involved in what.

To address the need for maintaining the admissibility of digital evidence, the fifth part of this book covers three chapters concerning with technical and legal issues surrounding the chain-of-custody for evidence.

Chapter 15, *Suspect Sciences? Evidentiary Problems with Emerging Technologies*, contributed by Gary Edmond, critically examine the response to new forms of incriminating expert opinion evidence in Australia based on recent developments surrounding the admission of expert evidence derived from images and sound recordings. This chapter argues that forensic sciences, biometrics and other forms of expert identification and comparison of evidence, along with incriminating expert opinion evidence, should all be demonstrably reliable before they are relied upon in criminal proceedings. The chapter begins with a succinct introduction to regulations governing the admissibility of expert evidence in Australia and then considers several cases exemplifying the ways Australian courts have responded to new and emerging modalities of expert opinion evidence in order to explain some of the problems with contemporary jurisprudence and practice. Gary Edmond concludes that emerging fields and disciplines should be thinking about forms of *self-regulation* that is scientifically legitimate. These forms of self-regulation should not rely on judges to come up with lists of qualified experts or devise standards and protocols. Judges usually are not expected to undertake such tasks. While self-regulation may involve sanctions and exclusion, perhaps the better approach is to have consensus statements about techniques and processes that have been tested along with the practices. If such statements are grounded in scientific research, developed in conjunction with scientists and experts from other fields, and widely accepted, they will provide practitioners with genuine assistance.

Recent technological advances in mobile phones functionalities and the development of smart phones technologies have provided enormous convenience for people to go about their daily life. However, they also provide powerful aids to criminals operating in many walks of the modern society. This entails effective measures for mobile phone forensic analysis in the fight against crime. Chapter 16, authored by Curran *et al.*, study many aspects of mobile phone forensic analysis, what it means, who avails of it and the commonly used software tools. The author start the chapter with an overview of forensic guidelines drafted by the British Association of Chief Police Officers (ACPO) for handling computer (including mobile phone) based electronic evidence. The authors also examine the process of the extraction of data from the Subscriber Identity Module (SIM) and phones and highlight some popular mobile phone forensics applications.

Cloud computing has emerged, not just as a new concept, but as a new paradigm for applications of information and communications technologies. The last few years has witnessed ICT providers investing heavily in developing technologies and enormous server facilities which allow global end users to access web-based applications and store their data off-site. However new concerns go hand in hand with new wave of ICT evolution. In chapter 17, *Grey Areas? The Legal Dimensions of Cloud Computing*, Michael Davis and Alice Sedsman start with the introduction of the benefits cloud computing has brought about and covers many aspects of human society where cloud computing can have significant impact. These includes payment models, free cloud services, access to data, centralised service, privacy issues and security, some cause of concerns regarding terms of use, intellectual property, and jurisdiction for disputes. The authors believe that in the face of this legal uncertainty, end users and industrial practitioners should be educated about the risks involved in the use of the cloud so that they can make informed choices about the applications for which cloud computing is an appropriate platform. The protection of end users is particularly important when cloud computing end user licence agreements give small players little or no opportunity to negotiate the terms. They conclude that as the world moves online, there is greater need for the laws that apply to these new activities to become more adaptive to international realities.

Narrative information in general is about the account of real-life or fictional scenarios ("narratives") that involve physical or imaginary characters, who would attempt to experience particular situations, attain specific results, manipulate tangible or abstract materials, send or receive messages, conduct transactions, et cetera. Narratives consist of temporally ordered sequences of elementary events. Chapter 18 - *A Conceptual Methodology for Dealing with Terrorism "Narratives"*, contributed by Gian Piero Zarri, concerns the use of in-depth symbolic techniques pertaining to the artificial intelligence domain to deal with "narratives" in the crime- and terrorism-related areas in the Intelligent Information Retrieval (IIR) style. The author provides some details about the Narrative Knowledge Representation Language (NKRL), which is a representation and querying/inferencing environment especially designed for advanced exploitations of all sorts of narrative information. This description is integrated with real-life examples that illustrate the use of NKRL tools in two recent defence applications, the first dealing with a corpus of "Southern Philippines terrorism" news stories used in an R&D European project, the second, carried out in collaboration with the French "Délégation Générale pour l'Armement" (DGA, Central Bureau for Armament), which handles news stories about Afghanistan's war.

Chang-Tsun Li
University of Warwick, UK

Anthony T. S. Ho
University of Surrey, UK

Section 1
Multimedia Forensics Based on Intrinsic Data

Chapter 1
A DFT–Based Analysis to Discern Between Camera and Scanned Images

Roberto Caldelli
University of Florence, Italy

Irene Amerini
University of Florence, Italy

Francesco Picchioni
University of Florence, Italy

ABSTRACT

Digital images are generated by different sensors, understanding which kind of sensor has acquired a certain image could be crucial in many application scenarios where digital forensic techniques operate. In this paper a new methodology which permits to establish if a digital photo has been taken by a photo-camera or has been scanned by a scanner is presented. The specific geometrical features of the sensor pattern noise introduced by the sensor are investigated by resorting to a DFT (Discrete Fourier Transform) analysis and consequently the origin of the digital content is assessed. Experimental results are provided to witness the reliability of the proposed technique.

1. INTRODUCTION

Digital images are nowadays used in the majority of the application fields in place of "old" analog images because of their easiness of usage, quality and above all manageability. These favourable issues bring anyway an intrinsic disadvantage: digital content can be simply manipulated by ordinary users for disparate purposes so that origin and authenticity of the digital content we are looking at is often very difficult to be assessed with a sufficient degree of certainty. Scientific instruments which allow to give answers to basic questions regarding image origin and image authenticity are needed (Chen, 2008). Both these issues are anyway connected and sometimes are investigated together. In particular, by focusing on assessing image origin, two are the main aspects

DOI: 10.4018/978-1-4666-1758-2.ch001

to be studied: the first one is to understand which kind of device has generated that digital image (e.g., a scanner, a digital camera or it is computer-generated) (Lyu, 2005; Khanna, 2008) and the second one is to succeed in determining which kind of sensor has acquired that content (i.e., the specific camera or scanner, recognizing model and brand) (Chen, 2008; Khanna, 2007; Gou, 2007). The main idea behind this kind of researches is that each sensor leaves a sort of unique fingerprint on the digital content it acquires due to some intrinsic imperfections and/or due to the specific acquisition process. Various solutions have been proposed in literature among these the use of CFA (Color Filter Array) characteristics (Swaminathan, 2008) is quite well-know, nevertheless two seem to be the main followed approaches. The first one is based on the extraction, from images belonging to different categories (e.g., scanned images, photos, etc.), of some robust features which can be used to train a SVM (Support Vector Machine). When training is performed and whether features grant a good characterization, the system is able to classify the digital asset it is asked to check. The second approach is based on the computation of fingerprints of the different sensors (this is particularly used in sensor identification) through the analysis of a certain number of digital contents acquired by a device (e.g., images scanned by a particular scanner, photos taken by a camera and so on). Usually fingerprints are computed by means of the extraction of PRNU noise (Photo Response Non-Uniformity) (Chen, 2008; Mondaini, 2007) through a digital filtering operation; PRNU presence is induced by intrinsic disconformities in the manufacturing process of silicon CCD/CMOSs. After that the PRNU of the to-be-checked content is compared with the fingerprints and then it is classified. In this paper a new technique to distinguish which kind of device, a digital scanner or a digital camera, has acquired a specific image is proposed. Because of the structure of CCD set, the (PRNU) noise pattern, left over a

digital image, will have a completely different distribution: in the scanner case it should show a mono-dimensional structure repeated row after row in the scanning direction, on the other hand, in the camera case, the noise pattern should present a bi-dimensional template. On the basis of this consideration we construct a 1-D signal and by resorting to a DFT analysis, which exploits the possible existence of a periodicity, understanding which has been the acquisition device. The paper lay-out is the following: Section 2 introduces a characterization of the sensor pattern noise and the periodicity is discussed, in Section 3 the proposed methodology is presented and Section 4 describes thresholds selection based on ROC curves. In Section 5 some experimental results are brought to support theoretical theses and conclusions are drawn in Section 6.

2. SENSOR PATTERN NOISE CHARACTERIZATION

PRNU (Photo Response Non-Uniformity) noise is quite well-known as being an effective instrument for sensor identification because it is deterministically generated over each digital image it acquires. Such a noise is therefore an intrinsic characteristic of that specific sensor. The extraction of this noise is usually accomplished by denoising filters (Mihcak, 1999) and information it contains are used to assess something on the sensor characteristics. If we focus our attention on the acquisition process, it is easy to comprehend that when a photo is taken by a digital camera, basically a PRNU with a bi-dimensional structure is superimposed to it; on the contrary, when a digital image is created by means of a scanning operation the sensor array which slides over the to-be-acquired asset located on the scanner plate leaves its mono-dimensional fingerprint row by row during scanning. So in the last case, it is expected that a certain periodicity of the 1-D noise signal is evidenced along the scanning direction. This behaviour should be absent in the camera case and this difference can be investigated to discern between images coming from the two different kinds of device. Being $R(i, j)$ with $1 \leq i \leq N$ and $1 \leq j \leq M$, the noise extracted by the scanned image of size $N \times M$, and assuming i (row) as scanning direction, it can, at least ideally, be expected that all the rows are equal (see Equation 1).

$$R(i, j) = R(k, j), \forall 1 \leq j \leq M, 1 \leq i, k \leq N \tag{1}$$

So if a 1-D signal, $\mathbf{S}$ of $N \times M$ samples, is constructed by concatenating all the rows, it happens that $\mathbf{S}$ is a periodical signal of period M (Equation 2).

$$\mathbf{S} = [R(1,1), \cdots, R(1, M), \cdots, R(N, 1), \cdots, R(N, M)] \tag{2}$$

It is also worthy to point out that if the 1-D signal is mounted along columns direction (i.e. this would be right assuming that j is the scanning direction), $\mathbf{S}$ is not periodical anymore, but it is constituted by diverse constant steps each of length M. A periodical signal such as $\mathbf{S}$, represented in Equation 2, contains a number of repetitions equal to N and therefore will have basically a frequency spectrum made by equispaced spikes. Such spikes will be spaced of $(N \times M) / M = N$ and will be weighted by the spectrum of the basic replica of the signal. So most of the energy of such a signal is located in these spikes. Obviously this is what should happen, in practice the 1-D signal will be corrupted and its periodical structure altered. Consequently the spectral spikes will be reduced and their magnitude partially spread over the other frequencies. If it is still possible to individuate such peaks, it will be simple to distinguish between a scanned image and a digital photo.

3. THE PROPOSED METHODOLOGY

According to the idea presented in Section 2, let us describe in detail which is the proposed methodology to achieve that aim. The to-be-checked image I (size $N \times M$) is denoise filtered [8] obtaining I_d which is subtracted to the initial image to extract the sensor pattern noise R (see Equation 3).

$$R = I - I_d \tag{3}$$

To improve the possible presence of the deterministic contribution due to the 1-D PRNU pattern noise, R is divided into non-overlapping stripes (both horizontally and vertically, because both possible scanning directions have to be taken into account) and then all the different rows (columns) belonging to a stripe are averaged according to Equation 4 where L is the width of the stripe.

$$R_r(k) = \frac{1}{L} \sum_{i=1}^{L} R[i + (k-1)L], 1 \leq k \leq N / L \tag{4}$$

After that two new noise images, named *bar codes*, respectively R_r (size $N / L \times M$) and R_c (size $N \times M / L$), have been obtained; R_r and R_c have the same number of samples. If an image has been scanned in the row direction, for instance, it is expected that R_r will be composed by equal (ideally) rows, on the other side such a characterization can not be expected in the column direction for R_c and, above all, for an image coming from a digital camera (both directions): this circumstance is presented in Figure 1. *Bar codes* are then used to create the mono-dimensional signal by concatenating respectively rows of R_r and columns of R_c and then periodicity is checked. Sometimes to reduce randomness a low pass

Figure 1. Bar codes of size N/L × M (scanning direction = row): camera image (top), scanned image (center) and ideal bar code for a scanned image (bottom)

filtering operation (usually a median filter) is applied to bar codes, along the rows and the columns separately, before constructing 1-D signals.

For the sake of clarity, let us call S_r and S_c the two mono-dimensional signal, obtained as previously described, from R_r and R_c respectively. DFT (Discrete Fourier Transform) is applied to both these signals and the magnitude of the coefficients is considered. After that a selection is carried out on the basis of the following criterion: amplitude values above a threshold T_1 (see Equation 5 where α is a weighting factor where choice is discussed in Section 4) and at the same time located in the expected positions within the spectrum (see Section 2) are taken.

$$T_1 = \alpha * max(max(abs(DFT(S_r))), \\ max(abs(DFT(S_c)))) \qquad (5)$$

In the end all the values satisfying the previous selection criterion are added, separately for row and column cases, yielding to two energy factors, F_r and F_c respectively and their ratio $RATIO = F_r / F_c$ is computed. If the digital image has been scanned in the row direction, a high value of $RATIO$ is expected (if the scanning direction has been along columns $RATIO$ will be very small), otherwise if the image has been taken by a digital camera the two energy factors should be comparable and a value of $RATIO$ around one is foreseen. Doing so it is

possible not only distinguishing between images coming from a scanner or from a camera but, in the scanner case, determining the scanning direction. To improve robustness, this technique is applied to all the three image channels (R, G, B) and three energy contributions are collected in each factor F_r and F_c.

4. ANALYSIS OF THRESHOLDS THROUGH ROC CURVES

As seen in Section 3, the threshold T_1, that is used to evaluate energy of DFT of signals S_r and S_c, depends upon α parameter, besides there is another threshold T_2, for the $RATIO$ value, that makes possible to distinguish between images taken from scanners or digital cameras. Proper choice of these two parameters is a key problem to adequately control discrimination. To find optimal value for T_1 and T_2, is possible to use ROC (Receive Operating Characteristic or Relative Operating Characteristic) Curve. To introduce ROC Curve is necessary to define two new parameters:

- *Se* (Sensitivity): the fraction of images taken from a scanner correctly identified as such.
- *Sp* (Specificity): the fraction of images taken from a digital camera that are correctly identified as such.

Finding optimal thresholds is not limited to the statistical minimization of wrong classification, but it is also related to the minimization of the FRR (False Rejection Rate) for scanner images or digital camera images. ROC Curve permits to analyze more values of the thresholds to determine which obtains the best results. The ROC Curves analysis is performed through the function that binds the probability of True Positive to recognize scanned images (*Se*) and the probability to obtain a False Positive ($1-Sp$). The relationship between these parameters can be represented by plotting Se on the y-axis and $(1-Sp)$ on the x-axis (see Figure 2). A single confusion matrix (see Table 1) thus produces a single point in ROC space. A ROC curve is formed from a sequence of such points, including $(0,0)$ and $(1,1)$.

To determine the best value of α for T_1 is necessary to plot multiple ROC curves for a certain range of T_2. To get results for ROC curves a training-set composed by 380 images taken from different scanners and 380 images taken from different digital cameras, diverse from the images of test-set used in Section 5 for the experimental tests, have been provided. The training-set has been tested by selecting for T_2 three values (0.1, 0.15, 0.2) and for each of this thresholds, the pa-

rameter α ranges in [0.1, 0.9] with steps of 0.1. This determines the ROC curves in Figure 2.

The area under a ROC curve (AUC) quantifies the overall ability of the test to discriminate between scanner and digital camera images. A truly useless test (no better to identify true positive than flipping a coin) has a relative area of 0.5. A perfect test (one that has zero false positive and zero false negative) has a relative area of 1. Real tests will present after that an area between these two values. As it can be noticed, the greater AUC is obtained with T_2 equal to 0.2

Next step is to analyze the single ROC Curve (see Figure 3). A point in ROC space dominates another one if it has a higher true positive rate and a lower false positive rate. So the best value for α is the closest point to $(0,1)$; in this case, it is achieved for α equal to 0.4.

Finally on the basis of such an analysis, in the experimental tests, the values of parameters have been set to $\alpha = 0.4$ and $T_2 = 0.2$ respectively.

Table 1. Confusion matrix

	Camera	Scanner
Camera	S_p	$1 - \mathbf{S}_p$
Scanner	$1 - S_e$	$\mathbf{S}_e$

Figure 2. Roc curves

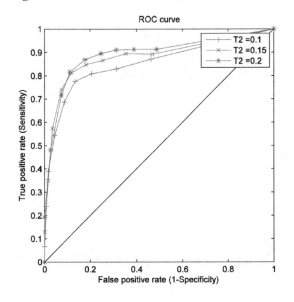

Figure 3. The selected ROC curve

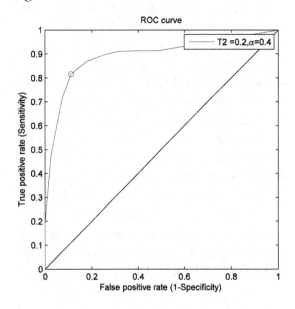

5. EXPERIMENTAL RESULTS

Experimental tests have been carried out to support the theoretical framework. Digital images coming from 4 different scanners (Epson Expression XL 10000 2400x4200 dpi, HP Scanjet 8300 4800x4800 dpi, HP Deskjet F4180 1200x2400 dpi, Brother DCP 7010 600x2.400 dpi) and from 7 commercial cameras (Canon DIGITAL IXUS i ZOOM, Nikon COOLPIX L12, Fuji Finepix F10, HP Photosmart C935, Nikon D80, Samsung VP-MS11, Sony DSC-P200) have been acquired in TIFF and JPEG format.

Because of the diverse size of the contents, the analysis have been done by dividing them into images of fixed dimension $N \times M$ (1024×768). Obtained results have confirmed theoretical assumptions as it can be seen in Figure 4 (a) where $RATIO$ values are plotted and a separate clustering is observed (for sake of clarity when $RATIO$ was over 1 the inverse was taken, due to this, information about scanning direction is lost). In Figure 4 (b), only scanned images, correctly detected, are figured: in this case inversion of $RATIO$ has not been done and, to make visualization easier, high values are saturated at 6. It is simply to distinguish the two different scanning directions individuated by high and low values of $RATIO$; in particular it is interesting to note the left and the right side of the plot related to column scanning direction and the central part related to row direction. In Figure 5 the statistical distribution of $RATIO$ for 1000 camera images (*a*) and 1000 scanned ones (*b*) are pictured where, in this case, higher values have been saturated at 50; a strong concentration is evidenced on the tails of the graph for the scanner case. Finally, a massive test has been carried out on a data set of 2000 images (half scanned images and half photos) by setting the decision threshold T_2 at 0.2 with $RATIO$ normalized between 0 and 1 (as done for Figure 4 (a)): percentages are presented in the rows of Table 2 (left). In Table 2 (right),

percentages related to the scanning directions in the scanner successful cases (85.35% of Table 2, left) are reported.

6. CONCLUSION

In this paper a new technique to distinguish between digital images acquired by a scanner and photos taken by a digital camera has been proposed. Sensor pattern noise periodicity along the scanning direction is checked for classification through a frequency analysis. Experimental results

Figure 4. Energy RATIO for 200 scanned (circle) and 200 camera (cross) images (a). Energy RATIO only for 950 scanned images, correctly detected: scanning directions are evidenced (b)

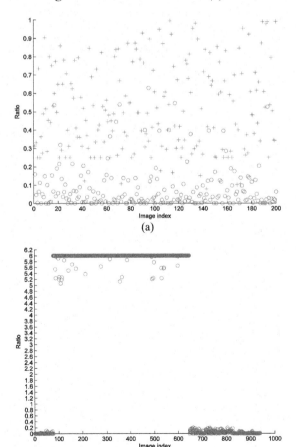

(a)

(b)

Figure 5. Statistical distribution of RATIO: camera (a) and scanned images (b)

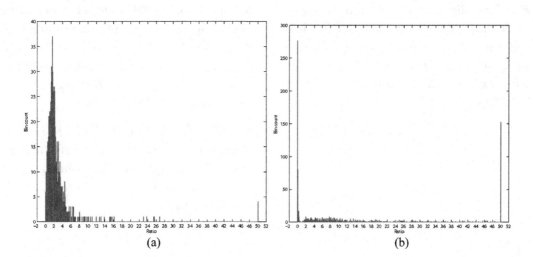

(a)   (b)

Table 2. Confusion matrix for scanned and camera images over a data set of 2000 images (left) and scanning direction recovery for scanner correct answers (right)

	Camera	Scanner
Camera	89.74%	10.26%
Scanner	14.65%	85.35%
	Row	Column
Row	100.00%	0.00%
Column	0.00%	100.00%

have been presented to support the theoretical framework. Future developments will regard the integration of this feature within a SVM classification.

REFERENCES

Chen, M., Fridrich, J., Goljan, M., & Lukas, J. (2008). Determining image origin and integrity using sensor noise. *IEEE Transactions on Information Forensics and Security*, *3*(1), 74–90. doi:10.1109/TIFS.2007.916285

Gou, H., Swaminathan, A., & Wu, M. (2007). Robust scanner identification based on noise features. In E. J. Delp III & P. W. Wong (Eds.), *Security, steganography, and watermarking of multimedia contents IX* (Vol. 6505, pp. 6505). Bellingham, WA: SPIE Press.

Khanna, N., Chiu, G. T.-C., Allebach, J. P., & Delp, E. J. (2008). Forensic techniques for classifying scanner, computer generated and digital camera images. In *Proceedings of the IEEE International Conference on Acoustics, Speech and Signal Processing, 2008 (ICASSP 2008)* (Vol. 6, pp. 1653-1656).

Khanna, N., Mikkilineni, A. K., Chiu, G. T.-C., Allebach, J. P., & Delp, E. J. (2007). Scanner identification using sensor pattern noise. In E. J. Delp III & P. W. Wong (Eds.), *Security, steganography, and watermarking of multimedia contents IX* (Vol. 6505, pp. 6505- 65051K). Bellingham, WA: SPIE Press.

Lyu, S., & Farid, H. (2005). How realistic is photorealistic? *IEEE Transactions on Signal Processing*, *53*(2), 845–850. doi:10.1109/TSP.2004.839896

Mihcak, M. K., Kozintsev, I., & Ramchandran, K. (1999). Spatially adaptive statistical modeling of wavelet image coefficients and its application to denoising. In *Proceedings of the IEEE International Conference on Acoustics, Speech and Signal Processing, 2008 (ICASSP 2008)* (Vol. 6, pp. 3253-3256).

Mondaini, N., Caldelli, R., Piva, A., Barni, M., & Cappellini, V. (2007). Detection of malevolent changes in digital video for forensic applications. In E. J. Delp III & P. W. Wong (Eds.), *Security, steganography, and watermarking of multimedia contents IX* (Vol. 6505, 65050T1-65050T12). Bellingham, WA: SPIE Press.

Swaminathan, A., Wu, M., & Liu, K. J. R. (2008). Digital image forensics via intrinsic fingerprints. *IEEE Transactions on Information Forensics and Security*, *3*(1), 101–117. doi:10.1109/TIFS.2007.916010

This work was previously published in the International Journal of Digital Crime and Forensics, Volume 2, Issue 1, edited by Chang-Tsun Li and Anthony TS Ho, pp. 21-29, copyright 2010 by IGI Publishing (an imprint of IGI Global).

Chapter 2
Estimate of PRNU Noise Based on Different Noise Models for Source Camera Identification

Irene Amerini
University of Florence, Italy

Vito Cappellini
University of Florence, Italy

Roberto Caldelli
University of Florence, Italy

Francesco Picchioni
University of Florence, Italy

Alessandro Piva
University of Florence, Italy

ABSTRACT

Identification of the source that has generated a digital content is considered one of the main open issues in multimedia forensics community. The extraction of photo-response non-uniformity (PRNU) noise has been so far indicated as a mean to identify sensor fingerprint. Such a fingerprint can be estimated from multiple images taken by the same camera by means of a de-noising filtering operation. In this paper, the authors propose a novel method for estimating the PRNU noise in source camera identification. In particular, a MMSE digital filter in the un-decimated wavelet domain, based on a signal-dependent noise model, is introduced and compared with others commonly adopted for this purpose. A theoretical framework and experimental results are provided and discussed.

INTRODUCTION

Digital forensics science emerged in the last decade in response to the escalation of crimes committed by the use of electronic devices as an instrument used to commit a crime or as a repository of evidences related to a crime (e.g., piracy and child-pornography). For instance a digital camera could be the instrument used to commit a crime and/or a digital photograph, being the evidence related to an illegal action, might have been altered to mislead the judgment. One important element of digital forensics is the credibility of the digital evidence in order to assess digital data origin and authenticity. In this paper digital images are taken in account focusing on evaluating image origin

DOI: 10.4018/978-1-4666-1758-2.ch002

determining the specific digital camera which has acquired that content. It is possible to split the source identification problem in two fields (Lanh, 2007): the first is devoted to determine the specific digital camera or scanner and also identify the model and brand that acquired an image (Bayram, 2005; Chen, 2008; Lukas, 2006; Swaminathan, 2008; Sorell, 2009), the second one is dedicated to investigate the kind of device (Caldelli, 2009a; Caldelli, 2009b; Khanna, 2008) that has generated the image under examination (digital camera, scanner, computer graphics images). Various solutions have been proposed in literature to solve the source identification problem analyzing the digital device acquisition process in order to find a fingerprint left by the device like the use of Color Filter Array (CFA) characteristics (Swaminathan, 2008; Bayram, 2005) and the Photo Response Non-Uniformity (PRNU) noise (Caldelli, 2009b; Khanna, 2008; Chen, 2008; Lukas, 2006). The PRNU noise is induced by intrinsic in-homogeneities over the silicon wafer and imperfections generated during sensor manufacturing process of CCD/CMOSs. The PRNU is used as sensor fingerprint and it is commonly employed to solve the problem of digital camera sensor identification. Such a technique is investigated in this paper. The extraction of PRNU noise happens through a digital filtering operation from a set of digital images taken by a camera. After that, the PRNU noise of the to-be-checked image is extracted and compared with the available fingerprints and then the image is classified as taken (or not) by a certain camera. It is important to point out, for the further discussion, that the PRNU noise is deterministically embedded in each image the sensor acquired.

In this paper we propose a method for estimating the PRNU noise introducing a MMSE filter in the un-decimated wavelet domain described in (Alparone, 2006). The application of this filter in forensic domain is novel, generally it is adopted for speckle and film-grain noise removal in coherent radiation imaging systems including ultrasound, infrared and laser imaging and synthetic aperture radar (SAR).

So we present a theoretical and experimental comparative analysis of different wavelet de-noising filters to estimate the PRNU in order to solve the digital camera identification problem. We used the filter described before and the filter proposed in (Mihcak, 1999) and then used in (Chen, 2008).

Introducing the filter in (Alparone, 2006) we make an assumption that the digital camera noise is considered as dependent on the sensed signal, while using the already known filter described in (Mihcak, 1999) a signal-independent noise model is supposed. Furthermore, the two filters are based on different noise models and in particular the novel filter noise model (Alparone, 2006) more accurately captures the image generation model of a digital camera.

The paper layout is the following: the two de-noising filters are introduced, in we then describe the digital camera sensor output model that will be used to derive the estimation of PRNU and the noise models for the two filters will be discussed. Some experimental results are the presented to evaluate the de-noising filters performances.

DE-NOISING FILTERS

According to PRNU methodology, it is crucial to analyze the type of de-noising filter to be used for the extraction of such a noise. In this work we have decided to compare the MMSE filter operating in the un-decimated wavelet domain (Alparone, 2006), named Argenti's Filter, with a spatially adaptive statistical modelling of wavelet coefficients filter (Mihcak, 1999), and named Mihcak's Filter. The first one is based on a signal dependent noise model; on the contrary the second one adopts a simple additive noise model. For sake of completeness a simple low-pass filter in the wavelets domain (LP Filter) has been considered too, to provide a performance lower bound during the experimental tests. In this case, after a 4 level Discrete Wavelets Transform (DWT), all the detail coefficients are set to zero and the Inverse Discrete Wavelets Transform (IDWT) is performed to reconstruct the de-noised image. The extreme simplicity of this filter is inversely proportional to its accuracy, because setting to zero the coefficients of detail equally removes noise and details that are part of the content of the image. Therefore, the results obtained when we used this filter are presumably coarser.

Argenti's Filter (Alparone, 2006)

This filter is based on a signal-dependent noise model (see Equation 1):

$$\mathbf{I} = \mathbf{I}_o + [\mathbf{I}_o]^\alpha \cdot \mathbf{U} + \mathbf{W}, \tag{1}$$

where $\mathbf{I}$ and $\mathbf{I}_o$ represent the noisy and noise-free images respectively, while $\mathbf{U}$ states for a stationary zero-mean uncorrelated random process independent of $\mathbf{I}_o$ and $\mathbf{W}$ takes into account of electronics noise (zero-mean white and Gaussian). The term α is the exponent that rules the dependence of noise from the signal. It is a parametric model which meets different situations of acquisition (Jain, 1989). The parameters to be estimated are: α, σ_U^2 which is the variance of $\mathbf{U}$ and σ_W^2 which is the variance of electronic noise $\mathbf{W}$, which can simply be estimated from black image area. The de-noising method is based on MMSE filtering in un-decimated wavelet domain: after the estimation of the parameters α and $\mathbf{I} = \mathbf{I}_o + [\mathbf{I}_o]^\alpha \cdot \mathbf{U} + \mathbf{W}$, σ_U^2 in the spatial domain, the un-decimated wavelet transform of the image is computed and then a MMSE filtering in this domain is applied according to the supplied parameters. IDWT to reconstruct the estimated noise-free image is finally performed.

The Estimation of α and σ_U

As described above two are the parameters to be estimated in the noise model (Equation (1)): α and σ_U^2. In (Torricelli, 2002) has been proposed an iterative algorithm to estimate these parameters which utilizes an adaptive filter (a MMSE noise filter in the spatial domain). After simple calculation (Torricelli, 2002), it is possible to obtain the relationship among the variance estimation $\tilde{\sigma}_I^2$ of the image $\mathbf{I}$, the image $\mathbf{I}$ and σ_U^2, expressed in Equation (2), which is valid on homogeneous pixels:

$$\tilde{\sigma}_{\text{TM}}^2 = E[\mathbf{I}]^{2\alpha} \cdot \sigma_U^2 \tag{2}$$

Then, by taking the logarithm of both sides, it is possible to derive the Equation (3):

$$\log[\tilde{\sigma}_\mathbf{I}] = \alpha \cdot \log\{E[\mathbf{I}]\} + \log(\sigma_U). \tag{3}$$

So on homogeneous pixels, the ensemble statistics of $\mathbf{I}$ are aligned along a straight line having α as a slope and $\log(\sigma_U)$ as intercept. At each step of the algorithm, the α and σ_U estimate are substituted in the MMSE spatial filter in order to obtain the noise free image on which the homogeneous pixels are selected through an homogeneity equation described in detail in (Torricelli, 2002). On these homogeneous pixels a log scatter plot is computed, the regression line is estimated and then the α and σ_U are found.

Mihcak's Filter (Mihcak, 1999)

Unlike the filter seen before this filter is based on a spatially adaptive statistical modelling of wavelet coefficients; such noisy coefficients $G(k)$ are considered as the addition of the noise-free image $X(k)$ (a locally stationary i.i.d. signal with zero mean) and the noise component $n(k)$ (a stationary white Gaussian noise with known variance σ_n^2). The target is to retrieve the original image coefficients as well as possible from the noisy observation. By using a local Wiener filter (Equation (4)) we obtain an estimate of the de-noised image in the wavelet domain and then apply the IDWT (Inverse DWT).

$$\hat{X}(k) = \frac{\sigma_x^2(k)}{\sigma_x^2(k) + \sigma_n^2} G(k) \qquad (4)$$

However, we cannot use the true signal variance $\sigma_x^2(k)$ since it is unknown, but only an estimate $\hat{\sigma}_x^2(k)$ achieved by previously using a MAP (Maximum A-posteriori Probability) approach on noisy wavelet coefficients.

DIGITAL CAMERA SENSOR OUTPUT MODEL

Digital camera acquisition process is well-known as being composed by different processes such as signal quantization, white balance, color and gamma correction, filtering and usually JPEG compression. This variety of effects, together with the diversities due to the specific kind of camera, determine that a precise modelling is difficult to be achieved. In (Chen, 2008) a quite complete model, which takes into account most of the components relevant for forensic task, is introduced. Such a model is reported in Equation (5), where $\mathbf{I}$ is the 2-D sensor output (noisy image), g and γ are the gain factor and the gamma correction respectively, and $\mathbf{Y}$ is the 2-D incident light:

$$\mathbf{I} = g^\gamma \cdot [(1 + \mathbf{K})\mathbf{Y} + \Lambda]^\gamma + \Theta_q. \qquad (5)$$

The term that is useful for the forensic analysis is $\mathbf{K}$ which represents a zero-mean noise-like signal that is the PRNU (Photo Response Non-

Uniformity) (i.e., the 2-D sensor fingerprint deterministically superimposed to each taken digital image), while Θ_q is the quantization noise and Λ takes into account a combination of different noise sources.

According to the discussion presented in (Chen, 2008), this expression can be simplified to get to a more concise representation (see Equation (6)), where $\mathbf{I}_0$ is the noise-free sensor output, $\mathbf{K}_1 = \mathbf{K} \cdot \gamma$ is basically considered again as the PRNU and Θ is an ensemble of independent random noise components.

$$\mathbf{I} = \mathbf{I}_0 + \mathbf{I}_0 \cdot \mathbf{K}_1 + \Theta \qquad (6)$$

This expression points out an additive-multiplicative relation between the signal without noise and the noise terms. An estimate $\hat{\mathbf{I}}_0 = F_M(\mathbf{I})$ of the de-noised image $\mathbf{I}_0$ is usually obtained by a wavelet-based de-noising filter F_M (Mihcak, 1999), though such a filter is built on an additive noise model as explained in Section 2. It is immediate to comprehend that Equation (1) coincides with Equation (6) ($\mathbf{U}$ and $\mathbf{W}$ are the same of $\mathbf{K}_1$ and of Θ respectively) except for the term α ($|\alpha| \leq 1$) which determines signal-dependency. When α is equal to 1 for purely multiplicative noise the two models are identical. On the basis of this consideration, it is interesting to analyze how this difference in modelling can influence filtering and consequently PRNU detection.

The two digital filters F_M and F_A will yield two estimates $F_M(\mathbf{I})$ and $F_A(\mathbf{I})$, and when are tested against signal-dependent generated noisy images, results achieved in de-noising operation are generally superior with F_A filter (e.g., 2 or 3 dB of PSNR improvement), as expected. This witnesses the goodness of the Argenti's filter when the noise model is exactly matched.

When the noise-free image is obtained, the PRNU noise is computed, at least in a rough approach, by subtracting from the noisy image the de-noised one. The more accurate the de-noised image estimate, the more reliable the fingerprint extraction so high relevance is given to the kind de-noising filter used. The sensor fingerprint **N** is obtained, as indicated in Equation (7), by suppressing the scene content:

$$\mathbf{N} = \mathbf{I} - \hat{\mathbf{I}}_0 \qquad (7)$$

Successively a refinement of the fingerprint is carried out by averaging the results got over a set of M training images (usually M is around 50). This operation yields to delete different noise components that are present on the acquired images but which are not systematic like PRNU.

EXPERIMENTAL RESULTS

In the first part of this section the de-noising filters performances are discussed in relation with the digital camera identification. In the second part of this section experimental measures of the model parameters associated to the Argenti's filter are reported and analyzed.

De-Noising Filters Performances

In this section experimental results for digital camera identification, carried out to compare the three filters (LP, Mihcak and Argenti) used to estimate the PRNU noise are collected and analyzed. The data set is composed by images coming from 10 digital cameras of various brand and model taken by generic users in different kinds of settings. We have created the fingerprint for each camera in the data set, averaging residual noises from 40 images; the remaining photos have composed the test-set (approximately 250 images for each camera). For each camera we obtained three fingerprints, one for each de-noising filter under investigation.

The correlation between each fingerprint and the residual noises of the test images is performed.

In Table 1 a numerical example of the correlation values for a selection of images from a Concord 2000 is shown. Each fingerprint calculated for the Nikon E4600, Samsung MS11 etc., through the three filters under examination (Low Pass, Mihcak and Argenti) is compared with the residual noise of a selection of Concord 2000 test images (from 30 to 38). It is worth to point out that the correlation values in the last column of the Table 1 have the higher values, so the images taken by the Concord 2000 are correctly identified as belonging to Concord 2000 digital camera. Moreover it is interesting to observe that higher values of the last column are encountered when the correlation is made between the fingerprint and the PRNU noise residual calculated with the Argenti filter (see the lower part of the Table 1).

To decide if an image has been acquired or not by a specific camera we introduced a statistical threshold for the correlation value. To calculate the threshold we used the Neyman-Pearson approach based on two parameters: the False Acceptance Ratio (FAR) and False Rejection Ratio (FRR).

The FAR establishes a limit to the number of cases in which an image is wrongly identified as related to a given fingerprint. The FRR is the rate that indicates the number of images that, though related to the given fingerprint, are not recognized as such. With this method we set an *a priori* FAR and we found the threshold that minimize FRR. We suppose that the distribution of the correlation between the fingerprint of the camera C_0 and the noise residuals coming from images taken by different cameras is Generalized Gaussian (see Equation (8)).

$$f(x; \delta, \beta, \mu) = \frac{1}{2\delta\,\Gamma(1 + 1/\beta)}\, e^{-\left(\frac{|x-\mu|}{\delta}\right)^{\beta}} \qquad (8)$$

Table 1. Correlation values (values are to be scaled by 10⁻³) for a selection of 9 test images (30 to 38) from a Concord 2000 digital camera with the fingerprints of 6 cameras (Concord 2000 included)

Filter Type	n.	Nikon E4600	Samsung MS11	Olympus FE120	Sony S650	Nikon L12	Concord 2000
Low Pass	30	-1.714	0.735	-0.234	0.778	0.262	**67.969**
	31	0.083	-0.160	0.469	-0.056	-0.265	**83.186**
	32	-1.007	0.593	-0.254	0.090	0.147	**67.926**
	33	-0.722	-0.522	0.411	-0.158	-0.456	**39.619**
	34	-1.815	0.700	0.322	0.883	1.037	**43.593**
	35	0.613	-1.261	-0.028	-0.340	-0.444	**68.18**
	36	-0.280	0.292	-0.539	0.294	-0.229	**69.173**
	37	0.477	0.016	0.347	-0.082	0.341	**99.602**
	38	0.416	-0.013	-0.001	-0.239	0.481	**63.028**
Mihcak	30	1.210	-0.487	0.365	0.173	-1.997	**101.070**
	31	-0.370	-1.152	0.263	-0.880	-1.157	**98.416**
	32	0.190	0.923	0.171	0.619	0.043	**100.710**
	33	-1.486	1.226	-0.524	0.595	0.026	**74.502**
	34	1.154	-0.621	0.031	1.368	0.449	**70.787**
	35	0.288	-0.594	0.917	-0.645	0.440	**105.400**
	36	0.166	0.470	-0.736	0.001	-0.064	**102.320**
	37	0.219	0.946	-0.048	0.185	0.736	**145.380**
	38	0.525	0.948	-0.282	0.679	0.996	**92.319**
Argenti	30	0.884	-0.469	0.026	0.334	-0.471	**111.530**
	31	-3.362	-4.128	3.466	-1.883	-1.879	**111.290**
	32	0.046	1.355	-1.608	1.026	0.787	**102.050**
	33	-0.591	-0.238	-0.547	-0.162	-0.959	**84.691**
	34	1.292	-0.762	-0.549	-1.179	-0.720	**79.884**
	35	0.174	-0.423	0.252	-0.421	-0.577	**113.380**
	36	-0.046	-1.253	-0.212	-1.235	-0.060	**105.320**
	37	1.291	0.051	-0.839	1.217	-0.629	**143.020**
	38	1.556	0.216	-1.395	0.889	1.211	**96.836**

In Figure 1 the distribution of correlation between the Nikon D40x with noise residual from a selection of images taken by the others cameras in the database (except the Nikon D40x) is shown.

It is possible to fit the data with a Generalized Gaussian distribution centered close to zero. Furthermore, the standard deviation is bigger in the Low wwPass filter case and decrease in the other two filters. So it's possible to consider the standard deviation as a performance marker of the three filter, and it is possible to presume that Argenti's and Mihcak's filter will show better results. The method of moments (Lukas, 2006) is used to estimate the parameters of Equation (8) and then we calculate the cumulative density function of $f(x; \delta, \beta, \mu)$ over all the cameras at disposal, except C_0. By using the Neyman-Pearson approach we determine the threshold by minimizing the probability of rejection, given an upper bound on the FAR = 10^{-3}. In Table 2 the

Figure 1. Distribution of the correlation values between Nikon D40x fingerprint with residual noises taken by a random selection of 300 images belonging to different cameras. The continuous line is the Generalized Gaussian fitting.

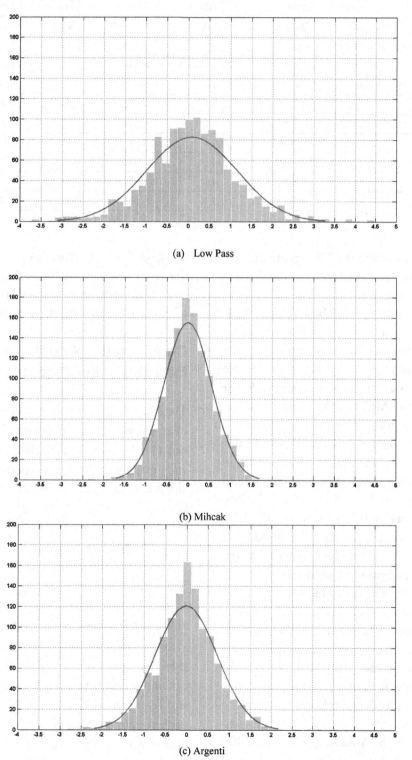

(a)   Low Pass

(b) Mihcak

(c) Argenti

Table 2. Thresholds t and FRR for all 10 cameras with a FAR=10⁻³ for the three different de-noising filters.

Camera	t (10^{-3})	LP FRR	t (10^{-3})	Mihcak FRR	t (10^{-3})	Argenti FRR
Nikon E4600	3.0	3×10^{-2}	3.0	8.11×10^{-3}	9.3	8.11×10^{-3}
Samsung MS11	15.5	2×10^{-2}	4.6	1.8×10^{-10}	9.9	8×10^{-12}
Olympus FE120	4.2	2.8×10^{-2}	2.6	1.2×10^{-2}	9.9	8×10^{-4}
Sony S650	4.9	2.6×10^{-2}	2.0	3.1×10^{-3}	7.7	1.8×10^{-2}
Nikon L12	5.6	$1.18 10^{-1}$	4.1	8.8×10^{-3}	8.4	9.4×10^{-3}
Canon DI50	5.7	$5.2 10^{-1}$	4.2	4.5×10^{-2}	7.7	4.7×10^{-2}
Nikon D40x	2.1	$1.76 10^{-1}$	2.4	7×10^{-3}	4.8	1.5×10^{-2}
Canon Diiz	7.7	$2.72 10^{-1}$	4.5	9.3×10^{-2}	5.2	5.7×10^{-2}
HP PSC935	4.6	$4.5 10^{-1}$	4.1	1.9×10^{-10}	5.0	7×10^{-2}
Concord 2000	3.3	1.3×10^{-2}	3.7	5×10^{-4}	5.8	9×10^{-4}

decision thresholds and the FRR computed for each de-noising filter relatively to the 10 test cameras are shown.

The LP filter has the worst behaviour as obviously expected. The other two filters showed a comparable behaviour; in fact in most cases the value of FRR has the same order of magnitude though Argenti's filter has a significative lower FRR for Samsung MS11 and Olympus FE120.

However Argenti's filter does not exhibit a considerable improvement in the results of camera identification compared to Mihcak's filter. According to our analysis, this is mainly due to the sensibility of the filter itself to the reliability of the parameters estimation. In fact we noted, by acting on noisy images generated by introducing a speckle noise, that filter performances drastically decreased, when an incorrect estimation was done, specifically for the parameter α.

In Figure 2 the correlation values for images from a Olympus FE120 with 5 fingerprints of various cameras are pictured. The distributions of the correlation values in all the three cases are always well separated; in fact the higher values are those related to the correlation between the noise residual of the Olympus FE120 images and its fingerprint. In the Mihcak and Argenti filter cases (Figure 2 (b),(c)) the two classes are better clustered than in Figure 2 (a). This result confirms that using a de-noising filter adequate at the noise model there is an improvement in the performance of the camera identification method.

Consideration About α and σ_U Estimate in the Argenti's Filter

The Argenti's filter proposes, an iterative estimate of α and σ_U in the parametric noise model (Equation (1)). So some tests to check the reliability of such estimation have been performed. We consider a noise free computer generated image (Figure 3), then we corrupted this image with a noise in order to achieve a $SNR = 3dB$, driven by the parameters α and σ_U.

Then using the estimation algorithm proposed in 2 we obtained the $\hat{\alpha}$ and σ_U estimated values. In Table 3 the results of this test are listed: in the first and the second columns there are the actual α and σ_U values while in the third and the forth there are the corresponding estimated values obtained by implementing the algorithm proposed in (Torricelli, 2002). In general the estimate of each couple of value (α, σ_U) seems to be consistent with the real ones.

Figure 2. Correlation values of residual noises (values are to be scaled by 10^{-3}) of 20 images coming from an Olympus FE120 with 5 fingerprints. Legend: + Nikon E4600, ○ Samsung MS11, ∗ Olympus FE120, × Sony S650, ◇ Nikon L12

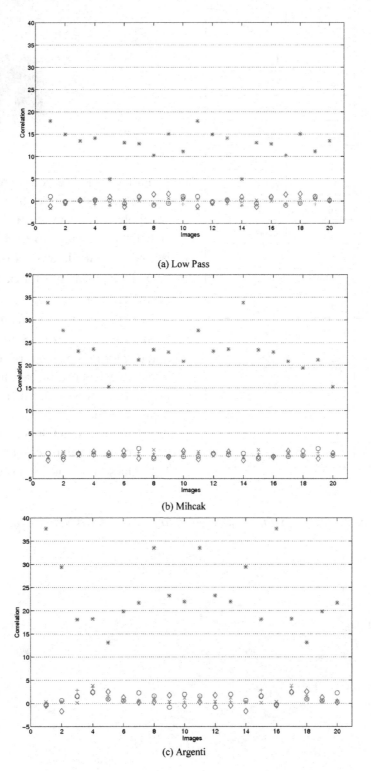

(a) Low Pass

(b) Mihcak

(c) Argenti

Table 3. The real α and σ_U and their estimate $\hat{\alpha}$ and σ_U over different measures

α	σ_U	$\hat{\alpha}$	σ_U
-0.80	1340.66	-0.77	1187.47
-0.70	885.20	-0.66	751.36
-0.60	578.87	-0.55	461.65
-0.50	375.11	-0.45	298.65
-0.40	241.01	-0.35	188.70
-0.30	153.63	-0.25	121.34
-0.20	97.22	-0.16	80.27
-0.10	61.12	-0.08	54.00
0.00	38.19	0.01	36.31
0.10	23.74	0.09	24.70
0.20	14.68	0.17	16.78
0.30	9.04	0.24	11.67
0.40	5.55	0.32	7.84
0.50	3.39	0.40	5.35
0.60	2.07	0.48	3.57
0.70	1.25	0.57	2.36
0.80	0.76	0.65	1.54

Figure 3. A computer graphics image "Room"

Furthermore we considered the estimate of these parameters in relation to the correlation value obtained from the fingerprint and the residual noise when the Argenti's de-noising filter is used. We calculated the first estimate (α^1 and σ_U^1) of the parameters for each photo taken by a certain camera C.

We computed new α and σ_U values calculated in the range of [-50%, +50%] from the initial value (121 values are considered in total). Then we calculated the residual noises for each of the 121 couples and then the correlation of them with the fingerprint of the camera C is measured. In the majority of the observed cases the correlation value does not improve using the 121 values of α and σ_U instead the initial one.

Figure 4. Trend of the correlation values with respect to (α, σ_U) for a Nikon E4600

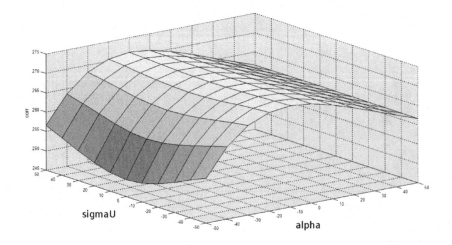

In Figure 4 an example of this situation for Nikon E4600 is presented. The values of (α, σ_U) in the (x, y) axes, and in z axes the value of the correlation are reported. The higher value of correlation is in the central point of the graph ($x = 0$, $y = 0$) that corresponds at the initial estimate of the two parameters. According to these observations we used the first estimate of the α and σ_U parameters for the computation of the PRNU noise. So it is necessary to find a new technique to estimate α and σ_U parameters in order to improve their reliability.

CONCLUSION

In this paper, we have analyzed how different de-noising filters based on diverse noise models can be adopted for PRNU extraction in source camera identification. In particular, a novel de-noising filter has been adopted to estimate the PRNU in source camera identification problem. Experimental results have demonstrated that when the noise model exactly matches the actual situation (i.e., digital image acquisition process), the filter based on such a model grants better performances if the parameters, needed for filtering, are reliably estimated (e.g., Argenti's filter). This is an input in proceeding to research appropriate solutions which can permit a better PRNU detection.

Future works will be dedicated to deeply investigate how parameters estimate really affects the successive filtering operation and furthermore to study a more effective methodology for PRNU extraction instead of that roughly adopted in Equation (7). Other tests will be performed for the source identification, in the case of digital cameras of the same brand and model to better understand both filters behaviour.

REFERENCES

Alparone, L., Argenti, F., & Torricelli, G. (2006). MMSE filtering of generalised signal-dependent noise in spatial and shift-invariant wavelet domain. *Signal Process Journal, 86*(8), 2056–2066. doi:10.1016/j.sigpro.2005.10.014

Bayram, S., Sencar, H. T., & Memon, N. (2005). Source Camera Identification Based on CFA Interpolation. In *Proceedings of the IEEE ICIP*.

Caldelli, R., Amerini, I., & Picchioni, F. (2009). Distinguishing between camera and scanned images by means of frequency analysis. In M. Sorell (Ed.), *Second International Conference, e-Forensics* (pp. 95-101).

Caldelli, R., Amerini, I., & Picchioni, F. (2010). A DFT-Based Analysis to Discern Between Camera and Scanner Images. *International Journal of Digital Crime and Forensics, 2*(1).

Chen, M., Fridrich, J., Goljan, M., & Lukas, J. (2008). Determining Image Origin and Integrity Using Sensor Noise. *IEEE Trans. on Information Forensics and Security, 3*(1), 74–90. doi:10.1109/TIFS.2007.916285

Jain, A. K. (1989). *Fundamentals of Digital Image Processing*. Upper Saddle River, NJ: Prentice Hall.

Khanna, N., Chiu, G. T.-C., Allebach, J. P., & Delp, E. J. (2008). Forensic techniques for classifying scanner, computer generated and digital camera images. In *Proceedings of the IEEE ICASSP*.

Lanh, T. V., Chong, K. S., Emmanuel, S., & Kankanhalli, M. S. (2007). A Survey on Digital Camera Image Forensic Methods. In *Proceedings of the IEEE International Conference on Multimedia and Expo* (pp.16-19).

Lukas, J., Fridrich, J., & Goljan, M. (2006). Digital Camera Identification from Sensor Pattern Noise. *IEEE Trans. on Information Forensics and Security, 1*(2), 205–214. doi:10.1109/TIFS.2006.873602

Mihcak, M. K., Kozintsev, I., & Ramchandran, K. (1999). Spatially Adaptive Statistical Modeling of Wavelet Image Coefficients and its Application to Denoising. In *Proceedings of the IEEE ICASSP, 6*, 3253–3256.

Sorell, M. J. (2009). Conditions for Effective Detection and Identification of Primary Quantisation of Re-Quantized JPEG Images. *International Journal of Digital Crime and Forensics, 1*(2), 13–27.

Swaminathan, A., Wu, M., & Liu, K. J. R. (2008). Digital Image Forensics via Intrinsic Fingerprints. *IEEE Transactions on Information Forensics and Security, 3*(1), 101–117. doi:10.1109/TIFS.2007.916010

Torricelli, G., Argenti, F., & Alparone, L. (2002). Modelling and assessment of signal-dependent noise for image de-noising. In *Proceedings of the EUSIPCO* (pp. 287-290).

This work was previously published in the International Journal of Digital Crime and Forensics, Volume 2, Issue 2, edited by Chang-Tsun Li and Anthony TS Ho, pp. 21-33, copyright 2010 by IGI Publishing (an imprint of IGI Global).

Chapter 3
Source Camera Identification Based on Sensor Readout Noise

H. R. Chennamma
University of Mysore, India

Lalitha Rangarajan
University of Mysore, India

ABSTRACT

A digitally developed image is a viewable image (TIFF/JPG) produced by a camera's sensor data (raw image) using computer software tools. Such images might use different colour space, demosaicing algorithms or by different post processing parameter settings which are not the one coded in the source camera. In this regard, the most reliable method of source camera identification is linking the given image with the sensor of camera. In this paper, the authors propose a novel approach for camera identification based on sensor's readout noise. Readout noise is an important intrinsic characteristic of a digital imaging sensor (CCD or CMOS) and it cannot be removed. This paper quantitatively measures readout noise of the sensor from an image using the mean-standard deviation plot, while in order to evaluate the performance of the proposed approach, the authors tested against the images captured at two different exposure levels. Results show datasets containing 1200 images acquired from six different cameras of three different brands. The success of proposed method is corroborated through experiments.

1. INTRODUCTION

An interesting question in digital image forensics is: can we prove a given digital image is an output of a suspected camera? In film photography, there are some methods for camera identification using

camera imperfections, such as scratches on the negative caused by the film transport mechanism (Lukas, 2005). In digital photography, raw image files are called digital negatives, as they fulfil the same role as negatives in film photography; that is, the negative is not directly usable as an image, but has all the information needed to create an image. The process of converting a raw image file into a

DOI: 10.4018/978-1-4666-1758-2.ch003

viewable format is called developing a raw image. A raw image file contains minimally processed data from the imaging sensor of a digital camera. If we set camera's output as raw, it means we are bypassing certain in-camera processing steps like colour space transformation, demosaicing and post processing operations such as white balancing, bit depth reduction, gamma correction and compression. Raw image conversion software allows user to select different processing algorithms or parameters which may often encode the image in a source device-independent format. Using such images in device linking process may lead to misclassification. In this work, we determine origin of the digitally developed image (using raw image conversion software) based on sensor imperfections. Such solutions would provide useful forensic information to law enforcement and intelligence agencies about the authenticity of an image. All compact cameras are not facilitated to produce raw images. However, the so called high end cameras like DSLR cameras are also getting popular very fast and being increasingly used by both professionals and ordinary users due to their falling costs.

Although image file header contains information regarding camera make and model, in addition to the shooting data and image file information, the content of the file header is editable and can be removed. Hence the photo file header can no longer provide reliable information for identifying source camera. Watermarking is also a powerful tool for the determination of image origin (Blythe, 2004), but most digital cameras available in the market do not have this facility.

The rest of the paper is organized as follows: Section 2 discusses the related work about source camera identification. Section 3 describes the basic processing stages carried out inside a typical digital camera. Section 4 explains origin of readout noise in digital camera and how to measure it using the mean-standard deviation plot. Section 5 describes the proposed approach for the identification of source camera model based on readout noise. Sec-

tion 6 demonstrates the preparation of dataset and the experimental results. Section 7 discusses the limitations of the proposed approach and Section 8 concludes the paper.

2. RELATED WORK

A decade of research in identifying source camera of digital images, researchers mostly concentrated to link the given image with its device, based on sensor imperfections, CFA interpolation, JPEG quantization (Sorell, 2008) and lens aberration (Choi, 2006).

Since digital imaging sensor is not a perfect device, the determination of image origin based on inherent sensor imperfections is identified as a reliable method. Kurusawa et al. (1999) have initially addressed the problem of source camera identification. They have developed a method for individual video camera identification method using the correlation coefficient of the Fixed Pattern Noise (FPN). FPN is caused by the dark current which is a signal collected from the sensor when it is not exposed to light. The authors have extracted FPN from dark frames. This limits the method to use only dark frames. Another approach proposed by Geradts et al. (2001) is the analysis of pixel defects. The authors have shown that hot pixels or dead pixels (defective pixels) could be used for reliable camera identification even from lossy JPEG compressed images. However, recent cameras do not contain any defective pixels or it is possible to eliminate defects by post processing their images on-board. Lukas et al. (2006) have proposed a method for the problem of digital camera identification based on sensor's pattern noise. The authors have used high quality images like raw, tiff etc. with native resolution. The method uses pixel non-uniformity noise which is a stochastic component of the pattern noise to all digital imaging sensors. This is determined by averaging the noise obtained from multiple images taken by the same camera using a denoising filter. The presence of this noise in a given image is established using correlation as in the detection of spread-spectrum watermark. Further the sensor fingerprint (i.e., sensor pattern noise) has been used for camera model identification (Filler, 2008). Camera identification from printed images (Goljan, 2008a) and cropped & scaled images (Goljan, 2008b) have also been attempted. Sensor pattern noise has also been used for determining the image integrity (Chen, 2008) and for identifying whether the given image is computer generated or digital camera image (Dehnie, 2006).

Chang-Tsun Li has investigated the limitation in extracting the Sensor Pattern Noise (SPN). The SPNs extracted from images can be severely contaminated by the details of scenes. This is because; the absence of the camera prohibits the acquisition of a clean fingerprint of the camera. To circumvent this limitation Chang-Tsun Li (2009) envisaged the hypothesis that the stronger a component of the sensor pattern noise is, the less trustworthy the component should be and demonstrated five enhancing models for realising the hypothesis. Recently Knight et al. (2009) have improved the technique of extracting sensor pattern noise proposed by Lukas (2006). They have modified denoising filter for raw sensor data. The approach of using raw sensor data allows analysis of the noise pattern separate from any artifacts introduced by on-board camera processing. This extension is utilized for investigating the reliability of the technique when using different lenses between the same camera and between cameras of the same manufacturer.

An alternative method for extracting the Pixel-to-pixel Response Non-Uniformity (PRNU) noise is proposed by Amerini et al. (2010) for source camera identification. The Argenti's filter operating in the undecimated wavelet domain, based on a signal-dependant noise model, is introduced for the extraction of such a noise. They have also presented a theoretical and experimental comparative analysis of different wavelet denoising filters to estimate the PRNU and shown that the proposed filter noise model captures the image more accurately and hence is useful in camera identification. Caldelli et al. (2010) have proposed a new technique to distinguish between digital images acquired by a scanner and photos taken by a digital camera. Because of the structure of CCD set, the (PRNU) noise pattern, left over a digital image, will have a completely different distribution. In the scanner case, it should show a mono-dimensional structure repeated row after row in the scanning direction, on the other hand, in the camera case, the noise pattern should present a bi-dimensional template. On the basis of this consideration they have constructed a 1-D signal and by resorting to a DFT analysis, which exploits the possible existence of a periodicity, there by understanding the acquisition device. Thus the sensor pattern noise periodicity along the scanning direction is checked for classification through a frequency analysis.

Dirik et al. (2008) have investigated a method for Digital Single Lens Reflex (DSLR) camera identification based on detection and matching of sensor dust–spot characteristics. Since DSLR cameras suffer from sensor dust problem due to its interchangeable lenses, dust specks on the image are detected using intensity variations and shape features to form the dust pattern of the DSLR camera. As authors mentioned, the problems with this approach is that for wide apertures dust specks become almost invisible and the detection of dust specks in non-smooth, complex regions becomes a challenging task.

Another promising approach in this area has been attempted by Bayram et al. (2005). In their work, they have identified the source camera of an image based on traces of the proprietary CFA interpolation algorithm deployed by a digital camera. Due to cost considerations, most of the digital cameras employ a single mosaic structure Colour Filter Array (CFA) rather than having different filters for each colour component. As a consequence, each pixel in the sensor has only one colour component associated with it and then each digital camera employs a proprietary interpolation algorithm in obtaining the missing colour values. To determine the source camera model of a digital image, new features that can detect traces of low-order interpolation are introduced and used in conjunction with a support vector machine based multi-class classifier (Bayram, 2006). To identify demosaicing artifacts associated with different camera models, Bayram et al. (2008) have defined a set of image characteristics which are used as features in designing classifiers that distinguishes between digital camera models. Swaminathan et al. (2007, 2008) have proposed a unified methodology for forensic analysis of digital camera images. This method is based on the intrinsic fingerprints of various in-camera processing operations. The processing applied to the camera captured image is modelled as a manipulation filter, for which a blind deconvolution technique is employed to obtain a linear time-invariant approximation and estimate the intrinsic fingerprints associated with post-camera operations. Sorell (2008) proposed that the implementation of the JPEG compression algorithm represents a manufacturer and model-series specific as means of identification of the source camera of a digital photographic image. The choice of JPEG quantization table, acts as an effective discriminator between model series with a high level of differentiation. Furthermore, he demonstrated that even after recompression of an image, residual artifacts of double quantization continue to provide limited means of source camera identification, provided that certain conditions are met. However, if an image is digitally developed by computer software tool which allows user to use different demosaicing algorithm or post-processing operations, which is not the one coded in the camera. Thus such images may lead to misclassification of camera.

Choi et al. (2006) have noticed that the majority of digital cameras are equipped with lenses having spherical surfaces, whose inherent radial distortions serve as unique fingerprints in the images. They have extracted distortion parameters from pixel intensities and aberration measurements, and then employed a classifier to identify the source camera of an image. But this method works only for structural images where straight edges with significant length are available.

We are motivated by the method proposed by Chen et al. (2007) for source camera identification based on gain histogram. We used similar dataset in our work for camera model identification based on readout noise of the sensor. The main advantage of our method is that readout noise of the camera can be estimated from single image but a set of 5 photos of the same camera are required to compute camera gain histogram and extract features per colour channel. Thus our proposed approach has high practical significance.

3. SIGNAL PROCESSING IN DIGITAL CAMERAS

In this section, we briefly describe the processing stages inside a typical digital camera. Figure 1 shows the basic structure of a high-end digital camera. In particular, we focus on the formation of raw image and its properties.

The light from the scene enters a set of lenses and goes through an optical path which constitutes various filters. Most important and common are antialiasing filter and infrared filter. The imaging sensor is the main component of every digital camera. The sensor is divided into a minimally addressable picture element (pixels) that converts light into electrical signal. Currently, the most frequently used sensors are Charge Coupled Device (CCD) or Complementary Metal Oxide Semiconductor (CMOS) sensors. Each element of the sensor is monochromatic. In other words it can only sense one band of wavelengths. Therefore most digital cameras use a Colour Filter Array (CFA) to sample real-world scenes. A CFA consists of an array of colour sensors, each of which captures corresponding colour of the real-world scene at an appropriate pixel location. The photons collected

Figure 1. Basic structure of a high-end digital camera

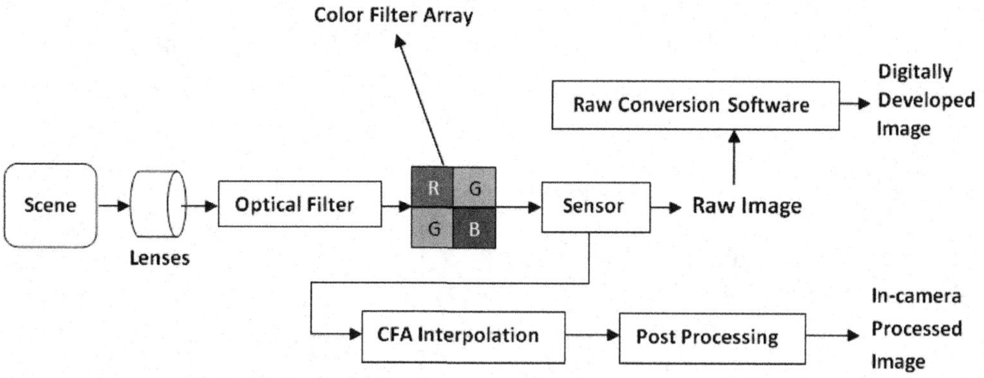

in each element of the sensor induce voltage. The voltage is converted into a digital number as a pixel value is also called Analog-to-Digital Unit (ADU) by an Analog-to-Digital Converter (ADC). Thus the raw image collected from the sensor array is a mosaic of red, green and blue pixels. If camera is set to raw then this raw image data that is what the imaging chip recorded along with the metadata (the camera settings and other technical information) is saved in the memory card. Note that the image is not changed by these settings; they are simply tagged onto the raw image data. Now the raw image can be developed or converted to viewable image (TIFF/JPG) format by using raw conversion software in user convenient form.

If the camera is not set to raw, then the digitized sensor output is further interpolated (demosaiced) using colour interpolation algorithms to obtain all three basic colours for each pixel. The resulting output is then further processed like white balance adjustment, gamma correction and compression. Finally, the in-camera processed image is written to the camera memory device in a user selected image format.

4. ORIGIN OF READOUT NOISE

This paper aims to discuss the source camera identification problem by estimating readout noise of the sensor. The photon transfer technique has proven to be one of the most valuable CCD transfer curves for characterizing readout noise (Janesick, 2001).

Sensor Noise Model

The sensor imperfections at various signal levels can be represented by the model called Photon Transfer Curve (PTC). The analysis of the PTC is the most common and standardized procedure used during camera manufacturing to provide consistent, quantitative and verifiable performance data such as readout noise, dark current, full well capacity, sensitivity, dynamic range, gain and linearity (Janesick, 2001). Figure 2 shows the PTC which shows the typical noise profile seen at the output of a digital camera. In this figure, the three distinct noise regions of the sensor are shown: read noise, shot noise and fixed pattern noise.

Read noise or readout noise is represented by the first (flat) region of the graph shown in Figure 2. It is the minimum signal ever present in all output images. The readout noise is the noise which is seen in the bias frame. A bias frame is a zero second exposure in the absence of light. Readout noise is produced by the on-chip amplifier and other sources of noise in the data transmission before the signal is converted into a digital representation by the analog-to-digital converter.

Figure 2. Photon transfer curve (adapted from Chen, 2007)

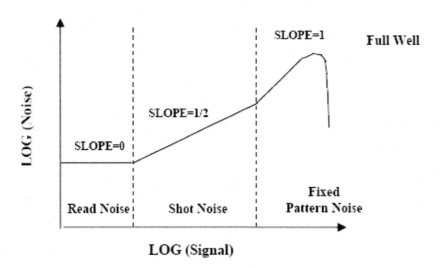

As the illumination increases, the noise becomes dominated by the shot noise of the signal, shown in the middle region of the curve. Shot noise is the noise associated with the random arrival of photons on the sensor. The shot noise is characterized by a line of slope ½. This specific slope arises because the uncertainty in the quantity of charge collected in any given pixel is proportional to the square root of the number of incident photons.

The third region is associated with fixed pattern or pixel non-uniformity noise that results from sensitivity differences among pixels. Pixel non-uniformity is a manifestation of processing variations and photo mask alignment errors when the CCD is fabricated. This problem generates pixels with different responsivities. Pixel non-uniformity noise is proportional to signal and consequently produces a characteristic slope of unity on the plot.

Full-Well is the peak of photon transfer curve. Full well capacity is the maximum charge level that a pixel can hold. As illumination levels are further increased, the individual CCD pixels are unable to hold any additional charge without spilling over into adjacent pixels; such a process is called blooming. Blooming occurs when a CCD chip is overexposed. At this point on the noise curve, output noise abruptly drops because charge sharing between adjacent pixels averages the signal and suppresses random noise.

Measuring Readout Noise

The readout noise or read noise is an important characteristic of a digital sensor. It is a consequence of the imperfect operation of physical electronic devices. As discussed in section 3 the sensor converts light into electrical signal and then the electrons are transferred to amplifier. But the amplifier cannot do a perfect job of measuring the charge. Typically, it gives the right value on average, but with some random scatter. Readout noise is simply a measure of this scatter around the true value. Thus the read noise is uniformly added to the image. The actual readout noise of the camera can be represented by one value which is derived as the average standard deviation of bias frames (Shang, 2009).

Dark current noise is thermally generated electrons in the CCD device itself. All CCDs have dark current, which can cause each pixel to fill with electrons in only few seconds at room temperature even in the absence of light. This dark current varies from pixel-to-pixel and this variation is called Fixed Pattern Noise (FPN). FPN does not change significantly from frame-to-frame. Such pattern noise is usually removed by subtracting one image from another and the difference image is used for the estimation of readout noise. In practical sense, for making difference image from two images (under investigation) of the same scene taken with same camera settings is often impossible to get. However, fixed pattern noise does not vary significantly at room temperature. In this proposed work readout noise of an image is computed in the presence of fixed pattern noise and yet it can successfully distinguish camera models. Thus the source camera of an image is identified correctly if the estimated readout noise of an image is within the threshold specified, defined by actual readout noise of the camera.

5. PROPOSED APPROACH

An ideal CCD sensor should exhibit linear response from the lowest detectable light level to the maximum well depth. It is also evident from Figure 2 that intensity is directly proportional to the noise until full well is reached. Now if we plot the intensity versus standard deviation for images taken under various illumination levels, then we should obtain a linear plot where the standard deviation at zero intensity represents readout noise. Shang et al. (2009) have showed this linear plot by taking a series of images with stepped exposure times at fixed illumination. But it is obvious in statistics of the raw frames; the illumination is in fact not constant. Thus the linear plot can also be obtained by plotting the average intensity values versus standard deviation of a sub-region typical at the centre of images (Kimbrough, 2004).

In order to estimate readout noise from real case images, we plot the mean versus standard deviation of different sub-regions having minimum variation, of an image and a straight line fit is obtained which represents linearity then y-intercept is taken

as readout noise which is the standard deviation at zero mean intensity. The proposed method for source camera identification based on readout noise consists of three processing steps:

- Extract sub-regions from each image
- Compute the mean and standard deviation for each sub-region
- Plot a set of mean versus standard deviation and estimate readout noise

Extract sub-regions from each image: This is a crucial step for accurate determination of readout noise. We extract different non-overlapping image sections of size 100x100 pixels from each image such that an image section must have less than 5% variation among intensity values. Such image sections are apparently free from defect or hot pixels. As photon transfer curve (Figure 2) shows that once the intensity reaches full well capacity, the noise curve abruptly drops because charge sharing between adjacent pixels averages the signal and suppresses random noise. Such pixels are called saturated pixels. Thus the extracted image sections must also be free from saturated pixels. The number of image sections detected may vary from one image to another depending on the texture of image and the distribution of light over the scene. Experimental studies showed that there are at least 5 image sections from an image are required for the accurate estimation of readout noise. Figure 3 shows a sample image acquired by Nikon D40x camera. The detected image sections are shown in white lined blocks.

Compute the mean and standard deviation for each sub-region: Compute the mean (μ) and standard deviation (σ) of intensity values of each detected image section and are derived from the following equations:

$$\mu = \frac{1}{n} \sum_{i=1}^{n} x_i$$

Figure 3. A sample Nikon D40x image with extracted image sections

$$\sigma = \left[\frac{1}{n}\sum_{i=1}^{n}(x_i - \mu)^2\right]^{\frac{1}{2}}$$

Let 'm' be the number of image sections extracted from an image. Let 'I_m' be the set of mean values computed for 'm' image sections and is defined as:

$I_m = \{\mu_1, \mu_2, \mu_3, ..., \mu_m\}$

Let 'I_{sd}' be the set of standard deviation computed for 'm' image sections and is defined as:

$I_{sd} = \{\sigma_1, \sigma_2, \sigma_3, ..., \sigma_m\}$

Plot a set of mean versus standard deviation and estimate readout noise: A scatter plot is drawn for a set of mean (I_m) versus standard deviation (I_{sd}) which are computed in the previous step for each image or a set of images. A straight line fit is obtained by robust regression method using *robustfit* function available in MATLAB and then y-intercept is taken as readout noise in ADU. Figure 4 shows scatter plot and straight line fit for the image in Figure 3.

6. EXPERIMENTAL SETUP

In order to evaluate the efficacy of our proposed method for the identification of source camera model based on readout noise of the sensor, 2 sets of experiments were conducted. In the first experiment, we estimate the readout noise from a set of 2 images taken at two different exposure levels. In the second experiment, we estimate readout noise for an individual image irrespective of its exposure level.

Data Set

The dataset of our experiment consists of 1200 images acquired from six high-end digital cameras of three different brands. In order to compare the performance of the proposed method in identifying source camera, the test images are standardized. So we have taken photos of the same scene with same camera settings in all six cameras. Dataset contains 1200 photos of 100 scenes taken at two exposure levels. Few sample images of the dataset are shown in Figure 5. Same parameter settings were fixed in all cameras except varying exposure time. Photos were taken with no flash, ISO 400 and other default settings. Table 1 shows for

Figure 4. Plot of a set of mean vs. standard deviation of image sections in Figure 3

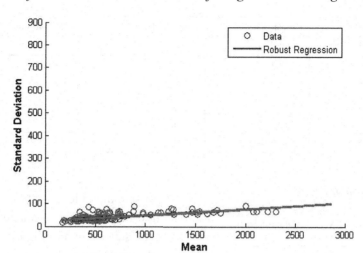

each camera, the type of imaging sensor, different exposure levels, native resolution and image format in which the images were taken. In addition we have also acquired 25 bias images from each camera. We have taken such bias images from a camera in total darkness with no light is allowed to hit the sensor. These images were used for the estimation of actual readout noise of the sensor.

Images in the Nikon NEF raw format were converted by Nikon's ViewNX version 1.5.0 raw conversion software into the 16-bit TIFF format. Images taken in Canon CR2 raw format were converted using the Canon Utilities raw image converter to the 16-bit TIFF format. Images in the Olympus ORF raw format were converted using the Olympus Camedia software to 8-bit TIFF format (since no option available to convert 16-bit TIFF format).

Results

The actual readout noise of a camera is computed from its bias images. A bias image is logically divided into 'm' non-overlapping blocks of size 100x100 pixels and then the standard deviation of intensity values is computed for each block. The standard deviation of a bias image is estimated as the average standard deviation of 'm' blocks. The actual readout noise of the camera is estimated as the average standard deviation of 25 bias images and is for each camera is shown in Table. 2.

In the first experiment, we investigate the source camera identification by combining photo data sets from two different exposure levels of the same camera. The photos belong to one of the

Figure 5. Sample images of the dataset

Table 1. Cameras used in experiments and their settings

Camera Model	Sensor	Exposure level 1	Exposure level 2	Native Resolution	Image Format
Nikon D80	CCD	F5.6/60	F5.6/125	3872x2592	NEF
Nikon D40x	CCD	F5.6/60	F5.6/125	3872x2592	NEF
Olympus C-5060	CCD	F5.6/60	F5.6/125	2592x1944	ORF
Canon EOS 30D	CMOS	F5.6/60	F5.6/125	3504x2336	CR2
Canon EOS 500D	CMOS	F5.6/60	F5.6/125	4752x3168	CR2
Nikon D70s	CCD	F5.6/60	F5.6/125	3008x2000	NEF

Table. 2. Actual readout noise of each camera

Camera Model	Actual readout noise in ADU
Nikon D80	54.39
Nikon D40x	24.77
Olympus C-5060	1.55
Canon EOS 30D	36.98
Canon EOS 500D	16.15
Nikon D70s	27.52

six cameras are divided into 100 sets and every set contains 2 photos. For each set, estimate readout noise as described in section 5. The identification results are shown in Table 3. The plot of image index versus readout noise is shown in Figure 6. In the second experiment, we compute readout noise for each individual image in the dataset irrespective of its exposure level. The corresponding identification results are shown in Table 4 and the plot of image index versus readout noise is shown in Figure 7.

Experimental studies showed that the estimated readout noise may not be the exact true value of readout noise. Thus in our experiments, the source camera of an image is correctly identified if the predicted readout noise of an image lies in the range (actual readout noise ± 5). We can observe from scatter plots (Figure 6 and Figure 7) that Nikon D70s and Nikon D40x are not clearly distinguished. Similarly, we can also observe from the confusion matrix (Table 3 and Table 4) that Nikon D70s and Nikon D40x have more number of false positives. This is because of the both cameras have nearly the same actual readout noise (Table 2). Thus those cameras are not clearly distinguishable. The average identification accuracy for first experiment and second experiment are 88.3% and 79%. The average ac-

Table 3. Camera identification results for combined exposure levels

	Nikon D40x	Nikon D80	Canon 30D	Olympus C-5060	Canon EOS 500D	Nikon D70s	Others	Correctly Identified (aprox.)
Nikon D40x	82	0	6	0	4	68	0	82%
Nikon D80	6	86	0	0	0	0	8	86%
Canon 30D	2	2	90	0	0	0	6	90%
Olympus C-5060	0	0	0	100	0	0	0	100%
Canon EOS 500D	0	0	6	1	85	3	5	85%
Nikon D70s	67	0	6	2	0	87	0	87%

Figure 6. Scatter plot of readout noise for combined exposure levels

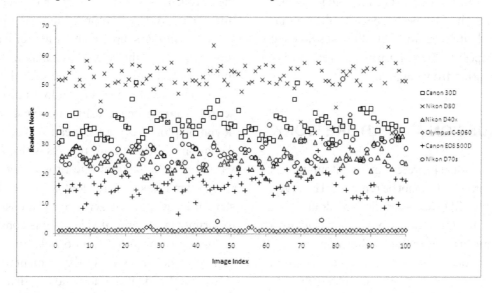

Table 4. Camera identification results

	Nikon D40x	Nikon D80	Canon 30D	Olympus C-5060	Canon EOS 500D	Nikon D70s	Others	Correctly Identified (aprox.)
Nikon D40x	147	1	8	3	21	112	6	74%
Nikon D80	1	150	0	0	0	9	40	75%
Canon 30D	4	1	155	0	0	13	23	78%
Olympus C-5060	0	0	0	200	0	0	0	100%
Canon EOS 500D	4	0	18	1	145	3	9	73%
Nikon D70s	123	2	8	2	0	148	2	74%

Figure 7. Scatter plot of readout noise for each image

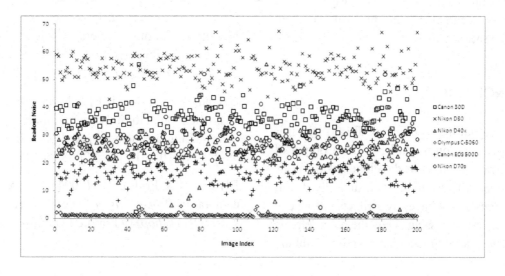

curacy is high for first experiment than second experiment. This is expected because the estimation of readout noise from set of images taken at stepped exposure time is always more accurate than computing from single image.

7. DISCUSSION AND FUTURE WORK

The readout noise is present in all output images of the camera and it cannot be removed. However, the modern CCDs have very low readout noise. Measuring readout noise from real images is a challenging task. Sometimes the proposed approach for source camera identification based on readout noise may not give conclusive result. The experimental results can be improved by using a more sophisticated method to estimate the readout noise from an image. We believe that our research work makes an initial attempt to explore readout noise as an evidence for the process of device linking.

Currently, we have adopted only indoor photos as our dataset. In outdoor images, the variation among pixels is very high, thus uncertainty in the estimation of readout noise is also high. However, more research and analysis is needed to determine the influence of higher illumination levels (near full well) for the estimation of readout noise.

In future, we want to study how to distinguish between cameras if they posses nearly the same readout noise and also from images in which all pixels are saturated.

8. CONCLUSION

A given digital image (TIFF or JPEG) which is under investigation might be a direct output of the camera or it might be developed using a raw conversion software tool. Such digitally developed images do not have any artifacts introduced by in-camera processing. Thus the most reliable method of source camera identification is linking the given image with the sensor of camera. In this paper, we have proposed a novel approach for determining source camera model based on readout noise of the sensor. Readout noise is the inherent electronic noise of the digital camera. We quantitatively measure readout noise of the sensor from an image using the mean-standard deviation plot. We plot the mean versus standard deviation of different sub-regions with minimum variation and a straight line fit is obtained then y-intercept is taken as readout noise which is the standard deviation at zero mean intensity. The experimental dataset of size 1200 is constructed using photos acquired from 6 different cameras at two exposure levels. Experimental results show that the identification rate is satisfactory in distinguishing different camera models.

REFERENCES

Amerini, I., Caldelli, R., Cappellini, V., Picchioni, F., & Piva, A. (2010). Estimate of PRNU noise based on different noise models for source camera identification. *International Journal of Digital Crime and Forensics*, 2(2).

Bayram, S., Sencar, H. T., & Menon, N. (2005). Source camera identification based on CFA interpolation. In *Proceedings of IEEE International Conference on Image Processing*, 3, 69–72.

Bayram, S., Sencar, H. T., & Menon, N. (2006). Identifying Digital Cameras Using CFA Interpolation. In *Proceedings of the International Conference on Digital Forensics* (pp. 289-299).

Bayram, S., Sencar, H. T., & Menon, N. (2008). Classification of digital camera-models based on demosaicing artifacts. *Digital Investigation*, 5, 49–59. doi:10.1016/j.diin.2008.06.004

Blythe, P., & Fridrich, J. (2004). Secure digital camera. In *Proceedings of Digital Forensic Research Workshop*, Baltimore (pp. 12-47).

Caldelli, I., Amerini, I., & Picchioni, F. (2010). A DFT-Based Analysis to Discern Between Camera and Scanned Images. *International Journal of Digital Crime and Forensics, 2*(1), 21–29.

Chang-Tsun, L. (2009). Source Camera Linking Using Enhanced Sensor Pattern Noise Extracted from Images. In *Proceedings of the 3rd International Conference on Imaging for Crime Detection and Prevention*, London.

Chen, M., Fridrich, J., Goljan, M., & Lukás, J. (2008). Determining Image Origin and Integrity Using Sensor Noise. *IEEE Transactions on Information Forensics and Security, 3*(1), 74–90. doi:10.1109/TIFS.2007.916285

Chen, S.-H., & Hsu, C.-T. (2007). Source camera identification based on camera gain histogram. In *Proceedings of the IEEE International Conference on Image Processing* (pp. 429-432).

Choi, K. S., Lam, E. Y., & Wong, K. K. Y. (2006). Automatic source camera identification using the intrinsic lens radial distortion. *Optics Express, 14*(24), 11551–11565. doi:10.1364/OE.14.011551

Dehnie, S., Sencar, T., & Memon, N. (2006). Digital Image Forensics for Identifying Computer Generated and Digital Camera Images. In *Proceedings of the International Conference on Image Processing*, Atlanta, GA (pp. 2313-2316).

Dirik, A. E., Sencar, H. T., & Manon, N. (2008). Digital single lens reflex camera identification from traces of sensor dust. *IEEE Transactions on Information Forensics and Security, 3*(3), 539–552. doi:10.1109/TIFS.2008.926987

Filler, T., Fridrich, J., & Goljan, M. (2008). Using sensor pattern noise for camera model identification. In *Proceedings of the International Conference on Image Processing*, San Diego, CA (pp. 1296-1299).

Geradts, Z., Bijhold, J., Kieft, M., Kurosawa, K., Kuroki, K., & Saitoh, N. (2001). Methods for identification of images acquired with digital cameras. In *Proceedings of the Enabling Technologies for Law Enforcement and Security, 4232*, 505–512.

Goljan, M., & Fridrich, J. (2008b). Camera Identification from Scaled and Cropped Images. In *Proceedings of the SPIE, Electronic Imaging, Forensics, Security, Steganography, and Watermarking of Multimedia Contents*, San Jose, CA (pp. OE-1-OE-13).

Goljan, M., Fridrich, J., & Lukas, J. (2008a). Camera Identification from Printed Images. In *Proceedings of the SPIE Electronic Imaging, Forensics, Security, Steganography, and Watermarking of Multimedia Contents*, San Jose, CA (pp. OI-1-OI-12).

Janesick, J. R. (2001). *Scientific Charged-Coupled Devices (Vol. PM83)*. Bellingham, WA: SPIE. doi:10.1117/3.374903

Kimbrough, J. R., Moody, J. D., Bell, P. M., & Landen, O. L. (2004). Characterization of the series 1000 camera system. *The Review of Scientific Instruments, 75*(10), 4060–4062. doi:10.1063/1.1789261

Knight, S., Moschou, S., & Sorell, M. (2009). Analysis of Sensor Photo Response Non-Uniformity in RAW Images. In *Proceedings of e-Forensics (Vol. 8*, pp. 130–141). Lecture Notes of the Institute for Computer Sciences, Social Informatics and Telecommunications Engineering.

Kurosawa, K., Kuroki, K., & Saitoh, N. (1999). CCD fingerprint method – identification of a video camera from videotaped images. In *Proceedings of the International Conference on Image Processing*, Kobe, Japan (pp. 537-540).

Lukas, J., Fridrich, J., & Goljan, M. (2005). Determining Digital Image Origin Using Sensor Imperfections. In *Proceedings of the SPIE Electronic Imaging, Image and Video Communication and Processing*, San Jose, CA (pp. 249-260).

Lukas, J., Fridrich, J., & Goljan, M. (2006). Digital camera identification from sensor pattern noise. *IEEE Trans. Information Forensics and Security*, *1*(2), 205–214. doi:10.1109/TIFS.2006.873602

Shang, Y., Zhang, J., Guan, Y., Zhang, W., Pan, W., & Liu, H. (2009). Design and evaluation of a high-performance charge coupled device camera for astronomical imaging. *Measurement Science & Technology*, *20*, 104002–104009. doi:10.1088/0957-0233/20/10/104002

Sorell, M. J. (2008). Digital camera source identification through JPEG quantization. In Li, C.-T. (Ed.), *Multimedia Forensics and Security*. Hershey, PA: IGI Global.

Swaminathan, A., Wu, M., & Ray Liu, K. J. (2007). Nonintrusive Component Forensics of Visual Sensors Using Output Images. *IEEE Transactions on Information Forensics and Security*, *2*(1), 91–106. doi:10.1109/TIFS.2006.890307

Swaminathan, A., Wu, M., & Ray Liu, K. J. (2008). Digital Image Forensics via Intrinsic Fingerprints. *IEEE Transactions on Information Forensics and Security*, *3*(1), 101–117. doi:10.1109/TIFS.2007.916010

This work was previously published in the International Journal of Digital Crime and Forensics, Volume 2, Issue 3, edited by Chang-Tsun Li and Anthony TS Ho, pp. 28-42, copyright 2010 by IGI Publishing (an imprint of IGI Global).

Section 2
Multimedia Security Based on Extrinsic Data

Chapter 4

Image Forensics Using Generalised Benford's Law for Improving Image Authentication Detection Rates in Semi-Fragile Watermarking

Xi Zhao
University of Surrey, UK

Anthony T. S. Ho
University of Surrey, UK

Yun Q. Shi
New Jersey Institute of Technology, USA

ABSTRACT

In the past few years, semi-fragile watermarking has become increasingly important to verify the content of images and localise the tampered areas, while tolerating some non-malicious manipulations. In the literature, the majority of semi-fragile algorithms have applied a predetermined threshold to tolerate errors caused by JPEG compression. However, this predetermined threshold is typically fixed and cannot be easily adapted to different amounts of errors caused by unknown JPEG compression at different quality factors (QFs). In this paper, the authors analyse the relationship between QF and threshold, and propose the use of generalised Benford's Law as an image forensics technique for semi-fragile watermarking. The results show an overall average QF correct detection rate of approximately 99%, when 5%, 20% and 30% of the pixels are subjected to image content tampering and compression using different QFs (ranging from 95 to 65). In addition, the authors applied different image enhancement techniques to these test images. The proposed image forensics method can adaptively adjust the threshold for images based on the estimated QF, improving accuracy rates in authenticating and localising the tampered regions for semi-fragile watermarking.

DOI: 10.4018/978-1-4666-1758-2.ch004

INTRODUCTION

Nowadays, the popularity and affordability of advanced digital image editing tools, allow users to manipulate images relatively easily and professionally. Consequently, the proof of authenticity of digital images has become increasingly challenging and difficult. Moreover, image authentication and forensics techniques have recently attracted much attention and interest from the Police, particularly in law enforcement applications such as crime scene investigation and traffic enforcement applications.

Semi-fragile watermarking has been used to authenticate and localise malicious tampering of image content, while permitting some non-malicious or unintentional manipulations. These manipulations can include some mild signal processing operations such as those caused by transmission and storage of JPEG images. In the literature, a significant amount of research has been focused on the design of semi-fragile algorithms that could tolerate JPEG compression and other common non-malicious manipulations (Lin & Chang, 2000; Lin et al., 2000; Zou et al., 2006; Zhu et al., 2007a; Zhu et al., 2007b; Yu et al., 2000; Kundur & Hatzinakos, 1999). However, watermarked images could be compressed by unknown JPEG QFs. As a result, in order to authenticate the images, these algorithms have to set a pre-determined threshold that could allow them to tolerate different QF values when extracting the watermarks.

The art of determining the threshold values for semi-fragile watermarking schemes has been extensively documented by several researchers. In this paper, we review three common approaches. The first approach uses a threshold for authenticating each block of the image (Lin et al., 2000; Zhu et al., 2007a). In this scheme, if a block of correlation coefficients cr (between the extracted watermark w' and its corresponding original watermark w) is smaller than threshold τ, this block is classified as a tampered block, and vice versa. This is represented in Equation (1):

$$cr\left(w, w'\right) < \tau, \ \max\left(\tau\right) - \tau = TM \qquad (1)$$

where $\max\left(\tau\right)$ is the maximum threshold value with $w = w'$, and TM is the JPEG compression tolerance margin. We discuss this approach in more detail in the next section. The second approach uses a threshold, which has been pre-determined during the watermark embedding process (Zou et al., 2006; Zhu et al., 2007a). An example is illustrated in Figure 1, where the watermarks w are embedded into each side of threshold τ according to the watermark value (e.g., 0 or 1), by shifting or substituting the corresponding coefficient. The value of T and $-T$ controls the perceptual quality of the watermarked image. Threshold τ is determined empirically to detect the watermark while extracting the watermarks w'. TM is the JPEG compression tolerance margin. If $w' > \tau$ then $w' = 1$, otherwise $w' = 0$ (Zhu et al., 2007a).

The third approach uses a threshold for comparison with the result of applying the Tamper Assessment Function (TAF) during the authentication of images (Kundur & Hatzinakos, 1999). The extracted watermarks w' and their corresponding original watermarks w are calculated by using TAF, as in Equation (2):

$$TAF\left(w, w'\right) = \frac{1}{N_w} \sum_{i=1}^{N_w} w\left(i\right) \oplus w'\left(i\right) \qquad (2)$$

where N_w is the length of the watermark. The TAF value is compared with a threshold τ, where $0 \leq \tau \leq 1$. If $TAF(w, w') > \tau$, then the watermarked image is considered as a tampered image, otherwise it is not. The tolerance margin can also be denoted as $TM = 1 - \tau$. The thresholds τ mentioned previously are pre-determined which will result in some fixed tolerance margins. A significant amount of research has been dedicated to improving the watermark embedding algorithms by analysing the characteristics of

Figure 1. The pre-determined threshold during the watermark embedding process

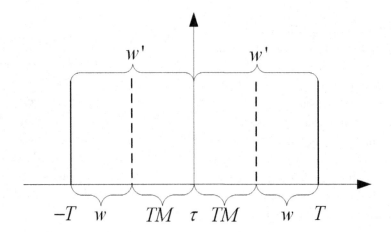

JPEG coefficients of the compressed watermarked image (Zhu et al., 2007b; Yu et al., 2000; Kundur & Hatzinakos, 1999). Alternatively, Error Correction Coding (ECC) has been used for improving watermark detection and authentication rates (Zou et al., 2006). However, the relationship between QF and threshold has not been discussed in the literature. If the QF could be estimated, then appropriate thresholds could be adapted for each test image, before initialising the watermark extraction and authentication process. The use of Benford's Law has already been applied to image forensics of JPEG compressed images (Fu et al., 2007). In (Zhao et al., 2009), we analysed the relationship between the QF and threshold for semi-fragile watermarking, and proposed a framework that further explores generalised Benford's Law as an image forensics technique. The objective was to accurately detect the unknown JPEG compression QF used for semi-fragile watermarking schemes. In this paper, we extend our proposed method in (Zhao et al., 2009) to further analyse the results. Our experiments include applying different percentages of image content tampering to the test images, as well as applying four image enhancement techniques.

The rest of this paper is organised as follows. A simple semi-fragile watermarking scheme to explain the relationship between threshold, QF,

missed detection rate and false alarm rate when authenticating test images. The background of Benford's Law, generalised Benford's Law and their relationship with the watermarked image, JPEG compressed watermarked image also described as well as the proposed image forensics method and experimental results are then presented.

THRESHOLD IN SEMI-FRAGILE WATERMARKING

In this section, the feasibility of our proposed method is investigated in detail. By analysing the first approach previously reviewed in (Lin et al., 2000; Zhu et al., 2007a), a simple semi-fragile watermarking algorithm based on discrete cosine transform (DCT) and the importance of threshold is also described.

Watermark Embedding Process

As shown in Figure 2, the original image is divided into non-overlapping sub-blocks of 8×8 pixels and DCT is applied to each block.

The watermark embedding process is achieved by modifying the random selected mid-frequency (shaded blocks in Figure 3) of the DCT coefficients in each block as follows:

Figure 2. The watermark embedding process

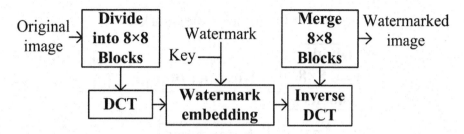

Figure 3. Examples of three 8×8 blocks for watermark embedding

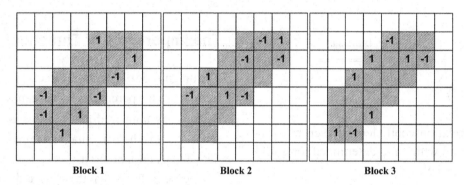

$$coef' =$$
$$\begin{cases} coef, & \left(coef \geq T \wedge w = 1\right) \vee \left(w \leq -T \wedge w = -1\right) \\ \alpha, & \left(coef < T \wedge w = 1\right) \\ -\alpha, & \left(coef > T \wedge w = -1\right) \end{cases}$$

$$(3)$$

where $coef$ is the original DCT coefficient, $coef'$ is the modified DCT coefficient. w is the watermark bits generated via a pseudo-random sequence (1 and -1) using a secret key. $T > 0$ determines the perceptual quality of the watermarked image and $\alpha \in [T/2, T]$ is a constant. The inverse DCT is then applied to each block to obtain the watermarked image. Figure 3 illustrates examples of 8 × 8 DCT block with different watermark sequences and embedding locations for each block.

Watermark Detection and Authentication Process

In Figure 4, the test image is first divided into non-overlapping sub-blocks of 8 × 8 pixels, and DCT is then applied to each block.

The watermark detection algorithm shown in Equation (4) is then applied.

$$w' = \begin{cases} 1, & coef' \geq 0 \\ -1, & coef' < 0 \end{cases} \qquad (4)$$

where w' is the extracted watermark bits and $coef'$ is the DCT coefficient of the test image. The extracted watermark bits from each block are compared with its corresponding original watermark w bits to obtain the correlation coefficient cr as shown in Equation (5):

Figure 4. An illustration of the watermark detection and authentication processes

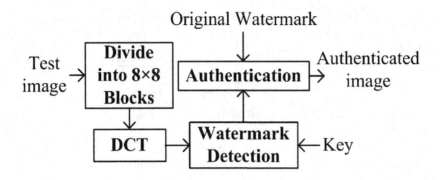

$$cr(w,w') = \frac{\sum \left(w' - \overline{w}'\right)\left(w - \overline{w}\right)}{\sqrt{\sum \left(w' - \overline{w}'\right)^2 \sum \left(w - \overline{w}\right)^2}} \qquad (5)$$

The correlation coefficient of each block is then compared with a pre-determined threshold $-1 \leq \tau \leq 1$ as below:

$$Block = \begin{cases} un-tampered, & cr(w,w') \geq \tau \\ tampered, & cr(w,w') < \tau \end{cases}$$

$$(6)$$

The Importance of Threshold

The magnitude of threshold affects the false alarm rate (P_F) is the percentage of un-tampered blocks detected as tampered and the missed detection rate (P_{MDR}) is the percentage of tampered blocks detected as un-tampered.

Figure 5 shows that the missed detection rate decreases if the threshold is in close proximity to 1. This also leads to an increase in the false alarm rate. However, if the threshold is set to be of a close proximity to -1, then the missed detection rate increases and the false alarm rate will decrease. This results in a dilemma in determining a suitable threshold. For the proposed semi-fragile water-

Figure 5. The relationship among threshold, P_F and P_{MDR}

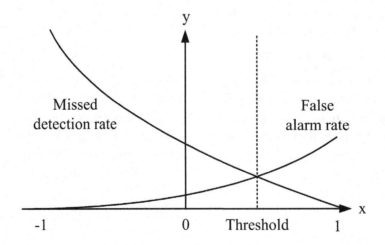

marking scheme, the threshold is set as 0.5, which provides a good trade-off between P_F and P_{MDR}.

Figure 6 illustrates the overall relationship between threshold, P_F and P_{MDR} for the proposed semi-fragile watermarking scheme. The water-marked image 'Lena' has been tampered with a rectangular block and JPEG compressed at QF=75. Figure 6 (a) shows the pre-determined threshold $\tau = 0.5$ used for authentication. The authenticated image shows that the proposed semi-fragile watermarking scheme can localise the tampered region with reasonable accuracy, but with some false detection errors.

In Figures 6 (b) and 6 (c), the lower and upper thresholds $\tau = 0.3$ and $\tau = 0.7$ were used for comparison, respectively. Figure 6 (b) shows that the false alarm rate has decreased whilst the missed detection rate has increased in the authenticated

image. Figure 6 (c) shows the image has a lower missed detection rate but with a higher false alarm rate. From this comparison, $\tau = 0.5$ was chosen for JPEG compression at QF=75. However, if QF =95, then $\tau = 0.5$ may not be adequate as shown in Figure 7 (a). The missed detection rate is higher than Figure 7 (b) with $\tau = 0.9$. Therefore, it would be advantageous to be able to estimate the QF of JPEG compression, so that an adaptive threshold can be applied for increasing the authentication accuracy. In this paper, we propose the use of generalised Benford's Law to estimate the QF, and this will be explained in the next section.

Figure 6. Different thresholds for QF=75

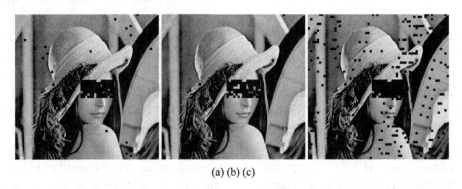

(a) (b) (c)

Figure 7. Different thresholds for QF=95

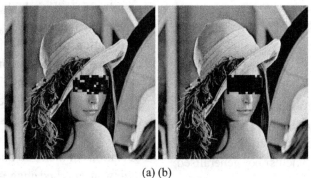

(a) (b)

BENFORD'S LAW FOR SEMI-FRAGILE WATERMARKING

Background of Benford's Law

Benford's Law was introduced by Frank Benford (1938) and then was developed by Hill (1995) for analysis of the probability distribution of the first digit (1-9) of the number from natural data in statistics. Benford's Law has also been applied to accounting forensics (Nigrini, 1999; Durtschi et al., 2004). Since the DCT coefficients of a digital image obey Benford's Law, it has recently attracted a significant amount of research interests in image processing and image forensics (Fu et al., 2007; Jolion, 2001; Perez-Gonzalez et al., 2007). The basic principle of Benford's Law is given as follows:

$$p(x) = \log_{10}\left(1 + \frac{1}{x}\right), \qquad x = 1, 2, \ldots 9 \qquad (7)$$

where x is the first digit of the number and $p(x)$ is the probability distribution of x.

In contrast to digital image watermarking which is an "active" approach by embedding bits into an image for authentication, image forensics is essentially a "passive" approach of analysing the image statistically to determine whether it has been tampered with. Fu et al. (2007) proposed a generalised Benford's Law, used for estimating the QF of the JPEG compressed image, as shown in Equation (8).

$$p(x) = N \log_{10}\left(1 + \frac{1}{s + x^q}\right), \qquad x = 1, 2, \ldots 9 \qquad (8)$$

where N is a normalisation, and s and q are model parameters (Fu *et al.,* 2007). Their research indicated that the probability distribution of the first digit of the JPEG coefficients obey generalised

Benford's Law after the quantisation. Moreover, the probability distributions were not following the generalized Benford's Law if the image had been compressed twice with different quality factors. Thus, by utilizing this property, the QF of the image can be estimated. In this paper, we propose to use generalised Benford's Law for detecting unknown JPEG compression QF to improve the authentication process, during the semi-fragile watermarking authentication process.

Benford's Law, Generalised Benford's Law vs. Watermarked Images

The feasibility of generalised Benford's Law for use in semi-fragile watermarking was first investigated. In our experiment, we selected 1338 uncompressed grayscale images from the Uncompressed Image Database (UCID) (Schaefer & Stich, 2004) for analysis to ensure that there was no compression performed on the images previously. Throughout this section we adhere to the same terminology as used in (Fu et al., 2007), where "Block-DCT coefficients" refers to the 8 × 8 block-DCT coefficients before the quantisation, and "JPEG coefficients" refers to the 8 × 8 block-DCT coefficients after the quantisation.

Figure 8 illustrates the comparison between the probability distribution of Benford's Law, mean distribution of 1st digit of block-DCT coefficients of 1338 images and the watermarked images. The average PSNR between the original images and watermarked images was approximately 35.71dB, which is considered to be of acceptable image quality. Figure 8 shows that the distribution of the 1st digits of the block-DCT coefficients for the uncompressed images obeys Benford's Law closely. This was also observed by Fu et al. (2007) in their analysis. In terms of the watermarked images, the mean distribution also follows Benford's Law. The mean standard deviations of the 1338 uncompressed images and their watermarked images are considerably small, as shown in Table 1. The average χ^2 divergence (Fu et al., 2007) for watermarked images is also small at 0.0115. This indicates a good fitting between Benford's Law and watermarked images. The χ^2 divergence is shown in Equation (9).

$$\chi^2 = \sum_{i=1}^{9} \frac{\left(p_i{}' - p_i\right)^2}{p_i} \tag{9}$$

where $p_i{}'$ is the actual 1st digit probability of the DCT coefficients of the watermarked images and p_i is the 1st digit probability from Benford's Law in Equation (7). Hence, the results indicated that the probability distribution 1st digits of the block-DCT coefficients of the watermarked images follow Benford's Law. Figure 9 (a) illustrates an example of 8×8 DCT coefficients. The 1st digits of the AC coefficients are then extracted as shown in Figure 9 (b).

Figures 10-12 illustrate the comparisons between the probability distribution of Benford's Law, generalized Benford's Law and the mean distributions of the 1st digits of block JPEG coefficients of the watermarked images compressed

Table 1. Mean standard deviations of 1338 images

1st digit	Original images	Watermarked images
1	0.0139	0.0145
2	0.0084	0.0078
3	0.0067	0.0068
4	0.0050	0.0049
5	0.0037	0.0030
6	0.0032	0.0023
7	0.0028	0.0021
8	0.0028	0.0023
9	0.0022	0.0021

at QF=100, 75, 50, respectively. Table 2 summarises the mean standard deviations obtained for the 1338 original and watermarked images, JPEG compressed at the three QF rates are considerably small. Furthermore, as shown in Table 3, the χ^2 divergences are also calculated by using Equation (9), where $p_i{}'$ is the actual 1st digit probability of the JPEG coefficients of the compressed watermarked images, p_i is the 1st digit probability from generalised Benford's Law in Equation (8) and N, s and q are model param-

Figure 8. 1st digit of block-DCT coefficients

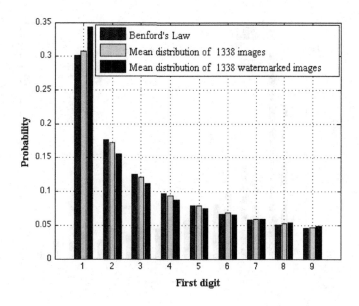

Figure 9. 1ˢᵗ digit of 8 × 8 block-DCT coefficients

1.3e+3	4.7	3.2	−0.19	0.25	−0.5	−4.5	5.6
7.9	−0.7	0.6	−4.9	1.9	2.9	−3.7	3.3
−5.0	−0.2	−1.6	1.7	−0.6	−0.4	1.8	−2.2
2.3	1.1	1.7	0.9	−0.7	−1.3	0.2	1.1
−1.0	−1.2	−0.3	−1.4	1.7	1.1	−1.4	−0.6
1.2	0.4	−1.8	−0.1	−2.0	−0.7	1.6	0.7
−1.7	0.2	3.1	1.6	1.6	−2.2	−1.2	−0.9
1.3	−0.4	−2.4	−1.6	−0.8	1.9	0.5	0.6

(a)

	4	3	1	2	5	4	5
7	7	6	4	1	2	3	3
5	2	1	1	6	4	1	2
2	1	1	9	7	1	2	1
1	1	3	1	1	1	1	6
1	4	1	1	2	7	1	7
1	2	3	1	1	2	1	9
1	4	2	1	8	1	5	6

(b)

eters gained from (Fu et al., 2007). These results also indicate the good fitting between generalized Benford's Law and watermarked images compressed with different QFs, respectively.

The results indicated that the probability distributions of the 1ˢᵗ digits of JPEG coefficients of the watermarked images, in Figures 10 to 12, obey generalised Benford's Law model proposed by Fu et al. (2007), in Equation (8). Hence, we could employ their model to estimate the unknown QF of test images to adjust the threshold for authentication. The improved authentication process is described in next section.

THE IMPROVED AUTHENTICATION METHOD

In this section, we explain the improved authentication process which uses the generalised Benford Law model. In Figure 13, the test image is divided into non-overlapping blocks of 8×8 pixels and DCT is then applied to each block. The watermark detection process then extracts the watermark bits using a secret key.

The same test image is also used for detecting the QF by the quality factor estimation process. This process works by firstly classifying the test image as compressed or uncompressed by adapt-

Figure 10. 1ˢᵗ digit of JPEG coefficients (QF=100)

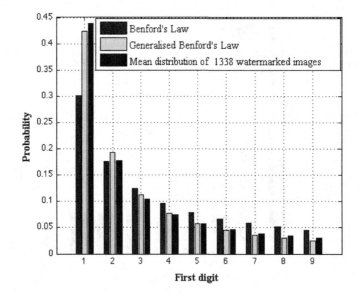

Figure 12. 1ˢᵗ digit of JPEG coefficients (QF=50)

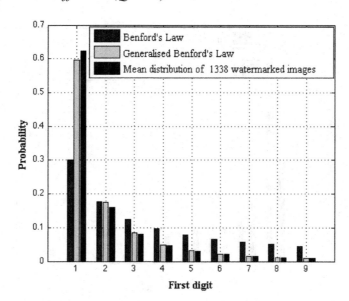

Table 2. Mean standard deviations of 1338 JPEG compressed images

1ˢᵗ digit	Original images			Watermarked images		
	QF100	QF75	QF50	QF100	QF75	QF50
1	0.0828	0.0327	0.0399	0.0664	0.0514	0.0509
2	0.0165	0.0067	0.0089	0.0122	0.0132	0.0149
3	0.0169	0.0066	0.0088	0.0143	0.0111	0.0112
4	0.0163	0.0058	0.0072	0.014	0.0082	0.0084
5	0.0142	0.0049	0.0059	0.0121	0.0064	0.0065
6	0.0123	0.0043	0.0048	0.0102	0.0052	0.0051
7	0.0107	0.0037	0.0039	0.0087	0.0042	0.0041
8	0.0094	0.0032	0.0033	0.0075	0.0035	0.0034
9	0.0084	0.0027	0.0027	0.0065	0.003	0.0028

Table 3. Average χ^2 of 1338 compressed watermarked images

QF	Model Parameters			χ^2
	N	q	s	
100	1.456	1.47	0.0372	0.0257
70	1.412	1.732	-0.337	0.0292
50	1.579	1.882	-0.2725	0.0166

ing from (Fu *et al.*, 2007). If the test image has been compressed, the test image is then recompressed with the largest QF, from QF=100 to QF=50, in decreasing steps of 5. We decrease in steps of 5 as this gives us the most frequently used quality factors for JPEG compressed images (i.e., 95%, 90%, 85% etc.). For each compressed test image, the probability distribution of the 1ˢᵗ digits of JPEG coefficients is obtained. Each set of values are then analysed by employing the generalized Benford's Law equation and using the

Figure 11. 1ˢᵗ digit of JPEG coefficients (QF=75)

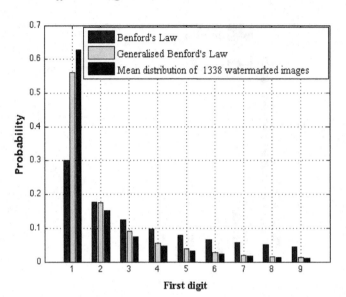

Figure 13. Improved authentication process

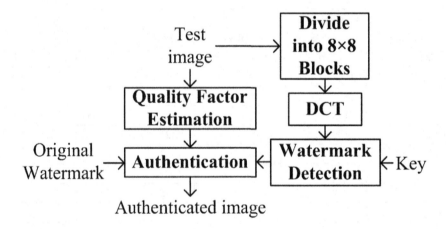

best curve-fitting to plot the data. In order to obtain the goodness of fit, we calculate the sum of squares due to error (SSE) of the recompressed images. We can detect the QF of the test image by iteratively calculating the SSE for all QFs (starting at QF=100, and decreasing in steps of 5), and as soon as $SSE \leq 10^{-6}$, we have reached the estimated QF for the test image. As per the pseudocode below, the threshold 10^{-6} has been set to allow us to detect the QF of the test image. This threshold value was reported in (Fu et al., 2007),

and has been verified by the results in our experiment.

```
If SSE ≤ 10⁻⁶
  Then QF has been detected.
  Break,
End
```

Figure 14 illustrates the results of estimating the QF for a test image that has previously been compressed with QF=70. Three curves have

Figure 14. Estimating the QF of a watermarked image

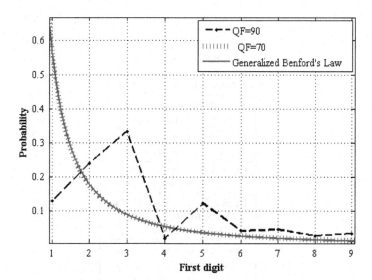

been drawn in order to fit the three probability distribution data sets: generalized Benford's Law for QF=70, the test image recompressed with QF=70, and separately recompressed at QF=90. The distribution of QF=90 shows the worst fit and is considerably fluctuated, while the distribution of QF=70 is a generally decreasing curve, which also follows the trend of generalized Benford Law. These results indicate that if the test image has been double compressed without the same quality factor, the probability distribution would not obey the generalised Benford's Law.

Once the QF is estimated, the threshold τ can be adapted according to different estimated QFs, based on the following conditions:

$$\tau = \begin{cases} 0.9 & QF \geq 90 \\ 0.7 & 90 < QF < 75 \\ 0.5 & QF \leq 75 \end{cases} \qquad (10)$$

Finally, the correlation coefficient between original watermarks and extracted watermarks for each block is compared using the attuned threshold τ to authenticate, in order to determine whether any blocks have been tampered with.

This is similar to the authentication process as described previously.

EXPERIMENTAL RESULTS

The watermarked images are generated by our proposed semi-fragile watermarking algorithm using the 1338 test images from UCID (Schaefer & Stich, 2004). In order to achieve a fair comparison, different embedding parameters are randomised for each image such as the watermarks location, watermark string and watermark bits. For our analysis, ten types of test images with and without attacks are considered as shown in Figure 15. Each set illustrated in Figure 15 is performed individually for the 1338 watermarked images.

Table 4 summaries the results obtained for test images that have been JPEG compressed only. To evaluate the accuracy of the quality factor estimation process, each test image has been blind compressed from QF=100 to QF=50 in decreasing steps of 5. For each compression, the quality factor estimation process was used to determine the QF. The mean estimated QFs for all 1338 test images and each correctly identified detection

Figure 15. Ten types of test images with and without attacks

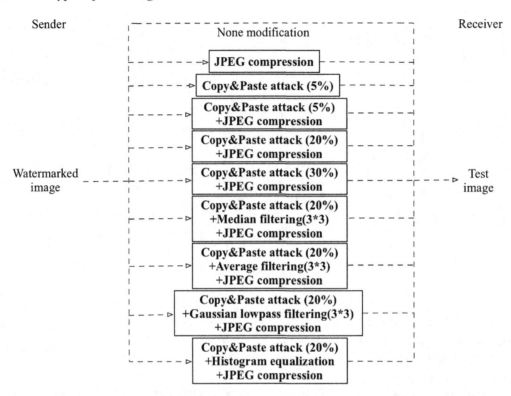

accuracy rate P_{de} for each JPEG compression quality factor are shown in Table 4, based on Equation (11).

$$P_{de} = \frac{\partial}{\beta} \times 100\% \qquad (11)$$

where ∂ is the number of correctly detected QF and β is the number of images tested. The mean estimated QF results indicate the QFs can be estimated with high accuracy. The only exceptions for lower correct detection rates, P_{de}, were obtained for QF=50, QF=60, and QF=100. In the case of QF=50, P_{de} was very low at approximately 18.2%, meaning that the process was probably detecting QFs close to QF=55. For QF=60, and QF=100, the detection rates were slightly better at 38.6% and 65.7%, respectively. For comparison, both the mean estimated QF value and correct detection rate were used for

each result to estimate the actual QF for the images. The QFs were then grouped into three different ranges: $QF \geq 90$, $90 > QF > 75$ and $QF \leq 75$. The grouping into three QF ranges did

Table 4. JPEG compression only

Actual QF	Mean Estimated QF	P_{de}	τ	P_{de2}
100	98.2	65.7%		
95	94.9	97.3%	0.9	98.8%
90	90.0	98.2%		
85	84.2	91.4%	0.7	99.1%
80	79.8	97.5%		
75	75.4	97.0%		
70	69.8	98.8%		
65	64.4	93.7%	0.5	99.4%
60	62.4	38.6%		
55	55.2	94.1%		
50	54.3	18.2%		

not have an overall effect on the authentication process. Results obtained for P_{de2} also showed the correct detection accuracy rates in these QF ranges were on average at 99%. Two further experiments were performed with the test image: no modification, and copy and paste attack (5%). All of the detected QFs achieved for both experiments were approximately 99%, and fit well in the upper range of $QF \geq 90$.

Table 5 summaries the results obtained for test images that have been attacked via copy & paste and then JPEG compressed. Each watermarked image has been tampered randomly in different regions by applying a copy & paste attack to 5% of the watermarked image (9830 pixels in 384512 pixels image), and also compressed with different QF values. In order to further investigate our proposed method, we undertake the analysis of increasing the copy & paste attack area in the watermarked image. Tables 6 and 7 illustrate the average QF estimation rates based on 1338 watermarked images, each attacked via copy & paste (20% and 30%), and then JPEG compression. Tables 5 to 7 show that each watermarked image was exposed to three different volumes of tampering: 5%, 20%, and 30%. Each tampering iteration was performed by selecting random

blocks from the watermarked images. Each tampered watermarked image is then blind JPEG compressed from QF=100 to QF=50 in decreasing steps of 5. Consequently, 44154 test images are obtained during these copy & paste attack and JPEG compression simulations. The results showed that the quality factor estimation process was highly accurate even under these attacks.

From Table 4, the lowest correct detection rates P_{de} were obtained for QF=50, QF=60, and QF=100 with a tamper region of 5%. However, in Tables 6 and 7, the correct detection rates P_{de} for QF=100 are relatively increased to 94% and 100% when the tampered regions are 20% and 30%, respectively. However, the correct detection rates P_{de} for QF=50 and QF=60 are still maintaining the lowest in Tables 6 and 7. Nevertheless, from Tables 5 to 7, all of the results of P_{de2} showed the correct detection rates in the three ranges, with an overall average of 99%. As such, the threshold can be adapted into the three QF ranges according to the estimated QF of each test image as described in Section 4.

As mentioned semi-fragile watermarking techniques can permit some non-malicious or uninten-

Table 5. Copy and paste (5%) + JPEG compression

Actual QF	Mean Estimated QF	P_{de}	τ	P_{de2}
100	98.6	72%		
95	95.0	100%	0.9	99.1%
90	90.1	98.6%		
85	84.8	97.9%	0.7	99.3%
80	79.9	99.6%		
75	75.2	99.1%		
70	69.9	99.5%		
65	64.5	98.7%	0.5	99.2%
60	61.5	63.9%		
55	54.9	96.6%		
50	53.3	20.4%		

Table 6. Copy and paste (20%) + JPEG compression

Actual QF	Mean Estimated QF	P_{de}	τ	P_{de2}
100	99.7	94%		
95	95.0	100%	0.9	100%
90	90.0	100%		
85	85.0	100%	0.7	99.9%
80	80.0	100%		
75	75.5	98%		
70	70.0	100%		
65	65.2	96%	0.5	99.9%
60	61.6	68%		
55	55.0	100%		
50	54.9	20%		

Table 7. Copy and paste (30%) + JPEG compression

Actual QF	Mean Estimated QF	P_{de}	τ	P_{de2}
100	100.0	100%		
95	95.0	100%	0.9	99.9%
90	90.2	99.8%		
85	84.8	98%	0.7	99.9%
80	79.1	99.8%		
75	75.2	99.7%		
70	69.4	99.6%		
65	65.3	99.5%	0.5	99.9%
60	62.1	58%		
55	55.0	100%		
50	55.2	14%		

tional manipulations. Aside from JPEG compression as one of major unintentional manipulations, some other non-malicious manipulation can include image enhancement techniques such as median filtering, average filtering, Gaussian low pass filtering, and histogram equalisation. Hence, we simulated the experiments to obtain 58872 test images by firstly tampering 20% of the watermarked image, before applying these image enhancement techniques along with blind JPEG compression from QF=100 to QF=50 in decreasing steps of 5. The results are shown in Tables 8 to 11. Table 8 indicates that the average performance of the correct detection rates P_{de} is increased when the median filtering is added to the test images. When QF=95 to QF=65, the correct detection rates P_{de} reach 100%, which implies that all of corresponding QFs for each test images are correctly detected. In Table 9, the test images are subjected to average filtering. The results illustrate that the P_{de} have been decreased insignificantly, while the results of QF=95 to QF=65 still remaining high at over 96%. Table 10 shows that the highest correct detection rates (100%) are achieved when Gaussian low pass filtering is applied to the test images with QF=100 to QF=80. However, the P_{de} declined approxi-

mately 8% from QF=75 to QF=50, and the P_{de2} decreased to the lowest at 96.6%. In Table 11, we evaluated the results of the test images after histogram equalisation. We found that the P_{de} for QF=60 increased to 87.5% (the highest P_{de} for QF=60), whereas the P_{de} for QF=50 decreased to the lowest at 4%, as shown in Tables 4 to 11. Tables 8 to 11 showed the correct detection rates P_{de2} were highly accurate with an overall average of 99.5%, which can also be adapted to adjust the threshold into three ranges.

SUMMARY

In this paper, we presented the relationship between QF and threshold, and proposed a framework incorporating the generalised Benford's Law as an image forensics technique to accurately detect unknown JPEG compression levels in semi-fragile watermarked images. We reviewed three typical methods of employing predetermined thresholds in semi-fragile watermarking algorithms and the limitations of using predetermined thresholds were also highlighted.

Table 8. Copy and paste (20%) + median filtering (3*3) + JPEG compression

Actual QF	Mean Estimated QF	P_{de}	τ	P_{de2}
100	99.9	98.0%		
95	95.1	100%	0.9	100%
90	90.3	100%		
85	85.0	100%	0.7	100%
80	80.0	100%		
75	75.0	100%		
70	70.0	100%		
65	65.0	100%	0.5	98.0%
60	62.4	52.0%		
55	56.6	92.0%		
50	54.0	30.0%		

Table 9. Copy and paste (20%) + average filtering (3*3) + JPEG compression

Actual QF	Mean Estimated QF	P_{de}	τ	P_{de2}
100	99.8	96%		
95	94.9	98%	0.9	100%
90	90.0	100%		
85	85.0	100%	0.7	100%
80	80.0	100%		
75	74.5	98%		
70	67.2	96%		
65	58.5	90%	0.5	100%
60	59.7	54%		
55	48.4	88%		
50	44.4	58%		

Table 10. Copy and paste (20%) + Gaussian low pass filtering (3*3) + JPEG compression

Actual QF	Mean Estimated QF	P_{de}	τ	P_{de2}
100	100.0	100%		
95	95.0	100%	0.9	100%
90	90.0	100%		
85	85.0	100%	0.7	100%
80	80.0	100%		
75	72.9	89.8%		
70	68.4	85.7%		
65	59.7	91.8%	0.5	96.6%
60	61.3	46.9%		
55	57.0	91.8%		
50	57.9	32.7%		

Table 11. Copy and paste (20%) + histogram equalization + JPEG compression

Actual QF	Mean Estimated QF	P_{de}	τ	P_{de2}
100	99.7	93.9%		
95	94.9	97.9%	0.9	100%
90	90.0	100%		
85	84.9	97.9%	0.7	98.9%
80	79.7	97.9%		
75	75.0	100%		
70	70.0	100%		
65	65.0	100%		
60	60.6	87.8%	0.5	100%
55	55.1	97.9%		
50	54.8	4.1%		

In our proposed semi-fragile watermarking method, the test image was first analysed to detect its previously unknown quality factor for JPEG compression, before proceeding with the semi-fragile authentication process. The results showed that QFs can be accurately detected for most unknown JPEG compressions. In particular, the average QF detection rate was as high as 96% for watermarked images compressed with QFs between 95-65, and 99% when the image was subjected to tampering of 5%, 20% and 30% pixels of the image and compressed with QFs between 95-65. In addition, we applied different image enhancement techniques, such as median filtering, average filtering, Gaussian low pass filtering, and histogram equalisation, to these test images, and the results show that the QF correct detection rates are also high as above 90%. Consequently, the threshold was adapted into three specific ranges according to the estimated QF of each test image. For future work, we plan to analyse and estimate double JPEG compression and print-scan processes for semi-fragile watermarking images, as well as in robust watermarking.

REFERENCES

Benford, F. (1938). The law of anomalous numbers. *Proceedings of the American Philosophical Society, 78*, 551–572.

Durtschi, C., Hillison, W., & Pacini, C. (2004). The effective use of Benford's Law to assist in detecting fraud in accounting data. *Journal of Forensic Accounting, 5*, 17–34.

Fu, D., Shi, Y. Q., & Su, Q. (2007). A generalized Benford's law for JPEG coefficients and its applications in image forensics. In *Proceedings of the SPIE Security, Steganography, and Watermarking of Multimedia Contents IX* (Vol. 6505, pp. 1L1-1L11).

Hill, T. P. (1995). The significant-Digit Phenomenon. *The American Mathematical Monthly, 102,* 322–327. doi:10.2307/2974952

Jolion, J. M. (2001). Images and Benford's Law. *Journal of Mathematical Imaging and Vision, 14,* 73–81. doi:10.1023/A:1008363415314

Kundur, D., & Hatzinakos, D. (1999). Digital watermarking for telltale tamper proofing and authentication. *Proceedings of the IEEE, 87*(7), 1167–1180. doi:10.1109/5.771070

Lin, C. Y., & Chang, S. F. (2000). Semi-fragile watermarking for authenticating JPEG visual content. *In Proceedings of the SPIE Security and Watermarking of Multimedia Contents II EI '00.*

Lin, E. T., Podilchuk, C. I., & Delp, J. (2000). Detection of image alterations using semi-fragile watermarks. *In Proceedings of the SPIE International Conference on Security and Watermarking of Multimedia Contents II* (Vol. 3971, No. 14).

Nigrini, M. J. (1999, May). I've got your number. *Journal of Accountancy.*

Perez-Gonzalez, F., Heileman, G. L., & Abdallah, C. T. (2007). Benford's Law in image processing. In *Proceedings of the IEEE International Conference on Image Processing, 1,* 405–408.

Schaefer, G., & Stich, M. (2004). UCID - an uncompressed colour image database. In *Proceedings of the SPIE, Storage and Retrieval Methods and Applications for Multimedia* (pp. 472-480).

Yu, G. J., Lu, C. S., Liao, H. Y. M., & Sheu, J. P. (2000). Mean quantization blind watermarking for image authentication. In *Proceedings of the IEEE International Conference on Image Processing, 3,* 706–709.

Zhao, X., Ho, A. T. S., & Shi, Y. Q. (2009). Image Forensics using Generalized Benford's Law for Accurate Detection of Unknown JPEG Compression in Watermarked Images. In *Proceedings of the 16th International Conference on Digital Signal Processing (DSP2009)* (pp. 1-8).

Zhu, X. Z., Ho, A. T. S., & Marziliano, P. (2007a). A new semi-fragile image watermarking with robust tampering restoration using irregular sampling. *Elsevier Signal Processing: Image Communication, 22*(5), 515–528. doi:10.1016/j.image.2007.03.004

Zhu, Y., Li, C. T., & Zhao, H. J. (2007b). Structural digital signature and semi-fragile fingerprinting for image authentication in wavelet domain. *In Proceedings of the Third International Symposium on Information Assurance and Security* (pp. 478-483).

Zou, D., Shi, Y. Q., Ni, Z., & Su, W. (2006). A semi-fragile lossless digital watermarking scheme based on Integer Wavelet Transform. *IEEE Trans. Circuits and Systems for Video Technology, 16*(10), 1294–1300. doi:10.1109/TCSVT.2006.881857

This work was previously published in the International Journal of Digital Crime and Forensics, Volume 2, Issue 2, edited by Chang-Tsun Li and Anthony TS Ho, pp. 1-20, copyright 2010 by IGI Publishing (an imprint of IGI Global).

Chapter 5
Blind Detection of Additive Spread-Spectrum Watermarking in the Dual-Tree Complex Wavelet Transform Domain

Roland Kwitt
University of Salzburg, Austria

Peter Meerwald
University of Salzburg, Austria

Andreas Uhl
University of Salzburg, Austria

ABSTRACT

In this paper, the authors adapt two blind detector structures for additive spread-spectrum image watermarking to the host signal characteristics of the Dual-Tree Complex Wavelet Transform (DT-CWT) domain coefficients. The research is motivated by the superior perceptual characteristics of the DT-CWT and its active use in watermarking. To improve the numerous existing watermarking schemes in which the host signal is modeled by a Gaussian distribution, the authors show that the Generalized Gaussian nature of Dual-Tree detail subband statistics can be exploited for better detector performance. This paper finds that the Rao detector is more practical than the likelihood-ratio test for their detection problem. The authors experimentally investigate the robustness of the proposed detectors under JPEG and JPEG2000 attacks and assess the perceptual quality of the watermarked images. The results demonstrate that their alterations allow significantly better blind watermark detection performance in the DT-CWT domain than the widely used linear-correlation detector. As only the detection side has to be modified, the proposed methods can be easily adopted in existing DT-CWT watermarking schemes.

DOI: 10.4018/978-1-4666-1758-2.ch005

INTRODUCTION

Watermarking has been proposed as a technology to ensure copyright protection by embedding an imperceptible, yet detectable signal in digital multimedia content such as images or video. Transform domains such as the DCT or DWT facilitate modeling human perception and permit selection of signal components which can be watermarked in a robust but unobtrusive way.

Loo (2000) first proposed to use Kingsbury's dual-tree complex wavelet transform (DT-CWT) (Kingsbury, 1998) for blind watermarking. The DT-CWT is a complex wavelet transform variant which is only four-times redundant in 2-D and offers approximate shift invariance together with the property of directional selectivity. Thus, it remedies two commonly-known shortcomings of the classic, maximally decimated DWT. Furthermore, it can be implemented very efficiently on the basis of four parallel 2-D DWTs.

For these reasons, the DT-CWT domain has become a very popular choice for watermark embedding recently (Loo & Kingsbury, 2000; Woo et al., 2006; Earl & Kingsbury, 2003; Wang et al., 2007; Coria et al., 2008; Mabtoul et al., 2008; Mabtoul et al., 2009; Tang & Chen, 2009; Zhuang & Jiang, 2006). However, for blind watermarking detection, i.e. when detection is performed without reference to the unwatermarked host signal, the host interferes with the watermark signal. Hence informed embedding/coding techniques at the embedder side, e.g., ISS (Malvar & Florencio, 2003),

and, at the detector side, accurate modelling of the host signal is crucial for the overall performance of a blind watermarking scheme. In this paper, we focus on improving the detector part.

In Section 2 we argue that the real and imaginary parts of DT-CWT subband coefficients can be accurately modeled by a Generalized Gaussian distribution (GGD). After reviewing the literature on complex wavelet domain watermarking in Section 3, we adopt and compare the applicability of two blind spread-spectrum watermark detectors in Section 4 which exploits the DT-CWT domain subband statistics. We experimentally compare the detection performance of the proposed schemes also under JPEG and JPEG2000 attacks and assess the perceptual quality of DT-CWT embedding in Section 5. Section 6 offers concluding remarks.

2. DT-CWT SUBBAND STATISTICS

In order to obtain a good signal detector in noise, i.e. the host signal for blind watermarking in the absence of attacks, we have to find a reasonable noise model first. By employing a J-scale 2-D DT-CWT we obtain six complex subbands per decomposition level, oriented along approximately +/- 15, +/- 45, +/- 75 degree. To visualize the directional selectivity, Figure 1 shows the magnitude of the six complex detail subbands at level two of the decomposed Bridge image (see Figure 1).

Figure 1. Complex coefficient magnitudes of the 2ⁿᵈ level detail subbands with the MLEs of the GGD's shape parameter β fitted to the marginal distributions of concatenated real and imaginary parts

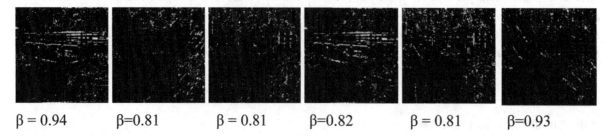

$\beta = 0.94$ $\beta=0.81$ $\beta = 0.81$ $\beta=0.82$ $\beta = 0.81$ $\beta=0.93$

The subbands will be denoted by $\mathbf{D}_{sk} = \{d_{sk,ij}\}_{1 <= i,j <= ns}$, where the decomposition level is given by s, $1 <= s <= J$ and k, $1 <= k <= 6$ denotes the orientation. Further, we recognize that $d_{sk,ij} \in C$. The number of coefficients per subband on level s is given by $n_s n_s$ (for square subbands). The matrix $\mathbf{D}_{sk}$ can also be written in vector notation as $\mathbf{d}_{sk} = [d_{sk,11}, d_{sk,21}, ..., d_{sk,ns1}, ... d_{sk,1ns}, ..., d_{sk,nsns}]$, where we have simply rearranged the column vectors into one big row vector. We propose that the marginal distributions of the real and imaginary parts of complex wavelet coefficients of scales s >= 2 can be modeled by two-parameter GGDs. The probability density function (PDF) of a GGD is given by (Nadarajah, 2005)

$$p(x; \alpha, \beta) = \frac{\beta}{2\alpha\Gamma(1/\beta)} e^{-\left|\frac{x}{\alpha}\right|^\beta}, \infty \leq x \leq -\infty$$

(1)

with parameters $\alpha > 0$ (scale) and $\beta > 0$ (shape). In case of $\beta = 1$ the PDF reduces to the Laplace distribution, in case of $\beta = 2$ we obtain the Gaussian distribution. To verify the suitability of the proposed distributional model, we employ a Chi-Square Goodness-of-Fit (GoF) test at the 1% significance level on the subband statistics for a three-scale DT-CWT. The null-hypothesis of the Chi-Square GoF test is that the data originates from a GGD. Regarding the filter parameterization of the DT-CWT, we use near-orthogonal (13,19)-tap filters on level one and Q-shift (14,14)-tap filters (Kingsbury, 2001) on levels >= 2. Table 1 summarizes the outcomes of the Chi-Square test for our six test images. A 0 signifies that the null-hypothesis could not be rejected at the given significance level for all images, while a number > 0 signifies the corresponding number of rejections. The first number gives the outcome for the real part, the second number gives the outcome for the imaginary part. As we can see, the null-hypothesis cannot be rejected for many of the tests at decomposition levels >= 2. Considering

the fact that in case we assume a Normal distribution all null-hypothesis are rejected without exception, the GGD seems to be a quite good model here.

We further suggest that the real and imaginary parts of the coefficients of a given subband are realizations of i.i.d. random variables following one GGD with parameters α and β. Given that this assumption is actually valid, we can concatenate the real and imaginary parts to form a row vector $\mathbf{v}_{sk} = [R(\mathbf{d}_{sk}) I(\mathbf{d}_{sk})]$ of dimensionality $2n_s n_s$. Here, R() denotes the real parts and I() denotes the imaginary parts. To verify if the assumption holds, we conduct a number of two-sample Kolmogorow-Smirnow (KS) tests at the 1% significance level on the corresponding subband statistics. The null-hypothesis for the test is that both parts are drawn from the same underlying population. Table 2 lists the corresponding outcomes. Again a 0 denotes that the null-hypothesis cannot be rejected, numbers > 0 denote the number of rejections for our six test images.

We observe that for levels >= 2 our assumption cannot be rejected for the majority of cases. Thus, concatenation is reasonable and we can estimate the GGD parameters from $\mathbf{v}_{sk}$. For readability, we set $\mathbf{x} = \mathbf{v}_{sk}$. Further, let $N = 2n_s n_s$ denote the dimensionality of $\mathbf{x}$. We use Maximum-Likelihood Estimation (MLE) to determine the GGD parameters throughout this work. The ML estimate for β is given as the solution to the transcendental, non-linear equation

Table 1. Rejected null-hypothesis for the Chi-Square GoF outcomes at 1 % significance (6 images)

Orientation						
Scale	15°	45°	75°	-75°	-45°	-15°
1	6,5	4,3	6,6	6,5	4,4	6,6
2	4,5	2,4	4,4	3,3	3,3	5,4
	2,0	0,0	1,2	1,2	1,0	1,1

Table 2. Rejections for the two-sample KS tests at 1 % significance (6 images)

	Orientation					
Scale	15°	45°	75°	-75°	-45°	-15°
1	6	6	6	6	6	6
2	0	0	0	1	0	0
3	1	0	0	1	0	0

$$0 = 1 + \frac{\Psi(1/\hat{\beta})}{\hat{\beta}} - \frac{\sum_{i=1}^{N} |x_i|^{\hat{\beta}} \log|x_i|}{\sum_{i=1}^{N} |x_i|^{\hat{\beta}}} + \log\left(\frac{\hat{\beta}}{N} \sum_{i=1}^{N} |x_i|^{\hat{\beta}}}{\hat{\beta}}\right) \quad (2)$$

The parameter estimate β is then used to compute the MLE of the second parameter α as follows

$$\hat{\alpha} = \left(\frac{\hat{\beta}}{L} \sum_{i=1}^{N} |x_i|^{\hat{\beta}}\right)^{1/\hat{\beta}} \quad (3)$$

To find the root of Equation (2) we will resort to the classic Newton-Raphson root-finding iteration, which was proposed in (Do & Vetterli, 2000) for example. An alternative would be to use moment estimate methods (Nadarajah, 2005).

3. COMPLEX WAVELET TRANSFORM WATERMARKING

Generally speaking, additive spread-spectrum watermarking in the DT-CWT domain adds a pseudo-random watermark **w** to the host signal **x** to compute the watermarked signal **y** as **y** = **x** + **gw**, where the mask **g** is used to perceptually shape the watermark (Note: **gw** denotes a point-wise multiplication). Since the CWT coefficients closely relate to human perception, a simple

perceptual model can be used (Loo, 2002), where the elements of the mask **g** for subband $\mathbf{D}_{sk}$ are computed by

$$g_{sk} = \sqrt{r^2 \overline{|d_{sk}|}_U^2 + \gamma^2} \quad (4)$$

Here, $\overline{|d_{sk}|}_U^2$ represents the averaged squared magnitude of neighboring CWT coefficients and $r \; \varepsilon \; R$ and $\gamma \; \varepsilon \; R$ are parameters depending on the decomposition level as well as orientation of the embedding subband (Loo & Kingsbury, 2000). The advantage of the DT-CWT over the DWT with biorthogonal 7/9 filters can be seen in the difference images of Figure 2. Due to the better directional selectivity of the DT-CWT, the embed-

Figure 2. Difference between original and watermarked images: DWT domain embedding (top) and DT-CWT domain embedding (bottom) at 40 dB PSNR

ded watermark better aligns with the texture of the image (especially visible in the lower-right area of Barbara's trousers). For a quantitative comparison see the results in Section 5.1.

We note that the components of the random watermark **W** which lie in the null-space of the inverse transform of the redundant DT-CWT domain will be lost. The problem of embedding a spread-spectrum watermark in the DT-CWT domain can be overcome by adding the DT-CWT transformed watermark **W'** to the detail subbands, rather then adding the bipolar pseudo-random watermark **W** directly (Loo, 2002). The watermark vector $\mathbf{w'}_{sk}$ used to watermark the host signal vector $\mathbf{v}_{sk}$ is obtained by decomposing the bipolar watermark image **W** in the same way as to host signal and again rearranging the watermark subband $\mathbf{W'}_{sk}$ into a row vector. In this work, we only use a scalar scaling factor g_{sk} per subband rather than a perceptual mask $\mathbf{g}_{sk}$.

In the literature, complex wavelet domain watermarking has been employed because its shift-invariance allows to compensate geometrical attacks and because of the superior perceptual characteristics due to the better directional sensitivity of its subbands compared to the DWT (Loo, 2002). Woo et al. (2006) construct an embedding domain invariant to geometric desynchronization attacks by applying the DT-CWT on top of the FFT and a log-polar mapping. For video watermarking, Earl and Kingsbury (2003) presents a spread-transform, quantization-based scheme operating on a series on frames, exploiting the shift invariance property of the DT-CWT to resist spatial jitter. Tang and Chen (2009) employ motion estimation in the DT-CWT domain to embed a energy-adaptive watermark which allows for blind detection. Wang et al. (2007) employ scene-segmentation together with a 3D CWT for video watermarking. Coria et al. (2008) embed a spread-spectrum watermark in the coarse subbands and correlate over multiple frames of a video sequence to achieve robustness against geometrical distortions. Kumaran and Thangavel (2008) turn

to the recently proposed double-density dual-tree DWT domain (Selesnick, 2004) and investigate two quantization-based embedding strategies with genetic optimization. Two non-blind watermarking methods incorporate color images and describe combined visible/invisible watermarking (Mabtoul et al., 2007; Zhuang & Jiang, 2006). An assessment of non-blind watermark robustness for CWT versus DWT embedding is performed by Terzija and Geisselhardt (2004). Two semi-blind watermarking techniques in the DT-CWT and DWT domain are compared by Mabtoul et al. (2009) w.r.t. robustness and perceptual image quality, indicating better performance for the DT-CWT embedding approach.

We now turn to blind watermark detection adapted to the DT-CWT domain host signal statistics. Previous work relies on linear correlation detection which is suboptimal for the non-Gaussian DT-CWT detail subbands.

4. BLIND DT-CWT WATERMARK DETECTION

In this section, we will first discuss the detection of the embedded watermark sequence using the classic GGD detector (Hernandez et al., 2000) and the problems w.r.t. to our watermarking approach. Second, we introduce our proposed solution and discuss its advantages. For the following illustrations, we will omit the position indices s,k of the subbands in the DT-CWT decomposition structure and use y to denote a watermarked subband vector with $N = 2n_s n_s$ coefficients.

Hernandez et al. (2000) have derived a blind detector structure for host signals that can be modeled by a two-parameter GGD. Since the detector can be adapted to a given host signal via the GGD's shape parameter β, the detector demonstrates superior performance compared to a linear-correlation (LC) detector, which is optimal for a Gaussian host signal only. The log-likelihood ratio test (LRT) between the PDFs under H0 (no watermark present) and H1 (watermarked) of the GGD detector is given by

$$\rho_{LRT} = \sum_{i=1}^{N} \frac{1}{\alpha^{\beta}} \left(|y_i|^{\beta} - |y_i - g w_i|^{\beta} \right), \qquad (5)$$

for a single scaling factor g ε R$^+$. We note that the random elements in Equation (5) are the coefficients of the watermark, not the y$_i$ itself. Under the central limit theorem (n $\rightarrow \infty$)the log-likelihood ratio ρLRT (i.e. the detector response) follows a Gaussian distribution for which under H0 the expectation value $E[\rho LRT | H0] = \mu_{H0}$ can be computed according to

$$\mu_{H_0} = \sum_{i=1}^{N} \frac{1}{\alpha^{\beta}} |y_i|^{\beta} - \frac{1}{2} \sum_{i=1}^{N} \frac{1}{\alpha^{\beta}} \left(|y_i - g|^{\beta} + |y_i + g|^{\beta} \right)$$

$$. \qquad (6)$$

The variance $V[\rho LRT | H0] = \sigma^2_{H_0}$ can be easily derived,

$$\sigma^2_{H_0} = \frac{1}{4} \sum_{i=1}^{N} \frac{1}{\alpha^{2\beta}} \left(|y_i + g|^{\beta} - |y_i - g|^{\beta} \right)^2 .$$

$$\qquad (7)$$

The expectation and variance under the alternative hypothesis H1, denoted as μ_{H1}, β, have been shown to be $\mu_{H1} = \mu_{H0}$ and $\sigma^2_{H1} = \sigma^2_{H0}$, respectively. According to the Neyman-Pearson criterion, we can select the detection threshold T based on a desired probability of false-alarm P$_f$ as $T = \sigma_{H0} \cdot Q^{-1}(P_f) - \mu_{H0}$ where Q() denotes the Q-function to express right-tail probabilities of the Normal distribution. The probability of miss P$_m$ is given by

$$P_m = P\left(\rho_{LRT} < T | H_1\right) = 1 - Q\left(Q^{-1}(P_f) - 2\frac{\mu_{H_1}}{\sigma_{H_1}}\right)$$

$$. \qquad (8)$$

However, there is one important restriction to be considered. Equations (6) and (7) only hold for watermarks following a discrete distribution with equiprobable values {-1,+1}. Our experimental results based on 1000 randomly generated watermarks with equiprobable values {+1,-1} show that the transformed watermark **W'** follows a Gaussian distribution with zero mean and approximate variance of 0.25. Therefore, Equations (6) and (7) cannot be applied any longer. Since we do not have a closed form expression for Equations (6) and (7) for the normally distributed subband statistics of **W'**, we have to resort to empirical estimates of μ_{H0} and σ^2_{H0} for a given signal, in order to determine a reasonable detection threshold T. Unfortunately, this is a cumbersome procedure in practice.

We can find a solution to that problem in signal detection theory (Kay, 1998). In particular, we adopt a Rao hypothesis test which has already been extensively discussed in a general signal detection setting (Kay, 1989) and was proposed by Nikolaidis and Pitas (2003) for the purpose of blind spread-spectrum watermark detection in the DWT domain. However, our setup is slightly different from the one presented by Nikolaidis and Pitas (2003). First, our watermark is not bipolar but Normal and second, we use another, but equivalent parametrization of the GGD (see Equation (1) Provided that $\rho(.)$ denotes a symmetric PDF, the general formulation of the Rao hypothesis test derived in Kay (1989) is given by

$$\rho_{Rao} = \frac{\left[\sum_{i=1}^{N} \left. \frac{\partial \log(p(y_i - g w_i, \gamma))}{\partial g} \right|_{g=0} \right]^2}{\frac{1}{N} \sum_{i=1}^{N} w_i^2 \left[\sum_{i=1}^{N} \frac{p'(y_i, \gamma)}{p(y_i, \gamma)} \right]},$$

$$\qquad (9)$$

where ρ' denotes the first derivative of the PDF w.r.t. y$_i$ and γ ε R^d denotes an arbitrary d-dimensional parameter vector. In signal detection theory, the elements of γ are termed the *nuisance* parameters, which are unknown and have to be estimated. Inserting the PDF of the GGD α now leads to our desired detection statistic

$$\rho_{Rao} = \frac{\left[\sum_{i=1}^{N} w_i \, \mathrm{sgn}(y_i) \, |y_i|^{\beta-1}\right]^2}{\frac{1}{N}\sum_{i=1}^{N} w_i^2 \left[\sum_{i=1}^{N} |y_i|^{2\beta-2}\right]}, \qquad (10)$$

where sgn() denotes the signum function. We note that in contrast to the Rao detector for bipolar watermarks, the sum over the squared watermark elements in the denominator of Equation (10) cannot be dropped. From the theory of statistical signal detection we know that detection statistic under H0 follows a Chi-Square distribution with one degree of freedom. Under the alternative hypothesis H1, the detection statistic follows a Non-Central Chi-Square distribution with one degree of freedom and non-centrality parameter λ. We can determine the detection threshold T based on a desired P_f as $T = Q^{-1}(P_f/2)^2$. The probability of missing the watermark (P_m) is given by

$$P_m = P(\rho_{Rao} < T \mid H_1)$$
$$= 1 - Q\left(Q^{-1}(P_f/2) - \sqrt{\lambda}\right) - Q\left(Q^{-1}(P_f/2) + \sqrt{\lambda}\right) \qquad (11)$$

Alternatively, P_m can be computed using the CDF of the Non-Central Chi-Square distribution. To illustrate the difference in the detector output statistics, Figure 3 shows exemplary histograms of the detector responses (Lena) for the linear-correlation (LC) detector, the likelihood-ratio test (LRT) and the Rao detector. We note that the responses of the first two detectors follow Normal distributions with approximately equal variances under H0 and H1 while the detection responses of the Rao test can be modeled by the aforementioned Chi-Square distributions.

5. EXPERIMENTAL RESULTS

In this section, we present the experimental results of our work[1]. Our six 256x256 grayscale test images are shown in Figure 4. We begin by justifying the more involved DT-CWT domain embedding over the use of the DWT domain and then report detection performance results.

5.1. Perceptual Assessment

We have already observed the superior perceptual characteristics of DT-CWT embedding in Figure 2, Section 3. For an objective assessment of the distortion caused by DT-CWT and DWT embedding with the same PSNR, we employ four perceptual metrics, wPSNR/PQS (Miyahara, 1998),

Figure 3. Exemplary histograms of the LC, LRT and Rao detector responses under H0 and H1

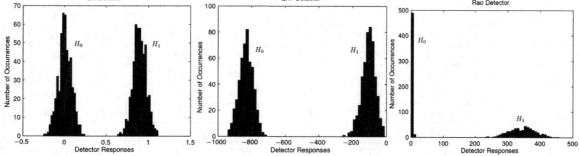

Figure 4. Example images (Lena, Barbara, Fabric, Bridge, Dromedary, Models)

Komparator[2] (Barba & Callet, 2003), C4 (Carnec et al., 2008) and VSNR[3] (Chandler & Hemami, 2007) which all have been proposed to assess compression artifacts without making assumptions about the type of degradation introduced by coding schemes. Komparator and C4 have already been successfully applied to the perceptual assessment of watermarking schemes (Marini et al., 2007). In Table 3 we present the perceptual quality measures for DWT and DT-CWT embedding according to our chosen metrics. The embedding strength has been adjusted to obtain watermarked images of 36 dB PSNR, so that the watermark becomes slightly noticeable in smooth and edge regions. DT-CWT embedding results in better image quality with the exception of the texture image Fabric which lacks any diagonal features. Note that for Komparator, lower values correspond to better perceptual quality, and vice-versa for wPSNR/PQS, C4 and VSNR.

In addition to our selected example images, the objective quality assessment has also been performed on 500 other natural grayscale images of size 512x512 (taken from the BOWS-2 image

Table 3. wPSNR/PQS, Komparator, C4 and VSNR quality metric for DWT and DT-CWT embedding with 36 dB PSNR

Image	wPSNR/PQS		Komparator		C4		VSNR	
	DWT	DT-CWT	DWT	DT-CWT	DWT	DT-CWT	DWT	DT-CWT
Lena	45.88	**46.49**	992.28	**799.57**	0.939	**0.950**	23.48	**26.53**
Barbara	46.81	**47.26**	1045.24	**400.61**	0.954	**0.957**	24.63	**27.78**
Fabric	46.19	**46.90**	**198.86**	320.72	**0.966**	0.965	30.88	**34.67**
Bridge	45.96	**46.49**	556.72	**506.75**	0.941	**0.960**	26.21	**29.43**
Dromedary	45.95	**46.52**	1059.48	**387.69**	0.923	**0.946**	22.78	**25.56**
Models	45.75	**46.29**	672.59	**444.81**	0.957	**0.963**	28.60	**31.90**

set[4]. Komparator claimed superior quality for the DT-CWT embedding in 382 cases versus 118 for DWT, while C4 votes 422 times for DT-CWT and 78 times for DWT. wPSNR/PQS and VSNR decided in all cases in favour of the DT-CWT embedding approach. To our knowledge, this is the first objective quality assessment comparing two watermark embedding domains -- further study is needed.

5.2. Detection Results

For a comparison of the detection performance, we arbitrary choose to embed the watermark sequence at decomposition level two (subband +45 degree). The resulting PSNRs for the watermarked images (16 dB Document-to-Watermark Ratio, DWR) are shown in Table 4.

First, we analyze the performance of our detectors in the absence of attacks, see Figure 5. We determine the experimental ROC curves from test runs with 1000 randomly generated watermarks (simulating the H1 hypothesis). Only in case of

Table 4. Average PSNR (dB) for our watermarked images (embedding with 16 dB DWR)

Image	PSNR	Image	PSNR
Barbara	48.21	Bridge	46.73
Dromedary	52.42	Fabric	38.60
Lena	47.16	Models	44.55

the LRT detector, we have to resort to estimating the mean and variance of the normally distributed detection statistic under H0 as well. We have further verified that the detector responses of the Rao detector under H0 actually follow a Chi-Square distribution with one degree of freedom using a GoF test at 1% significance.

To compute the ROC curves of the Rao detector we estimate the non-centrality parameter λ from the ρ_{Rao} as follows: since we know that under H1 the square-root of the detection statistic will follow a Normal distribution $N(\lambda^{1/2}, 1)$, we can simply estimate λ by raising the arithmetic mean of $\rho_{Rao}^{1/2}$ to the power of two. Then, we can determine P_m at a given P_f from the Equation (11). As expected, the LC detector employed by previous DT-CWT domain watermarking schemes (Loo, 2002; Earl & Kingsbury, 2003; Woo et al., 2006; Wang et al., 2007; Coria et al., 2008) performs worst. Interestingly, using the MLE of the shape parameter β did not result in the best detection performance for the Rao and LRT detector. To find a reasonable explanation for this behavior, we have to take a closer look at the embedding process. What we actually do, is to add a scaled random sequence (the watermark), which follows a Gaussian law, to the transform coefficients following a Generalized Gaussian law. Depending on the embedding strength, this has the effect that the shape parameter β is altered. Due to the redundancy of the DT-CWT, the marked coefficients

Figure 5. Detector ROC plots for 16 dB DWR

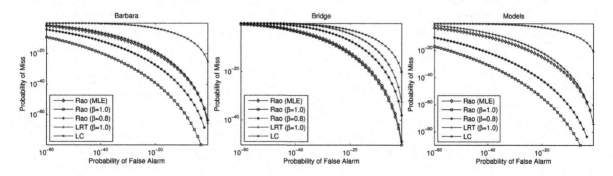

Figure 6. JPEG attack results for $P_f = 10^{-10}$ and DWR 16 dB

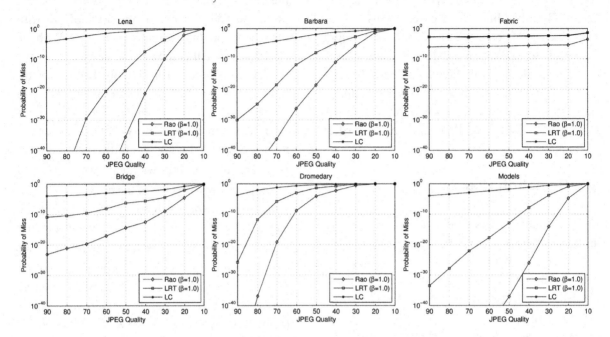

will be partly lost during the inverse transform. This leads to the situation that at the detection stage, β be accurately estimated any longer, which in turn leads to poor detection performance.

However, our experiments show that for reasonable DWRs, a fixed shape parameter $\beta = 1$ performs very well, since after embedding the GGD shape is close to one for natural images.

Figure 7. JPEG2000 attack results for $P_f = 10^{-10}$ and DWR 16 dB

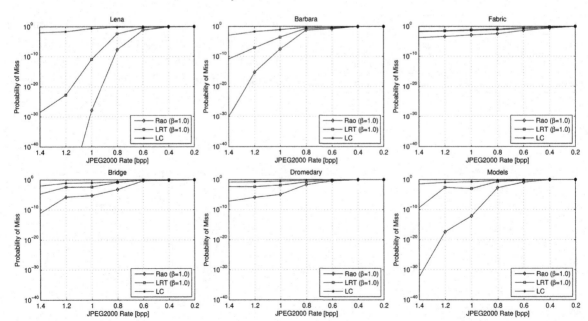

Therefore, we will perform the detection performance analysis under attacks with this fixed shape parameter $\beta = 1$. The ROC results for the other test images are similar but we omit them due to space limitations.

We consider JPEG and JPEG 2000 compression with varying quality factors and bit rates to evaluate the detectors' performance under attack in Figures 6 and 7. For the JPEG attacks we use MATLAB's functionality to write JPEG images with quality factors ranging from 10 to 90. In case of JPEG2000, we employ the Kakadu toolkit[5] with bit rates ranging from 0.2 bpp to 1.4 bpp. The LC detector shows the worst performance. Concerning the LRT and Rao detector, Rao is consistently better than LRT for both attacks at the P_f of 10^{-10}. Setting the GGD's shape parameter $\beta = 1$ only limits the detection performance for the texture image Fabric, where the true shape of the GGD significantly differs from $\beta = 1$ and is close to two.

6. CONCLUSION

The contribution of this paper is threefold: First, we show that the concatenated marginal statistics of the real and imaginary coefficient components of the DT-CWT detail subbands can be modeled by GGDs. Since the shape parameters of fitted GGDs differ significantly from the Gaussian distribution in case of natural images, the blind linear correlation detection employed by earlier DT-CWT watermarking schemes (Loo, 2002; Earl & Kingsbury, 2003; Woo et al., 2006; Wang et al., 2007; Coria et al., 2008) can be improved. To this end, we have adapted the GGD detector structure proposed (Hernandez et al., 2000) to work with the DT-CWT and discussed the problem of threshold determination. Further, we have proposed a modification of the Rao detector presented (Nikolaidis & Pitas, 2003) to work with our watermarking setup in order to overcome the problems re-

lated to the LRT detector. Second, our experimental results indicate that an estimation of the shape parameter of the GGD leads to poorer detection performance than setting β to a fixed value. The explanation of this behavior is strongly related to the redundancy of the DT-CWT and the distributional properties of the transformed watermark. Last, detection results under JPEG and JPEG2000 attacks highlight the advantages of the Rao detector and justify our approach. Further work will include a detailed examination of the parameter estimation issues, investigate the impact of perceptual modelling and continue the perceptual assessment of the watermarked images.

REFERENCES

Barba, D., & Callet, P.-L. (2003). A robust quality metric for color image quality assessment. In *Proceedings of the IEEE International Conference on Image Processing (ICIP '03)*, Barcelona, Spain (Vol. 1, pp. 437-440). Washington, DC: IEEE.

Carnec, M., Callet, P.-L., & Barba, D. (2008). Objective quality assessment of color images based on a generic perceptual reduced reference. *Signal Processing Image Communication, 23*(4), 239–256. doi:10.1016/j.image.2008.02.003

Chandler, D., & Hemami, S. (2007). VSNR: A wavelet-based visual signal-to-noise ratio for natural images. *IEEE Transactions on Image Processing, 16*(9), 2284–2298. doi:10.1109/TIP.2007.901820

Coria, L., Pickering, M., Nasiopoulos, P., & Ward, R. (2008). A video watermarking scheme based on the dual-tree complex wavelet transform. *IEEE Transactions on Information Forensics and Security, 3*(3), 466–474. doi:10.1109/TIFS.2008.927421

Do, M., & Vetterli, M. (2000). Texture Similarity Measurement using Kullback-Leibler Distance on Wavelet Subbands. In *Proceedings of the IEEE International Conference on Image Processing (ICIP '00)*, Vancouver, Canada (Vol. 3, pp. 703-733).

Earl, J., & Kingsbury, N. (2003). Spread transform watermarking for video sources. In *Proceedings of the IEEE International Conference on Image Processing (ICIP '03)*, Barcelona, Spain (Vol. 2, pp. 491-494).

Hernandez, J., Amado, M., & Perez-Gonzalez, F. (2000). DCT-domain watermarking techniques for still images: Detector performance analysis and a new structure. *IEEE Transactions on Image Processing, 9*(1), 55–68. doi:10.1109/83.817598

Kay, S. (1989). Asymptotically optimal detection in incompletely characterized non-Gaussian noise. *IEEE Transactions on Acoustics, Speech, and Signal Processing, 37*(5), 627–633. doi:10.1109/29.17554

Kay, S. (1998). *Fundamentals of Statistical Signal Processing: Detection Theory* (*Vol. 2*). Upper Saddle River, NJ: Prentice-Hall.

Kingsbury, N. (1998). The Dual-Tree Complex Wavelet Transform: A new Technique for Shift-Invariance and Directional Filters. In *Proceedings of the 8th IEEE DSP Workshop*, Bryce Canyon, UT (pp. 9-12).

Kingsbury, N. (2001). Complex Wavelets for Shift-Invariant Analysis and Filtering of Signals. *Journal of Applied Computational Harmonic Analysis, 10*(3), 234–253. doi:10.1006/acha.2000.0343

Kumaran, T., & Thangavel, P. (2008). Genetic algorithm based watermarking in double-density dual-tree DWT. In *Proceedings of the International Conference on Wavelet Analysis and Pattern Recognition (ICWAPR '08)* (pp. 585-590).

Loo, P. (2002). *Digital Watermarking with Complex Wavelets*. PhD thesis, University of Cambridge, UK.

Loo, P., & Kingsbury, N. (2000). Digital watermarking using complex wavelets. In *Proceedings of the IEEE International Conference on Image Processing (ICIP '00)*, Vancouver, Canada (Vol. 3, pp. 29-32).

Mabtoul, S., Elhaj, E., & Aboutajdine, D. (2007). Robust color image watermarking based on singular value decomposition and dual tree complex wavelet transform. In *Proceedings of the 14th IEEE International Conference on Electronics, Circuits and Systems (ICECS '07)* (pp. 534-537). Washington, DC: IEEE.

Mabtoul, S., Elhaj, E., & Aboutajdine, D. (2009). Robust Semi-Blind Digital Image Watermarking Technique in DT-CWT Domain. *International Journal of Computer Science, 4*(1), 8–12.

Malvar, H., & Florencio, D. (2003). Improved spread spectrum: A new modulation technique for robust watermarking. *IEEE Transactions on Signal Processing, 51*(4), 898–905. doi:10.1109/TSP.2003.809385

Marini, E., Autrusseau, F., Callet, P.-L., & Campisi, P. (2007). Evaluation of standard watermarking techniques. In *Proceedings of SPIE, Security, Steganography and Watermarking of Multimedia Contents IX*, San Jose, CA (Vol. 6505).

MIT Vision and Modeling Group. (n.d.). *VisTeX* (Online). Retrieved May 13, 2009 from http://vismod.media.mit.edu

Miyahara, M. (1998). Objective picture quality scale (PQS) for image coding. *IEEE Transactions on Communications, 46*(9), 1215–1226. doi:10.1109/26.718563

Nadarajah, S. (2005). A generalized normal distribution. *Journal of Applied Statistics, 32*(7), 685–694. doi:10.1080/02664760500079464

Nikolaidis, A., & Pitas, I. (2003). Asymptotically optimal detection for additive watermarking in the DCT and DWT domains. *IEEE Transactions on Image Processing, 12*(5), 563–571. doi:10.1109/TIP.2003.810586

Selesnick, I. (2004). The Double-Density Dual-Tree DWT. *IEEE Transactions on Signal Processing, 52*(5), 1304–1314. doi:10.1109/TSP.2004.826174

Tang, X., & Chen, L. (2009). A Color Video Watermarking Algorithm Based on DTCWT and Motion Estimation. In *Proceedings of the 2009 WRI International Conference on Communications and Mobile Computing (CMC '09)* (Vol. 3, pp. 413-417).

Terzija, N., & Geisselhardt, W. (2004). Digital image watermarking using complex wavelet transform. In *Proceedings of the ACM Multimedia and Security Workshop (MMSEC '04),* Magdeburg, Germany (pp. 193-198). New York: ACM.

Wang, J., Gao, X., & Zhong, J. (2007). A video watermarking based on 3-D complex wavelet. In *Proceedings of the IEEE International Conference on Image Processing (ICIP '07)*, San Antonio, TX (Vol. 5, pp. 493-496). Washington, DC: IEEE.

Woo, C., Du, J., & Pham, B. (2006). Geometric invariant domain for image watermarking. In *Proceedings of the International Workshop on Digital Watermarking (IWDW '06),* South, Korea (LNCS 4283, pp. 294-307). New York: Springer.

Zhuang, L., & Jiang, M. (2006). Multipurpose digital watermarking algorithm based on dual-tree CWT. In *Proceedings of the 6th International Conference on Intelligent Systems, Design and Applications (ISDA '06)* (Vol. 2, pp. 316-320).

ENDNOTES

[1] Our MATLAB source is available online at http://www.wavelab.at/sources.

[2] Komparator source code is available at http://autrusseau.florent.club.fr/Komparator.

[3] VSNR source code is available at http://foulard.ece.cornell.edu/dmc27/vsnr/vsnr.html.

[4] BOWS-2 is online at http://bows2.gipsa-lab.inpg.fr/.

[5] Kakadu binaries are available at http://kakadusoftware.com.

This work was previously published in the International Journal of Digital Crime and Forensics, Volume 2, Issue 2, edited by Chang-Tsun Li and Anthony TS Ho, pp. 34-46, copyright 2010 by IGI Publishing (an imprint of IGI Global).

Chapter 6
Spatio–Temporal Just Noticeable Distortion Model Guided Video Watermarking

Yaqing Niu
Communication University of China, China

Sridhar Krishnan
Ryerson University, Canada

Qin Zhang
Communication University of China, China

ABSTRACT

Perceptual Watermarking should take full advantage of the results from human visual system (HVS) studies. Just noticeable distortion (JND), which refers to the maximum distortion that the HVS does not perceive, gives a way to model the HVS accurately. An effective Spatio-Temporal JND model guided video watermarking scheme in DCT domain is proposed in this paper. The watermarking scheme is based on the design of an additional accurate JND visual model which incorporates spatial Contrast Sensitivity Function. (CSF), temporal modulation factor, retinal velocity, luminance adaptation and contrast masking. The proposed watermarking scheme, where the JND model is fully used to determine scene-adaptive upper bounds on watermark insertion, allows providing the maximum strength transparent watermark. Experimental results confirm the improved performance of the Spatio-Temporal JND model. The authors' Spatio-Temporal JND model is capable of yielding higher injected-watermark energy without introducing noticeable distortion to the original video sequences and outperforms the relevant existing visual models. Simulation results show that the proposed Spatio-Temporal JND model guided video watermarking scheme is more robust than other algorithms based on the relevant existing perceptual models while retaining the watermark transparency.

DOI: 10.4018/978-1-4666-1758-2.ch006

INTRODUCTION

The rapid growth of the Internet has created a need for techniques that can be used for copyright protection of digital images and videos. One approach is to introduce digital watermark into images or video sequences. For a well-designed watermark there are many requirements including imperceptibility, robustness and capacity. However, in order to maintain the image quality and at the same time increase the probability of the watermark detection, it is necessary to take the human visual system (HVS) into consideration when engaging in watermarking research (Wolfgang, Podilchuk, & Delp, 1999; Podilchuk & Zeng, 1998; Doerr & Dugelay, 2003).

HVS makes final evaluations on the quality of videos that are processed and displayed. Just noticeable distortion (JND), which refers to the maximum distortion that the HVS does not perceive gives us a way to model the HVS accurately and can serve as a perceptual visibility threshold to guide video watermarking. JND estimation for still images has been relatively well developed. An early perceptual threshold estimation in DCT domain was proposed by Ahumada and Peterson (1992), which gives the threshold for each DCT component by incorporating the spatial Contrast Sensitivity Function (CSF). This scheme was improved by Watson (1993) after the luminance adaptation effect had been added to the base threshold, and contrast masking (Legge, 1981) had been calculated as the elevation factor. In Zhang, Lin, and Xue (2005) an additional block classification based contrast masking and luminance adaptation was considered by Zhang for digital images. A spatial JND model proposed by Wei and Ngan (2008) incorporates new spatial CSF, luminance adaptation and contrast masking. Since motion is a specific feature of videos, temporal dimension needs to be taken into account for human perceptual visibility analysis. JND estimation for video sequences need to incorporate not only the spatial CSF, but the temporal CSF as well. A

spatio-temporal CSF model was proposed by Kelly (1979) from experiments on visibility thresholds under stabilized viewing conditions. Daly (1998) extended Kelly's model to fit unconstrained natural viewing conditions with a consideration of eye movements. Based on Daly's model, Jia, Lin, and Kassim (2006) estimated the JND thresholds for videos by combining other visual effects such as the luminance adaptation and contrast masking. An improved temporal modulation factor proposed by Wei and Ngan (2008) incorporates not only temporal CSF, but the directionality of motion is also considered. In Niu, Zhang, Krishnan, and Zhang (2009) a video-driven JND profile which incorporates the temporal modulation factor, retinal velocity, luminance adaptation, and block classification was developed.

Previous Watermarking schemes have only partially used the results of the HVS studies (Wolfgang, Podilchuk, & Delp, 1999; Ling, Lu, Zou, & Li, 2006; Podlilchuk & Zeng, 1998; Huang, Shi, & Shi, 1998; Kankanhalli & Ramakrishnan, 1998). Many video watermarking algorithms utilize visual models for still images to increase the robustness and transparency. The perceptual adjustment of the watermark is mainly based on Watson's spatial JND model (Wolfgang, Podilchuk, & Delp, 1999; Ling, Lu, Zou, & Li, 2006; Podilchuk & Zeng, 1998). An image-adaptive watermarking procedure based on Watson's spatial JND model was proposed in Podilchuk and Zeng (1998). In Wolfgang, Podilchuk, and Delp (1999), the DCT-based watermarking approach uses Watson's spatial JND model in which the threshold consists of spatial frequency sensitivity, luminance sensitivity and contrast masking. An Energy Modulated Watermarking Algorithm Based on Watson's spatial JND model was proposed in Ling, Lu, Zou, and Li (2006). During the modulation, Watson's perceptual model is used to restrict the modified magnitude of DCT coefficients. The main drawback of utilizing visual models for still images in video watermarking to increase the robustness and transparency is that it does not satisfactorily take into account the temporal dimension. Thus, the obtained watermark is not optimal in terms of imperceptibility and robustness since it does not consider the temporal sensitivity of the human eye. As we discussed, motion is a specific feature of video, temporal HVS properties needs to be taken into account to design more efficient watermarking algorithms. In Niu, Liu, Krishnan, and Zhang (2009) we exploit a combined Spatio-Temporal JND model to guide watermarking for digital videos.

In this study, we propose an effective Spatio-Temporal JND model guided video watermarking scheme in DCT domain. The watermarking scheme is based on the design of additional accurate JND visual model which incorporates spatial CSF, temporal modulation factor, retinal velocity, luminance adaptation and contrast masking. The proposed watermarking scheme, where JND model are fully used to determine scene-adaptive upper bounds on watermark insertion, allows us to provide the maximum strength transparent watermark.

This paper is organized as follows. In the next section, a detailed combined Spatio-Temporal JND model is presented. Section 3 gives the details of the proposed Spatio-Temporal JND model guided watermarking scheme. The proposed scheme is tested against attacks, such as additive Gaussian noise, lossy video compression, and valumetric scaling in Section 4. A detailed comparison of the proposed Spatio-Temporal JND model guided watermarking scheme with three relevant existing perceptual models guided watermarking scheme is also presented in this section. Finally, the paper is concluded in Section 5.

2 COMBINED SPATIO-TEMPORAL JND MODEL

Spatio-Temporal Just noticeable distortion (JND) is an efficient model incorporating spatial and temporal sensitivity of the human eye to represent the additional accurate perceptual redundancies for digital videos. Here we compute the visibility threshold of each DCT coefficient with a combined Spatio-Temporal JND model which incorporates spatial CSF, temporal modulation factor, retinal velocity, luminance adaptation and contrast masking all together.

2.1 Retinal Velocity

Motion is a specific feature of video imagery. Human eyes tend to track a moving object to keep retinal image of the object in the fovea (Daly, 1998; Tourancheau, Callet, & Barba, 2007; Laird, Rosen, Pelz, Montag, & Daly, 2006; Shutz, Delipetkos, Braun, Kerzel, & Gegenfurtner, 2007). It is necessary to take into account the observers' eye movements to see how well the traced objects can be seen during the presentation of motion imagery for human perceptual visibility analysis.

There are three types of eye movements (Daly, 1998): natural drift eye movements, smooth pursuit eye movements (SPEM) and saccadic eye movements. The natural drift eye movements are present even when the observer is intentionally fixating on a single position and these movements are responsible for the perception of static imagery during fixation. The saccadic eye movements are responsible for rapidly moving the fixation point from one location to another; thus, the HVS sensitivity is very low. The former are very slow (0.8-1.5 deg/s) and the latter are fast (80-300 deg/s). Fast object motion blurs the HVS perception. The SPEM tend to track the moving object and reduce the retinal velocity, and thus, compensate for the loss of sensitivity due to motion. Future experiments should test the limit of SPEM (Laird, Rosen, Pelz, Montag, & Daly, 2006).

Based on eye movements in Daly (1998), the retinal velocity v_R is different from the image velocity v_I, which can be obtained through motion estimation. The retinal velocity v_R can be expressed as (1)

$$v_{Rh} = v_{lh} - v_{Eh} \; (\hbar = x, y), \tag{1}$$

where eye movement velocity v_E is determined as (2)

$$v_{Eh} = \min\left[g_{sp} \times v_{lh} + v_{MIN}, v_{MAX}\right], \tag{2}$$

where g_{sp} is the gain of the SPEM, v_{MIN} is the minimum eye velocity due to drift, and v_{MAX} is the maximum eye velocity before saccadic movements. The average g_{sp} over all observers was 0.956 +/- 0.017 (Tourancheau, Callet, & Barba, 2007). The values v_{MIN} and v_{MAX} are set to 0.15 and 80.0 deg/s.

The image velocity v_I can be obtained with a motion estimation technique as follows

$$v_{lh} = f_{frame} \times MV \times \theta_h, \tag{3}$$

where f_{frame} is the frame rate of video and MV is the motion vector of each block; θ_h is the visual angle of a pixel obtained by (4)

$$\theta_\hbar = 2 \times \arctan\left(\frac{\Lambda_\hbar}{2l}\right), \tag{4}$$

where l is the viewing distance and Λ_h stands for the display width/length of a pixel on the monitor (Kelly, 1979).

2.2 Joint Spatio-Temporal CSF

Human eyes show a band-pass property in the spatial frequency domain. In comparison with various Spatial CSF models for still images (Watson, 1993; Zhang, Lin, & Xue, 2005), the CSF model for videos need to take into account the temporal dimension in addition to the spatial properties. The Joint Spatio-Temporal CSF describes the effect of spatial frequency and temporal frequency on the HVS sensitivity. The Spatio-Temporal CSF model is the reciprocal of the base distortion

threshold which can be tolerated for each DCT coefficient. In Wei and Ngan (2008a), and Wei and Ngan (2008b) it is shown that the base threshold for the DCT domain T_{BASE} corresponding to the Spatio-Temporal CSF model can be expressed by

$$T_{BASE}(k,n,i,j) = T_{BASEs}(k,n,i,j) \times F_T(k,n,i,j), \tag{5}$$

where T_{BASEs} is the base threshold corresponding to the Spatial CSF model and F_T is the temporal modulation factor; k is the index of the frame in the video sequences, and n is the index of a block in the k_{th} frame; i and j are the DCT coefficient indices. For still images, the T_{BASE} corresponding to the Spatio-Temporal CSF is equivalent to T_{BASEs} corresponding to the Spatial (static) CSF, so the JND model derived in this paper is also applicable for guiding image watermarking.

In Wei and Ngan (2008b) the base threshold T_{BASEs} is computed by (6)

$$T_{BASEs}(n,i,j) = s \times \frac{1}{\varphi_i \varphi_j} \times \frac{\exp\left(c\omega_{ij}\right)/\left(a + b\omega_{ij}\right)}{r + (1-r) \times \cos^2 \phi_{ij}}, \tag{6}$$

where a=1.33, b=0.11, c=0.18, s=0.25. φ_i and φ_j are DCT normalization factors by (7); ω_{ij} is the spatial frequency which can be calculated by (8); N is the dimension of the DCT block; θ_x and θ_y are the horizontal and vertical visual angles of a pixel by (4). r is set to 0.6, and φ_{ij} stands for the directional angle of the corresponding DCT component by (9).

$$\phi_m = \begin{cases} \sqrt{1/N}, & m = 0 \\ \sqrt{2/N}, & m > 0 \end{cases} \tag{7}$$

$$\omega_{ij} = \frac{1}{2N}\sqrt{(1/\theta_x)^2 + (j/\theta_y)^2} \tag{8}$$

$$\varphi_{ij} = \arcsin\left(\frac{2\omega_{i,0}\omega_{0,j}}{\omega^2_{ij}}\right) \tag{9}$$

In Wei and Ngan (2008a) the temporal modulation factor F_T is computed by (10)

$$F_T(k,n,i,j) = \begin{cases} 1 & f_s < 5cpd \ \& \ f_t < 10Hz \\ 1.07^{(f_t-10)} & f_s < 5cpd \ \& \ f_t \geq 10Hz \\ 1.07^{f_t} & f_s \geq 5cpd \end{cases} \tag{10}$$

where the *cpd* is cycles per degree, the temporal frequency f_t which depends not only on the motion, but also on the spatial frequency of the object is given by (11)

$$f_t = f_{sx}v_{Rx} + f_{sy}v_{Ry}, \tag{11}$$

where f_{sx} and f_{sy} are the horizontal and vertical components of the spatial frequency, which can be calculated by (12).

$$f_{sx} = \frac{i}{2N\theta_x} \quad f_{sy} = \frac{j}{2N\theta_y} \tag{12}$$

As discussed in Section 2.1, human eyes can automatically move to track an observed object. The retinal velocity v_{Rx} and v_{Ry} can be calculated by (1).

2.3 Luminance Adaptation

HVS is more sensitive to the noise in medium gray regions, so the visibility threshold is higher in very dark or very light regions. Because our base threshold is detected at the 128 intensity value, for other intensity values, a modification factor needs to be included. This effect is called the luminance adaptation effect. The curve of the luminance adaptation factor is a U-shape which means the factor at the lower and higher intensity regions is larger than the middle intensity region. An empirical formula for the luminance adaptation factor a_{Lum} in Wei and Ngan (2008b) it is shown as (13) where $I(k,n)$ is the average intensity value of the n_{th} block in the k_{th} frame.

$$a_{Lum}(k,n) = \begin{cases} (60 - I(k,n))/150 + 1 & I(k,n) \leq 60 \\ 1 & 60 < I(k,n) < 170 \\ (I(k,n) - 170)/425 + 1 & I(k,n) \geq 170 \end{cases} \tag{13}$$

2.4 Contrast Masking

Contrast masking refers to the reduction in the visibility of one visual component in the presence of another one. The masking is strongest when both components are of the same spatial frequency, orientation, and location. To incorporate contrast masking effect, we employ contrast masking $a_{contrast}$ (Legge, 1981) measured as

$$a_{contrast}(k,n,i,j) = \\ \max\left(1, \left(\frac{C(k,n,i,j)}{T_{BASE}(k,n,i,j) \times a_{Lum}(k,n)}\right)^{\varepsilon}\right) \tag{14}$$

where $C(k,n,i,j)$ is the $(i,j)_{-th}$ DCT coefficient in the n_{th} block of the k_{th} frame, and $\varepsilon=0.7$.

To find a suitable value for ε, Zhang, Lin, and Xue's (2005) perceptual model proposed a much lower value 0.36; But Zhang's model tends to underestimate JND in edgy blocks (Damnjanovic & Izquierdo, 2006). We exploit ε fixed to 0.7 as the value of this parameter chosen in Watson's perceptual model (Legge, 1981) which generates more accurate JND in edgy blocks.

2.5 Complete JND Estimator

The overall JND given in Equ (15) can be determined by the base threshold T_{BASE}, the luminance adaptation factor a_{Lum} and the contrast masking factor $a_{Contrast}$.

$$T_{JND}(k,n,i,j) =$$
$$T_{BASE}(k,n,i,j) \times a_{Lum}(k,n) \times a_{contrast}(k,n,i,j)$$
$$(15)$$

$T_{JND}(k,n,i,j)$ is the complete scene-driven Spatio-Temporal JND estimator which represents the additional accurate perceptual visibility threshold profile to guide watermarking.

3 THE SPATIO-TEMPORAL JND MODEL GUIDED WATERMARKING SCHEME

We exploit the combined Spatio-Temporal JND model guided watermarking scheme to embed and extract watermarking. The scheme first constructs a set of approximate energy sub-regions using the Improved Longest Processing Time (ILPT) algorithm (Zou, 2006), and then enforces an energy difference between every two sub-regions to embed watermarking bits (Langelaar & Lagendijk, 2001; Ling, Lu, & Zou, 2004) under the control of our combined Spatio-Temporal JND model.

3.1 The Construction of Approximate Energy Sub-Regions

The watermark bit string is embedded bit-by-bit in a set of regions (each region is composed of 2n 8x8 DCT blocks) of the original video frame. Each region is divided into two sub-regions (each sub-region is composed of n 8x8 DCT blocks). A single bit is embedded by modifying the energy of two sub-regions separately. However, for better imperceptibility, approximate energy sub-regions has to be constructed using ILPT, so that the original energy of each sub-region in one region are approximate.

Each bit of the watermark bit string is embedded in its constructed bit-carrying-region. For instance, in Figure 1 each bit is embedded in a region of 2n=16 8x8 DCT blocks. The value of the bit is encoded by introducing an energy difference between the low frequency DCT coefficients of the top half of the region (denoted by sub-region A) containing in this case n=8 8x8 DCT blocks, and the bottom half (denoted by sub-region B) also containing n=8 8x8 DCT blocks. The number of watermark bits that can be embedded is determined by the number of blocks in a region which is used to embed one watermark bit.

Figure 1. Watermark bit corresponding to approximate energy sub-regions constructed by ILPT

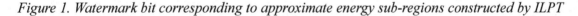
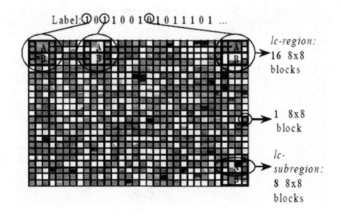

3.2 The Embedding Procedure

Diagram of combined Spatio-Temporal JND model guided watermark embedding is shown in Figure 2. The embedding procedure of the scheme is described as the following steps:

a) Decompose the original video frames into non-overlapping 8x8 blocks and compute the energy of the low-frequency DCT coefficients in the zigzag sequence.

b) Obtain approximate energy sub-regions by ILPT algorithm.

c) Map the index of the DCT blocks in a sub-region according to ILPT.

d) Use our combined Spatio-Temporal JND model described in Section 2 to calculate the perceptual visibility threshold profile for DCT coefficients calculated over blocks in video frames which makes the watermark imperceptible and robust.

e) If the watermark to be embedded is 1, the energy of sub-region A should be increased (positive modulation) and the energy of sub-region B should be decreased (negative modulation). If the watermark to be embedded is 0, the energy of sub-region A should be decreased (negative modulation) and the energy of sub-region B should be

increased (positive modulation). The energy of each sub-region is modified by adjusting the low-frequency DCT coefficients according to the combined Spatio-Temporal JND model as Equation 16 where $C(k,n,i,j)^m$ is the modified DCT coefficient, Sign(.) is the sign function, PM is positive modulation which means increase the energy and NM is negative modulation which means decrease the energy, $T_{JND}(k,n,i,j)$ is the perceptual visibility threshold by our combined Spatio-Temporal JND model and $f(.)$ can be expressed by

$$f(C(k,n,i,j), T_{JND}(k,n,i,j)) = \begin{cases} 0 & \text{if} \quad C(k,n,i,j) < T_{JND}(k,n,i,j) \\ T_{JND}(k,n,i,j), & \text{if} \quad C(k,n,i,j) \geq T_{JND}(k,n,i,j) \end{cases}$$

$$(17)$$

f) Conduct IDCT to the energy modified result to obtain the watermark embedded video frames.

3.3 The Extraction Procedure

Diagram of combined Spatio-Temporal JND model guided watermark extraction is shown in

Figure 2. Diagram of combined Spatio-Temporal JND model guided watermark embedding

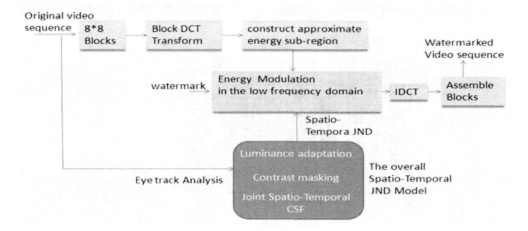

Equation 16.

$$C\left(k,n,i,j\right)^{m} = \begin{cases} C\left(k,n,i,j\right) + Sign\left(C\left(k,n,i,j\right)\right) \times f\left(C\left(k,n,i,j\right), T_{JND}(k,n,i,j)\right), & PM \\ C\left(k,n,i,j\right) - Sign\left(C\left(k,n,i,j\right)\right) \times f\left(C\left(k,n,i,j\right), T_{JND}(k,n,i,j)\right), & NM \end{cases}$$

Figure 3. The extraction procedure is described as follows:

a) Decompose the watermark embedded video frames into non-overlapping 8x8 blocks and compute the energy of the low-frequency DCT coefficients in the zigzag sequence.

b) Energy of each sub-region is calculated according to the index map.

c) Compare the energy of sub-region A with sub-region B. If the energy of sub-region A is greater than the energy of sub-region B, the watermark embedded is 1. If the energy of sub-region A is smaller than the energy of sub-region B, the watermark embedded is 0. The watermark is extracted accordingly.

4 EXPERIMENTAL RESULTS AND PERFORMANCE ANALYSIS

The proposed algorithm is composed of two parts. The first part of the proposed algorithm is in Section 2 which derived the combined Spatio-Temporal JND model. And in Section 3 which is the second part of the proposed algorithm gives the details of how to utilize the combined Spatio-Temporal JND model to guide video watermarking. And the experimental results are given according to these two parts. For the first part, we performed experiments in Section 4.1 to evaluate the performance of our combined Spatio-Temporal JND model. For the second part, we performed experiments in Section 4.2 to evaluate the performance of our JND model guided watermarking scheme focusing on the watermark's visual quality, capacity and robustness.

4.1 Evaluation on Spatio-Temporal JND Profile for Videos

In this experiment, the generated JND profile can be used to guide noise shaping in video sequences to evaluate the performance of different JND models. Watson's spatial JND model (Watson 1993) (referred to as Model 1 hereinafter), Zhang's spatial JND model (Zhang, Lin, & Xue, 2005) (referred to as Model 2 hereinafter) and Zhenyu

Figure 3. Diagram of combined Spatio-Temporal JND model guided watermark extraction

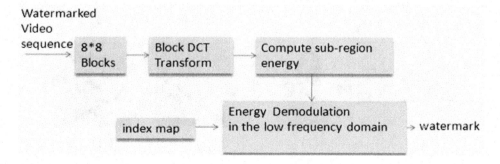

Wei's Spatio-Temporal JND model (Wei & Ngan, 2008a) (referred to as Model 3 hereinafter) were also implemented and compared with our JND estimator.

Eight video sequences are chosen as test sequences for this experiment ("akiyo", "bus", "flower", "foreman", "Stefan", "silent", "waterfall" and "suzie" shown in Figure 4 with different visual contents and object motion).

Noise is added to each DCT coefficients of the video sequences as (18), where f takes +1 or -1 randomly, $T_{JND}(k, n, i, j)$ represents the JND obtained via each model, $C'(k, n, i, j)$ is the noise-injected DCT coefficient.

$$C'(k, n, i, j) = C(k, n, i, j) + f \times T_{JND}(k, n, i, j) \tag{18}$$

For a convincing evaluation of our spatial JND estimator for videos, we tested in two aspects. One is to measure how much the visual content variations are after each JND model guided noise injection and the second is to assess the quality of each noise injected video frame. The PSNR tests were used to measure the variations introduced by noise injection. On the other hand, the subjective viewing tests were used to assess the quality of the resultant visual content. A better JND model allows higher injected-noise energy (corresponding to lower PSNR) without jeopardizing visual quality (measured by the subjective viewing tests). In the mean while, we performed tests to evaluate how our Spatio-Temporal JND model performs in the presence of motion as well.

4.1.1 PSNR Tests

Figure 5 shows the first frame of resultant "waterfall" video sequences after the JND guided noise injection as (18) by Models 1 to 3, and our model. We find the noise hardly noticeable in all four resultant frames which showed the four models yield values no larger than the actual HVS thresholds. The proposed model yields the lowest PSNR (Model 1 PSNR=29.8; Model 2 PSNR=29.4; Model 3 PSNR=27.3; Proposed model PSNR= 26.9) that reflects our JND model allows higher injected-noise energy without introducing noticeable visual distortions.

As aforementioned, at the same level of perceived picture quality, a better JND model yields more aggressive JNDs (resulting in lower PSNR). Figure 6 demonstrates the average PSNRs of noise injected frames of different sequences with four

Figure 4. Video sequences for the experiments (a) akiyo.cif (b) bus.cif (c) flower.cif (d) foreman. cif (e) stefan.qcif (f) silent. cif (g) waterfall. Cif (h) suzie. qcif

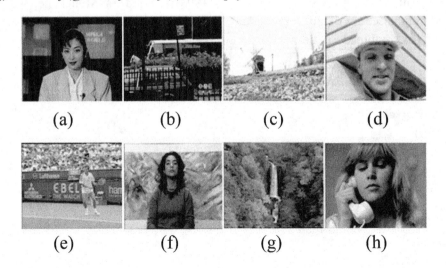

(a)   (b)   (c)   (d)

(e)   (f)   (g)   (h)

Figure 5. Resultant waterfall sequences (a) with Model 1, (b) with Model 2, (c) with Model 3, and (d) with Proposed model

(a) (b) (c) (d)

JND profiles. As can be seen, the proposed model yields the lowest average PSNR. The average PSNR by our model is 2.3 dB lower than that by Model 1, 1.8 dB lower than that by Model 2 and 1.1 dB lower than that by Model 3. Our model outperforms the other three models, since Model 1 and Model 2 does not exploit temporal sensitivity of HVS, while Model 3 does not exploit the more effective contrast masking properties. Thus, our Spatio-Temporal JND model is able to exploit the HVS bounds more optimally.

4.1.2 Motion Tests

Since we have discussed, motion is a specific feature of video, temporal HVS properties needs to be taken into account to design more efficient watermarking algorithms. To test how our Spatio-Temporal JND model performs in the presence of motion, we measure the motion of each frame using the average motion energy defined as (19), where N_b is the number of blocks in a frame.

$$Avg\_Motion\_Energy(k) = \frac{1}{N_b} \sum_n (MV_x^2(k,n) + MV_y^2(k,n)) \quad (19)$$

Figure 6. PSNR with four JND profiles

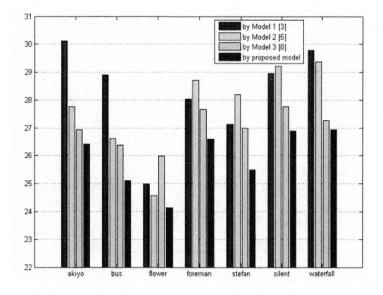

As discussed in Section 2.1, fast object motion blurs the HVS perception. Since the sensitivity of human eyes reduces when motion occurs, more visual content variations can be introduced without jeopardizing visual content quality. Figure 7 illustrates the average motion energy over the frames for the Suzie video sequences, while Figure 8 shows the PSNRs over the frames for the noise-injected Suzie sequences by the proposed Spatio-Temporal JND model. As shown in Figure 7, there is a large increase in average motion energy around frames 50 to 55; as expected, Figure 8 shows the corresponding drop of PSNR by our model. From evidence above, it can be concluded that our Spatio-Temporal JND model can respond to motion correctly and tolerate more distortion with higher motion.

4.1.3 Subjective Viewing Tests

The subjective viewing tests were conducted with a ThinkPad X61 12.1 TFT LCD display and the viewing distance was 50 cm. In order to test the perceptual quality, the Double Stimulus Continuous Quality Scale (DSCQS) method in ITU-R BT.500 is used (Methodology for the subjective assessment of the quality of television pictures, 2002). The method presents two videos (the original one and the processed one) to the viewers. Ten subjects were asked to give scores for all the video sequence pairs. The Mean Opinion Score (MOS) scales for the quality are: Excellent (100-80), Good (79-60), Fair (59-40), Poor (39-20), and Bad (19-0). Then, the difference MOS (DMOS) is calculated by subtracting the MOS of the processed one from that of the original one.

The experimental results show that the averaged DMOSs over the ten viewers for all test sequence pairs by Models 1 to 3, and our model are 12.8, 14.7, 13.8 and 13.9 respectively. The scores resulting from four models are very similar; hence, our model leads to similar visual quality on average as Models 1 to 3 in the noise-injected video sequences.

From the experimental results above, our Spatio-Temporal JND model for videos yields more aggressive JNDs than Models 1 to 3 with the evidence of lower PSNR, yet at the same level of perceived quality, and the modeling of temporal effect is effective. Our Spatio-Temporal JND profile for videos correlate with the human

Figure 7. Average motion energy of each frame

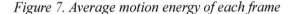
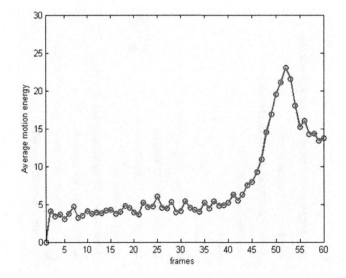

Figure 8. PSNR of each frame with the proposed Spatio-Temporal JND model

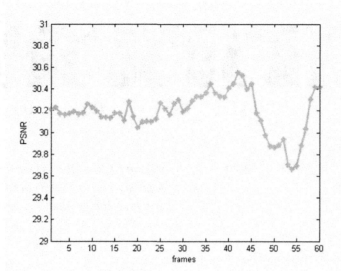

visual system very well and can obtain better performance in guiding video watermarking.

4.2 Evaluation on Performance of Combined Spatio-Temporal JND Model Guided Video Watermarking

We construct a series of tests to observe the performance of our combined Spatio-Temporal JND model guided video watermarking as well. The 720 x 576 "walk_pal" video sequences are used for experiments A, B, and C. The "suzie" video sequences are used for experiment D.

4.2.1 Visual Quality

As discussed in Section 4.1, the combined Spatio-Temporal JND model correlates with the human visual system very well. We can use the proposed model to guide noise shaping in each DCT coefficients of digital video frames yet the difference is hardly noticeable. To embed watermark with the guiding of our model is similar to the process of noise shaping. As described in section 3, not all the coefficients are modified with the consideration of Lossy Compression so the Visual quality is even

better than the test result in Section 4.1. Figure 9 (a) shows the first frame of the "walk_pal" video sequence. Figure 9 (b)-(e) are the first frame of the watermarked video sequence using four JND models. The section below compares the five mentioned figures, Figure 9 (a)-(e). We can see no obvious degradation in Figure 9 (b)-(e) where the PSNR are 35.5dB, 47.9dB, 43.9dB and 34.4dB respectively.

4.2.2 Capacity

The watermark bit string is embedded bit-by-bit in a set of regions of the original video frame. Each region is divided into two sub-regions. A single bit is embedded by modifying the energy of two sub-regions separately. For each 720x576 video frame the number of bits can be embedded is determined by the number of 8 x 8 DCT blocks in a region. We set the number of blocks at 8 in each region in the following experiments. That means each 720x576 video frame would embed 810 bits.

In Section 4.2 we focused on testing that for the same number of embedded bits (810 bits) which watermarking scheme is more robust based

Figure 9. Original "walk_pal" video (a) Watermarked pal video by Model 1 (b) Watermarked pal video by Model 2 (c) Watermarked pal video by Model 3 (d) Watermarked pal video by the proposed model (e)

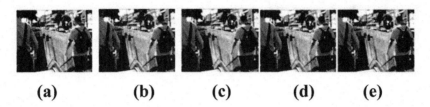

(a)   (b)   (c)   (d)   (e)

on the relevant JND model while retaining the watermark transparency.

4.2.3 Robustness

In practice, watermarked content may be subject to face a variety of distortions before reaching the detector. We present robustness results with different attacks such as MPEG2 compression, MPEG4 compression, Gaussian noise and valumetric scaling. Robustness results of algorithm based on Models 1 to 3 were compared with results of algorithm based on our JND model shown in Figure 10, Figure 11, Figure 12, and Figure 13. For each category of distortion, the watermarked images were modified with a varying magnitude of distortion and the BER of the extracted watermark was then computed.

4.2.3.a MPEG2 and MPEG4 Compression

We test the watermark robustness versus MPEG2 compression. The MPEG2 compression is added to the watermarked video sequences to get compressed video stream at different bit rates. After decompression and watermark extraction, the bit errors introduced by MPEG2 compression are represented in Figure 10 (a) and (b). From Figure 10 (a), we can see that the watermarking scheme based on our combined Spatio-Temporal JND Model performs better than algorithms based on Model 2 and Model 3. From the details of Figure 10 (b), we can see that if the video bit rate is compressed to 2Mb/s, there will be about 5.7% bit error rate introduced by Model 1, while only 3.1%

Figure 10. Robustness vs. MPEG2 compression by four models (a) Details of robustness vs. MPEG2 compression by model 1 and the proposed model (b)

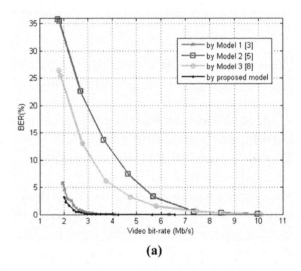

(a)

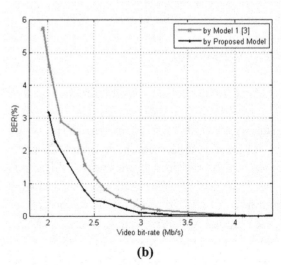

(b)

Figure 11. Robustness vs. MPEG4 compression by four models (a) Details of robustness vs. MPEG4 compression by model 1 and the proposed model (b)

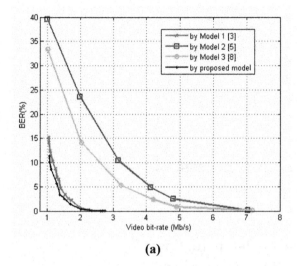

(a)

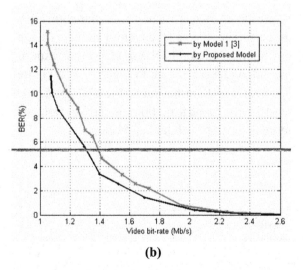

(b)

is based on our Model. As the compressed video bit rate decreases, the gap between the bit errors of Model 1 compared to our Model increases.

We test the watermark robustness versus MPEG4 compression as well. The bit errors introduced by MPEG4 compression are represented in Figure 11 (a) and (b). From Figure 11 (a), we can see that the watermarking scheme based on our combined Spatio-Temporal JND Model per-

forms better than algorithms based on Model 2 and Model 3. From the details of Figure 11 (b), we can see if the video bit rate is compressed to 1.1Mb/s, about 12.4% bit error rate is introduced by Model 1, while only 8.6% by our Model.

4.2.3.b Gaussian Noise

The normal distributed noise with mean 0 and standard deviation σ is added to the watermarked video sequences, where σ varies from 0 to 25. The experimental results are presented in Figure 12. From the robustness results with Gaussian noise in Figure 12, the watermarking scheme based on our combined Spatio-Temporal JND Model performs better than algorithms based on Models 1 to 3. Figure 12 demonstrates that our scheme's performance against Gaussian noise has an average bit error rate value 0.3% lower than algorithm based on Model 1, 11.1% lower than algorithm based on Model 2, and 8.0% lower than algorithm based on Model 3.

4.2.3.c Valumetric Scaling

From the robustness results with valumetric scaling in Figure 13, the watermarking scheme based on our combined Spatio-Temporal JND Model performs better than algorithms based on Models 1 to 3. The experiment shown in Figure 13 reduced the intensities as scaling factor varied from 1 to 0.1, and increased the intensities as scaling factor varied from 1 to 2. Figure 13 demonstrates that our scheme's performance against valumetric scaling has an average BER value equal to algorithm based on Model 1, 2.9% lower than algorithm based on Model 2, and 2.4% lower than algorithm based on Model 3.

We have presented the results of our investigation on the performance of our Spatio-Temporal JND model guided video watermarking scheme in terms of watermark visual quality, capacity and robustness. The improvement evident above is due to our Spatio-Temporal JND model for videos yields more aggressive JNDs than Models 1 to

Figure 12. Robustness vs. Gaussian noise

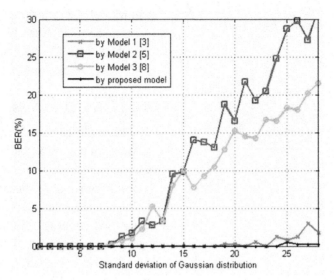

3, yet at the same level of perceived quality. Our Spatio-Temporal JND profile for videos, which correlates with the human visual system very well, can allow higher injected-watermark energy and obtain better robustness in video watermarking.

4.2.4 Temporal Effect

As we have tested in Section 4.1.2, temporal HVS properties have been taken into account to design our Spatio-Temporal JND model. From experimental evidences shown in Figure 7 and Figure 8, we can conclude that our Spatio-Temporal JND model can respond to motion correctly and tolerate more distortion with higher motion.

Figure 13. Robustness vs. Valumetric Scaling

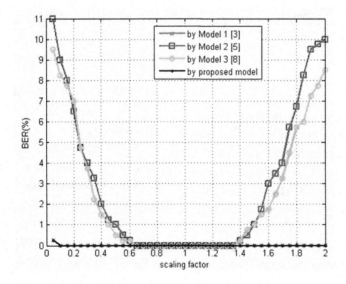

To test how our Spatio-Temporal JND model guided video watermarking scheme performs in the presence of motion; we measure the BER results of each extracted frame with different attacks such as MPEG2 compression, Gaussian noise and valumetric scaling shown in Figure 14, Figure 15, and Figure 16.

The MPEG2 compression is added to the watermarked video sequences to get compressed video stream at quality scale factor 10. The BER results of each extracted frame with our scheme are presented in Figure 14. As we have discussed, Our Spatio-Temporal JND model guided video watermarking scheme is capable of yielding higher injected-watermark energy without jeopardizing visual content quality when fast object motion occurs. As shown in Figure 7, there is a large increase in average motion energy around frames 50 to 55; as expected, Figure 15 shows the corresponding drop of BER results of frames 50 to 55.

The normal distributed noise with mean 0 and standard deviation 20 is added to the watermarked video sequences. The BER results of each extracted frame with our scheme are presented in Figure 15. As shown in Figure 7, there is a large increase in average motion energy around frames 50 to 55;

as expected, Figure 15 shows the corresponding drop of BER results of frames 50 to 55.

The frame intensities are increased with valumetric scaling factor 2 to the watermarked video sequences. The BER results of each extracted frame with our scheme are presented in Figure 16. As shown in Figure 7, there is a large increase in average motion energy around frames 50 to 55; as expected, Figure 16 shows the corresponding drop of BER results of frames 50 to 55.

From evidence above, it can be concluded that our Spatio-Temporal JND model guided video watermarking scheme can respond to motion correctly and be more robust with higher motion.

5 CONCLUSION

Perceptual Watermarking should take full advantage of the results from HVS studies. JND, which refers to the maximum distortion that the HVS does not perceive, gives us a way to model the HVS accurately. An effective Spatio-Temporal JND model guided video watermarking scheme in DCT domain is proposed in this paper. The watermarking scheme is based on the design of additional accurate JND visual model which incorporates

Figure 14. BER results of each frame vs. MPEG2 compression

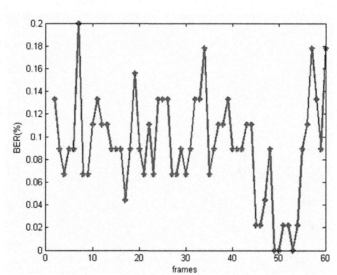

Figure 15. BER results of each frame vs. Gaussian noise

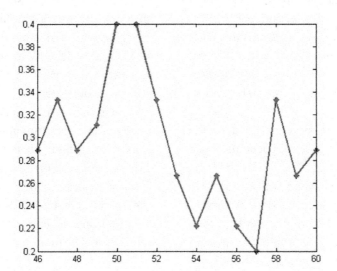

spatial CSF, temporal modulation factor, retinal velocity, luminance adaptation and contrast masking. The proposed watermarking scheme, where JND model are fully used to determine scene-adaptive upper bounds on watermark insertion, allows us to provide the maximum strength transparent watermark. Experimental results confirm the improved performance of our Spatio-Temporal JND model. Our Spatio-Temporal JND model is capable of yielding higher injected-watermark energy without introducing noticeable distortion to the original video sequences and outperforms the relevant existing visual models. Simulation results show that the proposed Spatio-Temporal JND model guided video watermarking scheme is more robust than other algorithms based on the relevant existing perceptual models while retaining the watermark transparency.

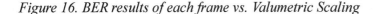

Figure 16. BER results of each frame vs. Valumetric Scaling

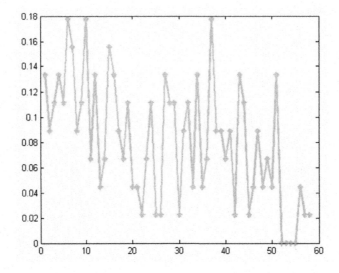

ACKNOWLEDGMENT

We acknowledge the funding provided by the National Natural Science Foundation of China (Grant No. 60832004) and Key Construction Program of the Communication University of China "211" Project.

REFERENCES

Ahumada, A. J. Jr, & Peterson, H. A. (1992). Luminance-Model-Based DCT Quantization for Color Image Compression. *Proceedings of the Society for Photo-Instrumentation Engineers, 1666*, 365–374.

Daly, S. (1998). Engineering observations from spatio velocity and spatiotemporal visual models. *Proceedings of the Society for Photo-Instrumentation Engineers, 3299*, 180–191.

Damnjanovic, I., & Izquierdo, E. (2006). Perceptual watermarking using just noticeable difference model based on block classification. In *Proceedings of the 2nd international conference on Mobile multimedia communications* (No. 36).

Doerr, G., & Dugelay, J. L. (2003). A guide tour of video watermarking. *Signal Processing Image Communication, 18*(4), 263–282. doi:10.1016/S0923-5965(02)00144-3

Huang, J., Shi, Y. Q., & Shi, Y. (1998). Adaptive image watermarking scheme based on visual masking. *Electronics Letters, 34*, 748–750. doi:10.1049/el:19980545

Jia, Y., Lin, W., & Kassim, A. A. (2006). Estimating justnoticeable distortion for video. *IEEE Transactions on Circuits and Systems for Video Technology, 16*(7), 820–829. doi:10.1109/TC-SVT.2006.877397

Kankanhalli, M. S., & Ramakrishnan, K. R. (1998). Content based watermarking of images. In *Proceedings of the sixth ACM international conference on Multimedia* (pp. 61-70).

Kelly, D. H. (1979). Motion and vision. II. Stabilized spatio-temporal threshold surface. *J. opt. Sot. Am., 69*, 1340–1349.

Laird, J., Rosen, M., Pelz, J., Montag, E., & Daly, S. (2006). Spatio-velocity CSF as a function of retinal velocity using unstabilized stimuli. *Proceedings of the Society for Photo-Instrumentation Engineers, 6057*, 32–43.

Langelaar, G. C., & Lagendijk, R. L. (2001). Optimal differential energy watermarking of DCT encoded images and video. *IEEE Transactions on Image Processing, 10*(1), 148–158. doi:10.1109/83.892451

Legge, G. E. (1981). A power law for contrast discrimination. *Vision Research, 21*, 457–467. doi:10.1016/0042-6989(81)90092-4

Ling, H. F., Lu, Z. D., & Zou, F. H. (2004). Improved Differential Energy Watermarking (IDEW) Algorithm for DCT-Encoded Imaged and Video. In *Proceedings of the Seventh International Conference on Signal Processing (ICSP'2004)* (pp. 2326-2329).

Ling, H. F., Lu, Z. D., Zou, F. H., & Li, R. X. (2006). An Energy Modulated Watermarking Algorithm Based on Watson Perceptual Model. *Journal of Software, 17*(5), 1124–1132. doi:10.1360/jos171124

Methodology for the subjective assessment of the quality of television pictures (ITU-R BT.500-11). (2002).

Niu, Y. Q., Liu, J. B., Krishnan, S., & Zhang, Q. (2009). Spatio-Temporal Just Noticeable Distortion Model Guided Video Watermarking. In *Proceedings of the 2009 IEEE Pacific-Rim Conference on Multimedia (PCM 2009)*.

Niu, Y. Q., Zhang, Y., Krishnan, S., & Zhang, Q. (2009). A Video-Driven Just Noticeable Distortion Profile for Watermarking. In *Proceedings of the 2009 International Conference on Engineering Management and Service Sciences (EMS 2009)*.

Podilchuk, C. I., & Zeng, W. (1998). Image-adaptive watermarking using visual models. *Proceedings of the IEEE, 16*, 525–539.

Schütz, A. C., Delipetkos, E., Braun, D. I., Kerzel, D., & Gegenfurtner, K. R. (2007). Temporal contrast sensitivity during smooth pursuit eye movements. *Journal of Vision (Charlottesville, Va.), 7*(13), 1–15. doi:10.1167/7.13.3

Tourancheau, S., Callet, P. L., & Barba, D. (2007). Influence of motion on contrast perception: supra-threshold spatio-velocity measurements. In *Proceedings of SPIE* (Vol. 6492).

Watson, A. B. (1993). *DCTune: A technique for visual optimization of DCT quantization matrices for individual images* (pp. 946–949). Soc. Information Display Dig. Tech. Papers XXIV.

Wei, Z., & Ngan, K. N. (2008a). A temporal just-noticeble distortion profile for video in DCT domain. In *Proceedings of the 15th IEEE International Conference on Image Processing* (pp. 1336-1339).

Wei, Z., & Ngan, K. N. (2008b). Spatial Just Noticeable Distortion Profile for Image in DCT Domain. In *Proceedings of IEEE International Conference on Multimedia and Expo* (pp. 925-928).

Wolfgang, R. B., Podilchuk, C. I., & Delp, E. J. (1999). Perceptual watermarks for digital images and video. In *Proceedings IEEE, Special Issue on Identification and Protection of Multimedia Information* (Vol. 87, pp. 1108-1126).

Zhang, X. K., Lin, W. S., & Xue, P. (2005). Improved estimation for just-noticeable visual distortion. *Signal Processing, 85*(4), 795–808. doi:10.1016/j.sigpro.2004.12.002

Zou, F. h. (2006). *Research of Robust Video Watermarking Algorithms and Related Techniques*. Unpublished doctoral dissertation, Hua zhong University of Science & Technology, China.

This work was previously published in the International Journal of Digital Crime and Forensics, Volume 2, Issue 4, edited by Chang-Tsun Li and Anthony TS Ho, pp. 16-36, copyright 2010 by IGI Publishing (an imprint of IGI Global).

Chapter 7

Watermark–Only Security Attack on DM–QIM Watermarking:
Vulnerability to Guided Key Guessing

B. R. Matam
Aston University, UK

David Lowe
Aston University, UK

ABSTRACT

This paper addresses the security of a specific class of common watermarking methods based on Dither modulation-quantisation index modulation (DM-QIM) and focusing on watermark-only attacks (WOA). The vulnerabilities of and probable attacks on lattice structure based watermark embedding methods have been presented in the literature. DM-QIM is one of the best known lattice structure based watermarking techniques. In this paper, the authors discuss a watermark-only attack scenario (the attacker has access to a single watermarked content only). In the literature it is an assumption that DM-QIM methods are secure to WOA. However, the authors show that the DM-QIM based embedding method is vulnerable against a guided key guessing attack by exploiting subtle statistical regularities in the feature space embeddings for time series and images. Using a distribution-free algorithm, this paper presents an analysis of the attack and numerical results for multiple examples of image and time series data.

1. INTRODUCTION

Data hiding, embedding information into digital media for the purpose of identification, annotation and copyright is a form of steganography (Bender et al., 1996). Embedding information into digital data (called cover data) is known as watermark-ing and the embedded information (watermark) signifies invisible information that can be detected and retrieved by authorised personnel or systems designed for that purpose (Lin et al., 2005). The watermarks hence extend the information content of the cover work. They are utilised as a means of securing the rights of the owner of the digital data, authentication of the source or as a tracing mechanism. Kalker (Kalker, 2001) defines the

DOI: 10.4018/978-1-4666-1758-2.ch007

security of a watermarking system as the inability of unauthorised users to remove, detect and estimate, write or modify the raw watermarking bits. Comesaña et al. (Comesaña et al., 2005) take a more restrictive view of the security of a watermarking system linking it to the gaining of knowledge about the secrets of the system in addition to destroying the embedded message. The current paper is consistent with both views since the random key locations will be estimated.

We consider the case where the watermark bits are embedded in selected samples of the cover data wherein the indices of the selected samples are referred to as the secret embedding key. The work presented in (Giakoumaki et al., 2006) states that the watermarks are secure because the key represents a random vector which cannot be easily guessed. Evaluation of the security of watermark embedding methods is still a nascent field though some limited analysis of the security of different lattice based embedding methods exists in the literature.

Based on Diffie-Hellman's Terminology, Cayre et al. (Cayre et al., 2005) grouped the attacks on watermarked content as 1. Watermark only attack (WOA) - wherein the attacker has access to a set of watermarked host data. 2. Known-message attack (KMA) - where the attacker has access to a set of watermarked content, watermarked with the same key and the associate messages. 3. Known-original attack (KOA), where the attacker has access to both the watermarked content and the original un-watermarked content.

Utilising the definition of watermarking security given by Kalker (Kalker, 2001) the work presented in this paper is a WOA analysis of the security of the DM-QIM method explicitly pertaining to the detection of the secret key based on the assumption that the cover work has been identified as watermarked content and the watermark embedding method is known. This paper proposes an efficient distribution-independent approach to attacking watermarks embedded using transform domain DM-QIM. It employs a method to estimate the probable location of the hidden information when only a single copy of the watermarked content is available, an extreme case of the WOA class of attacks, for both discrete wavelet transform (DWT) and independent component analysis (ICA) domain based DM-QIM watermarking methods. DWT and ICA is representative of current state-of-the-art transform domain methods where the signal space is spanned by either fixed orthogonal or data-adaptive non-orthogonal basis functions. Despite the use of a random key for message locations in the transform domain, departures from the natural distribution of the covertext are induced which are amenable to non-parametric density estimation models. The results illustrate the fallibility of DM-QIM against guided key guessing attacks for both image and time series data.

2. KEY SECURITY CLASSES

The concept of key security for QIM based watermarking has been investigated by various authors (Kalker, 2001; Holliman et al., 1999; Bas & Hurri, 2006; Cayre et al., 2005; Pérez-Freire et al., 2006; Cayre & Bas, 2008; Pérez-Freire & Pérez-González, 2007). Overwriting the information in the watermarked cover to partially or completely destroy the original information is possible if the embedding method is known. Even if the exact secret embedding key is not known, it is possible to destroy the embedded message by randomly overwriting the watermarked content to a large extent (although this could be interpreted as robustness rather than security). Cox et. al. in (Cox et al., 1996) claim that $O(\sqrt{l \, / \, ln(l)})$ similar watermarks must be added to the watermarked content to destroy the original watermark, where l represents the number of most perceptually significant frequency components of an image's discrete cosine transform used to embed the original watermark. The watermark used in their experiments is a sequence of real numbers drawn from a Gaussian distribution. This method of destroying the watermark in a watermarked cover has the disadvantage of destroying the usability of the watermarked cover. Any benefit that the attacker may wish to gain will be lost. Hence a non-blind method of estimating the location of the watermark samples is necessary in order to destroy or overwrite the embedded message and still maintain the viability of the watermarked cover for use. In watermarking applications using random keys, the security of the message content is considered to be assured since it lies hidden in the host signal distributed randomly and the random distribution pattern is known only to the owner of the host signal.

Cayre et al. (Cayre et al., 2005) state that it is possible to guess certain information about the secret key from the watermarked content. They define this term as information leakage and show that the information leakage can be quantified by measures such as mutual information. Using tools from information theory various measures to estimate information leakage about the secret embedding key from the observable data have also been discussed in the paper. Cayre and Bas (Cayre & Bas, 2008) state that 'an embedding function is key secure if and only if the secret subspace to which the secret key belongs cannot be estimated'. Though it may be impossible to estimate the secret key, if the secret subspace to which the secret key belongs can be estimated, the uncertainty of the secret key is reduced. Therefore the security of the secret key is then dependent on the number of possible keys that can be obtained in the subspace.

An in-depth estimation of the secret key for spread spectrum based watermarking methods for the WOA class can be found in (Cayre & Bas, 2008). Pérez-Friere and Pérez-González (Pérez-Freire & Pérez-González, 2007) have presented an extensive analysis of lattice-based data hiding methods. The work presented in (Pérez-Freire et al., 2006) is based on the assumption that the

attacker has access to several copies of the data watermarked with the same secret key. For the DM-QIM watermarking technique, Bas and Hurri (Bas & Hurri, 2006) showed how, under some assumptions on image statistics and sparsity of coding, the watermarked pixel locations can be estimated for images by using an independent component analysis approach. This latter method relies on the DM signal being independent of the image statistics and so an independent component analysis should isolate the watermark in one of the independent components. This is probably one of the most efficient current attacks. It relies on assumptions of independence of the DM watermark method from the natural image statistics, and hence can be circumvented by making the watermark embedding dependent on the image statistics. Though literature exists on the importance of key security for lattice based watermarking techniques, except for the work presented in (Bas & Hurri, 2006), the work is primarily theoretical.

References related to the investigation of key security applied to time series data seem absent, and hence is one of the focus points of this paper. The work presented by Giakoumaki et al. (Giakoumaki et al., 2006) for example, is directed towards biomedical images, and uses the concept of the secret embedding keys to show that the watermarking method adopted by them for biomedical images should be secure. By contrast, in addition to images in many of the experiments presented in the current paper, messages are embedded in time series data. A method to find the secret embedding keys thus enabling the modification of the watermarked samples is presented. The experiments are based on Kerckhoffs' principle assuming that the security of the communication process is based on the secret key. It is assumed that the attacker knows everything about the watermarking method chosen. Using measures from information theory (McKay, 2002) and inference techniques from neural networks (Bishop, 1995; Nabney, 2002) an efficient distribution-independent approach to attacking watermarks embedded using transform domain DM-QIM is proposed. The method estimates the probable location of the hidden information when only a single copy of the watermarked content is available, an extreme case of the WOA class of attacks. The method is demonstrated for the discrete wavelet transform domain and independent component analysis based DM-QIM watermarking methods. The consequence of the results is the fallibility of DM-QIM and hence that the embedding method is insecure.

3. THE ATTACKER'S CHALLENGE

Let $\mathbf{c}(t)$ represent the cover data. In this paper we consider both one-dimensional time series and two-dimensional images, such that $t \in \{1, ..., N_{ts}\}$ for one-dimensional time series data of length N_{ts} or $t \in \{1, ..., N_r\} \times \{1, ..., M_c\}$ for two-dimensional data of size $N_r \times M_c$ respectively. The watermark can be embedded in the spatial domain of the cover, $\mathbf{c}(t)$ or a transformed representation of $\mathbf{c}(t)$. Let T represent a suitable transform (for example discrete Fourier transform (DFT), discrete cosine transform (DCT), discrete wavelet transform (DWT), independent component analysis (ICA)). Details of the application of each transform to one-dimensional and 2D data can be obtained from the references listed. Let $C(t_T)$ represent $\mathbf{c}(t)$ in the transform space, where t_T is the transform domain conjugate to the spatial domain co-ordinate system.

$$C(t_T) = T(\mathbf{c}(t)). \tag{1}$$

The values and domain of C are defined by the application of T to $\mathbf{c}(t)$. Let N_{WM} represent the length of the random watermark, $\mathbf{m}$. Quantisation index modulation (QIM) (Chen & Wornell, 2001) refers to embedding information by first modulating an index or sequence of indices of

$\mathbf{c}(t)$ or $C(t_T)$ with $\mathbf{m}$ and then quantising $\mathbf{c}(t)$ or $C(t_T)$ with the associated quantiser or sequence of quantisers. Henceforth for simplicity we will consider that the watermark is embedded in the transformed space of the cover, $C(t_T)$.

Let $\mathbf{K}$ represent the vector of random indices of the samples of $C(t_T)$ which are selected based on the required design of the watermarking system. For example, the possible choice of $\mathbf{K}$ can be used to reflect robust, semi-fragile or fragile watermarking systems.

A robust watermarking system is one wherein the embedded watermark can be recovered from a cover which has been subjected to severe tampering. A semi-fragile system refers to a watermarking system wherein the embedded message should be recoverable from a cover subjected to common signal processing techniques such as compression, A/D and D/A conversions, filtering, addition of noise. A watermark embedded in a fragile watermarking method is destroyed when the cover is modified to any extent, small or large.

Let $[\mathbf{k}_1, \mathbf{k}_2, ..., \mathbf{k}_{Nk}] \in \mathbf{K}$ represent the number of different possible sub-sets of length N_{WM}. The watermark is embedded using one of the subsets chosen randomly, referred to as $\mathbf{k}$ which is considered as a secret embedding key.

Let $\Delta = [d_1, d_2, ...]$ represent a discrete lattice on which the elements of $C(t_T)$ are quantised. The probability distribution of the quantised $C(t_T)$ is then

$$\mathbf{Pr}[C(t_T) = \Delta] = p_\Delta(C(t_T)). \tag{2}$$

Let δ represent a uniform quantiser defining a new lattice structure $\Upsilon = [v_1, v_2, ...]$ whose elements are multiples of δ. The embedding function F_m modifies $C(\mathbf{k})$ as

$$F_m(C(t_T), \mathbf{k}, \mathbf{m}, \delta) \rightarrow \tilde{C}(t_T). \tag{3}$$

where $\tilde{C}(t_T)$ represents the watermarked $C(t_T)$. The probability distribution of the modified samples is

$$\mathbf{Pr}[C(\mathbf{k}) = \Upsilon] = p_\Upsilon(\mathbf{k}). \qquad (4)$$

Dither modulation (DM)-QIM adds a dither signal, $\mathbf{o}$ to the modified $C(\mathbf{k})$ to randomise the discrete lattice of Υ.

$$\mathbf{Pr}[C(\mathbf{k}) = \Upsilon + \mathbf{o}] = p_{\Upsilon+\mathbf{o}}(\mathbf{k}). \qquad (5)$$

The probability distribution of $\tilde{C}(t_T)$ is now $p_\Gamma(t_T)$ where $\Gamma = \Delta \cup (\Upsilon + \mathbf{o})$. The watermarked cover $\tilde{\mathbf{c}}$ is obtained as

$$\tilde{\mathbf{c}}(t) = T^{-1}(\tilde{C}(t_T)). \qquad (6)$$

The embedded watermark represents a distortion of $\mathbf{c}(t)$, say D_{Emb} subject to a distortion constraint.

$$D_{Emb} = |\mathbf{c} - \tilde{\mathbf{c}}|; D_{Emb} \leq \zeta; \qquad (7)$$

where $\zeta \geq 0$ and is defined by the application of the watermark (for example a watermark used for copyright purposes must be robust while a watermark used for tamper detection is fragile). This is achieved by the choice of the levels of the three main characteristics of a watermark, imperceptibility, rate of information and robustness. Imperceptibility refers to the indistinguishability of the watermark from the cover, the rate of information is the ratio of the number of watermark samples (bits) to the number of samples of $\mathbf{c}$ (bits) and robustness of the watermark is the ability of the watermark to remain undistorted when $\tilde{\mathbf{c}}$ is attacked. These three properties form a trade-off against each other and in QIM based embedding techniques the parameter δ defines the position of the watermark in the trade-off triangle. For the embedded watermark to be robust against attacks the value of δ should be large and to comply with $\zeta \approx 0$ for D_{Emb}, the function F_m should be close to the identity mapping. This implies $\Upsilon \cong \Delta$.

During storage/transmission $\tilde{\mathbf{c}}(t)$ is subjected to various signal processing attacks such as compression, addition of noise during transmission over the channel. Let η represent the distortion of $\tilde{\mathbf{c}}(t)$ which we consider to be additive. This results in an attacked watermarked document $\hat{\mathbf{c}}(t)$. The attacked watermarked transform domain representation is

$$T(\hat{\mathbf{c}}(t)) = \hat{C}(t_T). \qquad (8)$$

where $\hat{C}(t_T) \neq \tilde{C}(t_T)$. The probability distribution of $\hat{C}(t_T)$ is hence

$$\mathbf{Pr}[\hat{C}(t_T) = \Gamma + \xi] = p_{\Gamma+\xi}(t_T), \qquad (9)$$

where ξ represents the distortion of $\tilde{\mathbf{c}}(t)$ due to η in the transformed domain space.

The attacker's challenge is to estimate the probability distribution over Υ from the probability distribution of the observations over $\Gamma + \xi$. The following analysis illustrates one mechanism to resolve this problem.

4. GUIDED KEY GUESSING

The guided key guessing approach is based on the second order effects that the message quantiser distorts the distribution over Δ. In the approach illustrated here, the estimation of the probable δ and then probable $\mathbf{k}$ is made by investigating the distribution of differences in the ranked transform domain coefficients.

To illustrate, consider first the analysis of a one-dimensional EEG time series in which the embedding is performed in the fourth level DWT domain. Figure 1 is the plot of the detail

Figure 1. Histogram of detail coefficients of fourth level decomposition of one-dimensional EEG. No information on probable δ is apparent

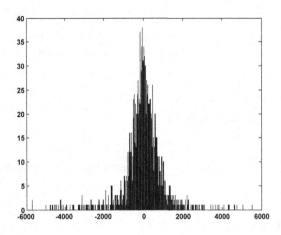

co-efficients obtained for the fourth level DWT decomposition of the one-dimensional EEG signal.

This figure represents the distribution of the elements of $\hat{C}(t_T)$, $p_{\Gamma+\varsigma}$ and does not provide any information about δ.

The effect of the message imposing on a second lattice can be seen as follows:

1. Construct the relevant transform domain $T(\hat{\mathbf{c}}(t)) \rightarrow \hat{C}(t_T)$.
2. Sort the samples of $\hat{C}(t_T)$.
3. Construct the differenced sequence: $\iota(j) = \hat{C}(j+1) - \hat{C}(j)$ for $j \in \{1, length(C(t_T)) - 1\}$.
4. Plot the histogram of ι.

The histogram (figure 2) depicts the spacing between two consecutive quantisers on the Γ lattice. The histograms observed in figures 1 and 2, vary largely because the two sets of plots represent different characteristics of C for the time series data. While figure 1 represents $p_\Gamma(\hat{C}(t_T)$ figure 2 represents $p(\Gamma)$.

The changes in the histogram when the value of N_{WM} is varied are also distinct. When N_{WM} is more than 90% of the length of the signal, the histogram resembles an impulse function. This is because $\Gamma \approx \Upsilon$ since most samples will be quantised on the watermark lattice and almost 90% of the elements in ι will have the same value. The mean of the elements of ι in this case will be close to zero.

Since $\tilde{\mathbf{c}}$ is distorted by a value η before and during transmission, $\tilde{C}$ is also distorted. Let this distortion to $\tilde{C}$ be represented by ξ.

$$\tilde{\mathbf{c}} + \eta \Rightarrow \hat{\mathbf{c}}; \tilde{C} + \xi \Rightarrow \hat{C}. \qquad (10)$$

This results in

$$\left| \frac{\hat{C}(k)}{\delta} \right| \neq \left| \frac{\tilde{C}(k)}{\delta} \right| \qquad (11)$$

From Equation 11 it can be seen that a large value of η and therefore ξ will destroy the embedded message. We assume that η is below a threshold such that knowledge of $\mathbf{k}$ and δ used to embed the message enables the retrieval of the hidden message. In order to gain any advantage the attacker has to be able to estimate $\mathbf{k}$ and this is possible if the quantiser levels defined by Υ could be separated from the quantiser levels de-

Figure 2. Histograms of the differences between successive sorted detail co-efficients obtained for the fourth level decomposition of one-dimensional EEG

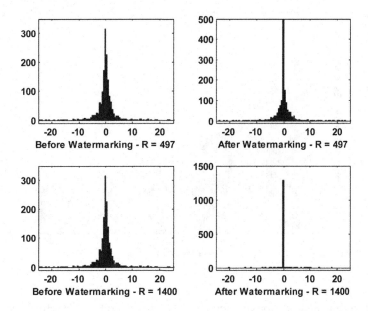

fined by Δ, in Υ and also estimate the probable **o**. Since an estimation of Υ without the knowledge of δ and a practical separation of the two grids is not possible, we estimate the possible value of δ with the help of the histogram of ι.

As mentioned earlier the histogram of ι represents $p(\Gamma)$, hence the value of δ should be contained in the range of $p(\Gamma)$. Therefore grids of probable δ, denoted $\breve{\delta}$ where $\breve{\delta} = [0, \ldots, \upsilon]$ are applied on $\hat{C}$. υ defines the maximum value of the domain of ι. The application of the dither signal shifts the watermarked samples $\tilde{C}(\mathbf{k})$ from the lattice of Υ by a value $\mathbf{o}(\mathbf{k})$. These samples are further shifted due to the addition of ξ. Hence the number of samples of $\hat{C}$ which lie in the range ε of the lattice defined by $\breve{\delta}$ are estimated. ε denotes an estimate of the probable shift of $\tilde{C}(\mathbf{k})$ due to $\mathbf{o}$ and ξ and is defined to be a fraction of the dynamic range of $\hat{C}$.

This result of this estimation method can be seen in figure 3 which is a plot of the number of estimated watermarked samples $|\breve{\mathbf{k}}|$ as a function of trial spacing $\breve{\delta}$.

4.1. Estimation of Probable δ

As indicated in Figure 3, the distribution of the number of estimated samples as a function of δ, $P(\delta)$, can be modelled as a baseline correction $b(\delta)$ plus background random noise fluctuations $n(\delta)$ and a superimposed structure $S(\delta)$ due to the distribution characteristics of the hidden message which distorts the distribution:

$$P(\delta) = b(\delta) + n(\delta) + S(\delta). \tag{12}$$

An estimation of the probable δ used to embed the message can be obtained by finding the area under the largest peak. Figure 4(a) represents $|\breve{\mathbf{k}}|$ as a function of $\breve{\delta}$, 4(b) the estimation of the peaks for baseline correction, 4(c) the baseline corrected estimation of $|\breve{\mathbf{k}}|$ and Figure 4(d) the peak with the largest area. The peak is estimated for $\breve{\delta} = 30$ which we consider to be $\hat{\delta}$.

To automate the process of detecting the likely value of δ used, we seek a maximum-likelihood-estimator. We use a simple model of a Cauchy-

Figure 3. for different values of $\breve{\delta}$

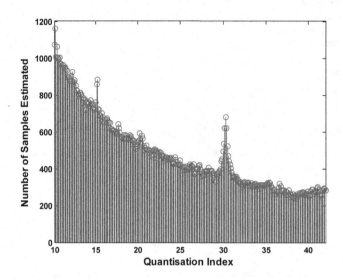

Lorentz distribution for the local distortions induced by the hidden message which is optimised assuming the data samples are i.i.d. The location parameter that maximises the likelihood of the data being represented by a Cauchy distribution indicates the most likely value of δ.

$b(\delta)$ arises from the reciprocal nature of the level spacing and the distribution of signal values

Figure 4. An estimation of the probable δ. 4(a) represents $|\breve{k}|$ as a function of $\breve{\delta}$, 4(b) the estimation of the peaks for baseline correction, 4(c) the baseline corrected estimation of $|\breve{k}|$ and Figure 4(d) the peak with the largest area. The peak is estimated for $\breve{\delta} = 30$ which we consider to be $\hat{\delta}$.

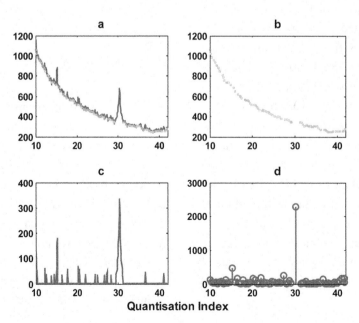

and distorts the structure due to the hidden message. Therefore in the automated process this baseline effect is first removed before the distribution modelling is performed. We use a thin-plate spline approach using knots determined by locally minimum values so as not to interpolate the structure $S(\delta)$. Once the background has been removed, the resulting distribution is analysed automatically for a point estimator of the most likely δ.

Specifically, we assume that the likelihood $P(K \mid \theta)$ of the sampled data $K = \{k(i), i = 1, \ldots, N\}$ given the parameter set $\theta = (d, \Gamma)$ (in the case of the Cauchy distribution assumed here, this equates to the location parameter d and a half-width parameter Γ) is simply $\prod_{i=1}^{N} P(k_i \mid \theta)$. Assuming a functional form for 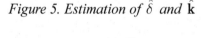 $P(k_i \mid \theta)$ as a Cauchy distribution parameterised by location d and width Γ, gradient optimisation of the likelihood based on the data can be performed to return the most likely parameter choice of location d and hence an estimate of $\hat{\delta}$.

This approach has no prior information on the distribution of the parameters, and so it assumes $P(\theta) = 1$, which is of course generally incorrect since we often know something about the location and the width parameters. If we have some knowledge of these parameters then we can consider estimating the posterior distribution of the model parameters given the data.

$$P(\theta \mid K) = P(K \mid \theta)P(\theta) / P(K). \qquad (13)$$

Since the prior over the data $P(K)$ does not depend on the model, it can be neglected in the optimisation process. So, although we can extend the method to consider a more Bayesian approach to estimating $\hat{\delta}$ if we have additional knowledge on the parameter priors, for the problem considered here across many signal examples we have found that the direct MLE approach provides a simple and robust point estimate of the useful $\hat{\delta}$.

For the example data used in Figure 3 for illustration, and from Figure 5, $\hat{\delta} = 30.2$. The value of δ used at the embedder for this case was

Figure 5. Estimation of $\hat{\delta}$ and $\hat{\mathbf{k}}$

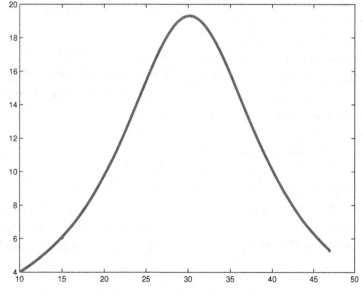

30.27. The quantised samples were also randomised using a dither signal of $N(0,1)$.

4.2. Estimation of k

An estimate of the probable watermarked samples $\hat{\mathbf{k}}$ is then obtained as $|\breve{\mathbf{k}}|$ obtained for $\hat{\delta}$.

$$\hat{\mathbf{k}} = [j : \frac{\hat{C}_j}{\hat{\delta}} \leq \varepsilon]. \tag{14}$$

In the DWT based experiments the method adopted is the method described in (Giakoumaki et al., 2006) to embed the robust watermark. The watermark is embedded in the vertical coefficients obtained for the fourth level decomposition of the image data, and the detail coefficients obtained for the fourth level of decomposition for the time series data. These coefficients are chosen as they contain significant energy (information content of $\mathbf{c}$) to survive compression attacks. But these coefficients do not contain the maximum information content of $\mathbf{c}$ that any distortion to these components results in a large D_{Emb}.

In the ICA method the watermark is embedded in the samples of one of the sources estimated from the cover work (either image or time series) which represents a broadband though informative source of $\mathbf{c}$. The image data of size 512×512 is divided into blocks of 8×8 and each block is converted to a vector. The 64 estimated sources are ranked according to their energy content. The sources which contain sufficient energy (information of $\mathbf{c}$) to be robust against compression and also not distort the cover work significantly represents $\mathbf{K}$. $\mathbf{k} \in \mathbf{K}$ are chosen randomly to embed the WM.

The application of the ICA algorithm to a single channel EEG signal to obtain an estimate of the underlying sources using the delay embedding method has been discussed in (Woon & Lowe, 2001).

Some concepts explaining the construction of the input matrix to the ICA are repeated here. The one-dimensional EEG is recorded from an adult. It is sampled at 250Hz and each sample is represented as a 16 bit unsigned integer. The slowest signal component is assumed to be 3Hz and a delay of 1 sample between two successive vectors is used. The embedding window size, $E_{mb}W_{in}$ is obtained as 83. $E_{mb}W_{in}$ sets the upper bound on the total number of sources p that can be estimated from the EEG. The number of delay vectors N_{ov} for a one-dimensional signal $\mathbf{c}$ of length N_c is given as

$$N_{ov} = N_c - E_{mb}W_{in} + 1. \tag{15}$$

The input to the ICA is $\mathbf{X}_{p \times N_{ov}}$,

$$[\mathbf{S}, \mathbf{W}] \xleftarrow{\ ICA\ } \mathbf{X}_{p \times N_{ov}}.$$

One of the sources, $\mathbf{s}_{wm}$ obtained from the ICA transform representing the low frequency component of $\mathbf{c}$ is used to embed the watermark. The samples of $\mathbf{s}_{wm}$ represent $\mathbf{K}$. A random subset of the selected samples representing $\mathbf{k} \in \mathbf{K}$ is chosen equal to the length of the watermark to be quantised.

$$F_m(\mathbf{s}_{wm}(\mathbf{k}), WM) \rightarrow \tilde{\mathbf{s}}_{wm}. \tag{16}$$

$\mathbf{S}$ is modified to $\tilde{\mathbf{S}}$ in the sense that one of the sources (rows) represented by $\mathbf{s}_{wm}$ is watermarked. The watermarked matrix representing the set of observations is obtained by multiplying $\tilde{\mathbf{S}}$ by the inverse of $\mathbf{W}$, $\mathbf{A}$.

$$\tilde{\mathbf{X}} = \mathbf{A} * \tilde{\mathbf{S}}. \tag{17}$$

A similar procedure is applied to one-dimensional audio signals to obtain the independent sources, one of which is used to embed the watermark.

All the following experiments are based on the assumption that the attacker knows everything about the system except the keys which are $\mathbf{k}$ and δ. The attacker's challenge is to estimate $\mathbf{k}$ and δ sufficiently close to allow isolation of $\mathbf{m}$ from an attacked $\tilde{\mathbf{c}}$, $\hat{\mathbf{c}}$.

5. RESULTS

In this section the evidence of the estimation method described in section 4 to determine the secret key $\mathbf{k}$ for both the DWT based method and the ICA based method are presented. Three different data types representing audio signals, EEGs and images are used as the cover data $\mathbf{c}$ to embed the watermarks.

The EEG signals were taken from two different data sets (no epileptic activity EEG_1, epileptic activity EEG_2). A total of 42 EEG signals were used. For the audio data 21 one-dimensional signals representing three different genres of music classical, pop and rock were considered. Similarly 40 2-D images divided into three different sets representing textures, objects and faces were considered.

Each one-dimensional signal/ 2D data was watermarked using a different value of δ and $\mathbf{k}$ using both DWT and ICA based approaches for different rates of information R. The watermarked data $\tilde{\mathbf{c}}$ is then processed by applying three different attacks representing filtering, addition of noise and compression. Each attack is applied separately to $\tilde{\mathbf{c}}$ and the estimation of $\mathbf{k}$ from the resulting attacked watermarked content $\hat{\mathbf{c}}$ is conducted.

5.1. Estimation of $\mathbf{k}$, DWT Based Approach

The watermarked image and time series data are subjected to compression, addition of noise and filtering attacks. $\hat{\mathbf{c}}$ obtained in each case is pro-cessed to obtain the corresponding $\hat{C}$. The experiments detailed in section 4 are conducted on the derived $\hat{C}$ to find $\hat{\delta}$.

Figures 6(a) (image) and 7(a) (time series) denote the samples of C which have been actually watermarked (dark shade) and the estimate of the samples for different values of $\breve{\delta}$ (light shade) using DM-QIM. The samples of C were quantised using $\delta = 0.2$ and randomised using a dither signal $N(0, 0.02)$ for the image and $\delta = 30.27$ and a dither signal $N(0, 1)$ for the time series data at the encoder. A large number of samples for most values of $\breve{\delta}$ were estimated, but as can be seen from Figures 6(a) and 7(a), the distribution of the estimated samples changes when $\breve{\delta}$ approaches the true value of δ. The detection method described in section 4 is applied to obtain $\hat{\delta}$ and $\hat{\mathbf{k}}$. By concentrating on the values around this $\hat{\delta}$ value, the results shown in Figures 6(c) and 7(c) are obtained. When $\hat{\delta} \approx \delta$ most of the samples of $\mathbf{k}$ were estimated and the number of false positives is less than one third the value of R.

The Figures 6(d) and 7(d) are obtained when C is watermarked using a dither signal with a large variance. The dither signal used for the image data is $N(0, 0.1)$ and in the case of the time series data, $N(0, 5)$. These large variance dither signals did not produce any distinguishing peaks (Figure 6(b)) for the image data but small changes in the structure were observed for the time series data (Figure 7(b)). This was due to the larger dynamic range of the time series data compared to the image data and the ratio of δ to the dynamic range for the different data. The detection mechanism identified the maximum peak at $\hat{\delta} = 0.123$ for the image data and a peak of 30.3 for the time series data. Dither signals with a variance almost equal to the δ value will not be used in practice as it has been observed that they increase the distortion of the cover data significantly. However as a test the watermark for this high variance was embedded. Figure 6(d) represents

Figure 6. a) Estimation of **k** *for image data using DWT where* δ = 0.2 *was used for WM embedding and randomised by adding a dither signal of* $N(0, 0.02)$. *b) Estimation of* **k** *for image data using DWT where* δ = 0.2 *used for WM embedding and randomised by adding a dither signal of* $N(0, 0.1)$. *c) Estimated samples of* $\hat{\mathbf{k}}$ *for* $\hat{\delta}$ *around the largest peak detected (light colour) and* $\hat{\mathbf{k}} \cap \mathbf{k}$ *(darker colour), the dither signal used to embed the WM is* $N(0, 0.02)$. *The star represents the number of true watermarked samples. d) Estimated samples of* $\hat{\mathbf{k}}$ *for* $\hat{\delta}$ *around the largest peak detected (light colour) and* $\hat{\mathbf{k}} \cap \mathbf{k}$ *(darker colour), the dither signal used to embed the WM is* $N(0, 0.1)$.

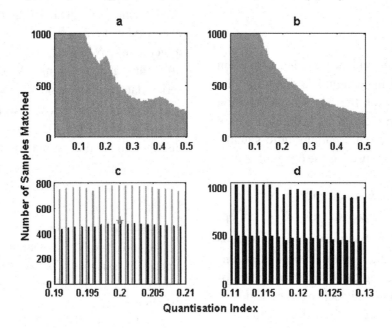

the values of $\hat{\mathbf{k}}$ (lighter shade) and $\hat{\mathbf{k}} \cap \mathbf{k}$ (darker shade). The number of false positives is quite high but all the values of **k** are estimated correctly.

5.2. Estimation of k, ICA Based Approach

The security of the embedding method in the ICA transform domain is now presented. In order to estimate the probable δ and **k** an estimate of the probable sources will need to be obtained. Hence $\hat{\mathbf{X}}$ is constructed from $\hat{c}$ using the delay embedding process explained earlier.

Two different experiments were conducted to find $\hat{\delta}$ and estimate $\hat{\mathbf{k}}$. One, given the separating matrix **W** used at the embedder to transform the

EEG to the estimated sources, is it possible to find the watermarked source and δ and **k**? Experiment two answers the question 'How close can an attacker get to recovering the message, given she knows the method and key factors such as segmentation blocking?'.

5.2.1. Estimation of k, Sources Estimated Using W Used at the Embedder

An estimate of the probable sources is obtained as the projection of $\hat{\mathbf{X}}$ onto the independent component rows of **W**, $\hat{\mathbf{S}} = \mathbf{W}\hat{\mathbf{X}}$. Histograms were plotted as explained in section 4 and a possible range for $\check{\delta}$ was obtained. The source whose histogram is plotted is chosen randomly but the

Figure 7. a) Estimation of $\mathbf{k}$ *for time series data using DWT where* $\delta = 30.27$ *used for WM embedding and randomised by adding a dither signal of* $N(0,1)$. *b) Estimation of* $\mathbf{k}$ *for time series data using DWT where* $\delta = 30.27$ *used for WM embedding and randomised by adding a dither signal of* $N(0,5)$. *c) Estimated samples of* $\hat{\mathbf{k}}$ *for* $\hat{\delta}$ *around the largest peak detected (light colour) and* $\hat{\mathbf{k}} \cap \mathbf{k}$ *(darker colour), the dither signal used to embed the WM is* $N(0,1)$. *The star represents the number of true watermarked samples. d) Estimated samples of* $\hat{\mathbf{k}}$ *for* $\hat{\delta}$ *around the largest peak detected (light colour) and* $\hat{\mathbf{k}} \cap \mathbf{k}$ *(darker colour), the dither signal used to embed the WM is* $N(0,5)$. *The star represents the number of true watermarked samples.*

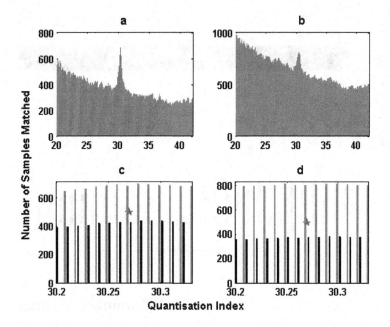

histograms of all the sources obtained, as explained in section 4, are nearly the same. The estimation of $\hat{\mathbf{k}}$ and $\hat{\delta}$ was conducted similar to that explained in the section 4. Figures 8 and 9 are the outputs of the estimation of $\hat{\mathbf{k}}$ for the watermarked source (image and time series respectively).

It is assumed that the attacker has no knowledge of the identity of $\hat{\mathbf{s}}_{wm}$ in the set of p sources. Therefore the estimation of $\hat{\delta}$ and $\hat{\mathbf{k}}$ is conducted on all the estimated sources. $\breve{\delta}$ takes values from zero to 13 for the image data and zero to 5 for the time series data.

Figure 10 is the estimation result obtained for $\mathbf{s} \neq \mathbf{s}_{wm}$ (time series data). Unlike the results obtained for $\mathbf{s}_{wm}$, there is no distinctive peak and

the output is varying randomly. Similar outputs to Figure 10 were observed $\forall \mathbf{s}_i; i \neq wm$.

5.2.2. Estimation of $\mathbf{k}$, Sources Estimated by Applying ICA to $\tilde{\mathbf{c}}$

The sources in this experiment were derived by applying the ICA to $\hat{\mathbf{X}}$. The independent components (the separating matrix $\mathbf{W}$) are derived from the input data. The input at this stage is $\hat{\mathbf{X}}$ the noise contaminated version of $\mathbf{X}$. Hence the independent components obtained from this input are denoted by $\hat{\mathbf{W}}$. Let the sources estimated as projections of $\hat{\mathbf{X}}$ on these independent components be represented as $\hat{\mathbf{S}}_{att}$.

Figure 8. Estimation of **k** *for image data using ICA, where* $\delta = 8.1$ *used for* WM *embedding and the sources are obtained from the watermarked image using the same separating matrix used by the embedder. The result shown is for the source which has been watermarked. a) Estimation of* $\hat{\mathbf{k}}$. *b) Estimated samples of* $\hat{\mathbf{k}}$ *for* $\hat{\delta}$ *around* δ *(light colour) and* $\hat{\mathbf{k}} \cap \mathbf{k}$ *(darker colour). The star represents the number of true watermarked samples.*

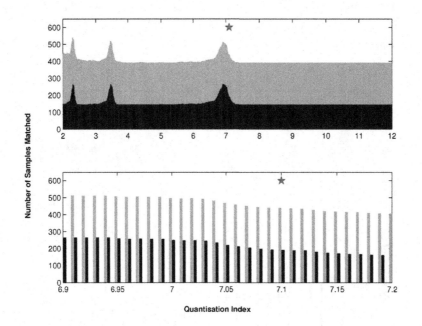

$$ICA(\hat{\mathbf{X}}) \rightarrow [\hat{\mathbf{S}}_{att}, \hat{\mathbf{W}}], \qquad (18)$$

$$\hat{\mathbf{S}}_{att} = [\hat{\mathbf{s}}_{1_{att}}; \hat{\mathbf{s}}_{2_{att}}; \dots; \hat{\mathbf{s}}_{wm_{att}}; \dots; \hat{\mathbf{s}}_{l_{att}}]'. \qquad (19)$$

The estimation of $\hat{\delta}$ and $\hat{\mathbf{k}}$ is conducted as explained in section 4. All the estimated sources (rows of $\hat{\mathbf{S}}_{att}$) are sampled for different values of $\breve{\delta}$.

No value of $\breve{\delta}$ positively identified the actual δ used at the embedder for either image or time series data. This result was observed for all the sources estimated. We conclude that an attacker applying the ICA to $\hat{\mathbf{c}}$ will not be able to estimate **k** and hence will be unable to destroy the embedded WM significantly without destroying the cover.

5.3. Summary of Results

The result of the estimation method discussed in section 4 for examples of one-dimensional and 2D data for both the DWT and ICA based watermarking methods are shown in Figures 6, 7, 8, 9 and 10.

Figures 11 and 12 show the relationship between the bit error rate (BER) and the number of samples of the secret embedding key **k**. BER is calculated as the Hamming distance between the actual embedded watermark and the watermark retrieved from $\hat{\mathbf{c}}$. Though the original embedded watermark is not available to the attacker, the BER has been calculated to depict the effect of the level of attack on the watermarked cover and our estimation method.

'True Positives' refers to the number of samples of **k** that are detected by the estimation method.

Figure 9. Above: Estimation of **k** *for ICA where* δ *= 3.1 is used for WM embedding and the sources are obtained from the watermarked EEG using the same separating matrix used by the embedder. The result shown is for the source which has been watermarked. Below: Estimated samples of* $\hat{\mathbf{k}}$ *for* $\hat{\delta}$ *around the largest peak detected (light colour) and* $\hat{\mathbf{k}} \cap \mathbf{k}$ *(darker colour). The star represents the true length of the watermarked samples.*

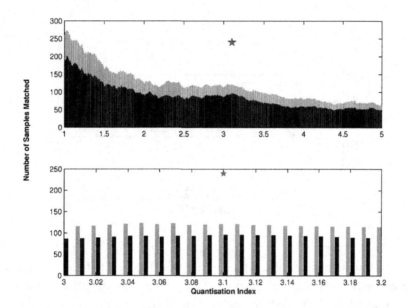

Figure 10. Estimation of **k** *for ICA where* δ *= 0.12 is used for WM embedding and the sources are obtained from the watermarked EEG using the same separating matrix used by the embedder. The result shown is for the source which is not watermarked.*

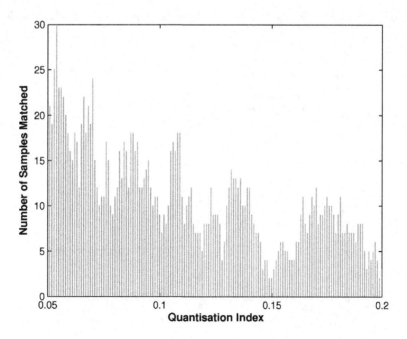

Figure 11. Result of estimation of $\hat{k}$ *and* $\hat{\delta}$ *for DWT based watermark embedding method, addition of noise attack*

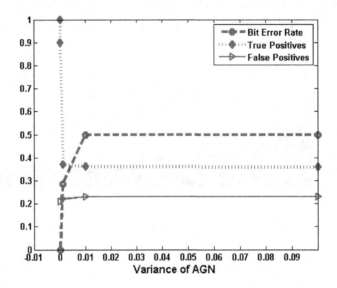

'False Positives' refers to the number of samples estimated by the estimation method that do not belong to **k**. The values of BER, 'True Positives' and 'False Positives' have been represented in terms of percentages.

In Figure 11 it can be seen that as the noise level increases the BER increases. The estimation method estimates an increasing number of 'False Positives' as the BER increases. The number of 'True Positives' on the other hand decrease with

Figure 12. Result of estimation of $\hat{k}$ *and* $\hat{\delta}$ *for DWT based watermark embedding method, compression attack*

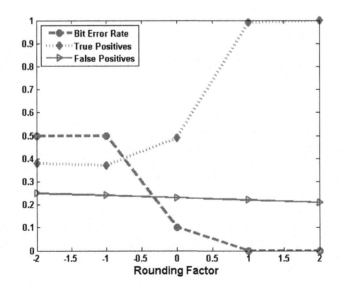

increasing BER. The opposite effect is observed in Figure 12. This is because the x-axis represents a decreasing level of compression. The BER decreases as the level of compression decreases. The number of 'True Positives' increases as the BER decreases whereas the number of 'False Positives' decreases to a smaller extent.

Tables 1 to 6 show the relationship between BER, R, 'True Positives' and 'False Positives' for the different types of data for both the DWT and ICA based approaches when the watermarked cover is filtered by applying a low-pass filter. The normalised cut-off frequency f_c of the filter was varied from 0.5 to 0.9. For simplicity the results obtained for f_c = 0.5 and f_c = 0.9 have been tabulated.

For the DWT based approach the BER and the number of 'True Positives' are affected by the level of filtering Tables 1 and 2. The BER decreases for a low-level of filtering but the number of 'True Positives' increases. The number of 'False Positives' are not affected by the level of filtering but are affected by R. This shows that if the value of R is high and the attack on the watermarked content is within a threshold that allows recovery of the embedded watermark then the detection mechanism is successful. The detection mechanism can detect 50 to 85% of $\mathbf{k}$ along with a small number (nearly zero) of un-watermarked samples. This enables the retrieval of the embedded message even without a knowledge of $\mathbf{k}$ and d.

A similar result is obtained for the ICA based watermark embedding approach, Tables 3 and 4, when the estimation method utilises the separating matrix used at the embedder to obtain the independent sources. It should be noted that in the case of the ICA based approach the number of 'True Positives' does not increase beyond 50% even when the BER is zero. The separating matrix used to obtain the sources at the embedder has been derived from the data and the attacker has no information about the segmentation blocking or the actual source that has been watermarked.

Tables 5 and 6 are the results of the estimation approach when the separating matrix is derived from the watermarked content which is distorted due to the application of various signal processing techniques and addition of noise during transmis-

Table 1. Result of estimation of $\hat{\mathbf{k}}$ and $\hat{\delta}$ for DWT based watermarking embedding method

FilterAttack, $f_c = 0.5$				
Data	R	**BER**	**True Positives**	**False Positives**
EEG_1	20	0.34	0.30±0.00	0.98±0.04
	40	0.33	0.28±0.00	0.36±0.04
	60	0.34	0.28±0.00	0.15±0.04
	80	0.34	0.27±0.00	0.05±0.04
	99	0.34	0.27±0.00	0.00±0.04
EEG_2	20	0.37	0.42±0.00	1.54±0.09
	40	0.37	0.41±0.00	0.58±0.01
	60	0.37	0.40±0.00	0.25±0.00
	80	0.36	0.40±0.00	0.09±0.00
	99	0.37	0.40±0.00	0.00±0.00
Classical	20	0	0.50±0.00	1.42±0.00
	40	0	0.51±0.00	0.50±0.00
	60	0.00	0.51±0.00	0.21±0.00
	80	0.00	0.52±0.00	0.08±0.00
	99	0.00	0.51±0.00	0.00±0.00
Pop	20	0.33	0.39±0.00	1.42±0.00
	40	0.31	0.38±0.00	0.52±0.00
	60	0.32	0.37±0.00	0.22±0.00
	80	0.32	0.37±0.00	0.08±0.00
	99	0.31	0.37±0.00	0.00±0.00
Rock	20	0.23	0.52±0.00	1.82±0.00
	40	0.24	0.51±0.00	0.66±0.00
	60	0.24	0.50±0.00	0.29±0.00
	80	0.24	0.51±0.00	0.10±0.00
	99	0.24	0.51±0.00	0.00±0.00
Textures	20	0.07	0.28±0.00	2.18±0.02
	40	0.07	0.29±0.00	0.97±0.00
	60	0.07	0.28±0.00	0.59±0.00
	80	0.07	0.28±0.00	0.41±0.00
	99	0.07	0.28±0.00	0.30±0.00
Objects	20	0.11	0.44±0.01	0.98±0.32
	40	0.09	0.47±0.01	0.41±0.07
	60	0.09	0.48±0.00	0.23±0.03
	80	0.10	0.47±0.00	0.14±0.01
	99	0.10	0.48±0.00	0.09±0.01
Faces	20	0.05	0.60±0.01	1.32±0.29
	40	0.05	0.58±0.00	0.57±0.07
	60	0.06	0.56±0.01	0.35±0.02
	80	0.05	0.56±0.01	0.23±0.01
	99	0.06	0.57±0.01	0.17±0.01

Table 2. Result of estimation of $\hat{k}$ and $\hat{\delta}$ for DWT based watermark embedding method

FilterAttack, $f_c = 0.9$				
Data	R	**BER**	**True Positives**	**False Positives**
EEG_1	20	0.00	0.81±0.00	0.86±0.03
	40	0.00	0.81±0.00	0.32±0.03
	60	0.00	0.81±0.00	0.14±0.03
	80	0.00	0.81±0.00	0.05±0.03
	99	0.00	0.81±0.00	0.00±0.03
EEG_2	20	0.01	0.77±0.00	1.41±0.07
	40	0.01	0.77±0.00	0.52±0.00
	60	0.01	0.77±0.00	0.23±0.00
	80	0.01	0.77±0.00	0.08±0.00
	99	0.01	0.77±0.00	0.00±0.00
Classical	20	0	0.56±0.00	1.42±0.00
	40	0	0.56±0.00	0.50±0.00
	60	0	0.56±0.00	0.21±0.00
	80	0.00	0.56±0.00	0.08±0.00
	99	0.00	0.56±0.00	0.00±0.00
Pop	20	0.06	0.47±0.00	1.36±0.00
	40	0.06	0.45±0.00	0.50±0.00
	60	0.07	0.45±0.00	0.21±0.00
	80	0.06	0.46±0.00	0.07±0.00
	99	0.06	0.45±0.00	0.00±0.00
Rock	20	0.04	0.65±0.00	1.75±0.00
	40	0.04	0.64±0.00	0.65±0.00
	60	0.04	0.64±0.00	0.29±0.00
	80	0.04	0.64±0.00	0.11±0.00
	99	0.04	0.64±0.00	0.00±0.00
Textures	20	0	0.71±0.03	1.95±0.02
	40	0	0.75±0.02	0.90±0.00
	60	0	0.74±0.02	0.55±0.00
	80	0	0.74±0.02	0.38±0.00
	99	0	0.73±0.02	0.29±0.00
Objects	20	0	0.77±0.01	1.00±0.33
	40	0	0.79±0.01	0.40±0.06
	60	0	0.80±0.01	0.22±0.02
	80	0	0.81±0.01	0.14±0.01
	99	0	0.81±0.01	0.08±0.00
Faces	20	0	0.85±0.00	1.22±0.24
	40	0	0.86±0.00	0.54±0.05
	60	0	0.85±0.00	0.32±0.02
	80	0	0.85±0.00	0.22±0.01
	99	0	0.85±0.00	0.16±0.00

Table 3. Result of estimation of $\hat{k}$ and $\hat{\delta}$ for ICA based watermark embedding method using the separating matrix used at the embedder

FilerAttack, $f_c = 0.5$				
Data	R	**BER**	**True Positives**	**False Positives**
EEG_1	20	0.13	0.15±0.00	0.63±0.00
	40	0.16	0.16±0.00	0.23±0.00
	60	0.20	0.14±0.00	0.10±0.00
	80	0.22	0.15±0.00	0.03±0.00
	99	0.25	0.15±0.00	0.00±0.00
EEG_2	20	0.17	0.17±0.00	0.64±0.00
	40	0.22	0.15±0.00	0.25±0.00
	60	0.23	0.16±0.00	0.10±0.00
	80	0.25	0.15±0.00	0.03±0.00
	99	0.26	0.16±0.00	0.00±0.00
Classical	20	0.45	0.32±0.00	1.04±0.00
	40	0.46	0.28±0.00	0.43±0.00
	60	0.42	0.26±0.00	0.20±0.00
	80	0.45	0.26±0.00	0.09±0.00
	99	0.46	0.25±0.00	0.02±0.00
Pop	20	0.49	0.30±0.01	1.05±0.00
	40	0.48	0.28±0.01	0.40±0.00
	60	0.49	0.25±0.00	0.20±0.00
	80	0.48	0.25±0.00	0.09±0.00
	99	0.48	0.24±0.00	0.02±0.00
Rock	20	0.49	0.38±0.01	1.50±0.01
	40	0.50	0.35±0.01	0.56±0.00
	60	0.50	0.35±0.01	0.27±0.00
	80	0.48	0.33±0.00	0.12±0.00
	99	0.50	0.34±0.00	0.03±0.00
Textures	20	0.50	0.16±0.00	3.07±0.00
	40	0.50	0.16±0.00	1.45±0.00
	60	0.50	0.16±0.00	0.92±0.00
	80	0.49	0.15±0.00	0.65±0.00
	99	0.49	0.16±0.00	0.48±0.00
Objects	20	0.49	0.18±0.00	1.73±0.75
	40	0.47	0.16±0.00	0.76±0.19
	60	0.48	0.17±0.00	0.43±0.08
	80	0.48	0.16±0.00	0.28±0.05
	99	0.48	0.16±0.00	0.20±0.03
Faces	20	0.48	0.17±0.00	2.05±0.75
	40	0.49	0.17±0.00	0.95±0.19
	60	0.50	0.16±0.00	0.58±0.08
	80	0.49	0.16±0.00	0.39±0.04
	99	0.50	0.16±0.00	0.28±0.03

Table 4. Result of estimation of $\hat{\mathbf{k}}$ and $\hat{\delta}$ for ICA based watermark embedding method using the separating matrix used at the embedder

FilterAttack, $f_c = 0.9$				
Data	R	BER	True Positives	False Positives
EEG_1	20	0	0.55±0.00	0.61±0.00
	40	0	0.46±0.00	0.24±0.00
	60	0.00	0.38±0.00	0.10±0.00
	80	0.00	0.35±0.00	0.04±0.00
	99	0.00	0.32±0.00	0.00±0.00
EEG_2	20	0	0.51±0.00	0.63±0.00
	40	0	0.44±0.00	0.24±0.00
	60	0.00	0.38±0.00	0.11±0.00
	80	0.00	0.35±0.00	0.03±0.00
	99	0.00	0.32±0.00	0.00±0.00
Classical	20	0	0.66±0.01	0.94±0.00
	40	0	0.54±0.00	0.34±0.00
	60	0	0.49±0.00	0.17±0.00
	80	0.00	0.45±0.00	0.07±0.00
	99	0.00	0.41±0.00	0.02±0.00
Pop	20	0.01	0.55±0.01	0.94±0.00
	40	0.02	0.50±0.01	0.37±0.00
	60	0.03	0.41±0.00	0.17±0.00
	80	0.03	0.42±0.00	0.08±0.00
	99	0.03	0.37±0.00	0.02±0.00
Rock	20	0.14	0.53±0.00	1.44±0.00
	40	0.14	0.50±0.00	0.52±0.00
	60	0.16	0.48±0.00	0.26±0.00
	80	0.15	0.46±0.00	0.11±0.00
	99	0.16	0.44±0.00	0.04±0.00
Textures	20	0	0.56±0.00	2.69±0.01
	40	0	0.56±0.00	1.05±0.00
	60	0	0.57±0.00	0.51±0.00
	80	0	0.57±0.00	0.31±0.00
	99	0	0.57±0.00	0.23±0.00
Objects	20	0	0.57±0.00	1.42±0.71
	40	0	0.57±0.00	0.53±0.10
	60	0	0.56±0.00	0.24±0.02
	80	0	0.57±0.00	0.14±0.01
	99	0	0.56±0.00	0.09±0.00
Faces	20	0	0.57±0.00	1.75±0.80
	40	0	0.57±0.00	0.69±0.12
	60	0	0.58±0.00	0.33±0.03
	80	0	0.58±0.00	0.18±0.01
	99	0	0.58±0.00	0.13±0.00

Table 5. Result of estimation of $\hat{\mathbf{k}}$ and $\hat{\delta}$ for ICA based watermark embedding method using the separating matrix estimated by applying the ICA to the attacked watermarked data

FilterAttack, $f_c = 0.9$				
Data	R	BER	True Positives	False Positives
EEG_1	20	0.49	0.16±0.00	0.62±0.00
	40	0.50	0.16±0.00	0.22±0.00
	60	0.50	0.15±0.00	0.10±0.00
	80	0.49	0.15±0.00	0.03±0.00
	99	0.48	0.15±0.00	0.00±0.00
EEG_2	20	0.50	0.16±0.00	0.63±0.00
	40	0.49	0.15±0.00	0.23±0.00
	60	0.50	0.16±0.00	0.10±0.00
	80	0.50	0.15±0.00	0.03±0.00
	99	0.48	0.15±0.00	0.00±0.00
Classical	20	0.50	0.30±0.00	1.08±0.00
	40	0.53	0.26±0.00	0.43±0.00
	60	0.52	0.26±0.00	0.20±0.00
	80	0.48	0.25±0.00	0.09±0.00
	99	0.49	0.25±0.00	0.02±0.00
Pop	20	0.54	0.40±0.00	1.45±0.00
	40	0.53	0.39±0.00	0.59±0.00
	60	0.49	0.35±0.00	0.26±0.00
	80	0.48	0.34±0.00	0.03±0.00
	99	0.49	0.34±0.00	0.03±0.00
Rock	20	0.48	0.39±0.00	1.45±0.00
	40	0.48	0.37±0.00	0.57±0.00
	60	0.50	0.36±0.00	0.26±0.00
	80	0.47	0.34±0.00	0.11±0.00
	99	0.49	0.33±0.00	0.03±0.00
Textures	20	0.46	0.23±0.01	2.78±0.24
	40	0.43	0.23±0.01	1.26±0.08
	60	0.44	0.24±0.01	0.77±0.04
	80	0.44	0.23±0.01	0.54±0.03
	99	0.44	0.23±0.01	0.39±0.02
Objects	20	0.48	0.18±0.00	1.72±0.76
	40	0.50	0.17±0.00	0.75±0.18
	60	0.49	0.18±0.00	0.44±0.08
	80	0.49	0.16±0.00	0.29±0.04
	99	0.50	0.16±0.00	0.19±0.03
Faces	20	0.50	0.17±0.00	2.16±0.78
	40	0.50	0.17±0.00	1.00±0.19
	60	0.49	0.16±0.00	0.60±0.08
	80	0.49	0.16±0.00	0.42±0.04
	99	0.49	0.16±0.00	0.30±0.03

Table 6. Result of estimation of $\hat{\mathbf{k}}$ and $\hat{\delta}$ for ICA based watermark embedding method using the separating matrix estimated by applying the ICA to the attacked watermarked data

FilterAttack, $f_c = 0.9$				
Data	R	BER	True Positives	False Positives
EEG_1	20	0.52	0.17±0.00	0.62±0.00
	40	0.49	0.16±0.00	0.23±0.00
	60	0.49	0.17±0.00	0.09±0.00
	80	0.50	0.16±0.00	0.03±0.00
	99	0.49	0.16±0.00	0.00±0.00
EEG_2	20	0.49	0.15±0.00	0.63±0.00
	40	0.50	0.16±0.00	0.22±0.00
	60	0.51	0.16±0.00	0.10±0.00
	80	0.51	0.15±0.00	0.03±0.00
	99	0.49	0.15±0.00	0.00±0.00
Classical	20	0.52	0.31±0.00	1.03±0.00
	40	0.53	0.26±0.00	0.40±0.00
	60	0.51	0.25±0.00	0.19±0.00
	80	0.48	0.25±0.00	0.08±0.00
	99	0.51	0.25±0.00	0.02±0.00
Pop	20	0.48	0.39±0.00	1.49±0.00
	40	0.50	0.37±0.00	0.58±0.00
	60	0.50	0.36±0.00	0.28±0.00
	80	0.49	0.34±0.00	0.12±0.00
	99	0.48	0.34±0.00	0.03±0.00
Rock	20	0.55	0.39±0.00	1.46±0.00
	40	0.49	0.36±0.00	0.57±0.00
	60	0.51	0.35±0.00	0.27±0.00
	80	0.48	0.34±0.00	0.12±0.00
	99	0.50	0.34±0.00	0.04±0.00
Textures	20	0.45	0.23±0.01	2.74±0.22
	40	0.44	0.23±0.01	1.23±0.08
	60	0.44	0.22±0.00	0.77±0.04
	80	0.44	0.23±0.01	0.53±0.02
	99	0.44	0.23±0.01	0.38±0.02
Objects	20	0.48	0.19±0.00	1.77±0.73
	40	0.50	0.18±0.00	0.79±0.17
	60	0.49	0.18±0.00	0.46±0.08
	80	0.49	0.18±0.00	0.29±0.04
	99	0.50	0.17±0.00	0.19±0.03
Faces	20	0.52	0.16±0.00	0.98±0.18
	40	0.50	0.17±0.00	1.00±0.19
	60	0.49	0.16±0.00	0.60±0.08
	80	0.50	0.16±0.00	0.41±0.04
	99	0.50	0.16±0.00	0.29±0.03

sion. It can be seen that the BER is around 50% indicating that the embedded watermark cannot be retrieved from the estimated sources using the new separating matrix. It should be noted that the number of 'True Positives' is less than 40% while the number of 'False Positives' is around 60%.

This shows that the separating matrix acts as an additional key in securing the embedded watermark thus making the ICA based approach better suited to watermark embedding in terms of security compared with the DWT based approach.

The approach advocated in this paper is based on a probability density function estimation of *differenced* watermarked transform domain, and so enjoys the benefits of being algorithmically simple and not reliant on assumptions about the distributions of cover text or watermark values.

It suffers when density estimation of high dimensional multivariate distributions is needed. However, for most applications this is limited to one or two dimensional distributions and so is computationally tractable. Our method failed when the strength of the attack applied to the watermarked signal resulted in a bit error rate of 30% or more.

These results are promising compared to existing attack methods of DM-QIM, especially for the DWT-based transform domain. The ICA based transform domain remains more resilient to attack. A brief analysis of the sensitivity of the ICA based approach has been presented in (Matam & Lowe, 2009a). An extensive statistical comparison between the method in this paper and recent attack methods is currently underway. Some of the results discussed in this paper have been presented in (Matam & Lowe, 2009b).

6. CONCLUSION

In this paper the claim that DM-QIM embedding techniques are secure was examined by investigating an estimation procedure of the unknown δ and $\mathbf{k}$. The experiments were conducted for two transform domain methods: DWT and ICA and were examined for multiple time series and images using multiple random realisations of embeddings. The results obtained illustrated that the DM-QIM method of embedding is not generally secure as has been claimed. Though retrieval of the exact message is not possible, deleting the existing message without destroying the covertext is possible. The results using the ICA method are not as precise as the results obtained for the DWT method. We believe this is due to the way the two transforms derive their basis vectors. Other variants of QIM based embedding techniques and different transform domain methods may give varying results, but for the watermarking methods described in this paper, it can be concluded that DWT based transform domain embedding is fallible, and the use of ICA as a transform domain for watermarking has the benefit of an extra inherent sensitivity to data snooping, which requires further investigation.

REFERENCES

Bas, P., & Hurri, J. (2006). Vulnerability of DM watermarking of non-IID host signals to attacks utilising the statistics of independent components. *IEEE Trans. Information Forensics and Security, 153*(3), 127–139.

Bender, W., Gruhl, D., Morimoto, N., & Lu, A. (1996). Techniques for data hiding. *IBM Systems Journal, 35*(3-4), 313–336. doi:10.1147/sj.353.0313

Bishop, C. M. (1995). *Neural networks for pattern recognition*. Oxford, UK: Oxford University Press.

Cayre, F., & Bas, P. (2008). Kerchkhoffs-based embedding security classes for WOA data hiding. *IEEE Trans. Information Forensics and Security, 3*(1), 1–15. doi:10.1109/TIFS.2007.916006

Cayre, F., Fontaine, C., & Furon, T. (2005). Watermarking security: Theory and practice. *IEEE Transactions on Signal Processing, 53*(10), 3976–3987. doi:10.1109/TSP.2005.855418

Chen, B., & Wornell, G. W. (2001). Quantization index modulation: a class of provably good methods for digital watermarking and information embedding. *IEEE Transactions on Information Theory, 47*(4), 1423–1443. doi:10.1109/18.923725

Comesaña, P., Pérez-Freire, L., & Pérez-González, F. (2005). An information-theoretic framework for assessing security in practical watermarking and data hiding scenarios. In *Proceedings of the International Workshop on Image Analysis for Multimedia Interactive Services*.

Cox, I., Killian, J., Leighton, T., & Shamoon, T. (1996). A secure, robust watermark for multimedia. In *Proceedings of the Workshop on Information Hiding* (pp. 175-190).

Giakoumaki, A., Pavlopoulos, S., & Koutsouris, D. (2006). *Multiple image watermarking applied to health information management*. IEEE Trans. Information.

Holliman, M., Memon, N., & Yeung, M. (1999). Watermark estimation through local pixel correlation. In *Proceedings of the SPIE Security and watermarking of multimedia content I, 3675*, 134-146.

Kalker, T. (2001). Considerations on watermarking security. In *Proceedings of the Multimedia Signal Processing, IEEE Fourth Workshop on* (pp. 201-206).

Lin, L., Doërr, G. J., Cox, I. J., & Miller, M. L. (2005). An efficient algorithm for informed embedding of dirty-paper trellis codes for watermarking. In *Proceedings of the ICIP (1)* (pp. 697-700).

Matam, B. R., & Lowe, D. (2009a). Exploiting sensitivity of nonorthogonal joint diagonalisation as a security mechanism in steganography. In *Proceedings of the Int. Conf. Digital Signal Processing* (pp. 532-538).

Matam, B. R., & Lowe, D. (2009b). Watermarking: How secure is the DM-QIM watermarking technique? In *Proceedings of the Int. Conf. Digital Signal Processing,* (pp. 401-408).

McKay, D. (2002). *Information theory, inference and learning algorithms.* Cambridge, MA: Cambridge University Press.

Nabney, I. T. (2002). *Netlab, algorithms for pattern recognition.* New York: Springer.

Pérez-Freire, L., & Pérez-González, F. (2007). Exploiting security holes in lattice data hiding. In *Proceedings of the 9th International Workshop on Information Hiding* (pp. 159-173).

Pérez-Freire, L., Pérez-González, F., Furon, T., & Comesaña, P. (2006). Security of lattice-based data hiding against the known message attack. *IEEE Trans. Information Forensics and Security, 1*(4), 421–439. doi:10.1109/TIFS.2006.885029

Woon, W. L., & Lowe, D. (2001). Nonlinear signal processing for noise reduction of unaveraged single channel MEG data. In *Proceedings of the International Conference on Artificial Neural Networks* (pp. 650-657).

This work was previously published in the International Journal of Digital Crime and Forensics, Volume 2, Issue 2, edited by Chang-Tsun Li and Anthony TS Ho, pp. 64-87, copyright 2010 by IGI Publishing (an imprint of IGI Global).

Section 3
Applications of Cryptography in Digital Forensics

Chapter 8
Cryptopometry as a Methodology for Investigating Encrypted Material

Niall McGrath
University College Dublin, Ireland

Pavel Gladyshev
University College Dublin, Ireland

Joe Carthy
University College Dublin, Ireland

ABSTRACT

When encrypted material is discovered during a digital investigation and the investigator cannot decrypt the material then he or she is faced with the problem of how to determine the evidential value of the material. This research is proposing a methodology titled Cryptopometry. Cryptopometry extracts probative value from the encrypted file of a hybrid cryptosystem. Cryptopometry also incorporates a technique for locating the original plaintext file. Since child pornography (KP) images and terrorist related information (TI) are transmitted in encrypted formats, the digital investigator must ask the question Cui Bono?—who benefits or who is the recipient? By following Cryptopometry, the scope of the digital investigation can be extended to reveal the intended recipient. The derivation of the term Cryptopometry is also described and explained.

INTRODUCTION

Law enforcement agencies (LEA) encounter encryption in relation to the distribution of KP (Carter, 2007) and of TI (Shahda, 2007) offences. For example a KP distributor encrypts the KP

material with PGP and posts it into a newsgroup or interest group via anonymous re-mailer or via an instant messenger system. The accomplice who is subscribed to that group receives encrypted material and can decrypt it. The anonymity of all involved parties is preserved and the content cannot be decrypted by bystanders. The use of PGP encryption in general has been cited (Sieg-

DOI: 10.4018/978-1-4666-1758-2.ch008

fried, Siedsma, Countryman, & Hosmer, 2004) as a major hurdle in these investigations. In addition, during digital investigations evidence is often discovered which extends the scope of the investigation. These are compelling reasons for the computer forensic investigator to be able to identify encrypted material, examine it and finally extract evidential value from it. This paper presents *Cryptopometry* which is a methodology that was experimentally formulated and it facilitates the identification of the recipient of PGP encrypted material. As an adjunct to this, a technique that identifies the plaintext file that was encrypted is presented. Subsequently a technical evaluation was carried out in a case study to validate the methodology. Following this, the performance and error-rate of *Cryptopometry* were evaluated through experimental means and finally the future work items are outlined.

1 RESEARCH CONTRIBUTION

The *Cryptopometry* methodology has been formulated for the investigation of encrypted material. This methodology extracts evidential value from the encrypted material to enable the identification of the recipient of the encrypted material. The incorporated search technique correlates the ciphertext file under investigation with the original plaintext file. The methodology has been validated and its performance has been evaluated to a high degree of success. In addition the error-rate of identifying the wrong file has been determined to be low. In general *Cryptopometry* reduces the investigation time by systematically carving the data under investigation into a significantly reduced file set. *Cryptopometry* is an entirely novel approach to investigating encrypted material and it is fully automated.

2 PROBLEM DESCRIPTION

The investigation of subject A is initiated and a forensic image of the hard disk drive (HDD) is taken. Analysis is carried out and it is found that there is a significant amount of ciphertext files and plaintext files containing evidence. Subject A is a suspected distributor/seller of KP and subject B whose identity is unknown is the recipient of the encrypted material. The objective of this research is to establish an evidential link between the encrypter and the recipient of PGP encrypted material and subsequently identify the plaintext file that was encrypted. In this scenario subject A must have had subject B's public key (PK_B) and PGP encrypted the plaintext material (M) to form the ciphertext (C_B). Subject B can decrypt the ciphertext when he receives it with his private key (PVK_B), please see Figure 1. PGP is a hybrid cryptosystem where the ciphertext created by it follows the OpenPGP message format specified in Callas et al. (2007). A hybrid cryptosystem is a combination of symmetric and asymmetric encryption. A symmetric key is session generated and then this is used to encrypt data. The symmetric key is then encrypted using the recipient's public key. The public key can be stored and distributed by a key server. The symmetrically encrypted data and the asymmetrically encrypted symmetric key are the major components of a PGP ciphertext data-packet. PGP also compresses data before encryption for added security because this helps remove redundancies and patterns that might facilitate cryptanalysis, compression is only applied to the symmetrically encrypted data-packet. PGP uses the Deflater (zip) algorithm for compression.

2.1 Methodology

The methodology which facilitates the investigation of PGP encryption is outlined in Figure 2 and consists of a number of steps that are described in the following sections. In order to carry out this research a framework of Java classes was created

Figure 1. Problem description

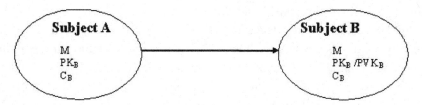

to do the following: generate OpenPGP encryption keys and data, create a file parser to extract and analyse information from data and create a test harness and a compression engine that examined ZIP compression.

2.1.1 Searching for Public Key and Ciphertext Artefacts

The first step of the methodology is to search for OpenPGP artefacts on the subject's HDD i.e. public keys and ciphertext files. Certain hexadecimal

values can be used as signatures when searching for OpenPGP artefacts. These values have been determined experimentally and are shown in Table 1 and Table 2.

When searching for public keys the linear relationship in equation 1 can be used to estimate the public key file size from the key strength. Key strength can be determined from section 3.1.3 below. Equation 1 was observed experimentally from the data of 300 generated RSA asymmetric keypairs, i.e., 100 keypairs each of 512, 1024 & 2048 bit strengths.

Figure 2. Methodology for investigating PGP encryption

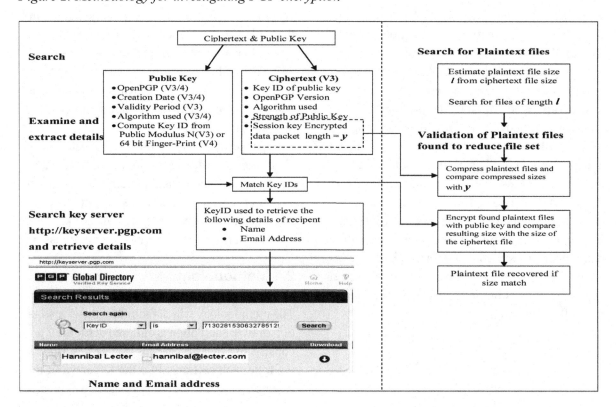

Table 1. OpenPGP version 4 Public Key Search Signatures

OpenPGP-PublicKey (V4)	Search Signature
512 Bit Key	\x98\x4d\x04
1024 Bit Key	\x98\x8d\x04
2048 Bit Key	\x99\x01\x0d\x04

Table 2. OpenPGP version 3 Ciphertext Search Signatures

OpenPGP-Ciphertext (V3)	Search Signature
512 Bit Key Encrypted	\x84\x4c\x03
1024 Bit Key Encrypted	\x84\x8c\x03
2048 Bit Key Encrypted	\x85\x01\x0c\x03

Equation 1. Estimating key size from key strength

$$y = 3.9802 * x184 - \qquad\qquad 184$$

where x=key size in bytes and y = key strength in bits

2.1.2 Analysis of Public Key Artefacts-Examine and Extract Details

For each found public key file the next step of the methodology is to determine the following components of the OpenPGP public key: (1) *Version* number which is currently at OpenPGP V4, (2) *Creation Date* which is a 4 byte timestamp measuring time (UTC: coordinated universal time) to the nearest millisecond of the creation date, (3) *Validity* Period (only for V3) indicates start date and time and expiration date and time, (4) *Algorithm* type indicates if the algorithm used is an RSA algorithm, Signature Algorithm, Elliptical curve algorithm etc. The numbers 1 to 3 are reserved for RSA (1 = RSA encryption algorithm). (5) The key strength can be determined from the length of Public Modulus (*N*).

The Public Modulus (*N*) is represented as a multi-precision integer (MPI) and the low order 64 bits of *N* are the *Key ID* for a V3 key, this can be represented as a *long* primitive type. The *Key ID* for a V4 key is the lower order 64 bits of the key finger print. This has to be computed because it is not an element of the OpenPGP specification however the method of computation is specified in the OpenPGP standard (Callas et al., 2007). Please

refer to appendix in section 10 where some java code snippets for extracting these components are listed. *Creation Date* and *Validity Period* are used to search for the corresponding ciphertext file because the timestamp of the ciphertext file will obviously be greater or equal to *Creation Date* of public key and less than or equal to *Validity Period* (if V3). The location of these items in the public key is specified in (Callas et al., 2007). For *key strength* the hexadecimal values "04 | 00" is equal to 1024 in decimal. Therefore 1024 bit strength can be concluded. For *Creation Date* the values "49 |66 |36| 2C" are used to initialise a Java *Date* object. The hexadecimal values evaluate to 1231435308 in decimal. This *long* number represents the specified number of seconds since the standard base time January 1, 1970, 00:00:00 GMT, i.e., Thu Jan 08 17:21:48 GMT 2009 is *Creation Date* of public key. The Java Date object constructor takes this value in milliseconds. Please see Figure 3 which shows the OpenPGP components and their indices in the public key file.

2.1.3 Analysis of Ciphertext Artefacts-Examine and Extract Details

For each ciphertext file found the following components of the OpenPGP ciphertext are determined: (1) *Version* number which is currently at OpenPGP V3, (2) *Key ID* of the public key used to encrypt the ciphertext which is embedded as an 8 byte hexadecimal number. This is extracted by retrieving the 8 bytes from indices 03 to 0a inclusive. This 8 byte *long* number is represented

Figure 3. Components from public key file (V4)

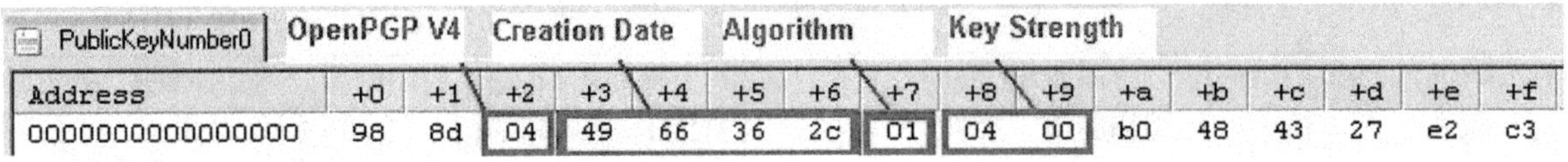

	Address	+0	+1	+2	+3	+4	+5	+6	+7	+8	+9	+a	+b	+c	+d	+e	+f
PublicKeyNumber0 / OpenPGP V4 / Creation Date / Algorithm / Key Strength	0000000000000000	98	8d	04	49	66	36	2c	01	04	00	b0	48	43	27	e2	c3

Figure 4. Components of ciphertext file (V3)

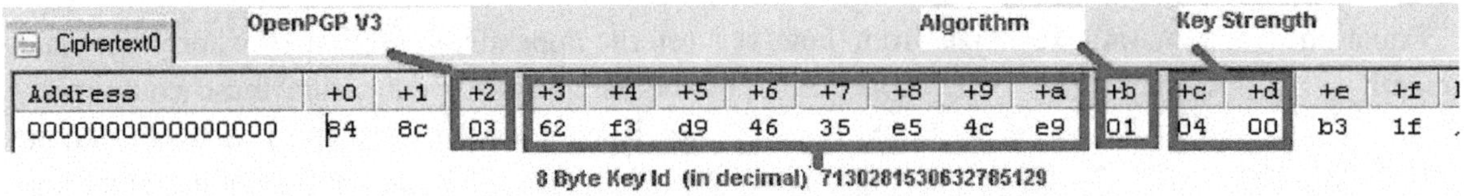

	Address	+0	+1	+2	+3	+4	+5	+6	+7	+8	+9	+a	+b	+c	+d	+e	+f	
Ciphertext0 / OpenPGP V3 / Algorithm / Key Strength	0000000000000000	84	8c	03	62	f3	d9	46	35	e5	4c	e9	01	04	00	b3	1f	

8 Byte Key Id (in decimal) 7130281530632785129

in decimal along with the other OpenPGP components in Figure 4. (3) Similar to Public Key analysis in section 3.1.2 above the *Algorithm* field and (4) *Key strength* of the public key used to create the ciphertext can be determined. Please refer to appendix in section 10 below where some java code snippets for extracting these components are listed.

Finally (5) the *length* of *Symmetric Key Encrypted Data Packet* can be extracted. Since the public key in question is 1024 bit, then the *public key encrypted data packet* must be 142 bytes long, index to offset 8E and read next 2 bytes. These 2 bytes in hexadecimal are C9 and FF. This is the header value for *session key encrypted data packet*. The next 4 byte values in hexadecimal are 00, 38, E9 and 92 and "00|38|E9|92" evaluates to 3729810 in decimal. 3729810 is the size in bytes of the *symmetric key encrypted data packet*. The size given here is the size of the data after compression has taken place i.e. size before symmetric encryption. Please see Figure 5 where this

size is retrieved from the ciphertext file. Note: if compression did not take place, this would be the size of the original plaintext file.

2.1.4 Matching the Key ID from Public Key and Ciphertext

In the next step the *Key ID* retrieved from ciphertext has to be compared with the computed *Key ID* from the public key. When a match occurs then it can be concluded that the public key was used to create the ciphertext under analysis.

2.1.5 Search Key Server: http://keyserver.pgp.com

Subsequently, the *Key Id* of public key is used to search a designated keyserver for *name* and *email address* of the owner of the public key, i.e., the recipient of the encrypted material. These details are easily retrieved by inputting the *Key ID* into the website.

Figure 5. Identifying size of compressed file before encryption

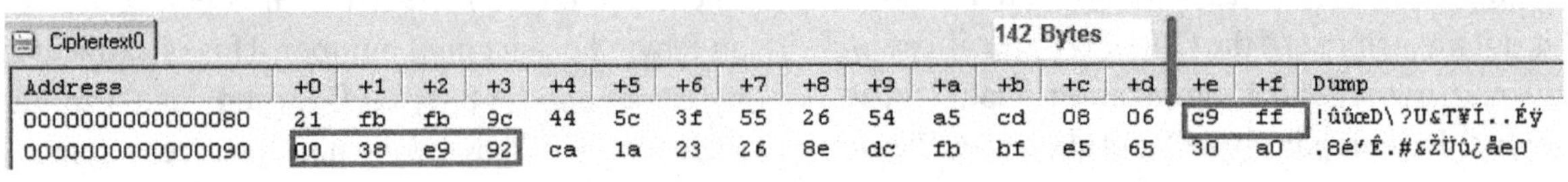

	Address	+0	+1	+2	+3	+4	+5	+6	+7	+8	+9	+a	+b	+c	+d	+e	+f	Dump
Ciphertext0 / 142 Bytes	0000000000000080	21	fb	fb	9c	44	5c	3f	55	26	54	a5	cd	08	06	c9	ff	!ûûœD\ ?U&T¥Í..Éÿ
	0000000000000090	00	38	e9	92	ca	1a	23	26	8e	dc	fb	bf	e5	65	30	a0	.8é'É.#&žÚû¿åeO

2.1.6 Approximating the Size of Plaintext File from Ciphertext File

This is the initial step to searching for the original plaintext file. A linear relationship between ciphertext file size and plaintext file size of JPEG files was determined, please see equation 2 below. Once l is evaluated then plaintext files of length l bytes can be searched for. This reduces the size of the candidate file set. Equation 2 was derived from the generated data of encrypting a number of JPEG files with a 100 RSA keys each of 1024 bit strength; using AES 256 bit symmetric encryption with ZIP compression.

Equation 2. Linear relationship between plaintext and ciphertext file lengths

$$l = 0.9924 * y + 30244$$

where y=length of encrypted JPEG file and l = length plaintext JPEG file

2.1.7 Validation

The next step is to validate the candidate plaintext file(s) that are identified by the approximating process above. This is done by passing the plaintext files through the *Deflater* engine, which compresses the files. The number of compressed bytes that the plaintext file deflates to closely approximates the *length* of the session key encrypted data packet to be session key (symmetrically) encrypted. This size is the *length* of data packet after compression has taken place. Finally each plaintext file in the validated file set is encrypted. This will definitively determine the original plaintext file that was encrypted and exchanged.

3 DERIVATION OF CRYPTOPOMETRY

In order to properly and accurately portray this research it is necessary to categorise it formally. However, the search for a suitable formalism was unsuccessful but there were similarities observed between this research and the contemporary system used for the identification of criminals i.e. anthropometry.

3.1 Background to Identification Systems: Anthropometry

In 1879 Alphonse Bertillon was the first person to invent a criminal identification system. This system consisted of taking eleven measurements, two photographs and a spoken narrative-type description of the criminal as outlined by (Reddy, 2005). This system came to be known as the *Bertillonage* system of identification. This system depended on measurements of parts of the human frame that remained constant during adolescent life and the sizes were unique and private to the individual. Reddy (2005) highlighted that the *Bertillonage* system was soon adapted to policing as both in preventing false impersonation and also a method of identifying repeat offenders. This system was formally known as anthropometry and it has come to be known as the "measurement of humans". Subsequently Francis Galton, a cousin of Charles Darwin, developed and refined a system of fingerprinting and identification. Then in 1896 Edward Henry's research resulted in a new classification system which was based on immutable biometric properties like the number of ridges, furrows, loops, arches and minutiae points (whorls) of the finger's/ thumb's delta. This is the fingerprinting system used today by police forces worldwide.

3.2 Cryptography and Anthropometry

The obvious overlap between anthropometry and cryptography is the use of fingerprinting as a means of identification. Anthropometric fingerprinting is used worldwide in criminalistics as a method of identification. Where cryptographic fingerprinting is the implementation of a mathematical one-way function called *hashing* which is the process of transforming a plaintext message into a string of fixed length. The practical applications here are to confirm message integrity and also to serve as a component of authentication and digital signatures.

In cryptography there are also properties that are constant, unique and private to each user. There are constant values like bit length of RSA modulus (key strength), the public exponent of the public key, version number of the PGP key and ciphertext, creation date of public key, length of encrypted session key etc. Then there are unique values like the key id of the public key and the encrypted octet streams of the session key and the actual data. Finally, there are private values like the two prime numbers whose product is the public modulus and the private key component that is calculated from the *Euler number* (*totient function*) of the public modulus. Where crimes are committed anonymously and concealed under the cover of encryption and when some of these (at least the constant and unique) values are revealed in an investigation it can contribute significant criminalistic information and also assist in identifying evidence.

This research endeavours to locate evidence and identify criminals where crimes are concealed and committed anonymously under the cover of encryption. However, similar parallels can be drawn with the use anthropometry outlined above. While anthropometry was used primarily to prevent false impersonation and also to identify repeat offenders by recording the physical dimensions of criminals, correspondingly this research removes the anonymity of criminals while also identifying certain values (dimensions) that contribute to evidential value. Subsequently, this presented methodology will be labelled with the title of "*CRYPTOPOMETRY*" i.e. *CRYPTO*-graphic anthro*POMETRY*.

4 CASE STUDY

This case study is modelled on the described problem above and the *Cryptopometry* methodology is applied practically to reveal the recipient of the exchanged encrypted material and to search for the original plaintext file. Techniques for investigating recently run programs, the registry and *NTUSER. dat* file and internet search history are outlined in Bunting (2008). In addition there are specialised techniques listed in Dickson (2006) for investigating AIM related incidents. An investigation was carried out based on these techniques and it was established that an incident where America Online Instant Messenger (AIM) is used in conjunction with PGP encryption took place. An encrypted file that was transferred to subject B using AIM was located. AIM provides real-time one-to-one messaging between computers and attachments can be encrypted with the recipient's PGP public key.

4.1 Search and Analysis of Artefacts: Extraction of Significant Information

An Encase® search was executed with the signatures in Table 1 and Table 2. Then the parser was run to carry out the automated analysis and matching of the public key and corresponding ciphertext *Key ID*s. When a match was detected between the two *Key ID*s output was generated from the parser, please see Figure 6.

Figure 6. Output from parser

Output from Parser
Analysis of PGP Public Key Artefact
Version 4. Computed *key ID* value is *7130281530632785129.* *Key Created Thu Jan 08 17:21:48 GMT 2009.* Validity Period: N/A because key is Version 4. *Value = 1, RSA -> Encryption* key strength is 1024.
Analysis of PGP Ciphertext Artefact
Version 3. *key ID retrieved from ciphertext is 7130281530632785129* *Value = 1, RSA -> Encryption* key strength is 1024. *Length of compressed data packet to be session key encrypted is 3729810.*
Match of Key IDs from Public Key & Ciphertext Files
Key ID from Public Key and Key ID from Ciphertext match -> Public Key was used to encrypt the Ciphertext.

4.2 Approximating the Size of Plaintext File from Ciphertext File

Since the size of the ciphertext file identified by the parser is 3,729,966 bytes, then using equation 2, *l* evaluated to 3,731,862. Then a search for plaintext files of length 3,731,862 bytes was carried out. This search yielded 7 candidate files. In order to further reduce this file set a validation process was carried out, which is explained below.

4.3 Validation

The *Deflator* engine was then used to determine what size the 7 plaintext files, short listed in the previous step, will compress to. Using the ciphertext file from the parser output; the length of data packet to be session key encrypted is 3729810. This is the size that the original plaintext data compresses to before encryption takes place. Therefore the number of compressed bytes, that the plaintext files *deflates* to, will closely approximate 3729810 bytes. Please refer to Figure 6 and Figure 5 above. This process reduces the file set down to 2 candidate files.

Finally these 2 plaintext files were encrypted giving 2 new ciphertext files of definitive sizes. These sizes were compared with the original ciphertext file size. Hence the original plaintext file that was encrypted and exchanged with AIM was conclusively determined. Incidentally, 3729810 is the size of the data after compression takes place and then after (symmetric) encryption this becomes 3729824. This is due to the fact that PGP uses CFB mode encryption and this mode operates on blocks of fixed length i.e. 16 bytes. This will give rise to the "stair casing effect" in terms of size of the encrypted file. The encrypted block size will be padded out to fit the block size. Note there is a difference of 142 bytes from this size (3729824) and the overall size (3729966) of the ciphertext file under investigation in section 5.2 above. This is due to the RSA asymmetrically encrypted datapacket which would be 142 bytes for a 1024 bit encryption key which would be suffixed to the symmetrically encrypted message datapacket.

5 EVALUATION: USING RECEIVER OPERATING CHARACTERISTIC (ROC) ANALYSIS

This section deals with establishing how to evaluate *Cryptopometry* in terms of performance and demonstrating experimentally how effective the methodology was. It had to be decided how the experimentation was going to be designed and what statistical modelling technique could be used to achieve evaluation of *Cryptopometry*. Narkundkar and Priestly (2006) provide direction on evaluation methods used to determine what statistical modelling techniques are more appropriate and better than others. The accuracy of the classification of three methods of evaluation are discussed, i.e., Classification Rates, The Kolmorgorov-Smirnov Test and ROC analysis. In all methods the outcomes would have some associated "loss" or "reward". The conclusion reached in that paper is that if an understanding of the problem domain and data are critical in deciding what model of evaluation method is used and also if there is no information available regarding the respective error costs then the ROC curve analysis would represent the most appropriate evaluation method. ROC analysis incorporates binary classification which is the task of classifying the members of a given set of objects into two groups on the basis of whether they have some property or not. The medical community applies this to testing techniques and a typical binary classification scenario is where medical testing is carried out to determine if a patient has a certain disease or not. Altman and Bland (1994) discuss that when measuring the performance of medical and quality control tests, the concepts *sensitivity* and *specificity* are used; these concepts are readily usable for the evaluation of any binary classifier. *Sensitivity* (true positive rate) is the proportion of the population that tested positive out of all of the population; (true positives)/ (true positives + false negatives). *Specificity* (or true negative rate) is the proportion of people that tested negative of all the negative people tested; (true negatives)/ (true negatives + false positives). Therefore (1 - *Specificity*) evaluates to the false positive rate because the number of true positives, false negatives, true negatives, and false positives add up to 100% of the set. Fisher (1966) explains that in statistical hypothesis testing of an experiment, there will be

a null hypothesis and an alternative hypothesis. Based on the outcome of the experiment it will be decided whether to reject the null hypothesis or not. If the result of the experiment is statistically significant then the null hypothesis is rejected in favour of the alternative hypothesis. Doing this when the null hypothesis is in fact true creates a false positive; doing this when the null hypothesis is false is a true positive. Fawcett (2006) highlights that ROC graphs are two-dimensional graphs in which true positive rate is plotted on the Y axis and false positive rate is plotted on the X axis. According to Narkundkar and Priestly (2004), ROC analysis is a useful technique for visualizing, organizing and selecting/evaluating classifiers based on their performance. ROC analysis also provides a better measure of classification performance than scalar measures such as accuracy or error rate. When the area under the ROC curve (AUC) is computed it will indicate the measure of performance as a scalar of the chosen classifier.

5.1 Experimentation

Based on the information presented above this research proceeded to implement experimentation for ROC analysis to illustrate how well the *Cryptopometry* chosen classifier performed. This was achieved by using a binary classification system that would highlight the measure of positives and positives for the classifier variable and then express its overall performance as a scalar. The objective, data and observations of experimentation are presented below.

5.1.1 Objective of Experimentation

The objective here was to evaluate the performance of the *Cryptopometry* methodology. To actually do this a variable of interest had to be identified—this was the ciphertext file length. This variable would be used as a 'predictor' or 'indicator' to illustrate how well the methodology performed over a set of file lengths - twenty different values of ciphertext file lengths were randomly selected. Next a classification variable (dichotomous) that would indicate results of instantiating *Cryptopometry* in finding the plaintext file (for this there are two classes where 1=success, 0=failure) was selected. From this it was possible to determine if there were any threshold points (ciphertext file length) where the classifier performed well or not. This objective was achieved by implementing ROC analysis (which included calculating the AUC). The AUC is a scalar measurement of performance-evaluation classifier of *Cryptopometry*. Since there is only one classifier of interest i.e. finding the right plaintext file or not, then by evaluating the performance of this classifier would serve to measure the performance of the methodology. The measurement is a real number in the range from 0 to 1. A maximum value of 1 for AUC represents a perfect classifier performance.

5.1.2 Procedure

A JPEG file (photograph) was selected from a subject HDD. The plaintext JPEG file was encrypted using a hybrid encryption with the following attributes: 1024 bit RSA Encryption with 256 bit AES symmetric encryption. This resulted in the creation of a ciphertext file which was placed under investigation. Using the *Cryptopometry* methodology the original plaintext JPEG photograph file was to be identified from the ciphertext file. The above process was carried out 20 times in total using 20 different random JPEG photograph files with file lengths of > 3 Mbytes and < 4 Mbytes. The sizes of the created 20 ciphertext files are listed in column A below in Table 3. The lengths of the original 20 plaintext file are estimated by using the linear equation that was derived in Equation 2, please see column B in Table 3 below. The upper and lower limits are calculated by the estimated lengths (in column B) $\pm$ 1 standard deviation (SD=2804). The values specified in column C reflect the number of plain-

text files on HDD that have file lengths which fall between the upper and lower limits. Then these identified files in columns C are retrieved. These plaintext files are compressed using the *Deflater* engine. The resulting files compress to various lengths but only the number of files (in column D) compress to the actual value (i.e. size before encryption) that is embedded in the metadata of the ciphertext file which is under investigation. Then the files (if there are more than one) in column D are encrypted and compared directly with the encrypted file under investigation. When the file found in column E matches that file in column A, and then there is a direct match, which indicates success (result = 1) otherwise there is no match, which indicates failure (result = 0).

Using the "1"s listed in column E Table 3 as the list of true positives (TPs) which are also listed in column B of Table 4, then a list of false positives (FPs) can be created - take the TPs and replace "0" with "1" and vice-versa. The FPs are listed in column C of Table 4. The TP rate is then calculated as being the proportion of files above this cut-off size that can be correctly identified. This is calculated by summing the number of TPs above this cut-off and then dividing by the total number of TPs. These values are listed in column D of Table 4. Similar calculations are carried out for the FP rate in column E. The true negative (TN) rate is simply calculated by subtracting the FPR from 1 because FPR=1-Specificity. These calculations constitute the ROC data and are listed in Table 4.

Using the data in Table 4, the TPR as Y-axis and the FPR as X-axis were graphed to give the ROC plot in Figure 7. Then the AUC was computed by calculating the area for each row using the *trapezoid rule* i.e.

$$\sum_{n=1}^{n=20}(((D_n + D_{n+1})/2)*(E_n - E_{n+1})) = AUC$$

Table 3. Methodology evaluation data

A	B	C	D	E
Ciphertext File Length (bytes)	Estimated Plaintext Length (bytes) using $y = 0.9924x + 30244$	Files Found within upper & lower limits	Files Found After Validation	Files Found After Encryption
3003076	3010496	1	0	0
3014468	3021802	0	0	0
3110324	3116930	1	0	0
3122708	3129219	18	0	0
3187844	3193860	1	0	0
3293252	3298467	1	1	1
3397252	3401677	2	1	1
3454180	3458172	2	1	1
3504932	3508539	1	1	1
3566404	3569543	1	1	1
3651108	3653604	6	2	1
3652900	3655382	5	2	1
3655380	3657843	4	0	0
3666292	3668672	15	1	1
3720404	3722373	2	1	1
3735748	3737600	2	1	1
3743300	3745095	0	0	0
3767700	3769309	4	2	1
3768612	3770215	4	2	1
3872884	3873694	2	1	1

Table 4. ROC data listing sensitivity and false positive rate for all possible threshold values

A	B	C	D	E	F	G	H
Ciphertext File Length	TP	FP	-TP Rate- Sensitivity	FP Rate (1-Specificity)	True Positives	False positives	-TN Rate- Specificity
3003076	0	1	1.000	0.857	13	7	0.143
3014468	0	1	1.000	0.714	13	6	0.286
3110324	0	1	1.000	0.571	13	5	0.429
3122708	0	1	1.000	0.429	13	4	0.429
3187844	0	1	1.000	0.285	13	3	0.571
3293252	1	0	1.000	0.285	13	2	0.715
3397252	1	0	0.923	0.285	12	2	0.715
3454180	1	0	0.846	0.285	11	2	0.715
3504932	1	0	0.769	0.285	10	2	0.715
3566404	1	0	0.692	0.285	9	2	0.715
3651108	1	0	0.615	0.285	8	2	0.715
3652900	1	0	0.538	0.285	7	2	0.715
3655380	0	1	0.462	0.285	6	2	0.715
3666292	1	0	0.462	0.142	6	1	0.858
3720404	1	0	0.385	0.142	5	1	0.858
3735748	1	0	0.308	0.142	4	1	0.858
3743300	0	1	0.231	0.142	3	1	0.858
3767700	1	0	0.231	0	3	0	1
3768612	1	0	0.154	0	2	0	1
3872884	1	0	0.077	0	1	0	1

where D is the TPR column and E is the FPR column. Then all the areas for the rows are summed up to give the AUC. Subsequently the decision plot in Figure 8 was drawn up based on the TPR and TNR data in Table 4. The decision plot allows the choice of the threshold value (decision value), i.e., ciphertext file length that minimizes the rate of false positives and aids in the selection of a specific value to use as a threshold that provides a desired trade-off between the true positive rate and the false positive rate.

5.1.3 Observations

The AUC in Figure 7 is computed to be 0.81. Altman and Bland (1994) point out that when the AUC is 1 the accuracy of the classifier is concluded to be excellent, when AUC is between 0.80 and 0.90 the accuracy of the test is regarded to be good, while 0.70 to 0.80 indicates a fair accuracy level, 0.60 to 0.70 is regarded to be poor and anything else warrants test failure. Therefore it can be inferred that the AUC for *Cryptopometry* classifier yielded a good result. Since this result verifies the selection of the classifier variable

Figure 7. ROC lot

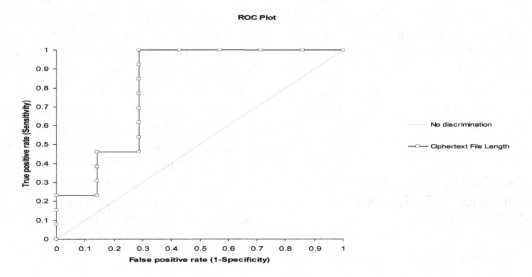

(Success/Failure) as a good classifier. It is reasonable to infer that *Cryptopometry* performed well over the selected thresholds of file lengths. Subsequently in relation to Hypothesis Testing; if the Null hypothesis is H_0 (indicating randomness) and the alternative hypothesis is H_1 (indicating non-randomness). Altman and Bland (1994) point out that where H_0: area ≤ 0.5. H_1: area > 0.5, then this means that the test is more powerful than a random rule, so H_0 is rejected and H_1 is accepted

i.e. results from the *Cryptopometry* classifier are not random. As a note - any points that lie under the line of no discrimination in Figure 7, represent where no discrimination can be made between TPR or FPR i.e. test failure. It was also interesting to note that there was a sharp improvement of the performance in *Cryptopometry* after ciphertext file length of 3187844 bytes, please see columns A and B in Table 4. This appears to be the threshold point above which *Cryptopometry* behaves most

Figure 8. ROC decision plot

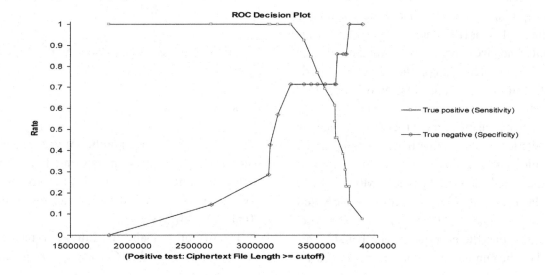

consistently and effectively. Finally, the decision (threshold) plot in Figure 8 shows the TPR and TNR over all of the file lengths and the point of intersection of the two lines is the optimum file size threshold where *Cryptopometry* identifies the original plaintext file with an equal success and failure rate- this occurs when ciphertext file is 3530000 bytes long.

6 PROBABILITY OF CORRECTLY IDENTIFYING THE ORIGINAL PLAINTEXT FILE

While the performance of *Cryptopometry* has been measured in the previous section it is necessary to determine the overall error rate and reliability with which the original plaintext file can be identified from the ciphertext file. The rationale in determining these rates is presented below followed by sections where the objective, procedure, data stratification and observations of the experimentation are presented.

6.1 Rationale

There are two questions to answer: (1) Given a particular encrypted file size, how likely is it that it has more than one file encrypting into the same size? This probability of collision can be estimated by computing the rate: number of encrypted sizes that has collisions (i.e. more than one file encrypting into that size) divided by the total number of distinct encrypted sizes produced by the experiment. Call this ratio P(c). Instead of computing this ratio over the entire set of compressed sizes produced by the experiment focus of the analysis was restricted to particular bands of compressed size, please see section 7.4 below. So looking at the encrypted file sizes between 3Mb and 4Mb, then P(c) for that range is number of encrypted sizes > 3Mb and < 4Mb that has collisions (i.e. more than one file encrypting into that size) divided by the number of distinct encrypted sizes >

3Mb and < 4Mb produced by the experiment. (2) The second question is as follows: if the method identifies a file whose encrypted size matches the encrypted size of the given encrypted file, then how likely is it that the right file is has been got? This probability is called P(right file) and it can be estimated by using the following reasoning. First observe that there is an encrypted file of a particular size, and then it may or may not have collisions on the suspect's HDD. These are mutually exclusive events, so the probability that there is no collision call it P(n) plus the probability that there is a collision P(c) equals 1: P(n) + P(c) = 1. P(c) has already been identified and therefore we can compute as:

Equation 3. Probability of no collision

$$P(n) = 1 - P(c).$$

There are two possibilities in estimating the probability of picking the right file: (a) If the given encrypted file did not have collisions, then the found file is always the right one, and the probability of that is P(n) and (b) If the encrypted file did have collision, in which case then the found file is one of several possible files all of which produce encrypted file with the given size. The chance of accidentally picking the right file out of x possibilities is 1/x. This rate is called P(choice). It can be estimated:

Equation 4. Rate of accidentally picking the right file

$$P(choice) = 1 / |x|$$

where $|x|$ is the average number of files in a collision (i.e. when collision happens, how many files encrypting to the same size it involves on average). Observe that $|x| >= 2$, which means that P(choice) is always <= 0.5.

The overall probability of the encrypted file having collisions and of *Cryptopometry* picking the right file out of several possibilities is P(c) * P(choice). Since cases (a) and (b) are mutually exclusive, we can simply add probabilities of (a) and (b) to get the overall probability of P(right file): P(right file) = P(n) + P(c)*P(choice). This formula agrees with common sense: If the given encrypted file size has no collisions, then the found file must be the right file- the probability of that is P(n), in addition if the given encrypted file size does have collision, we still have some chance of picking the right one- the probability of that is P(c)*P(choice). If 1-P(c) is substituted for P(n) and then substitute 1/|x| for P(choice), then:

Equation 5. Probability of selecting the right file

$$P(\text{right file}) = (1 - P(c)) + P(c) * 1/|x| = 1 - (P(c) * (1 - 1/|x|))$$

Subsequently, it can be concluded that the error-rate i.e. P(wrong file) would be:

Equation 6. Error rate

$$P(\text{wrong file}) = 1 - P(\text{right file})$$

6.2 Objective of Experimentation

The objective of this experimentation was to determine the reliability and error-rate with which the original plaintext file could be identified from the ciphertext file. P(right file) = p is the probability with which the right original plaintext file can be identified from the ciphertext file, p is a real number in the range from 0 to 1 and a maximum probability of 1 represents certainty of an event happening.

6.3 Procedure

The file length of all files on a HDD were measured, then these files were all encrypted using a hybrid cryptosystem key with the following properties, i.e., RSA 1024 bit asymmetric encryption with 256 bit AES symmetric encryption. Following this the file length of the created ciphertext files were measured. These measurements were subsequently used as a data sample. All of the steps above were carried out on a second HDD, giving a second sample set. The sample set taken from HDD1 contained 52,331 files, and the sample set taken from HDD2 contained 119,679 files.

6.4 Stratification of Data into Bands

Stratifying data allows the comparison of different segments of a population where the partitioning of data into distinct or non-overlapping groups is carried out. Dispersion is the term used to describe the study of variance in a sample and a box plot is one of the most effective visual tools used to view dispersion. A box plot was draw up from the data of HDD1 (lengths of every encrypted file on HDD1) and as can be seen in Figure 9 the length of the whiskers indicates how extreme the outliers are. Even though the files of two HDDs were encrypted it was sufficient to look at the box plot of one i.e. HDD1 and see that stratification of data was necessary. (Since the sample population of HDD1 was smaller than that of HDD2, it was inferred that a second box plot of HDD2 was not necessary). Since all of outliers were outside of ± 1 standard deviation (SD= 693978.1) and were > 1.5 IQR and < 3 IQR and > 3 IQR it was imperative that data stratification be carried out. A histogram of the frequency of same file size occurrence in HDD1 was generated and even from a visual inspection of this in Figure 10, it would indicate that the significant collision rates were happening in the file length > 0 Mbytes and < 5 Mbytes range. In order to give the sample sets a clear and structured meaning it was concluded that there was a case for data stratification.

6.5 Observations

It is clear from Equation 5 that the likelihood of picking the right file increase when the probability

Figure 9. Box plot of dispersion of file lengths on HDD1

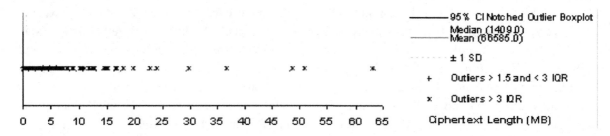

Figure 10. Histogram with normal fit of file lengths of HDD1

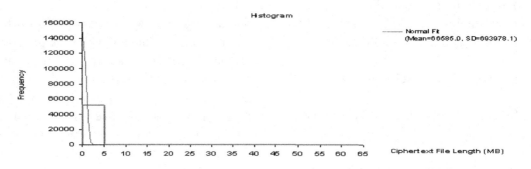

of collision P(c) decreases and when the number of files per collision (|x|) decreases. Please see columns C and D in Table 5 and Table 6 below. Table 5 and Table 6 below show the comparison of P(right file) at different file length bands for HDD1 and HDD2. As expected the collision rate is much higher for the smaller files and subsequently P(right file) is very poor. P(right file) is poorest for the 10-100 Kbyte file length band as this range scores the highest rate of collisions. However, the collision rate is smallest for the 4-10Mbyte file length band would result in an optimum usage for *Cryptopometry*. In general P(right file) performed consistently across the two HDDs however there was some fluctuation in some bands i.e. between bands 4 and 7 and this is evident by viewing Figure 13 below. In any case this fluctuation occurred above the line of P(right file)=0.5. This is because a probability > 0.5 implies a non random result for a sample where there are only 2 outcomes. The probability of identifying the correct file for band 6 i.e. 3-4Mbytes was calculated to be in a range from 0.612685 (HDD1) to 0.722439

(HDD2). Conversely from Equation 7 above, error-rate evaluates to 0.387315 to 0.277561. These error-rates can be inferred to be reasonably low as they are significantly below 0.5. Band 6 files (plaintext JPEG photographs and their corresponding ciphertext files) were the focus of these experimentations because of the capabilities of the camera used.

7 CONCLUSION

The proposed *Cryptopometry* methodology encompasses the searching for PGP public keys and encrypted material, the analysis of these and subsequently the extraction of the Key Id of the key used to encrypt the plaintext file. This enables the identification of the intended recipient (owner of public key) of the encrypted material by searching a global directory service like PGP key server. The integrated search technique facilitates the identification of the original plaintext file. Then by viewing the contents of the plaintext it can be

Table 5. HDD1 - P(right file)

	A	B	C	D
Band	File Length	|X|	P (c)	P (right file)
1	0-10 KB	521	0.904432133	0.097303821
2	10-00KB	625	0.998776758	0.002821285
3	100300KB	325	0.434166104	0.567169895
4	300B-1MB	97	0.36233766	0.637502361
5	1KB3MB	29	0.34459459	0.677074069
6	3-4MB	2.6	0.3958111	0.75643
7	4-1MB	4.2	0.044444444	0.966136952
8	10-0MB	3.09	0.306220096	0.792879674

Table 6. HDD2 - P(right file)

	A	B	C	D
Band	File Length	|X|	P (c)	P (right file)
1	0-10 KB	521	0.904432133	0.1124938
2	10-00KB	625	0.998776758	0.0015864
3	100300KB	325	0.434166104	0.5666666
4	300B-1MB	97	0.36233766	0.6407209
5	1-3B	28	0.34459459	0.8012039
6	3-4MB	2.4	0.185185000	0.8919001
7	4-1MB	4.2	0.044444444	0.9429788
8	10-0MB	3.11	0.306220096	0.8078664

Figure 11. P(right file) of HDD1 & HDD2

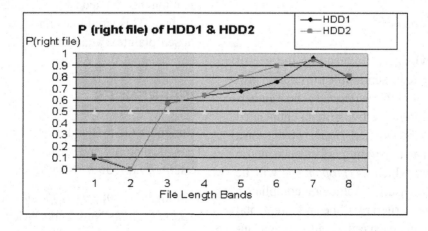

determined if it is evidence or not. *Cryptopometry* was evaluated through experimental means and proved to perform well with low error-rate.

It is assumed that the participation of subjects A and B in the exchange of encrypted material was wilful and knowing. The methodology adheres to computer forensic standards of evidence Search & Seizure, Acquisition and Retrieval. In addition the methodology which was carried out in the Irish jurisdiction does not violate any civil liberties and the subjects' right to privacy is upheld. Irish law operates exclusionary rules in respect of evidence which has been gathered illegally or in breach of constitutional rights. However, Section 8 of the Data Protection Law in Ireland provides an investigative clause, i.e., disclosure of personal data in certain cases. There is also the Anton Piller Order which deals with special investigative circumstances like serious crime which provides for the right to search premises and seize evidence without prior warning.

Note: In experimentation and research outside the scope of this paper, X.509 encryption has been explored and subsequently a similar methodological approach was developed. Abstract Syntax Notation (ASN) was used for data modelling and analysis. ASN is a data exchange framework that is used by X.509 cryptographic message systems and not by OpenPGP/PGP systems.

8 FUTURE WORK

In order for evidence, produced by the use of *Cryptopometry,* to be admissible to a court of law, it is mandatory that *Cryptopometry* be *Daubert* compliant, therefore the five criteria enunciated in *Daubert* must be satisfied. *Daubert* will form a conclusive and an important performance metric in itself against which *Cryptopometry* will be evaluated and measured. Achieving compliance with the *Daubert* criteria will be an incremental process of meeting each criterion's demands independently and with equal priority. However the current scope of this research has identified the following *Daubert* criteria for immediate future work targets.

It is necessary to get *Cryptopometry* tested in actual field conditions rather than just in laboratory conditions. Therefore, it is intended to recommend and promote the use of this methodology within a law LEA environment. Use of the methodology in this way would identify benefits and drawbacks of *Cryptopometry* and they would form the basis of future work, i.e., improvements and refinements to the methodology. It would also be very interesting to assemble a portfolio of cases where *Cryptopometry* was used and monitor how it was qualitatively accepted. Also, if *Cryptopometry* was used in an LEA environment it would be exposed to the main legal and operational controlling standards and if it was not compliant with these controlling standards it would be highlighted and subsequently the methodology would be enhanced to adapt to the standards.

Finally, after encrypting all the files on the HDDs and since *Cryptopometry*'s technique of identifying the original plaintext file is dependent on the relationship due to the compression applied before encryption, it would be worthwhile to determine the pile of data which is contained in the ciphertext and test for a match with the ciphertext created files. This could even be applied on every cluster of data on the file system, meaning that deleted files could also be matched this way. This would be similar to performing a chosen-plaintext attack on the data.

REFERENCES

Altman, D. G., & Bland, J. M. (1994). Diagnostic tests - sensitivity and specificity. *BMJ (Clinical Research Ed.)*, 308(6943), 1552.

Bunting, S. (2008). *The official EnCase certified examiner guide*. New York: Wiley.

Callas, J., et al. (2007, November). *OpenPGP message format*. Menlo Park, CA: PGP Corporation.

Carter, H. (2007). Paedophiles jailed for hatching plot on internet to rape two teenage sisters. *The Guardian*.

Dickson, M. (2006). An examination into AOL Instant Messenger 5.5. *Digital Investigation, 3*(4), 227–237. doi:10.1016/j.diin.2006.10.004

Fawcett, T. (2006). An introduction to ROC analysis. *Pattern Recognition Letters, 27*, 861–874. doi:10.1016/j.patrec.2005.10.010

Fisher, R. A. (1966). *The design of experiments and statistical estimation* (8th ed.). Edinburgh, UK: Hafner.

Narkundkar, S., & Priestly, L. (2004). *Assessment of evaluation methods for binary classification modelling*. Paper presented at DSI 2004.

Reddy, T. (2005). *Murder will out - Irish murder cases*. Park West, Ireland: Gill & Macmillan.

Shahda, J. (2007). *Paltalk hosts Al Qaeda, Hizballah and Hamas terror chat rooms*.

Siegfried, J., Siedsma, C., Countryman, B. J., & Hosmer, C. D. (2004). Examining the encryption threat. *International Journal of Digital Evidence, 2*(3).

9 APPENDIX: JAVA CODE SNIPPETS

9.1 A1: Extract Date from Public Key

```
long time = ((long)(bytes[3] & 0xff) << 24)
|((long)(bytes[4] & 0xff) << 16)|((long)(bytes[5] & 0xff) << 8)
|((bytes[6] & 0xff));
Date date = new Date(time*1000);
```

9.2 A2: Compute Key ID from Public Key (OpenPGP V3)

```
int length = ((int)(bytes[8] & 0xff) << 8) | ((int)(bytes[9] & 0xff));
int mpiByteArrayLength = (length + 7) / 8;
byte[] mpiBytes = new byte[mpiByteArrayLength];
for (int z =0; z < mpiByteArrayLength;z++){mpiBytes[z] = bytes[z+10];}
BigInteger value = new BigInteger(1, mpiBytes);
long keyID = value.longValue();
oLogger.writeLog("keyID value is "+keyID);
```

9.3 A3: Compute Key ID from Public Key (OpenPGP V4)

```
MessageDigest digest = MessageDigest.getInstance("SHA1")
digest.update((byte)0x99);
digest.update((byte)(bytes[1]& 0xff >> 8));
digest.update((byte)(bytes[1]& 0xff));
int parseBytesLength = bytes[1]& 0xff;
byte[] parseBytes = new byte[bytes[1]& 0xff];
for (int z =0; z < parseBytesLength;z++){
parseBytes[z] = bytes[z+2];}
digest.update(parseBytes);
byte[] fingerprint = digest.digest();
long keyID = ((long)(fingerprint[fingerprint.length - 8] & 0xff) << 56)
| ((long)(fingerprint[fingerprint.length - 7] & 0xff) << 48)
| ((long)(fingerprint[fingerprint.length - 6] & 0xff) << 40)
| ((long)(fingerprint[fingerprint.length - 5] & 0xff) << 32)
| ((long)(fingerprint[fingerprint.length - 4] & 0xff) << 24)
| ((long)(fingerprint[fingerprint.length - 3] & 0xff) << 16)
| ((long)(fingerprint[fingerprint.length - 2] & 0xff) << 8)
| ((fingerprint[fingerprint.length - 1] & 0xff));
```

9.4 A4: Extract N i.e. Public Modulus and Key Strength

```
//Public Key V4:start
int length = ((int)(bytes[8] & 0xff) << 8) | ((int)(bytes[9] & 0xff));
//Public Key V4:end
//Public Key V3: start
int mpiByteArrayLength = (length + 7) / 8;
byte[] mpiBytes = new byte[mpiByteArrayLength];
for (int z =0; z < mpiByteArrayLength;z++){ mpiBytes[z] = bytes[z+10]; }
BigInteger value = new BigInteger(1, mpiBytes);
int strength = value.bitLength();
oLogger.writeLog("key strength is "+strength);
//Public Key V3:end
```

9.5 A5: Extract Key ID from Ciphertext

```
keyID2 = ((long)(bytes[3+l] & 0xff) << 56) | ((long)(bytes[4+l] & 0xff) << 48)
|((long)(bytes[5+l] & 0xff) << 40) |((long)(bytes[6+l] & 0xff) << 32)
|((long)(bytes[7+l] & 0xff) << 24) | ((long)(bytes[8+l] & 0xff) << 16)
|((long)(bytes[9+l] & 0xff) << 8) | ((bytes[10+l] & 0xff));
String str1 = String.valueOf(keyID2);
output.writeBytes(str1);
oLogger.writeLog("KeyID is "+str1);
if (str1.equals(keyID)){oLogger.writeLog("KeyID "+str1+" is a Match ");}
```

This work was previously published in the International Journal of Digital Crime and Forensics, Volume 2, Issue 1, edited by Chang-Tsun Li and Anthony TS Ho, pp. 1-20, copyright 2010 by IGI Publishing (an imprint of IGI Global).

Chapter 9
Secure Robust Hash Functions and Their Applications in Non-Interactive Communications

Qiming Li
Institute for Infocomm Research, Singapore

Sujoy Roy
Institute for Infocomm Research, Singapore

ABSTRACT

A robust hash function allows different parties to extract a consistent key from a common fuzzy source, e.g., an image gone through noisy channels, which can then be used to establish a cryptographic session key among the parties without the need for interactions. These functions are useful in various communication scenarios, where the security notions are different. The authors study these different security notions in this paper and focus on forgery attacks, where the objective of the attack is to compute the extracted key (hash value) of a given message. This paper will examine information-theoretical security against forgery under chosen message attacks. The authors prove that it is not possible due to the entropy of the hash value of a given message can be reduced arbitrarily when sufficient message/hash pairs have been observed. In this regard, the authors give a computationally secure scheme, where it is computationally infeasible to compute the hash value even when its entropy may not be high.

A robust hash H is a function that maps an input message $X \in U$ to a binary string $b \in \{0,1\}^*$ such that, when given another message $X' \in M$ where X' is close to X, the hash of X' remains the same as b with high probability. In this regard,

a robust hash function is different from a cryptographic hash function, which does not tolerate even a single bit of error. Furthermore, the domain M can be real-valued, e.g., M can be feature vectors extracted from images.

Robust hash functions are very useful in secure non-interactive communications, where two or

DOI: 10.4018/978-1-4666-1758-2.ch009

more parties wish to derive a session key from a common fuzzy source without interaction. Such a session key can then be used, for example, in identity verification or encryption.

A typical application scenario of robust hash functions is the protection against copying attacks, where attackers attempt to copy a legitimate watermark from a marked multimedia object to an unmarked object (Kutter et al., 2000; Craver et al., 1998). In such scenarios, we could use a watermark that is dependent on the content of the multimedia object. To achieve this, a robust hash function could be employed to extract a key from the given multimedia object, and then a watermark could be generated from the extracted key. In this case, the communication parties would be the watermark embedder and detector, where the multimedia object serves both as a communication channel and the common fuzzy source to generate the watermarking key.

In this scenario, we would require that the hash function should be robust against the noise expected in the actual watermarking application, yet it should be difficult (if possible at all) to estimate this key generation process for an unmarked object.

We note that the central part of the above security application is the extraction of the session key from the common fuzzy source. Therefore, in this paper, we are concerned with the more abstract key extraction scenario as illustrated in Figure 1. Suppose two parties A and B have access to some correlated random sources X and X' respectively (e.g., X and X' could be the picture of the same scene taken at different times of the day), and they wish to agree on a common (secret) session key based on their own random source without communication. In this case, a keyed robust hash function $H(\cdot)$ can be applied to allow both parties to generate the same hash b using a shared key K. This allows both to decide upon a session key that they can use to do various tasks without directly using their shared secret key or exchanging any information as required by common key agreement protocols.

As we can see from Figure 1, if X is an original multimedia object, and X' is a watermarked object obtained by embedding a digital watermark into X, then the hash b that can be consistently extracted can be used to validate the authenticity of the multimedia object. Nevertheless, such a consistent string b can be used in many other scenarios, where it is desirable to extract a consistent key from noisy data.

Despite the potentials of robust hash functions, it is often not easy to analyze the security. This is perhaps partly due to the complexity of the interactions among many different parameters, which affect the robustness and security (such as collision and forgery resistance), and partly due to the lack of clear threat and attack models.

Roughly speaking, robustness of a robust hash function measures its tolerance to permissible noise, and collision resistance measures the difficulty of an attacker finding two dissimilar messages that yield the same hash value (more precise definitions will be given in later sections).

In this paper, we study *forgery resistance* of robust hash functions (Swaminathan et al., 2006), which measures the difficulty for attackers to compute the hash value of a given message without knowing the secret key. Similar to settings used by Swaminathan et al. (2006), we first investigate information theoretical security measured by conditional entropy. However, instead of considering just one message X_1 and its hash

Figure 1. Session key extraction

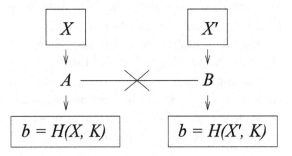

b_1, we consider *chosen message attacks*, where the attacker is allowed to observe (or probe the system to obtain) polynomially many message/hash pairs $\{X_2, b_2, \cdots, (X_p, b_p)\}$ before attacking on a given message. We say that a robust hash function is *non-forgeable* if it is difficult for attackers to compute the hash of a given message X_1 even under chosen message attacks. We also investigate collision resistance of robust hash functions, since a hash function, no matter how robust, would not be so useful if it is easy to create collisions.

Our main contributions are as follows: (1) We give formal definitions of both information-theoretic and computational security of non-forgeable hash functions; (2) We show that information-theoretic security is not possible under chosen message attacks; (3) We give a computationally secure and practical scheme based on random quantization; (4) We give a sufficient condition for a robust hash function to be collision resistant, and show that it is achievable with practical constraints.

RELATED WORK

Swaminathan et al. (2006) give a security model for analyzing the security of a robust hash, where they use differential entropy as a measure of security for randomized image features. It is also suggested that the security of a hashing scheme should be measured by the conditional entropy of the hashing key, when the hashing algorithm, and pairs of images and their hashes are known. We formalize this notion and show that such information-theoretic security is impossible.

The robust hash proposed by Swaminathan et al. (2006) is specifically designed for an authentication application. There are existing works that analyze security models for authentication application scenarios. Some examples of proposed scenarios are as follows. Ge et al. (2006) analyze

a scenario where A sends a message and an approximate message authentication code (AMAC) to B for verification. The AMAC serves as a keyed similarity-preserving function. Another scenario as discussed by Li and Chang (2006) is when A sends a message, some helper data and a cryptographic MAC to B, where the noise during communication can be corrected using the helper data. In both cases, A and B share a secret key. If public-private key pairs are used instead of secret keys in these scenarios, it would become a digital signature. Another scenario focusing on key extraction is studied by Dodis et al. (2004) where A and B have access to content X and its corrupted version X' respectively. A extracts a key k_a and some helper data which is sent to B. B uses X' and the helper data to generate another key k_b, and $k_a = k_b$ if X and X' are close enough. In all the above three scenarios there is need for communication between A and B. In the scenario proposed in this paper there is no communication between A and B.

We highlight that the scenario considered in this work represents a more general applicability of robust hash. In fact Mihcak and Venkatesan (2001) also propose a robust hashing algorithm to extract a consistent key from certain content but for watermarking application. Note that we also extract a consistent key, which can be used for authentication. Hence it is interesting to study the security of robust hash under the proposed scenario.

DEFINITIONS AND NOTATIONS

Let M be the message space. We do not impose any constraint on M. For example, it can be the set of feature vectors from a database of images. The distribution of the message can be either discrete or continuous. Here we mainly use discrete distributions and entropies as examples. Similar definitions and proofs based on differential entropies can be easily adapted. Let D be a distance function $D : M \times M \to \Re^+$ defined over M. We consider the following definitions of hash functions and their properties.

Definition 1 (Hash Function) *A hash function H* is an efficiently computable function, $H : M \times \{0,1\}^k \to \{0,1\}^{poly(k)}$, where $k \in Z^+$ and $poly(\cdot)$ is some positive polynomial.

Here being "efficiently computable" means that H can be computed with a polynomial time deterministic algorithm. Such a hash function may have the following properties.

Definition 2 (Robustness) *A hash function H is* $(D, \delta_r, \varepsilon_r)$-robust w.r.t. key length k if for any $X, Y \in M$ such that $D(X,Y) \leq \delta_1$, $H(X,K) = H(Y,K)$ with probability at least $1 - \varepsilon_r$.

Definition 3 (Sensitivity) *A hash function H is* $(D, \delta_s, \varepsilon_s)$-sensitive w.r.t. key length k if for random $K \in \{0,1\}^k$ and random $X, Y \in M$ such that $D(X,Y) \geq \delta_s$, we have $\Pr[H(X,K) \neq H(Y,K)] \geq 1 - \varepsilon_s$.

In many signal processing applications, sensitivity (i.e., resistance to random collisions) may be good enough. However, in security applications, we may need stronger notions of collision resistance.

Definition 4 (Negligible Function) *A function* $\sigma : Z \to \Re^+$ is negligible if for any positive polynomial $poly(\cdot)$ and any sufficiently large $n \in Z$, it holds that $\sigma(n) < 1 / poly(n)$.

When we say a task is computationally infeasible w.r.t. a parameter k, we mean that the probability that this task can be done is a negligible function of k.

Definition 5 (Collision Resistance) *A hash function H is* (D, δ_c)-collision-resistant w.r.t. key length k if for random $K \in \{0,1\}^k$ and any polynomial time probabilistic algorithm A, the probability $\Pr[A(1^k) = (X,Y) s.t. D(X,Y) \geq \delta_c, H(X,K) = H(Y,K)]$ is a negligible function of k.

In other words, a hash function is collision resistant if it is computationally infeasible to find two dissimilar messages that can be hashed to the same value. Here 1^k indicates that algorithm A is poly-time w.r.t. parameter k.

Furthermore, it is often desirable to make it difficult to forge hash values of noisy data without the secret key. It is worth to note that the forgery attacks as defined later are different from collision attacks. In forgery attacks, the goal of the attacker is to find the hash value of a given message, whereas in collision attacks, the goal is to find two dissimilar messages that yield the same hash. There are, however, certain connections between these two types of attacks. For example, if the collision probability of the hash function is high, a given message could itself collide with a message that has been observed by the attacker, which would lead to a successful forgery attack. In other words, security against forgery attacks implies collision resistance.

Furthermore, we consider chosen message attacks, where the attacker has the access to polynomial number of messages and their corresponding hash values, and the goal of the attacker is to find the hash value for another message that is not similar to any of the messages the attacker has seen.

Ideally, we would prefer information-theoretic security where it is possible, which is defined as the following.

Definition 6 (Perfect Forgery Resistance) *A hash function H is information-theoretically secure against forgery under chosen message attacks* if for all sufficiently large k, any positive polynomial $p(\cdot)$, any messages $X_1, ..., X_{p(k)} \in M$, such that $D(X, X_i) > \delta_c$ for all $1 \leq i \leq p(k)$, and for K uniformly distributed over $\{0, 1\}^k$, it holds that

$$\mathrm{H}(b_1 \mid X_1, (X_2, b_2), ..., (X_{p(k)}, b_{p(k)})) \geq s$$

where $\mathrm{H}(A \mid B)$ denotes the conditional entropy of A given B, $b_i = H(X_i, K)$, and s is a security parameter.

In other words, given the observations of $p(k) - 1$ dissimilar messages (which could be chosen by the attacker) and their corresponding hash values, there should still be sufficient amount of uncertainty about the hash value of another message X_1 that is dissimilar to all the observations. It should be noted that if a robust hash scheme is secure by the above definition, it would also imply

$$\mathrm{H}(K \mid (X_2, b_2), ..., (X_{p(k)}, b_{p(k)})) \geq s .$$

That is, it should also be difficult to find the key K, since otherwise the attacker could just work out the key first and then compute the hash value of X_1.

Correspondingly, we can define the security in terms of computationally bounded attackers as follows.

Definition 7 (Computational Forgery Resistance) *A hash function H* w.r.t. distance function D is computationally secure against forgery under chosen message attacks if, for any positive polynomial $p(\cdot)$, uniformly random $K \in \{0, 1\}^k$, and any poly-time probabilistic algorithm A, given any $X_1 \in M$, the probability

$$p = \Pr[A(X_1, (X_2, b_2), ..., (X_{p(k)}, b_{p(k)})) = b_1]$$

is a negligible function of k, where $b_i = H(X_i, K)$, $D(X_i, X_j) > \delta_c$ for all $1 \leq i, j \leq p(k)$, and the probability is taken over random choices of the key K and internal coin tosses of A.

In other words, it should be computationally infeasible for any attacker to come up with the correct hash value of a new message (which may be chosen by the attacker), even with observations of polynomial number of message/hash pairs. Furthermore, it is clear that forgery resistance implies collision resistance.

Lemma 1 *If a hash function H is computationally secure against forgery under chosen message attacks w.r.t. distance function D and threshold δ, it is also (D, δ)-collision-resistant.*

Proof: If H is not (D, δ)-collision-resistant, by definition there is a polynomial adversary A that can find, with a probability that is not negligible, a pair (X, Y) such that $H(X, K) = H(Y, K)$, and $D(X, Y) > \delta$. Hence, another adversary B can use A to find a collision pair (X, Y) first, inquire the hash oracle for the hash value $b = H(Y, K)$, and then output (X, b) as the result of a forgery. Clearly, B runs in polynomial time, and also succeeds with a probability that is not negligible. $\square$

On the other hand, collision resistance does not imply forgery resistance in general. For example, cryptographic hash functions such as SHA-1 are typically considered as collision resistant, but anyone can compute such hash functions for any given messages, and hence they are not forgery resistant by themselves. The same argument can be applied to robust hash functions.

IMPOSSIBILITY OF INFORMATION-THEORETIC FORGERY RESISTANCE

If the attacker has unbounded computation power and is able to *probe* the hash function with carefully chosen messages, or is able to *observe* previous independent message/hash pairs, we can see that it is not possible to have a robust hash scheme that is secure against forgery. In particular, we have the following result.

Theorem 2 For any hash function H, given any independently chosen $X_1, ..., X_{p(k)} \in M$, any positive polynomial $p(\cdot)$, uniformly chosen key $K \in \{0,1\}^k$, and any positive constant s ($s \leq k$), if

$$\mathrm{H}(K \mid X_1, ..., X_{p(k)}, b_1, ..., b_{p(k)}) \geq s \qquad (1)$$

where $b_i = H(X_i, K)$, it holds that

$$\mathrm{H}(b_1 \mid X_1, ..., X_{p(k)}, b_2, ..., b_{p(k)}) \leq (k - s) / p(k) \qquad (2)$$

Proof: Since the key is independently chosen,

$$\begin{aligned}
\mathrm{H}(K) &= \mathrm{H}(K \mid X_1, ..., X_{p(k)}) \\
&= \mathrm{H}(K, b_1, ..., b_{p(k)} \mid X_1, ..., X_{p(k)}) \\
&= \mathrm{H}(b_1, ..., b_{p(k)} \mid X_1, ..., X_{p(k)}) \\
&\quad + \mathrm{H}(K \mid b_1, ..., b_{p(k)}, X_1, ..., X_{p(k)})
\end{aligned}$$

The second equality is due to the fact that the hash values are deterministically computed from the messages and the key, and the third equality is obtained by applying the chain rule. Since $\mathrm{H}(K) = k$ and (1), we have

$$\mathrm{H}(b_1, ..., b_{p(k)} \mid X_1, ..., X_{p(k)}) \leq k - s .$$

By applying the chain rule, we have

$$\begin{aligned}
&\mathrm{H}(b_1, ..., b_{p(k)} \mid X_1, ..., X_{p(k)}) \\
&= \mathrm{H}(b_1 \mid b_2, ..., b_{p(k)}, X_1, ..., X_{p(k)}) \\
&+ \mathrm{H}(b_2 \mid b_3, ..., b_{p(k)}, X_1, ..., X_{p(k)}) . \\
&+ ... \\
&+ \mathrm{H}(b_{p(k)} \mid X_1, ..., X_{p(k)})
\end{aligned}$$

Clearly, the first term in the summation is no larger than the rest of the terms. Hence, we have proved (2).

In other words, no matter how we choose the parameters k and s, as long as the attacker has enough number of independent observations (i.e., large enough $p(k)$), the entropy of the hash value $H(X_1, K)$ can be reduced arbitrarily. Hence the scheme cannot be information-theoretically secure against forgery under chosen message attacks. As mentioned earlier, a similar proof using differential entropy for continuous distributions can be easily adapted.

It is also worth to note that even if the requirement (1) is relaxed such that the key K is only required to have conditional entropy the same as the hash value, the conclusion that the conditional entropy of the hash value can be reduced arbitrarily remains the same.

It is also noted that this proof does not depend on the robustness of the hash function. It is analogous to the known result that perfect secrecy cannot be achieved with fixed length keys.

A SUFFICIENT CONDITION FOR COLLISION RESISTANCE

As we have mentioned earlier, a robust hash that is $(D, \delta_s, \varepsilon_s)$-sensitive may be sufficient in some applications, but more rigorous collision resistance is needed in typical security applications. Here, we show that a robust and collision resistant hash function can be built using the robustness and sensitivity properties of the underlying hash function. Note that sensitivity differs from collision resistance in that the former only measures the collision probability of randomly chosen inputs. Therefore, what we need is a way to make it difficult for attackers to construct structured inputs to the hash function, and would be forced to choose random ones.

To achieve that, we will need a special type of transformation on M such that the neighborhood relationship among messages as measured by some distance function D will be roughly preserved under the transformation, yet the transformation looks random without the access to a secret key. First, we need to define a uniform transformation ensemble on M.

Definition 8 (Transformation Ensemble) *A transformation ensemble on M is a random variable Γ_M that assumes values from a set of functions on M. A **uniform transformation ensemble** on M, denoted by U_M, is uniformly distributed over all possible functions on M.*

Note that this definition differs from classical definition of uniform function ensembles in cryptography in that, the domain and co-domain of the functions (i.e., M) may not be a discrete space, and it is fixed in advance.

Next, let us consider an oracle adversary A^F as a probabilistic polynomial time algorithm A that can make polynomially many queries to an oracle that computes the function F, and each query costs constant time. We further consider a limited set of queries that the adversary can send as follows.

Definition 9 *A set of queries $X_1,...,X_n \in M$ is called well-formed w.r.t. distance function D and threshold δ if for any $1 \le i,j \le n$, we have $D(X_i, X_j) > \delta$.*

Definition 10 *A pseudo-random (D, δ_s)-sensitive transformation is a transformation ensemble $\Gamma_k : M \to M$ where*

1. *A function T_K drawn from Γ_k can be computed using a polynomial time algorithm $T_K(X) = T(X, K)$, where K is uniformly distributed over all k-bit strings.*

2. *For any polynomial time oracle adversary A, if the queries A sends to the oracle are well-formed, the probability*

$$p = | \Pr[A^{\Gamma_k}(1^k) = 1] - \Pr[A^{U_M}(1^k) = 1] |$$

is negligible in k. In other words, no efficient adversary A can distinguish a random function in Γ_k from a truly random function on M, even with oracle access to the function and is allowed to send polynomially many well-formed queries.

In the context of robust hash functions, it is typically required that such transformation is also robust.

Definition 11 *A pseudo-random (D, δ_s)-sensitive transformation Γ_k is $(\delta_r, \delta_w, \varepsilon_r)$-robust if, for any $X \in M$, it holds that, for a random $Y \in M$ such that $D(X,Y) < \delta_r$, we have $\Pr[D(\Gamma_k(X), \Gamma_k(Y)) < \delta_w] > 1 - \varepsilon_r$.*

To construct a collision resistant hash function, our main idea is that, given a message $X \in M$, we first apply a pseudo-random (D, δ_s)-sensitive transformation T on X to obtain $W \in M$, and then apply a $(D, \delta_s, \varepsilon_s)$-sensitive hash function H_s on W to obtain the final hash value. Due to the pseudo-randomness of the transformation T, it would be hard for any attacker to exploit the hash function H_s directly to find a collision. Hence, if ε_s is negligible in k, the hash function can be collision resistant. The robustness of the hash function can be achieved if the transformation T is robust.

Theorem 3 *Let* H_s *be a* $(D, \delta_s, \varepsilon_s)$ -*sensitive hash function, and* Γ_k *be a pseudo-random* (D, δ_s) -*sensitive transformation ensemble. The hash function* $H : M \times \{0,1\}^{2k} \to \{0,1\}^{poly(k)}$ *defined as* $H(X, K) = H_s(T(X, K_1), K_2)$ *is* (D, δ_s) -*collision-resistant if* ε_s *is negligible in* k, *where* $K = K_1 \| K_2$ *is uniformly selected, and* $| K_1 |=| K_2 |= k$.

Proof: Assume on the contrary that H is not (D, δ_s) -collision-resistant, by definition we have a polynomial adversary A that can find, with a probability that is not negligible, a pair of messages $X, Y \in M$ such that $D(X, Y) > \delta_s$, yet $H(X, K) = H(Y, K)$, for uniformly chosen $K \in \{0,1\}^{2k}$. We only need to show that we can construct another polynomial time algorithm B that can distinguish Γ_k from U_M. In particular, given an oracle O, the adversary B performs the following steps.

1. Invoke A to find a collision $X, Y \in M$ such that $D(X, Y) > \delta_s$. If A fails, output 0 and halt.
2. Randomly choose K_2 from $\{0,1\}^k$.
3. Send X and Y to the oracle O. Let the responses be W and Z respectively.
4. Compute $H_s(W, K_2)$ and $H_s(Z, K_2)$. If the results are the same, output 1. Otherwise output 0.

If the oracle O is indeed Γ_k, then by our assumption A should succeed with a probability that is not negligible. In this case, since X and Y are well-formed, B will output 1 with a probability that is not negligible. Otherwise, since U_M

is a random function and H_s is $(D, \delta_s, \varepsilon_s)$ -sensitive, B would output 1 with probability at most ε_s, which is negligible. Therefore, B can distinguish Γ_k from U_M with a probability that is not negligible, which is a contradiction. Hence the theorem is proved. $\square$

Basically, the attacker would not be able to exploit the weakness of the underlying hash function if the inputs are transformed using Γ_k, which the attacker cannot invert easily. In this way, no matter how the attacker tries to construct special pairs of inputs to create a collision, the resulting collision probability would not differ too much from that of a randomly chosen pairs.

It is worth to note that, in the above theorem, a key condition is the existence of a pseudo-random transformation ensemble. The construction of such a transformation ensemble relies heavily on the nature of M and the distance function D, and deserves further investigation in any actual application.

The robustness of the hash function as constructed in the above theorem can be similarly determined if the robustness of the transformation and hash function involved can be determined. In particular, we have the following.

Corollary 4 *Let* H_r *be a* $(D, \delta_r, \varepsilon_r)$ -*robust hash function, and* Γ_k *be a pseudo-random* (D, δ_s) -*sensitive transformation ensemble that is* $(D, \delta_r, \delta_w, \varepsilon_w)$ -*robust. The hash function* $H : M \times \{0,1\}^{2k} \to \{0,1\}^{poly(k)}$ *defined as* $H(X, K) = H_r(T(X, K_1), K_2)$ *is* $(D, \delta_w, (1 - \varepsilon_r), (1 - \varepsilon_w))$ -*robust where* $K = K_1 \| K_2$ *is uniformly selected, and* $| K_1 |=| K_2 |= k$.

The correctness of the above corollary directly follows from the definitions.

A ROBUST HASH SCHEME

In this section, we consider input space M to be real vectors of size n. This is a natural representation of many types of features that can be extracted from multimedia data.

Let Q be a random composite scalar quantizer, which consists of two sub-quantizers Q_0 and Q_1. Both sub-quantizers are uniform quantizers with the same step size 2λ, but the quantization levels are interleaved such that the minimum distance between the quantization levels of Q_0 and that of Q_1 is λ. The quantization levels of both sub-quantizers are labeled as interleaving 0's and 1's, and the output of the sub-quantizers will be the label of the nearest quantization level. The quantizer Q takes in two inputs, namely a random bit r and an x to be quantized. Based on the random bit r, Q either quantize x with Q_0 or Q_1. That is, $Q(r,x) = Q_r(x)$.

We assume that there exists an error-correcting code C that allows us to correct t errors in a binary string of length n, where t is a parameter depending on the number of bit flips to be tolerated for the required robustness.

We further assume that there exists an encryption scheme (Enc, Dec) with encryption algorithm Enc and decryption algorithm Dec, and the encryption scheme is secure against chosen ciphertext attacks.

Given $X = (x_1, ..., x_n)$ and random key $K = (k_1, k_2, k_3)$ consisting of three parts, the function H performs the following steps.

1. Randomize X by multiplying X with a random n by n matrix R generated using a pseudo-random number generator with seed k_1. Let $Y = RX = (y_1, y_2, ..., y_n)$.
2. Suppose $|k_2| = n$. Let the bits in k_2 be denoted as $r_1, ..., r_n \in \{0, 1\}$. Quantize Y by applying random quantizer Q on each y_i using randomness r_i. Let $\hat{Y} = (\hat{y}_1, ..., \hat{y}_n)$ where $\hat{y}_i = Q(r_i, y_i)$.
3. Decode $\hat{Y}$ using the error-correcting code C to obtain a binary string W.
4. Apply the decryption function Dec with key k_3 on W to obtain the final hash value h. That is, $h = Dec(k_3, W)$.

The first two steps are commonly used techniques to handle permissible noise, such that at the end of the second step, we would obtain a binary string that is close to the original, measured by some distance metric, say, Hamming distance. The error-correcting code in the third step is to correct a small number of bit flips in the binary string. The design of such an error-correcting code can be challenging if the length of $\hat{Y}$ is large, and the errors can be bursty. For typical applications, we can employ the two-layer error-correcting technique by Hao et al. (2006), or a suitable LDPC code (MacKay & Neal, 1997) such as those used by Martinian et al. (2005) and Draper et al. (2007). If the distance metric is not Hamming, the error-correcting code should be adapted accordingly (Mihcak & Venkatesan, 2001). The last step of decryption provides the actual security property that we need.

SECURITY ANALYSIS

The security of the hash function as stated at the beginning of this section largely depends on the security of the underlying encryption scheme. In particular, we require the encryption scheme to be secure under chosen ciphertext attacks.

Roughly speaking, an encryption scheme is secure if for any given ciphertext, it is computationally infeasible for any attacker to compute the corresponding plaintext. Furthermore, it is secure against chosen ciphertext attacks if the security can be maintained even the attackers observed *a priori* the plaintext corresponding to polynomial number of ciphertext at his choice. More formally, let Σ be the set of all possible binary plaintext, we have

Definition 12 *An encryption scheme* (Enc, Dec) *is secure against chosen ciphertext attacks if, for any positive polynomial* $q(\cdot)$, *uniform key* $K \in \{0,1\}^k$, *given any* $W_1 \in \Sigma$ *and any set of* $\{W_2, ..., W_{q(k)}\} \subset \Sigma$ *that does not contain* W_1, *the probability*

$$p = \Pr[A(W_1, W) = Dec(K, W_1)]$$

is a negligible function of k, *where* W *is the set of* $q(k) - 1$ *pairs*

$$W = \{(W_2, Dec(K, W_2)), ..., (W_{q(k)}, Dec(K, W_{q(k)}))\}.$$

In other words, given constant time access to a decryption oracle O_{Dec}, an encryption scheme is secure against chosen message attacks if and only if no polynomial-time attacker can decrypt a given message W_1 without sending W_1 itself to the oracle.

Now, the security of the hash function and that of the encryption scheme are related as the following.

Theorem 5 *The robust hash* H *is computationally secure against forgery under chosen message attacks if the encryption scheme* (Enc, Dec) *is secure against chosen ciphertext attacks.*

Proof: Suppose on the contrary that the hash function H is not secure against forgery under chosen message attacks, by definition, there is a polynomial-time probabilistic algorithm A such that for uniform K and any $X_1 \in M$, A can find the hash value of X_1 with a probability that is not negligible, provided that A has the oracle access to the hash function.

The idea of the proof is to show that we can use the algorithm A to construct another algorithm B that can break the underlying encryption scheme with the help of a decryption oracle O_{Dec}.

Firstly, we randomly select keys k_1 and k_2, and we construct the hash oracle O_H as follows. For any message X chosen by the algorithm A, we can perform steps 1 to 3 in the robust hash scheme to obtain a binary string W_X, which we then send to the decryption oracle O_{Dec} as our ``chosen ciphertext''. The result would be the hash value of X.

Now, given ciphertext W, we construct algorithm B as follows.

1. Invert the error-correcting code (by encoding W) to obtain a message $\hat{Y}$.
2. Invert quantization process (by finding any data that would be quantized to $\hat{Y}$) to obtain Y.
3. Invert the randomization (by multiplying with the inverse of R) to obtain an X.
4. Pass X to algorithm A as an original message and ask A to find a forged hash value.
5. Output the result of A.

If A is a successful attacker, the result would be exactly the plaintext corresponding to W, which means we would also be successful in attacking the underlying encryption scheme under chosen ciphertext attacks. This contradicts with the assumption, hence the theorem is proved. □

Further Discussions on Security

It should be noted that in many real applications, we are not given directly a sequence of numbers, but rather images, audio or video data. As a result, the security of the actual system depends not only on the security of the robust hash, but also depends on the *quality* of the features, in the sense that it should be difficult to find another multimedia object that is very different yet yields the same features. However, the similarity metric largely depends on the application scenario. How to select such good features is out of the scope of this paper.

It is also worth noting that we apply an error-correcting code to extract a consistent string from the noisy data. In practice, such codes are usually not perfect. As a result, to achieve required robustness, sometimes it would correct more errors than necessary. In this case, the attacker might be able to exploit the property of the error-correcting code to create a collision on a chosen message X by constructing dissimilar objects X' that have features that fall within the error-correcting capability, hence creating a forgery on the constructed object X' by re-using the hash value of X.

In our scheme, however, we include a randomization step (the first step) that will help to diffuse the feature coefficients in a key-dependent manner, such that it would be difficult for the attackers to make use of the error-correcting code. This step can be considered as a pseudo-random transformation as defined in Definition 10, when the number of message-hash pairs known by the attacker is not large enough to invert the randomization matrix. For example, when the messages are real vectors of length 600, the transformation is generally not invertible given less than 600 message-hash pairs, and we can achieve collision resistance as analyzed in previous sections.

CONCLUSION

A robust hash allows the extraction of a consistent key from noisy data, such as images. This can be useful in many application scenarios, ranging from authentication to session key agreement. An example of such applications is watermarking schemes resistant to copy attacks, where the watermarks are generated from a key extracted from the content, so that directly copying the watermark makes it useless. Another example

is key distribution with noisy data, where two or more parties agree on a consistent key based on a common noisy random source, without the need for communication as other key agreement protocols do.

In this paper we study the security of robust hash functions against forgery, under chosen message attacks. In these attacks, the attacker is allowed to observe or probe the system to access polynomial number of message/hash pairs, and the goal of the attacker is to compute the hash of another given message that is dissimilar to all previous observations.

We give formal definitions of the security of robust hash against forgery under chosen message attacks (both information-theoretic and computational). We show that information-theoretic security is not possible. This answers one of the open questions stated by Swaminathan et al. (2006). That is, it is not possible for the hash value in question to have conditional entropy that is not negligible, while keeping enough entropy for the secret key. Furthermore, we give a scheme that is computationally secure.

We also analyze the collision resistance of robust hash functions in the presence of smart attackers who attempt to carefully craft messages to create a collision. We give a sufficient condition that allows us to build a collision resistant robust hash function using a pseudo-random transformation and a robust and sensitive hash function. We show that such collision resistance can be achieved in our proposed scheme under practical constraints.

REFERENCES

Craver, S., Memon, N., Yeo, B., & Yeung, M. (1998). Resolv-ing rightful ownerships with invisible watermarking techniques: Limitations, attacks, and implications. *IEEE Journal on Selected Areas in Communications*, 16(4), 573–586. doi:10.1109/49.668979

Dodis, Y., Reyzin, L., & Smith, A. (2004). Fuzzy extractors: How to generate strong keys from biometrics and other noisy data. In *Eurocrypt* (LNCS 3027, pp. 523-540).

Draper, S., Khistiy, A., Martinianz, E., Vetro, A., & Yedidia, J. (2007, January). Secure storage of fingerprint biometrics using slepian-wolf codes. In *Proceedings of the Information theory and applications workshop*.

Ge, R., Arce, G. R., & DiCrescenzo, G. (2006). Approximate message authentication codes for n-ary alphabets. *IEEE Transactions on Information Forensics and Security, 1*(1), 56–67. doi:10.1109/TIFS.2005.863504

Hao, F., Anderson, R., & Daugman, J. (2006). Combining crypto with biometrics effectively. *IEEE Transactions on Computers, 55*(9), 1081–1088. doi:10.1109/TC.2006.138

Kutter, M., Voloshynovskiy, S., & Herrigel, A. (2000). The watermark copy attack. In *Proceedings of the SPIE, security and watermarking of multimedia contents II* (Vol. 3971).

Li, Q., & Chang, E.-C. (2006). Robust, short and sensitive authentication tags using secure sketch. In *Proceedings of the ACM multimedia and security workshop*.

MacKay, D., & Neal, R. (1997). Near Shannon limit performance of low density parity check codes. *Electronics Letters, 33*(6), 457–458. doi:10.1049/el:19970362

Martinian, E., Yekhanin, S., & Yedidia, J. (2005). Secure biometrics via syndromes. In *Proceedings of the Allerton conference on communications, control, and computing*.

Mihcak, M., & Venkatesan, R. (2001). A perceptual audio hashing algorithm: A tool for robust audio identification and information hiding. In *Proceedings of the Information hiding workshop* (Vol. 2137, pp. 51-65).

Swaminathan, A., Mao, Y., & Wu, M. (2006). Robust and secure image hashing. *IEEE Transactions on Information Forensics and security, 1*(2), 215-230.

This work was previously published in the International Journal of Digital Crime and Forensics, Volume 2, Issue 4, edited by Chang-Tsun Li and Anthony TS Ho, pp. 51-62, copyright 2010 by IGI Publishing (an imprint of IGI Global).

Chapter 10
Steganography in Thai Text

Natthawut Samphaiboon
Asian Institute of Technology, Thailand

Matthew N. Dailey
Asian Institute of Technology, Thailand

ABSTRACT

Steganography, or communication through covert channels, is desirable when the mere existence of an encrypted message might cause suspicion or provide useful information to eavesdroppers. Text is effective for steganography due to its ubiquity; however, text communication channels do not necessarily provide sufficient redundancy for covert communication. In this paper, the authors propose a novel steganographic embedding scheme for Thai plain text documents that exploits redundancies in the way particular vowel, diacritical, and tonal symbols are composed in TIS-620, the standard Thai character set. This paper provides a Thai text stegosystem following a provably secure construction that guarantees covertness, privacy, and integrity of the hiddentext message under meaningful attacks against computational adversaries. In an experimental evaluation, the authors find that the message embedding scheme allows 203 bytes of embedded hiddentext message per 100KB of covertext on average, and that the document modifications are not readily noticed by observers. The stegosystem is thus a practical and effective secure system for covert communication over Thai plain text channels.

INTRODUCTION

Privacy is a major concern for users of public networks such as the Internet. Traditionally, privacy is among the central concerns of cryptography, which achieves private communication through encryption. One problem with encryption, how-

ever, is that although it may hide the *contents* of a message, the mere *transmission* of an encrypted message may cause suspicion.

As a motivating example, consider a scenario in which a government officer from some country is sent to work in another country for purposes of deepening international relationships between the two countries. Any electronic communication with the guest could easily be monitored by the

DOI: 10.4018/978-1-4666-1758-2.ch010

host country's intelligence agency. If the guest is observed sending or receiving messages in encrypted form, he or she might be suspected of espionage. This could be illegal in some countries and could affect the relationship of mutual trust between the countries.

To avoid such suspicion, information hiding techniques collectively called *steganography* have received attention for a long time. Steganography dates at least as far back as ancient Greece (Ryder, 2004). In one story, a messenger had a message tattooed onto his shaved head, waited until his hair grew back, and then was sent to deliver the message. Since the secret message written on the messenger's head could not be read except by those who knew what to look for, his mission was successful. In modern times, steganography, which attempts to hide the existence of message transfer, has become a new major concern for the users of public communication networks.

The vast majority of practical steganographic schemes are instances of *embedding steganography*, in which a secret message is embedded in a given cover document to produce a normal-looking output. The secret message, cover document, and output are called the *hiddentext*, *covertext*, and *stegotext*, respectively. The covertext could be any kind of digital media, such as information in a Web site, Web board, blog, chat session, or email message. As such, steganographic schemes have been proposed for embedding secret messages in images (Lou & Liu, 2002), video (Su, Hartung, & Girod, 1998), audio (Cvejic & Seppänen, 2004), and text in multiple languages (Amano & Misaki, 1999; Brassil, Low, & Maxemchuk, 1999; Huang & Yan, 2001; Kim & Oh, 2004; Kim, Moon, & Oh, 2003; Muhammad, Rahman, & Shakil, 2009; Samphaiboon, in press; Shirali-Shahreza & Shirali-Shahreza, 2006; Shirali-Shahreza & Shirali-Shahreza, 2007; Sun, Luo, & Huang, 2004; Topkara, Taskiran, & Delp, 2005; Yuling, Xingming, Can, & Hong, 2007; Zhang, Zeng, Pu, & Zhu, 2006).

Among the existing practical steganographic schemes, images and video streams are the most popular covertext media, since they contain more redundancy than other types of covertext. However, in some situations, image and video steganography might not be effective, particularly when bandwidth is limited. Text documents are smaller in size than other types of covertext. Moreover, in the real world, people normally do their digital communications through text media such as email messages. Sending and receiving text messages has become normal daily behavior of humans everywhere. Therefore, text is an effective covertext medium for steganography.

It is widely recognized today that steganographic schemes should be secure against both *human observers* and *computational attacks*. There have been some recent attempts to formalize steganographic security notions and to construct stegosystems that are provably secure against computational attacks under those notions (Backes & Cachin, 2005; Cachin, 2004; Dailey, Namprempre, & Samphaiboon, 2010; Hopper, Langford, & Ahn, 2002; Kiayias, Raekow, & Russell, 2005; Mittelholzer, 2000; Moulin & O'Sullivan, 1999; Zollner et al., 1998). In these models, *covertness*, or hiding the existence of the hiddentext message is defined in terms of *statistical* or *computational* indistinguishability against computational attacks. Among the existing models, Dailey et al. (2010) propose a provably secure generic construction that provides not only covertness but also privacy and integrity of the embedded secret message. In the model, covertness requires that polynomial-time computational adversaries with practical resources cannot tell whether the stegotext contains a real hiddentext message or an empty hiddentext. Adversaries are allowed to attack the stegosystem both by observing stegotexts corresponding to chosen covertexts and secret messages and by observing hiddentext messages decoded from chosen stegotexts. Under similar attacks, privacy requires that adversaries cannot tell whether a stegotext contains which of two distinct chosen hiddentext messages of equal length, and integrity requires that such adversaries cannot forge a stegotext that can successfully be decoded to a hiddentext message with significant probability of success. The model of Dailey et al. (2010) can be applied to most practical embedding stegosystems whose constructions contain their own application-specific embedding and extracting algorithms.

In this paper, we introduce a new steganographic embedding scheme for Thai plain text documents and provide a secure Thai text stegosystem that is constructed following the generic construction proposed by Dailey et al. (2010). The scheme can be categorized as *text steganography*, in which the goal is to embed hiddentext messages in *plain text* files. Text steganography is among most challenging types of steganography. One reason text steganography is difficult is that text contains little redundancy compared to other media. Another is that humans are sensitive to abnormal-looking text. Because the grammatical and orthographic characteristics of every language are different, text steganographic schemes must be specifically designed to exploit the specific characteristics of the target language. There have been several successful attempts to design text steganographic schemes for English (Brassil et al., 1999; Huang et al., 2001; Kim et al., 2004; Kim et al., 2003; Shirali-Shahreza et al., 2007; Topkara et al., 2005), Japanese (Amano et al., 1999), Korean (Kim et al., 2004), Chinese (Kim et al., 2004; Sun et al., 2004; Yuling et al., 2007; Zhang et al., 2006), Persian and Arabic (Sharali-Shahreza et al., 2006), Thai (Samphaiboon, in press), and Bahasa Melayu (Muhammad et al., 2009).

The proposed steganographic embedding scheme exploits redundancies in the way certain Thai vowel, diacritical, and tonal symbols are combined to form compound characters in TIS-620, the standard Thai character set. The techniques we introduce are applicable to any language whose Unicode character sets contain redundancies. Our method takes special care to obey standard Thai character ordering rules when encoding and decoding hiddentext message bits.

To evaluate the efficiency and security of the new stegosystem, we report on a series of experiments using real Thai-language plain text documents as covertext. We find that the embedding capacity of the method is approximately 203 bytes per 100 KB of covertext on average, and that the document modifications are not readily noticed by observers. Moreover, since the proposed stegosystem is an instantiation of the provably secure generic construction, covertness, privacy and integrity of the embedded hiddentext message are simultaneously guaranteed. The stegosystem is thus practical and effective for covert communication through Thai plain text channels such as Web boards, blogs, and email messages.

The rest of the paper is organized as follows. First, we introduce Thai orthography, and then we show how it is possible to exploit redundancy in the Thai character set to embed and retrieve hidden bits. Then, we give definitions and a complete construction for the stegosystem and the underlying schemes. Finally, we describe two experimental evaluations of the stegosystem with an analysis of the scheme's security against computational attacks, and then give a discussion.

BACKGROUND: THAI ORTHOGRAPHY

Before introducing our Thai text steganographic embedding scheme, we introduce readers to the standard Thai character set and character encoding system.

Character Set

The Thai alphabet was created by King Ramkhamhaeng the Great in 1283. Although similar to the much simpler and more phonetic Lao alphabet, Thai is specific to the people of Thailand.

Figure 1. Thai character set

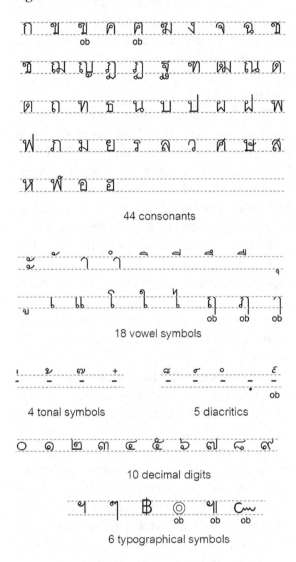

Figure 1. Thai character set

44 consonants

18 vowel symbols

4 tonal symbols   5 diacritics

10 decimal digits

6 typographical symbols

The standard for Thai characters is TIS-620-2533 (1990) (http://en.wikipedia.org/wiki/TIS-620), which is registered with the Internet Assigned Number Authority (IANA). TIS-620 extends ISO-646, the standard 7-bit ASCII character set, using the eighth bit in the code table. In Unicode 5.0, TIS-620 has been copied verbatim into the range U+0E00 to U+0E7F (http://en.wikipedia.org/wiki/Unicode).

The Thai character set is composed of 44 consonants, 18 vowel symbols, four tonal symbols, five diacritics, ten decimal digits, and six typographical symbols. The entire character set is shown in Figure 1.

Vertical Placement of Symbols

Thai characters can be placed vertically at four levels, namely at the *top* level, *above* level, *baseline* level, or *below* level (Karoonboonyanan, 1999). These four levels are shown in Figure 2.

Consonants, decimal symbols, and typographical symbols are always written at the baseline level while vowel symbols, tonal symbols, and diacritics might be written at any level depending on their characteristics and the surrounding context (Atsawaprecha, 1992).

Figure 3 classifies the symbols based on their vertical placement. In the table, NON, CONS, LV, FV, BV, BD, TONE, AD and AV represent non-composable characters, consonants, leading vowels, following vowels, below vowels, below diacritics, tonal symbols, above diacritics, and above vowels, respectively. Here, "non-composable" means baseline symbols that cannot be combined with symbols written at the top, above, or below level. The four tonal symbols normally written at the above level are shifted to the top level when they follow an above-level vowel.

Figure 2. Four levels of vertical placement of Thai symbols

top level
above level
base line
below level

Figure 3. Thai alphabetical character classification

Class	Characters	Writing level
NON	THAI NUMBERS, and ฯ, ฿, ๆ, ๏, ๚, ๛	BASE
CONS	44 CONSONANTS	BASE
LV	เ (SARA-E) แ (SARA-AE) โ (SARA-O) ใ (SARA-AI-MAI-MUAN) ไ (SARA-AI-MAI-MA-LAI)	BASE
FV1	ะ (SARA-A) า (SARA-AA) ำ (SARA-AM)	BASE
FV2	ๅ (LAK-KHANG-YAO)	BASE
FV3	ฤ (RU) ฦ (LU)	BASE
BV1	ุ (SARA-U)	BELOW
BV2	ู (SARA-UU)	BELOW
BD	ฺ (PHIN-THU)	BELOW
TONE	่ (MAI-EK) ้ (MAI-THO) ๊ (MAI-TRI)	ABOVE
	๋ (MAI-CHAT-TA-WA)	TOP
AD1	็ (NI-KHA-HIT) ์ (THAN-THA-KHAT)	ABOVE
AD2	็ (MAI-TAI-KHU)	ABOVE
AD3	์ (YA-MAK-KAN)	ABOVE
AV1	ิ (SARA-I)	ABOVE
AV2	ั (MAI-HAN-A-KAT) ึ (SARA-UE)	ABOVE
AV3	ี (SARA-II) ื (SARA-UEE)	ABOVE

NON = non-composible characters, CONS = consonants, LV = leading vowels,
FV = following vowels, BV = below vowels, BD = below diacritics, TONE = tonal symbols,
AD = above diacritics, AV = above vowels

Symbol Input Sequence Constraints

The standard Thai input/output method is WTT 2.0, proposed by the Thai API Consortium (TAPIC) in 1991. WTT 2.0 is *cell-oriented*. In cell-oriented input, the position of the cursor, called a *cell*, is determined when a character is input. The position of the cursor does not move forward to the next cell when above-level, top-level, or below-level vowel, diacritical, or tonal symbols are input. This is called *zero-width insertion*, and the zero-width characters are called *dead characters*. On the other hand, input characters for which the cursor always moves forward to the next cell are called *forward characters*. An example of zero-width insertion is shown in Figure 4.

WTT 2.0 defines improper symbol sequences that lead to illegal symbol compositions within the same cell (Koanantakool, 1991). There are three modes of input sequence checking: *pass-through* mode, *basic check* mode, and *strict* mode. In pass-through mode, all input sequences are allowed. In basic check mode, some input sequence patterns are prohibited, and in strict mode, even more sequences are prohibited. Here, "prohibited" means the character sequence cannot be input to a compliant text editor using a normal input device such as a keyboard. A diagram describing the legal input sequences in strict checking mode is shown in Figure 5.

As an example, the diagram shows that when one of the four tonal symbols is to be written at the top level, in the same cell as an above-level vowel symbol, it must be written after that vowel symbol, or the sequence is prohibited. Similarly, when a baseline consonant is composed with a below-level vowel symbol and a tonal symbol, the below-level vowel symbol must be input before the tonal symbol. Examples of these two cases in the CordiaUPC font are shown in Figure 6(a) and Figure 6(b), respectively.

Figure 4. Zero-width insertion

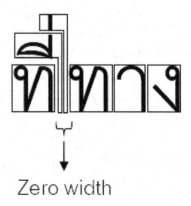

Zero width

Figure 5. Input sequence checking in strict mode

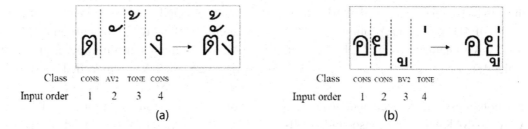

Figure 6. Proper input sequence examples (a) Example 1 (b) Example 2

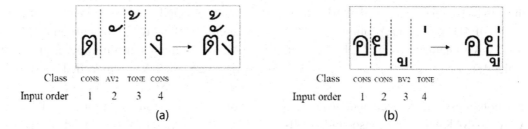

Output Method

WTT 2.0 also specifies how illegal character sequences should be displayed. This is necessary because it is possible to have an improper character string input in pass-through mode that then needs to be rendered. Two examples of Microsoft Word's rendering of improper input sequences are shown in Figure 7(a) and Figure 7(b).

METHOD

The essence of text steganography is to vary the way a document is written without changing its meaning. The encoder should embed the secret message in such a way that it can be reliably decoded, without producing stegotext that is distracting to readers.

To satisfy these design constraints, the embedding scheme must necessarily exploit redundancy, either in the language or in the character set. In

Figure 7. Examples of improper input sequence displayed in Microsoft Word (a) Example 1 (b) Example 2

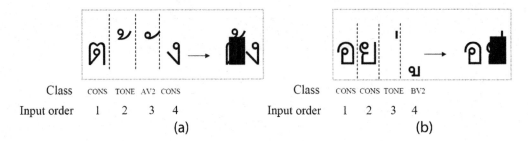

the case of Thai text steganography, a careful examination of the TIS-620 character set (or equivalently, the Thai Unicode character range) reveals two clear redundancies:

- The leading vowel SARA-AE can be written using either the compound character 0xE1 (แ, U+0E41 in Unicode) or separately using two SARA-E characters 0xE0 (เ, U+0E40 in Unicode).

- The trailing vowel SARA-AM, which can follow any consonant, can be written using either the compound character 0xD3 (ำ, U+0E33 in Unicode) or separately using the NI-KHA-HIT diacritical mark 0xED (◌ํ, U+0E4D in Unicode) followed by the SARA-AA character 0xD2 (า, U+0E32 in Unicode).

We denote these two replacement sequences by SARA-E→SARA-E and (consonant)→ NI-KHA-HIT→ SARA-AA, respectively. Since the replacement sequences are LV→LV and CONS→AD1→FV1, which follow the standard

input method, they are displayed properly by WTT 2.0-compliant renderers. The replacement combinations are shown in Figure 8.

The difficulty with this scheme for replacement of compound characters is that Thai words can contain SARA-AM composed with a tonal symbol MAI-EK (0xE8, ◌่, U+0E48 in Unicode), MAI-THO (0xE9, ◌้, U+0E49 in Unicode), MAI-TRI (0xEA, ◌๊, U+0E4A in Unicode), or MAI-CHAT-TA-WA (0xEB, ◌๋, U+0E4B in Unicode). In this situation, according to WTT 2.0, the tonal symbol must be input before SARA-AM. This means that the proper input sequence becomes (consonant)→(tonal symbol)→SARA-AM, or CONS→ TONE→FV1. This means a naive replacement of SARA-AM with NI-KHA-HIT→ SARA-AA creates an improper input sequence when the SARA-AM is preceded by a tonal symbol, since the final sequence would be (consonant)→(tonal symbol)→NI-KHA-HIT →SARA-AA, or CONS→TONE→AD1→FV1. An example of an improper input sequence created by naive replacement of SARA-AM is shown in Figure 9.

Figure 8. Replacement sequences for SARA-AE and SARA-AM

Vowel Symbol	Sequence of combination		Combined symbols
แ (SARA-AE)	เ (SARA-E)	→ เ (SARA-E)	แ
◌ำ (SARA-AM)	◌ํ (NI-KHA-HIT)	→ า (SARA-AA)	◌ำ

Figure 9. Invalid SARA-AM replacement (a) Original text (b) Improper input sequence

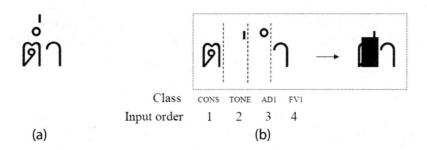

(a)   (b)

To understand the problem, note that the violating input sequence CONS→TONE→AD1→FV1 is a case of BASE→TOP→ABOVE→BASE, which violates the restriction that an above-level symbol in the same cell as a top-level symbol must come before the top-level symbol. To fix the inconsistency, we must swap the tonal symbol and the diacritical symbol, i.e., (consonant)→NIKHA-HIT→(tonal symbol)→SARA-AA or CONS→AD1→TONE→FV1. Figure 10 shows the example of Figure 9 with the input order fixed. Strictly speaking, the fixed input sequence violates the restrictions of WTT 2.0 strict checking mode (according to the diagram in Figure 6, there is no way to compose a consonant, diacritic, tonal symbol, and following vowel in the same cell). However, the sequence can nevertheless be entered in pass-through mode or constructed by a computer program, and it is properly displayed by WTT 2.0-compliant rendering engines.

A complete list of improper SARA-AM replacements with the corresponding correctly reordered sequences is shown in Figure 11.

We give samples of SARA-AE and SARA-AM symbols with the corresponding manipulated symbol sequences written in three of the most frequently used Thai fonts in Figure 12. We find that the SARA-AE manipulation can be visually noticeable by careful observers in some fonts, particularly when the size of the combined symbols is enlarged. However, when the manipulated symbols are written in typical text sizes, e.g., 12 to 16 points, the manipulation is effective. On the other hand, we find that the manipulation of SARA-AM is rendered identically to the corresponding normal sequence in all fonts. This makes the SARA-AM manipulation particularly effective.

THE STEGOSYSTEM

Here we provide complete definitions and constructions of our Thai text stegosystem and the underlying schemes, namely *authenticated encryption* and *embedding* schemes, by following

Figure 10. Valid SARA-AM replacement (a) Original text (b) Properly rendered input sequence

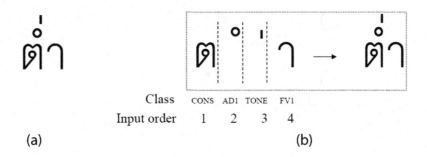

(a)   (b)

Figure 11. Invalid SARA-AM replacements and valid re-orderings

Patterns	Normal Sequence	Sequence of combined symbols	Sequence of re-combined symbols
	TOP → BASE	TOP → ABOVE → BASE	ABOVE → TOP → BASE
◌̇ำ	ı → ◌̇ำ	ı → ◌ → ำ	◌ → ı → ำ
◌̆ำ	◌̆ → ◌̇ำ	◌̆ → ◌ → ำ	◌ → ◌̆ → ำ
◌̃ำ	๗ → ◌̇ำ	๗ → ◌ → ำ	◌ → ๗ → ำ
◌̈ำ	·· → ◌̇ำ	·· → ◌ → ำ	◌ → ·· → ำ

Figure 12. Original symbols and corresponding manipulations written in different font types

Original Symbol	Combined Symbols	Font Type
แล	แล	Cordia New
แล	แล	Angsana New
แล	**แล**	Tahoma
น้ำ	น้ำ	Cordia New
น้ำ	น้ำ	Angsana New
น้ำ	น้ำ	Tahoma

the *generic construction* of the provably secure embedding stegosystem proposed in Dailey et al. (2010).

Definitions

Stegosystem. A stegosystem $Steg = (\text{KG}, \text{SE}, \text{SD}, \text{R})$ over character set $\sum$ consists of three algorithms and a relation, namely the *key generation, stego encoding, stego decoding* algorithms and a *compatibility relation*, respectively. We provide the syntax of these algorithms here.

The randomized *key generation* algorithm $\text{KG} : \varnothing \mapsto \{0,1\}^*$ takes no input and returns a key $K \in \{0,1\}^*$. The *stego encoding* algorithm $\text{SE} : \{0,1\}^* \times \sum^* \times \{0,1\}^* \mapsto \sum^* \cup \perp$, which may be randomized and/or stateful, takes the key $K \in \{0,1\}^*$, a character string as a covertext $C \in \sum^*$, and a hiddentext message $M \in \{0,1\}^*$ to return either a character string containing the hiddentext as a stegotext $S \in \sum^*$ or $\perp$ to indicate a rejection. The deterministic and stateless *stego decoding* algorithm

$$\text{SD} : \{0,1\}^* \times \sum^* \mapsto \{0,1\}^* \cup \perp$$

takes the key $K \in \{0,1\}^*$ and stegotext $S \in \sum^*$ to return either message $M \in \{0,1\}^*$ or $\perp$ to indicate that it rejects. The compatibility relation $\text{R} : \sum^* \times \sum^* \mapsto \{0,1\}$, which is a publicly, polynomial-time computable binary commutative equivalence relation on the stegotext space, takes two stegotexts $S_1, S_2 \in \sum^*$ to return either 1 to indicate that S_1 and S_2 are related under R or 0 otherwise.

We use $[\text{F}]$ to refer to the set of all possible outputs of any algorithm F. The correctness condition requires that for any $K \in [\text{KG}]$, for any covertext $C \in \sum^*$, for any hiddentext message $M \in \{0,1\}^*$, and for any stegotext $S \in [\text{SE}(K, C, M)]$, we have that the probabil-

ity of the event $S = \perp$ or $\text{SD}(K, S) = M$ is one, where the probability is taken over any coin tosses of KG and SE.

Authenticated encryption scheme. An authenticated encryption scheme $\mathcal{AE} = (\text{KG}, \text{E}, \text{D}, \text{LE})$ consists of four algorithms, namely the *key generation, encryption, decryption*, and *longest encryption* algorithms, respectively. KG, E, and D are standard algorithms, e.g., according to the model of Bellare & Namprempre (2008). LE is an additional algorithm associated with the authenticated encryption scheme $\mathcal{AE}$ in order to meet the requirements of embedding steganography. Since KG, E, and D are standard, we only give a definition of the associated algorithm LE and provide correctness conditions for the authenticated encryption scheme.

The deterministic and stateless *longest encryption* algorithm $\text{LE} : \mathbb{N} \mapsto \mathbb{N} \times \mathbb{N}$ takes as input a number of bits $b \in \mathbb{N}$ and computes and returns (1) the number of plaintext bits needed to be encrypted to produce a longest ciphertext Z whose length in bits does not exceed b and (2) the length in bits of the ciphertext Z. The correctness condition requires that for any $K \in [\text{KG}]$, for any plaintext $M \in \{0,1\}^*$, and for any ciphertext $Z \in [\text{E}(K, M)]$, we have that the probability of the event $Z = \perp$ or $\text{D}(K, C) = M$ is one, where the probability is taken over any coin tosses of KG and E.

Embedding scheme. An embedding scheme $\mathcal{EM} = (\text{Emb}, \text{Ext}, \text{Cap})$ consists of three algorithms, namely the *embedding, extracting* and *capacity* algorithms, respectively. Emb, Ext, and Cap are application-specific algorithms. Emb embeds an input string Z into a given covertext C and returns a stegotext S. Ext extracts the longest possible string Z embedded in the input string S. Cap returns the maximum number of bits cap that can be or could have been embedded in the input string C. In this section, we provide the syntax and correctness conditions of the required application-specific algorithms Emb, Ext, and Cap.

The deterministic and stateless *embedding* algorithm $\text{Emb}: \{0,1\}^* \times \sum^* \mapsto \sum^*$ takes two strings $Z \in \{0,1\}^*$ and $C \in \sum^*$ as inputs, embeds Z into C, and returns the resulting string $S \in \sum^*$. The deterministic and stateless *extracting* algorithm $\text{Ext}: \sum^* \mapsto \{0,1\}^*$ takes a string $S \in \sum^*$ and recovers the longest possible string $Z \in \{0,1\}^*$ embedded in S. The deterministic and stateless *capacity* algorithm $\text{Cap}: \sum^* \mapsto \mathbb{N}$ takes as input a string $C \in \sum^*$ and returns the maximum number of bits $cap \in \mathbb{N}$ that can be or could have been embedded in C. The correctness condition requires that, for any Z and C, we have that Z is a prefix of $\text{Ext}(\text{Emb}(Z,C))$ and that $\text{Cap}(C) = \text{Cap}(\text{Emb}(Z,C))$.

Constructions

If C is a string, the number of characters in C is called the *length* of C, denoted by $|C|$. A string of length 0 is called the *empty string*, denoted by ε. We write $C[i...j]$ to indicate the substring of C beginning at the ith character and ending at the jth character where $i, j \in \mathbb{N}$, and $1 \le i \le j \le |C|$. If C_1 and C_2 are strings, the concatenation of C_1 and C_2, denoted by $C_1 \parallel C_2$, is the characters of C_1 followed by the characters of C_2.

If F is a *stateless* and *deterministic* algorithm, we let $y \leftarrow \text{F}(x)$ denote the process of running F with input x and assigning the result to y, and we let $y \leftarrow \text{F}$ denote the process of running F with no input and assigning the result to y.

We provide a construction of a Thai text stegosystem $Steg^T = (\text{KG}, \text{SE}, \text{SD}, \text{R})$ that instantiates the generic construction, by specifying SE, SD,

and R in terms of an underlying authenticated encryption scheme and an application-specific embedding scheme. We let $\mathcal{AE} = (\text{KG}, \text{E}, \text{D}, \text{LE})$ be an underlying authenticated encryption scheme, and $\mathcal{EM}^T = (\text{Emb}^T, \text{Ext}^T, \text{Cap}^T)$ be an application-specific embedding scheme for $Steg^T$ stegosystem.

The key generation algorithm KG of $Steg^T$ is simply the key generation algorithm of the underlying authenticated encryption scheme $\mathcal{AE}$. The stego encoding algorithm SE, the stego decoding algorithm SD, and the compatibility relation R of $Steg^T$ are as provided by the generic construction. Therefore, next, we only describe how $Steg^T$ works with SE, SD, and R. Then, we specify the underlying authenticated encryption scheme $\mathcal{AE} = (\text{KG}, \text{E}, \text{D}, \text{LE})$ and the application-specific embedding scheme $\mathcal{EM}^T = (\text{Emb}^T, \text{Ext}^T, \text{Cap}^T)$ for $Steg^T$ stegosystem.

Stegosystem. In SE, first, the maximum embedding capacity cap of the input covertext C is calculated by Cap^T algorithm. Then, the number of plaintext bits l_p needed to be encrypted to produce the longest ciphertext whose length in bits does not exceed the cap is calculated by LE. After that, the n-bit binary encoding of the length of the hidden text message M (we use $n = 8$ in our experiments) is concatenated with the hiddentext message itself, and the hiddentext message is then further padded with 0s to create the longest possible plaintext M' for C. Here, the n-bit binary encoding of the length of M is for the purpose of blind decoding in which the length of the hiddentext message must be known from the stegotext. Next, the padded text M' and the stego key K are input to E, which returns an output ciphertext Z. Finally, the ciphertext Z and the covertext C are input to

Emb^T, which returns an output stegotext S. Here, it is possible that the covertext C passed to Emb^T contains instances of our steganographic modifications, e.g., SARA-E→SARA-E or NI-KHA-HIT→SARA-AA. For simplicity, to handle these cases, we assume the existence of a preprocessing algorithm $\text{Pre}: \Sigma^* \mapsto \Sigma^*$ that replaces any such combinations before the hiddentext message is embedded into the given covertext inside Cap^T and Emb^T algorithms. Pre takes covertext string $C \in \Sigma^*$ and returns the preprocessed covertext string $C' \in \Sigma^*$ where, for example, instances of SARA-E→SARA-E in C are replaced by SARA-AE. A flow diagram for SE is shown in Figure 13.

On the other hand, in SD, first, the maximum embedding capacity cap of the input stegotext S is calculated by Cap^T algorithm. Then, the length of the longest ciphertext l_c not exceeding cap that could have been produced in S is calculated by LE. After that, a string of embedded bits Z' is extracted from S by Ext^T algorithm,

and only the first l_c bits of the bit string Z' and the stego key K are input to D, which returns a decrypted plaintext M'. Next, the size of the hiddentext message included in M' is calculated by converting the first n bits of M' into an integer l_m. Finally, the l_m hiddentext message bits are retrieved from the $(n+1)^{th}$ position to the $(n+l_m)^{th}$ position in M' as a secret message M. A flow diagram for SD is shown in Figure 14.

In R, for input stegotexts S_1 and S_2, strings of embedded bits Z_1' and Z_2' are extracted by Ext^T, respectively. Then, R checks whether the first l_c bits of Z_1' and Z_2', i.e., Z_1 and Z_2, are the same or not. If Z_1 and Z_2 are the same, R outputs 1, (S_1 and S_2 are considered to be related under R). This means that S_1 and S_2 contains embedded bit strings which decoded to the same hiddentext message. Although the relation R is not used in the construction itself, it must exist in order to guarantee security of the stegosystem $Steg^T$ under the notions proposed

Figure 13. Flow diagram for stego encoding

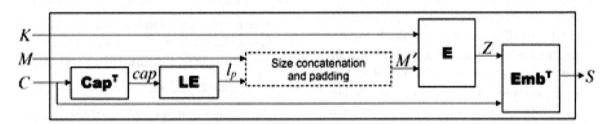

Figure 14. Flow diagram for stego decoding

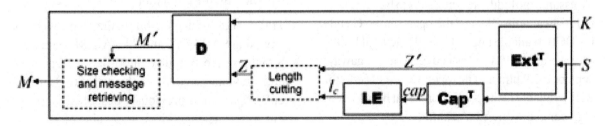

Figure 15. Flow diagram for compatibility relation

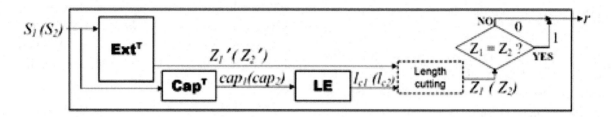

in Dailey et al. (2010). A flow diagram for R, is shown in Figure 15.

Authenticated encryption scheme. We instantiate the authenticated encryption scheme $\mathcal{AE} = (\mathrm{KG}, \mathrm{E}, \mathrm{D}, \mathrm{LE})$ using an *Offset Code-Book* (OCB) block-cipher mode of operation for symmetric authenticated encryption schemes. OCB is a provably secure block-cipher mode of operation that simultaneously provides privacy and integrity (Rogaway, Bellare, & Black, 2003) based on its underlying block cipher. The security properties of OCB require a new nonce every time one encrypts or decrypts. However, in OCB, the nonce does not have to be random, secret, or unpredictable. Therefore, for simplicity, we assume that the nonces used for encryption and decryption have previously been agreed upon between the sender and receiver.

In this paper, we use AES-128 as the block cipher for OCB. We call the resulting scheme OCB-AES. Hence, the key length for the underlying authenticated encryption scheme is 128 bits. OCB-AES uses the Encrypt-then-Mac composition (Bellare et al., 2008) for authenticated encryption. The scheme thus outputs a 128-bit tag for authenticating the encrypted ciphertext. OCB-AES can encrypt a plaintext of arbitrary length, but for simplicity, we assume the hiddentext message to be expressed in full-byte units. We use the open source C code for OCB available under the GNU General Public License at http://www.cs.ucdavis.edu/~rogaway/ocb/code-2.0.htm and the open source C code for AES available in the public domain at http://www.efgh.com/software/rijndael.htm.

Since the algorithms KG, E, and D are those of the underlying authenticated encryption scheme OCB-AES, We only specify the construction of LE as follows:

Algorithm $\mathrm{LE}(cap)$

    $bitsPerByte \leftarrow 8;\ tagLength \leftarrow 128$
    $l_c \leftarrow (\lfloor cap\,/\,bitsPerByte \rfloor) \times bitsPerByte$
    $l_p \leftarrow l_c - tagLength$
    Return (l_p, l_c)

Since we assume the hiddentext message to be written in full-byte units, first, the longest encryption algorithm LE rounds the capacity down to a multiple of 8 to get l_c and then calculates the number of plaintext bits l_p that would produce a ciphertext of that length.

Embedding scheme. We instantiate the application-specific embedding scheme $\mathcal{EM}^T = (\mathrm{Emb}^T, \mathrm{Ext}^T, \mathrm{Cap}^T)$ for $Steg^T$ assuming the existence of the preprocessing algorithm Pre are shown on Boxes 1-5.

The redundancies described in the method are exploited by the embedding algorithm Emb^T. Emb^T adds hiddentext bits to the Thai covertext bypassing SARA-AE and SARA-AM characters through to the output unmodified to represent hiddentext message bits with a value of 0 and by replacing them as previously described to represent secret message bits with a value of 1.

Box 1.

```
Algorithm Emb^T(Z, C)
    GLOBAL C' ← Pre(C)
    GLOBAL S ← ε
    char ← the first character in C'
    for each bit b in Z to be embedded do
        while char is not null
            if char is SARA-AE or SARA-AM then
                S ← S ‖ OutputPattern(b, char)
                char ← the next character in C'
                break
            else
                S ← S ‖ char
                char ← the next character in C'
            endif
        endwhile
    endfor
    S ← S ‖ C'
    Return S
```

The extracting algorithm $\mathtt{Ext}^T$ simply checks whether stegotext characters are SARA-AE or SARA-AM, or part of the replacement patterns as previously described, and outputs the corresponding bit string.

The capacity algorithm $\mathtt{Cap}^T$ counts the number of SARA-AE and SARA-AM characters in the preprocessed covertext C'. Since C is preprocessed, number of SARA-AE and SARA-AM in C' is the maximum embeddable capacity of C.

RESULTS

For purposes of evaluation, we implemented a prototype of the Thai text stegosystem $Steg^T = (\mathrm{KG, SE, SD, R})$. Two samples of original covertexts and the corresponding stegotexts are shown in Figure 16, Figure 17, Figure 18, and Figure 19. We performed two experiments: one to determine the embedding capacity of typical Thai text documents, and one to determine the visibility of the text modifications introduced by the encoding algorithm. Finally, we provide an analysis of security against computational attacks for the stegosystem $Steg^T$.

Embedding Capacity of Thai Text Documents

To determine the practical embedding capacity achievable with our algorithm, we collected a corpus of Thai text documents from many sources on

Box 2.

```
Subroutine OutputPattern(b, char)
    if bit is 0 then
        pattern ← char
    else
        if char is SARA-AE then
            pattern ← SARA-E ‖ SARA-E
        else if char is SARA-AM and the previous character is TONE then
            Replace S_{|S|} with NI-KHA-HIT
            pattern ← TONE ‖ SARA-AA
        else
            pattern ← NI-KHA-HIT ‖ SARA-AA
        endif
    endif
    Return pattern
```

Box 3.

```
Algorithm Ext^T(S)
    GLOBAL pos ← 1
    Z ← ε
    while S_{pos} is not null do
        Z ← Z ‖ ExtractBit(pos)
    endwhile
    Return Z
```

the Internet. We classified the documents into four categories: "news," "technical articles," "fiction," and "government documents." We subdivided the news category into six sub-categories: "general news," "economic news," "international news," "social news," "sports news," and "celebrity news." We collected 10 TIS-620 encoded text files for each document category and sub-category.

On average, the number of embeddable bits was 0.22% of the original covertext size. This means that on average, a 100KB Thai plain text file can be used to transmit a bit string of approximately 220 bytes or 1,760 bits. In the experiment, we used 8 bits to encode the hiddentext message length, and appended a 128-bit tag to the bit string, so the length of the embeddable hiddentext message itself was 203 bytes or 1,624 bits on average.

We also calculated the per-line embedding capacity for the corpus and found that 1.93 bits per line could be embedded on average. The detailed results are shown in Figure 20.

Visual Obtrusiveness

To determine the extent to which the text modifications introduced by the Thai text steganography encoding algorithm are visible to casual observers, we performed an informal study in which observers were asked if they could find any differences between two text documents.

Box 4.

Subroutine `ExtractBit`(pos)
    while S_{pos} is not null **do**
        if S_{pos} is SARA-AE or SARA-AM **then**
            $bit \leftarrow 0$; $pos \leftarrow pos + 1$; **break**
        else if S_{pos} is SARA-E and S_{pos+1} is SARA-E **then**
            $bit \leftarrow 1$; $pos \leftarrow pos + 2$; **break**
        else if S_{pos} is NI-KHA-HIT and S_{pos+1} is SARA-AA **then**
            $bit \leftarrow 1$; $pos \leftarrow pos + 2$; **break**
        else if S_{pos} is NI-KHA-HIT and S_{pos+1} is TONE and S_{pos+2} is SARA-AA **then**
            $bit \leftarrow 1$; $pos \leftarrow pos + 3$; **break**
        else
            $pos \leftarrow pos + 1$
        endif
    endwhile
    Return bit

Box 5.

Algorithm $\text{Cap}^T(C)$
    $cap \leftarrow 0$
    $C' \leftarrow \text{Pre}(C)$
    $char \leftarrow$ the first character in C'
    while $char$ is not null **do**
        if $char$ is SARA-AE or SARA-AM **then**
            Increase cap by 1
            $char \leftarrow$ the next character in C'
        endif
    endwhile
    Return cap

Figure 16. Sample 1 of original covertext

วันหนึ่งเหมือนโชคเข้าข้าง บุษบาได้มีโอกาสพบกับไมค์ซึ่งเป็นพนักงานใหม่
เข้ามาบรรจุในตำแหน่งครูฝึกสอนดำน้ำของบริษัททัวร์แห่งนั้น ไมค์เป็นชาย
หนุ่มจากเชียงรายที่มีรูปร่างดี อายุยี่สิบหกปี บิดามารดาแยกกันอยู่ตั้งแต่ไมค์
เรียนจบ ม.ปลาย และหน้าซ้ำยังแยกกันไปแต่งงานใหม่โดยไม่มีใครสนใจใน
ตัวไมค์อีกเลย โชคดีที่ไมค์ได้งานที่ร้านซ่อมรถมอเตอร์ไซค์ในละแวกบ้านทำ
จึงสามารถประทังชีวิตตัวเองมาได้ และแถมยังมีเงินเก็บจนกระทั่งตัวเองเรียน
จบวิชาช่างเทคนิคในระดับ ปวส.

Figure 17. Stegotext corresponding to Figure 9 with 16 secret message bits embedded

วันหนึ่งเหมือนโชคเข้าข้าง บุษบาได้มีโอกาสพบกับไมค์ซึ่งเป็นพนักงานใหม่
เข้ามาบรรจุในตำแหน่งครูฝึกสอนดำน้ำของบริษัททัวร์แห่งนั้น ไมค์เป็นชาย
หนุ่มจากเชียงรายที่มีรูปร่างดี อายุยี่สิบหกปี บิดามารดาแยกกันอยู่ตั้งแต่ไมค์
เรียนจบ ม.ปลาย และหน้าซ้ำยังแยกกันไปแต่งงานใหม่โดยไม่มีใครสนใจใน
ตัวไมค์อีกเลย โชคดีที่ไมค์ได้งานที่ร้านซ่อมรถมอเตอร์ไซค์ในละแวกบ้านทำ
จึงสามารถประทังชีวิตตัวเองมาได้ และแถมยังมีเงินเก็บจนกระทั่งตัวเองเรียน
จบวิชาช่างเทคนิคในระดับ ปวส.

Figure 18. Sample 2 of original covertext

ผู้สื่อข่าวรายงานเมื่อวันที่ 19 ต.ค.ว่า ที่ จ.นครราชสีมา น้ำจากลำน้ำมูลได้เอ่อล้นท่วม อ.เฉลิมพระเกียรติ
อ.โนนสูง และ อ.พิมาย ทำให้บ้านเรือนชาวบ้านและนาข้าวจมอยู่ใต้บาดาล โดยเฉพาะ อ.พิมาย ที่ว่าการอำเภอ
โรงพัก สภ.อ.พิมาย สำนักงานสาธารณสุขอำเภอ โรงเรียนกุลโน และโรงเรียนมัธยมพิมายวิทยาถูกน้ำท่วมหนัก
บางจุดสูงถึง 1.50 เมตร ส่วนที่ อ.เมืองนครราชสีมา ที่ได้รับผลกระทบจากลำน้ำลำตะคองนั้น ขณะนี้ระดับน้ำ
ลดลงเกือบเข้าสู่ภาวะปกติแล้ว เหลือยังท่วมขังบางพื้นที่ ขณะที่ อ.ด่านขุนทด มีผู้พบศพนายวิเชียร พันธนะ อายุ
35 ปี อยู่บ้านเลขที่ 30 หมู่ 4 ต.หนองบัวตะเกียด อ.ด่านขุนทด ที่ถูกน้ำซัดหายไปตั้งแต่เกิดน้ำท่วมเมื่อวันที่ 15
ต.ค. กระทั่งเจอศพอยู่ในบึงหนองกระเทียม หมู่ 5 ต.หนองบัวตะเกียด ส่วนการใส่ล่าจระเข้จำนวน 36 ตัว ที่ถูก
แม่น้ำมูลซัดหลุดออกจากฟาร์มของนายประจวบ ศิริแจ่ม ที่บ้านโต้งมะกอก หมู่ 4 ต.เมืองปราสาท อ.โนนสูง ทำให้
ชาวบ้าน หวาดผวานั้น ล่าสุด พล.ต.ต.ธัตรกนก เขียวแสงส่อง ผบก.ภ.จ.นครราชสีมา นำ ฮ.พร้อมนักแม่นปืนออก
ค้นหาทางอากาศ พร้อมกันนี้ ตำรวจ สภ.อ.โนนสูง และชาวบ้านนำเรือพายและเรือยนต์ขนาดเล็กล่องไปตามจุดที่
น้ำท่วม รวมทั้งเจ้าหน้าที่ประมงได้นำเครื่องช็อตไฟฟ้ามาช่วยช็อตจระเข้และสามารถจับตายจระเข้ได้แล้ว 11 ตัว
แต่ละตัวน้ำหนักประมาณ 50 กก. ยังเหลืออีก 25 ตัว ในจำนวนหนี้มีพ่อพันธุ์แม่พันธุ์รวมอยู่ด้วย

Figure 19. Stegotext corresponding to Figure 9 with 16 secret message bits embedded

ผู้สื่อข่าวรายงานเมื่อวันที่ 19 ต.ค.ว่า ที่ จ.นครราชสีมา น้ำจากลำน้ำมูลได้เอ่อล้นท่วม อ.เฉลิมพระเกียรติ
อ.โนนสูง และ อ.พิมาย ทำให้บ้านเรือนชาวบ้านและนาข้าวจมอยู่ได้บาดาล โดยเฉพาะ อ.พิมาย ที่ว่าการอำเภอ
โรงพัก สภ.อ.พิมาย สำนักงานสาธารณสุขอำเภอ โรงเรียนกุลโน และโรงเรียนมัธยมพิมายวิทยาถูกน้ำท่วมหนัก
บางจุดสูงถึง 1.50 เมตร ส่วนที่ อ.เมืองนครราชสีมา ที่ได้รับผลกระทบจากลำน้ำลำตะคองนั้น ขณะนี้ระดับน้ำ
ลดลงเกือบเข้าสู่ภาวะปกติแล้ว เหลือยังท่วมขังบางพื้นที่ ขณะที่ อ.ด่านขุนทด มีผู้พบศพนายวิเชียร พันธนะ อายุ
35 ปี อยู่บ้านเลขที่ 30 หมู่ 4 ต.หนองบัวตะเกียด อ.ด่านขุนทด ที่ถูกน้ำซัดหายไปตั้งแต่เกิดน้ำท่วมเมื่อวันที่ 15
ต.ค. กระทั่งเจอศพอยู่ในบึงหนองกระเทียม หมู่ 5 ต.หนองบัวตะเกียด ส่วนการใส่ล่าจระเข้จำนวน 36 ตัว ที่ถูก
แม่น้ำมูลซัดหลุดออกจากฟาร์มของนายประจวบ ศิริแจ่ม ที่บ้านโค้งมะกอก หมู่ 4 ต.เมืองปราสาท อ.โนนสูง ทำให้
ชาวบ้าน หวาดผวานั้น ล่าสุด พล.ต.ต.อัตรกนก เขียวแสงส่อง ผบก.ภ.จ.นครราชสีมา นำ อ.พร้อมนักแม่นปืนออก
ค้นหาทางอากาศ พร้อมกันนี้ ตำรวจ สภ.อ.โนนสูง และชาวบ้านนำเรือพายและเรือยนต์ขนาดเล็กล่องไปตามจุด
ที่น้ำท่วม รวมทั้งเจ้าหน้าที่ประมงได้นำเครื่องซ็อตไฟฟ้ามาช่วยซ็อตจระเข้และสามารถจับตายจระเข้ได้แล้ว 11 ตัว
แต่ละตัวน้ำหนักประมาณ 50 กก. ยังเหลืออีก 25 ตัว ในจำนวนหนึ่งมีพ่อพันธุ์แม่พันธุ์รวมอยู่ด้วย

Figure 20. Embedding capacity of Thai text documents

Category		Average Embeddable percentage	Average embeddable bits per line	Source
News	General	0.23	1.99	http://www.thairath.co.th http://www.dailynews.co.th http://www.komchadluek.net
	Economic	0.22	1.93	
	International	0.20	1.72	
	Social	0.21	1.86	
	Sports	0.22	1.98	
	Celebrity	0.23	2.05	
Technical articles		0.26	2.25	http://www.arts.chula.ac.th http://www.mbachula.info http://www.uniserv.buu.ac.th http://www.tga.or.th http://www.trsport8.com
Fiction		0.23	2.04	http://9nat.blogspot.com http://www.praphansarn.com http://www.sorcererwar.com http://www.aritaa.com http://www.yehyeh.com
Government documents		0.18	1.61	Royal Thai Air Force
Total average		**0.22**	**1.93**	

As covertext, we prepared approximately six A4 pages of Thai plain text in the AngsanaNew font at 16 points. We used our implementation of algorithm Emb^T to embed a secret message into this covertext. Each observer participated in one of three experimental conditions.

In the first condition, we presented participants with either printed or electronic versions of the plain text and stegotext, and gave them approximately 10 minutes to find any differences between the two versions of the document, without providing any background information. Ten Thai natives and five non-Thai natives participated. None of the participants were able to identify any differences between the two versions of the document.

In the second condition, we told participants that one of the versions of the document contained a secret message, and again asked them to find any differences between the two versions of the document. Ten Thai native and five non-Thai natives participated. None of the participants were able to identify any differences between the two versions of the document.

In the third condition, one non-Thai native familiar with steganography and the goals of the study was informed that the stegotext carried approximately 2 hiddentext bits per line and that the embedding algorithm was not based on document formatting. This participant was able to identify the SARA-AE modification but could not identify the SARA-AM modification.

Analysis of Security against Computational Attacks

As previously described, our proposed Thai text stegosystem $Steg^T$ is constructed following a secure generic construction guaranteeing covertness, privacy, and integrity of the embedded hiddentext message assuming security of the underlying cryptographic primitive (an authenticated encryption system). This means that the stegosystem itself and all related algorithms can be public and known to all, while only the secret key for the underlying authenticated encryption system, used as the key for the stegosystem, needs to be private.

Since we use OCB-AES, a secure block-cipher based authenticated encryption scheme, as the underlying cryptographic primitive in our Thai text stegosystem, covertness, privacy, and integrity of the embedded hiddentext message are all preserved even when the attacker knows the construction of the stegosystem and all related algorithms, except the key.

Covertness is the main steganographic-specific security property. When we say the scheme provides covertness, it means that even if the attacker knows the embedding algorithm and analyzes the sequence of modifiable characters (the leading vowel SARA-AE or the trailing vowel SARA-AM) or their manipulations in a stegotext document by eye or by some computational software tool, and transforms the sequence to the corresponding bit string following the public extracting algorithm, the attacker still could not tell the difference between a string decoding to a real message or the empty message, without knowing the key.

Note that in most of the work analyzing the security of a steganographic scheme, one formulates an attack model based on statistical distinguishability and adversaries with unlimited resources, then attempts to evaluate the scheme in question with respect to that attack model. It is usually impossible to prove a scheme absolutely secure in this approach. The notions for covertness, privacy, and integrity proposed in Dailey et al. (2010), on the other hand, are instead based on computational adversaries with practical resources and lend themselves to proofs of security based on the security of the underlying cryptographic primitives, giving concrete bounds on the security of a steganographic scheme.

DISCUSSION

In this paper, we propose a novel method for covert communication using text steganography with arbitrary documents written in the Thai language as cover media. The embedding scheme provides for embedding secret information bits in and retrieving secret information bits from digital Thai plain text documents by exploiting redundancies in the way TIS-620 represents compound characters combining vowel, diacritical, and tonal symbols. The techniques we introduce are applicable to any language whose Unicode character sets contain redundancies. The method is blind in that the original covertext document is not needed at decoding time. We find that the modifications made when information bits are embedded in the covertext are unnoticeable to casual observers, and that the embedding capacity of 203 bytes per 100 kilobytes makes the scheme practical and effective for covert communication through text.

The SARA-AE manipulation is visually detectable by careful observers in some fonts. However, in every Thai text rendering engine we have experimented with, input sequences containing the SARA-AM manipulation are rendered identically to the corresponding normal input sequence. This makes the SARA-AM manipulation particularly effective.

Since the proposed embedding scheme embeds hiddentext messages into Thai plain text documents, the scheme is robust to changes in font size, color, and so on. Similarly, the scheme is robust to format changes such as line space adjustment and insertion of whitespace between words. However, one limitation of the scheme is that it is not robust to insertion and deletion of SARA-AE, SARA-AM, and their replacements in the stegotext. Appropriate solutions to this problem will depend on the specific application (email, Web board, blog, and so on) in question and the characteristics of the possible insertions and deletions expected in that application.

We construct the Thai text stegosystem following a provably secure construction. Therefore, the stegotexts produced by our stegosystem are not only undetectable to human observers, but they are also produced in a way that simultaneously achieves steganographic security in terms of covertness, privacy, and integrity against computational attacks.

ACKNOWLEDGMENT

We are grateful to Chanathip Namprempre, Kiyoshi Honda, and Poompat Saengudomlert for helpful comments on this research. The first author is supported by a graduate fellowship from the Royal Thai Government.

REFERENCES

Amano, T., & Misaki, D. (1999). A feature calibration method for watermarking of document images. In *Proceedings of the fifth international conference on document analysis and recognition (ICDAR'99)*, Bangalore, India (pp. 91-94). Washington, DC: IEEE Computer Society.

Atsawaprecha, C. (1992). Thai input output methods. In *Computer and Thai language*.

Backes, M., & Cachin, C. (2005) Public-key steganography with active attacks. In *Proceedings of the Theory of cryptography conference* (LNCS 3378, pp. 210-226). New York: Springer.

Bellare, M., & Namprempre, C. (2008). Authenticated encryption: Relations among notions and analysis of the generic composition paradigm. *Journal of Cryptology, 21*(4), 469–491. doi:10.1007/s00145-008-9026-x

Brassil, J. T., Low, S., & Maxemchuk, N. F. (1999). Copyright protection for the electronic distribution of text documents. *Proceedings of the IEEE, 87*(7), 1181–1196. doi:10.1109/5.771071

Cachin, C. (2004). An information-theoretic model for steganography. *Information and Computation, 192*(1), 41–56. doi:10.1016/j.ic.2004.02.003

Cvejic, N., & Seppänen, T. (2004). Increasing robustness of LSB audio steganography using a novel embedding method. In *Proceedings of the international conference on information technology: Coding and computing (ITCC'04)*, Las Vegas, NV (Vol. 2, pp. 533). Washington, DC: IEEE Computer Society.

Dailey, M., Namprempre, C., & Samphaiboon, N. (2010). *How to do embedding steganography securely*. Retrieved from http:///www.cs.ait.ac.th/~mdailey/papers/DNS-ES-09.pdf

Hopper, N. J., Langford, J., & von Ahn, L. (2002). Provably secure steganography. In *Proceedings of the 22nd annual international cryptology conference on advances in cryptology*, Santa Barbara, CA (pp. 77-92). New York: Springer.

Huang, D., & Yan, H. (2001). Interword distance changes represented by sine waves for watermarking text images. *IEEE Transactions on Circuits and Systems for Video Technology, 11*(12), 1237–1245. doi:10.1109/76.974678

Karoonboonyanan, T. (1999). Standardization and implementation of Thai language. In *National electronics and computer technology center*, Bangkok, Thailand.

Kiayias, A., Raekow, Y., & Russell, A. (2005). Efficient steganography with provable security guarantees. In *Proceedings of the 7th international workshop on information hiding (IH'05)*, Barcelona, Spain (LNCS 3727, pp. 118-130). New York: Springer.

Kim, Y.-W., Moon, K.-A., & Oh, I.-S. (2003). A text watermarking algorithm based on word classification and inter-word space statistics. In *Proceedings of the seventh international conference on document analysis and recognition (ICDAR'03)*, Edinburgh, Scotland (pp. 775-779). Washington, DC: IEEE Computer Society.

Kim, Y.-W., & Oh, I.-S. (2004). Watermarking text document images using edge direction histograms. *Pattern Recognition Letters, 25*(11), 1243–1251. doi:10.1016/j.patrec.2004.04.002

Koanantakool, T. (1991). The keyboard layouts and input method of the Thai language. In *Information processing institute for education and development Thammasat university*, Bangkok, Thailand.

Lou, D.-C., & Liu, J.-L. (2002). Steganographic method for secure communications. *Computers & Security, 21*(5), 449–460. doi:10.1016/S0167-4048(02)00515-1

Mittelholzer, T. (2000). An information-theoretic approach to steganography and watermarking. In *Proceedings of the 3rd international workshop on information hiding (IH'99)*, Dresden, Germany (LNCS 1768, pp. 1-16). Berlin: Springer.

Moulin, P., & O'Sullivan, J. (1999). Information-theoretic analysis of information hiding. *IEEE Transactions on Information Theory, 49*, 563–593. doi:10.1109/TIT.2002.808134

Muhammad, H., Rahman, S., & Shakil, A. (2009). Synonym based Malay linguistic text steganography. In *Proceedings of the Innovative technologies in intelligent systems and industrial applications (CITISIA'09)*, Sunway Campus, Malaysia (pp. 423-427). Washington, DC: IEEE.

Rogaway, P., Bellare, M., & Black, J. (2003). OCB: A block-cipher mode of operation for efficient authenticated encryption. *ACM Transactions on Information and System Security, 6*(3), 365–403. doi:10.1145/937527.937529

Ryder, J. (2004). Steganography may increase learning everywhere. *Journal of Computing Sciences in Colleges, 19*(5), 154–162.

Samphaiboon, N. (in press). Steganography via running short text messages. *Multimedia Tools and Applications*.

Shirali-Shahreza, M., & Shirali-Shahreza, M. (2007). Text steganography in SMS. In *Proceedings of the International conference on convergence information technology (ICCIT'07)*, Gyeongju, Korea (pp. 2260-2265). Washington, DC: IEEE Computer Society.

Shirali-Shahreza, M. H., & Shirali-Shahreza, M. (2006). A new approach to Persian/Arabic text steganography. In *Proceedings of the 5th IEEE/ACIS international conference on computer and information science and 1st IEEE/ACIS international workshop on component-based software engineering, software architecture and reuse (ICIS-COMSAR'06)*, Honolulu, HI (pp. 310-315). Washington, DC: IEEE Computer Society.

Su, J. K., Hartung, F., & Girod, B. (1998). Digital watermarking of text, image, and video documents. *Computer Graphics, 22*(6), 687–695. doi:10.1016/S0097-8493(98)00089-2

Sun, X., Luo, G., & Huang, H. (2004). Component-based digital watermarking of Chinese texts. In *Proceedings of the 3rd international conference on information security*, Shanghai, China (pp. 76-81). New York: ACM.

Topkara, M., Taskiran, C. M., & Delp, E. J. (2005). Natural language watermarking. In *Proceedings of SPIE-IS & T electronic imaging 2005*, San Jose, CA (pp. 441-452). Washington, DC: SPIE.

Yuling, L., Xingming, S., Can, G., & Hong, W. (2007). An efficient linguistic steganography for Chinese text. In *Proceedings of the IEEE international conference on multimedia and expo (ICME'07)*, Beijing, China (pp. 2094-2097). Washington, DC: IEEE.

Zhang, W., Zeng, Z., Pu, G., & Zhu, H. (2006). Chinese text watermarking based on occlusive components. In *Proceedings of the 2nd IEEE international conference on information and communication technologies: from theory to applications (ICTTA'06)*, Damascus, Syria (pp. 1850-1854). Washington, DC: IEEE.

Zollner, J., Federrath, H., Klimant, H., Pfitzmann, A., Piotraschke, R., Westfeld, A., et al. (1998). Modeling the security of steganographic systems. In *Proceedings of the 2nd international workshop on information hiding*, Portland, OR (LNCS 1525, pp. 344-354). New York: Springer.

This work was previously published in the International Journal of Digital Crime and Forensics, Volume 2, Issue 3, edited by Chang-Tsun Li and Anthony TS Ho, pp. 43-64, copyright 2010 by IGI Publishing (an imprint of IGI Global).

Section 4
Applications of Pattern Recognition and Signal Processing Techniques to Digital Forensics

Chapter 11
Digital Image Forensics Using Multi-Resolution Histograms

Jin Liu
Huazhong University of Science and Technology, China

Hefei Ling
Huazhong University of Science and Technology, China

Fuhao Zou
Huazhong University of Science and Technology, China

Weiqi Yan
Queen's University Belfast, UK

Zhengding Lu
Huazhong University of Science and Technology, China

ABSTRACT

In this paper, the authors investigate the prospect of using multi-resolution histograms (MRH) in conjunction with digital image forensics, particularly in the detection of two kinds of copy-move manipulations, i.e., cloning and splicing. To the best of the authors' knowledge, this is the first work that uses the same feature in both cloning and splicing forensics. The experimental results show the simplicity and efficiency of using MRH for the purpose of clone detection and splicing detection.

INTRODUCTION

With the development of digital image processing technology, and wide spread use of digital image processing software, such as Photoshop, the modification of digital images has become much easier for people without professional knowledge. This makes our lives more colorful; however, a new problem is introduced. Is a digital image's authenticity trustworthy? How do we check the digital image's authenticity? Therefore, using digital image forensics to check a digital image's authenticity has become a significant research focus. We will review the current digital image forensics technology first.

DOI: 10.4018/978-1-4666-1758-2.ch011

INTRODUCTION TO DIGITAL IMAGE FORENSICS

To acquire a forged image, we first shoot a scene to get the original image with a camera, and then alter the image with different types of manipulation technologies. On one hand, during photographing process, the camera itself may introduce some distinct artifacts into an image because of its image processing mechanism. On the other hand, the manipulation technologies may introduce some distinct artifacts into the image. These two scenarios are both used in digital image forensics. We can divide current digital image forensics technologies into two classes, one is based on the camera's photographing mechanism, and the other is based on manipulation methods. The prior one uses camera artifacts introduced by different stages of image processing as evidence to detect manipulation: such as chromatic aberration introduced by an optical system (Micah, Johnson, & Farid, 2006), pixel's statistical correlations introduced by color filter array interpolation (Popescu & Farid, 2005; Swaminathan & Liu, 2006; Long & Huang, 2006), camera response function with camera sensors (Hsu & Chang, 2006; Lin, Wang, Tang, & Shum, 2005), and sensor noise introduced by whole processing steps (Chen, Fridrich, Luka, & Goljan, 2007; Gou, Swaminathan, & Wu, 2007; Lukas, Fridrich, & Goljan, 2006). Furthermore, there are a wide variety of manipulation methods, therefore, digital image forensic technologies which aim at manipulation methods are varied,

such as resampling detection (Gallagher, 2005; Popescu & Farid, 2005; Mahdian & Saic, 2008; Kirchner, 2008; Prasad & Ramakrishnan, 2006) and blur detection (Hsiao & Pei, 2005; Sutcu, Coskun, Sencar, & Memon, 2007). While the forensic method proposed in (Lyu & Farid, 2005; Tian-Tsong, Shih-Fu, Jessie, Lexing, & Mao-Pei, 2005) focus on how to distinguish a naturally occurred image from one computer-generated image.

In our opinion, the most general methods for tampering with an image include two kinds of copy-move manipulation: one is copying and moving a part to a different location within the same image, known as the clone operation; another is copying and moving a part of an image to another separate image, known as splicing. The examples of cloning and splicing are shown in Figure 1. Both of these two operations can easily misguide people's understanding about the content of the image. For example, in Figure 1 (c), (d), people may be confused as to the original environment within which the cheetah was present.

The initial thought to detect the clone operation is an exhaustive search (Fridrich, Soukal, & Lukas, 2003), as there are two or more completely identical parts within the same image. However, an exhaustive search is less practical, because it is computationally impossible. Therefore many kinds of methods to improve the computational efficiency have been studied in Huang, Guo, and Zhang (2008), Li, Wu, Tu, and Sun (2007), and Popescu and Farid (2004). Most of these methods divide the image into numbers of overlay blocks,

Figure 1. Cloned image and spliced image samples: (a) and (b) are cloned images, (c), (d) are spliced images (From Columbia Image Splicing Detection Evaluation Dataset. Used with permission[1])

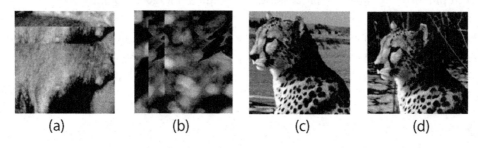

(a)   (b)   (c)   (d)

extract appropriate representation for each block, then sort and group the blocks to detect a clone region. Li et al. (2007) features of each block are extracted by applying singular value decomposition (SVD) to low frequency wavelet transform bands on each block. In Huang et al. (2008), SIFT features are extracted as representations for each block.

Obviously, the method of clone detection is inadequate for splicing detection because splicing uses separate images. Unless we know the original images that were used to create the composite image, an exhaust search is impossible. Recently, extensive work has been done on splicing detection. Parts of the work extract features from the image, and then perform classification with a classifier. The main difference is that many different features and classifiers are employed. In Ng, Chang, and Sun (2004), bi-coherence features are used to train a SVM to make the classification. In Zhang, Kang, and Ren (2008), moment features and selected Image Quality Metrics (IQMs) are used as features and trained by SVM to classify authentic and spliced images. In Zhen, Yukun, and Xijian (2008) of theirs, the classifier is an Artificial Neural Network. In Lu, Sun, Huang, and Lu, (2008), the authors use higher order statistical features and an RBF neural network to classify the fake and real images. In Hsu and Chang (2006), geometry invariants and camera characteristics consistency are used to detect image splicing. While in Zhang et al. (2008), the authors achieved 85% and above accuracy which is the best result among similar methods. Another part of the current work, such as Johnson and Farid (2007, 2008), and Johnson and Farid (2005), the authors studied how to detect splicing using inconsistencies in lighting. All the work mentioned above focuses on the accuracy of detection, but ignores the efficiency. For example, in Hsu and Chang (2006), feature extraction costs 11 minutes, and the training of the SVM costs 5 hours.

Though the methods of clone and splicing forensics are different, feature extraction from the image blocks/image and the use of features as representation of image blocks/image in detection are the same. This is the core challenge for most of the forensic methods. Currently, there are no works that use the same feature both in clone and splicing forensics. In this paper, our main contribution is that we endeavor to extract a multi-resolution histogram (MRH) from an image as its features which are used to characterize an image, and try to use these features in the detection of the clone and splicing operations. The MRH was first proposed in Hadjidemetriou, Grossberg, and Nayar (2004), and used in recognition. We will introduce the MRH briefly next.

INTRODUCTION TO MULTI-RESOLUTION HISTOGRAM

A MRH is the set of plain histograms of an image at multiple resolutions. It is an image representation since multi-resolution is applied to the image (Hadjidemetriou, Grossberg, & Nayar, 2001). The MRH can represent spatial information while the plain histogram cannot; meanwhile it retains the simplicity and efficiency of the plain histogram. To illuminate this, the equivalence between the histogram and the generalized image entropies have been analyzed, and extended to MRH in Hadjidemetriou et al. (2001), and Hadjidemetriou et al. (2004) as below.

Assume an image L has a continuous domain D with spatial coordinates $X = (x, y)$. The resolution of the image is decreased linearly with σ by convolving the image with a Gaussian kernel $G(\sigma)$. The convolution gives the image $L * G(\sigma)$ with histogram $h(L * G(\sigma))$, and one linear function of the histogram can express as the Tsallis generalized entropies with M graylevels as:

$$S_q = \sum_{j=0}^{M-1} \left(\frac{v_j - v_j^q}{q-1} \right) h_j \tag{1}$$

where q is a continuous parameter and h_j is the histogram density of the grayscale value v_j. In the limit $q \to 1$ the Tsallis generalized entropies reduce to the Shannon entropy.

The rate at which generalized image entropies change with respect to image resolution, $\frac{d}{d\sigma} S_q \left(L * G(\sigma) \right)$, are given by differentiating (1) with respect to σ:

$$\frac{d}{d\sigma} S_q \left(L * G(\sigma) \right) = \sum_{j=0}^{M-1} \left(\frac{v_j - v_j^q}{q-1} \right) \frac{dh_j \left(L * G(\sigma) \right)}{d\sigma} \tag{2}$$

Because the generalized Fisher information measures is

$$J_q(L) = \frac{l^2}{2} \frac{dS_q \left(L * G(\sigma) \right)}{d\sigma} \tag{3}$$

The substitution of (2) into the right side of (3) gives

$$J_q(L) = \frac{l^2}{2} \sum_{j=0}^{M-1} \left(\frac{v_j - v_j^q}{q-1} \right) \frac{dh_j \left(L * G(\sigma) \right)}{d\sigma} \tag{4}$$

As the generalized Fisher information measures can also be computed using

$$J_q(L) = \int_D \left| \frac{\nabla L(X)}{L(X)} \right|^2 L^q(X) d^2 x \tag{5}$$

The "sharpness" or spatial variation at a pixel is given by $|\nabla L(X) / L(X)|^2$. The average sharpness can be seen from Equation (5) is J_1,

namely the Fisher information. In general, functional J_q measures a weighted average "sharpness" of an image.

And from Equation (4), we can see that J_q is a linear function of the rate at which the histogram bins change with the resolution. The proportionality factors of J_q weigh heavier as the rate of change of the histogram bins corresponding to large intensity values increase. Then it is derived that the histogram bins change rate linearly with image resolution transforms of the values of J_q. In other words, the values of J_q are the measures of image variation that can encode shape and texture parameters. The MRH is sensitive to spatial information. Figure 2 shows this feature. In Figure 2, Row (a) and row (d) show the multiresolution decomposition of two original images. The left column shows the original images. Row (b) and row (c) show their MRH respectively. Although the histograms of two original images are the same, the MRH of each are different.

Compared with a plain histogram, the MRH possesses more spatial information and therefore has been widely used in the area of object recognition (Hadjidemetriou et al., 2004). Moreover, the MRH retains the simplicity and efficiency of the plain histogram. As described in Section 1, copy-move is a type of manipulation which may change image spatial information. Therefore in this paper, we investigate the prospect of using MRH of an image as features in order to detect the image clone and splicing operations.

METHOD

The most important challenge during clone detection and splicing detection is to describe the image blocks/image appropriately, as the follow-up processing is based on this abstract descriptor of the image. In this section, we will introduce how

Figure 2. Examples of two MRHs. Rows (a) and (d) show the multi-resolution decomposition of two images. The left column shows the original images. Rows (b) and (c) show their MRHs, respectively. Although the histograms of the two original images are the same, the MRH of each are different.

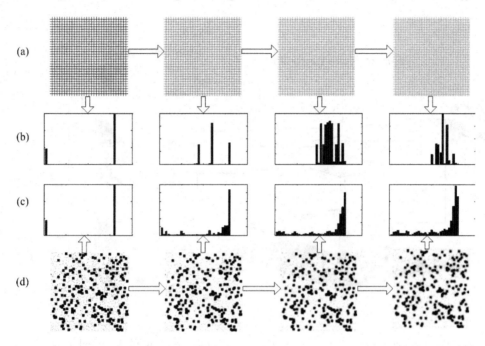

to obtain an image's MRH first, and then introduce the clone detection method and splicing detection method respectively.

EXTRACTION OF MULTI-RESOLUTION HISTOGRAMS

While a plain histogram with bin width w is described as $H_w = \{h_w(j) \mid j = 1, \cdots, n\}$, where n is the number of bins. Then the procedure of an image's MRH extraction is shown in Figure 3:

1) For an image, an 8-bit depth Burt-Adelson pyramid algorithm is used to build an l levels pyramid which is multi-resolution. That means each level of pyramid corresponds to one resolution of the image.

2) Compute the plain histogram H_w^i of each resolution of the image, where i corresponds to the level of multi-resolution pyramid, and $0 \leq i \leq l - 1$. w is the width of the bin.

3) Compute the cumulative histogram $H_w^i{}'$ corresponding to each resolution of the image. The cumulative histogram is used to eliminate the negative effects of the zero value in the plain histogram. Then all l cumulative histograms of an image are obtained.

4) Compute the differences between the cumulative histograms $H_w^i{}'$ of consecutive image resolutions, where $H_w^i{}'' = H_w^{i+1}{}' - H_w^i{}'$ $(0 \leq i \leq l - 2)$. An image with an l levels resolution pyramid has $l - 1$ difference histograms. If each of the difference histograms are regarded as an n dimensional feature vector (each dimension is corresponding to one bin), all of them compose $n \cdot (l - 1)$ dimensions feature vector of an image.

Figure 3. Obtain a MRH as features of an image. For l levels of a multi-resolution pyramid of an image, l corresponds to the cumulative histograms that are obtained, and $l-1$ difference histograms are computed.

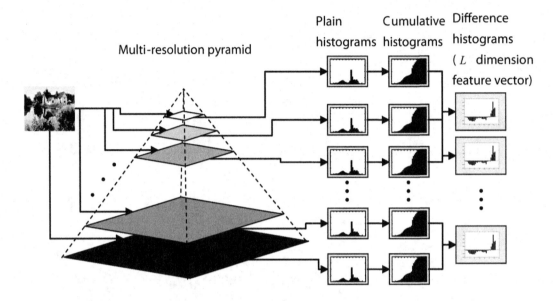

In this paper, considering the efficiency of the experiment, the bin width w is 8, and the pyramid level number l is 8. So, the number of bins of each histogram of the MRH n is 32 $\left(n = 2^8 / w = 32\right)$. The total number of bins in a MRH of an image is 224 $\left(n \cdot (l-1) = 32 \cdot (8-1) = 224\right)$. Then the MRH may be regarded as a 224-D vector, this is used as the features which characterize an image.

CLONE DETECTION

In Popescu and Farid (2004), the authors divide the image into a number of overlay blocks, and apply principal component analysis (PCA) on each of the blocks, and obtain features for each block. These features are then used to detect a cloned region. Other researchers also employed this method, the main differences among these methods is the feature selection process.

We also use a similar method for clone detection. To use MRHs in clone detection, we first divide the image into overlapping blocks. If each block's size is $a \times a$, then an image with size $m \times n$ will contain $(m - a + 1) \times (n - a + 1)$ blocks in total. The MRHs will be extracted from each block with the procedure described previously in this section. Therefore, in this paper, the feature of each block is a 224-D vector. There are $(m - a + 1) \times (n - a + 1)$ feature vectors in total for the whole image.

In other words, we slide a $a \times a$ sized window from the upper-left corner of the image to the lower-right corner of the image. The window slides pixel by pixel for each step, extracting features from the block on the current position of the window, and then the window slides to the next position.

We construct a matrix F with these extracted features: each row of the matrix F is the feature vector for each image block, and the number of rows is the number of blocks, $(m - a + 1) \times (n - a + 1)$; each column is the dimension of the feature, in this paper, that is the bins of the MRHs, and the number of columns is 224. The image is denoted as a matrix F.

If a pair of rows in the matrix F are the same or similar, that means the blocks that are denoted by the rows are the same or similar. This can be used to detect the clone operation, because the clone operation makes two or more completely identical parts appear in one image. Obviously, the size of the block/slide window should be smaller than the size of the clone region, otherwise the rows in Matrix F will be completely different and the detection process will fail. So the size a should be small enough. But on the other hand, smaller a makes the numbers of blocks larger, and increases the computational complexity. A suitable a must be chosen in order to balance computational complexity and detection accuracy.

Since the clone region consists of blocks, there should be blocks that are the same or similar with the others. These blocks are called same/similar block pairs, and the distance between them is called pair distance. Naturally, the authentic image may also contain numbers of same/similar block pairs, such as the image of blue sky. So the number of the same/similar block pairs on its own is not enough for deciding whether or not the clone operation has been performed. The number of the same/similar block pairs with same pair distance should be large enough for such a decision.

We sort the rows of matrix F lexicographically, and the features of the same or similar pairs will come successively. Then each of the same/similar block pair's pair distance is computed, and the number of same/similar block pairs with same pair distance is recorded. If the number is greater than a threshold that means there is a clone region within the image.

SPLICING DETECTION

As mentioned in the introduction, there are two methods available to assist in detecting and determining whether an image has been spliced. One method uses inconsistencies in lighting. This method has extreme restrictions in that the image must contain two or more people; this limits its range of use. So we employed the other method which was originally proposed in Ng et al. (2004). In this splicing detection method, the detection of splicing between different images is treated as a binary decision problem. What should be done is to estimate whether one image is an authentic image or a spliced image. Similar to (Ng et al., 2004), we also employed a support vector machine (SVM) as a classifier. In short, the estimation can be divided into two steps, training and testing. Using the procedure described in Section 2, each image is represented by a 224-D feature, which is used as data by the SVM. The SVM will be trained by using training data to obtain the model, then, in the next step, the SVM model is used to estimate which class new data belongs to. More about SVM could be found in Chen, Lin, and Scholkopf (2005).

LIBSVM (Chang & Lin), one of the implementations of the SVM classifier, was used in our experiment. In this paper, the images are divided into two classes, where +1 denotes an authentic image and -1 denotes a spliced image. We train LIBSVM with parts of our image database in order to obtain our SVM model. The SVM model is used to separate the test images into two classes; this is known as the prediction stage of the process.

EXPERIMENTATION AND RESULTS

Clone Detection Experiments

For our clone detection experiment, we employed parts of the Columbia Image Splicing Detection Evaluation Dataset (Lab, 2004). In detail, several images of an image block with an entirely homogeneous textured region or homogeneous smooth region from the authentic category are selected as authentic images, and their corresponding manipulated images with an entirely homogeneous textured region or homogeneous smooth region from spliced category are selected as clone images.

We implemented the clone detection method, and used it to detect clone regions in the cloned images. We used $a = 16$ as the block/window size. As the image's size is 128×128, the entire number of blocks is $(128 - 16 + 1)×(128 - 16 + 1)=12769$. All the clone region's size in this data set is 24×128, the number of same/similar block pairs with same pair distance is $(24 - 16 + 1)×(128 - 16 + 1)=1017$. Considering the noise and modification, the threshold is chosen as 500. The clone detection experimental results are shown in Figure 4.

We can see that in the result, the clone region of each cloned image is marked exactly in red, which means that the MRH in clone detection is effective.

Splicing Detection Experiments

For the experiment involving splicing detection, the Columbia Image Splicing Detection Evaluation Dataset (Lab, 2004) is further employed. The dataset is an open data set which includes 1845 image blocks with a fixed size of 128×128 pixels, 933 blocks of them are authentic images, and the remaining 912 blocks are spliced images. In this work, the Columbia Image Splicing Detection Evaluation Dataset is used for the experimental data, part of the set is used as training data, while the remainder is used as test data.

The experimental procedure is shown in Figure 5:

1) Randomly select parts of the spliced image and authentic image to compose a training sample set. The remainder of the images comprises the test sample set.

Figure 4. Experimental results of clone detection: the images in the left-hand column are the authentication images; the images in the middle column are the tampered images; the images in right-hand column are the detection results, the red regions are duplicated regions that have been detected. (The authentication image and tampered image are from Columbia Image Splicing Detection Evaluation Dataset. Used with permission)

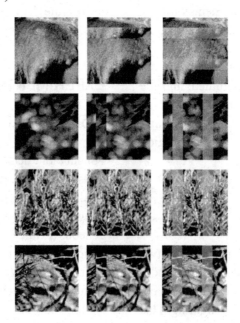

Figure 5. Experimental procedure. The procedure may be repeated several times because the size of the training image set is configurable and the experimental image set is randomly selected from the dataset.

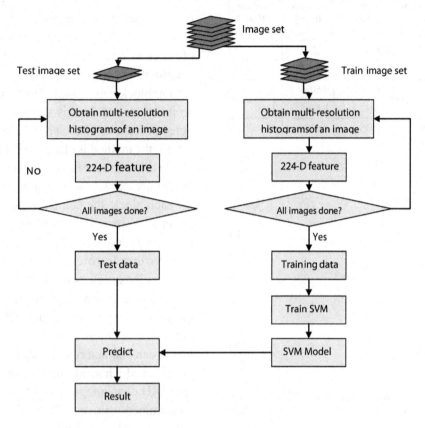

2) Obtain an image from training sample set, +1 denotes an authentic image, -1 denotes a spliced image.

3) Calculate MRH of the image using the procedure described in Section 2. Obtain a 224-D vector as features characterizing the image.

4) Repeat 2) to 4) for each image in the training sample set to obtain their features as training data for SVM.

5) Repeat 2) to 4) for each image in the test sample set to obtain their features.

6) Train the SVM with training data to obtain the SVM model and then use this SVM model to predict test data. The result is recorded.

If p denotes the percentage of training images from the total image set, and Set_A, Set_S denote the authentic image set and spliced image set in the total dataset respectively, then the training image set $Set_{training} = p \cdot (Set_A + Set_S)$, and the test image set $Set_{test} = (1-p) \cdot (Set_A + Set_S)$. The percentage p, which denotes the size of the training image set, may be set several times to generate different results. In this paper, p is set to 60%, 70%, 80%, and 90%. While the training image sample set is randomly selected from the total data set, considering experiment accuracy, the experimental procedure of each p is repeated several times to get average result.

The experimental results are shown in Table 1.

The accuracy mean $M_{accuracy}$, average precision $M_{precision}$, and average recall M_{recall} are slightly modified from the definition given in (TianTsong. Ng, et al., 2004):

Table 1. Experimental results

Ratio for training	Accuracy Mean	Average Precision	Average Recall	Average Time (minutes)
60%	0.5997	0.6184	0.5041	14
70%	0.6129	0.6264	0.5355	13
80%	0.6224	0.6206	0.6026	13
90%	0.6488	0.6447	0.6595	12
Average	0.6210	0.6275	0.5754	13

$$M_{accuracy} = \frac{1}{t} \sum_k \left(N_{S|S}^k + N_{A|A}^k \right) / \left(N_{\bullet|S}^k + N_{\bullet|A}^k \right) \tag{6}$$

$$M_{precision} = \frac{1}{t} \sum_k N_{S|S}^k / N_{S|\bullet}^k \tag{7}$$

$$M_{recall} = \frac{1}{t} \sum_k N_{S|S}^k / N_{\bullet|S}^k \tag{8}$$

where t denotes the computational cost of the experiment, and $0 \le k \le t - 1$. S and A represents Spliced and Authentic images respectively, $\bullet$ represents a Spliced or Authentic image, and $N_{X|Y}^k$ denotes the number of samples Y detected as X in the kth run.

The results closely resemble the experimental results in Ng et al. (2004) with the original feature set. We can see that the test score improves with the increase on the size of the training image set, and a better score is expected if the size of the dataset is large enough. Meanwhile, because of the MRH's simplicity and efficiency which extends from the plain histogram, the experiment's efficiency is high, as one turn of the experiment which includes feature extraction and training the SVM costs no more than 15 minutes. This improves upon the results presented in (Hsu & Chang, 2006).

DISCUSSION

In this paper, we endeavored to use MRH both in clone detection and splicing detection. Detection of the clone operation within an image is done by examining whether there are a number of same/similar block pairs with the same pair distance in an image or not. In this method, MRHs are adopted as features of each block. Because MRH is robust, the method is effective in clone detection. While the number of overlay blocks is great, and the feature extraction procedure must be repeated for each block, the computation complexity can increase. Further study is needed to reduce computational complexity. Further experimentation is required in order to test the robustness with regard to operations such as rotation and compression.

As the detection of splicing between different images is treated as a binary decision problem, there are two important issues: one is the features which can characterize the image; another is the classifier which makes the decision. In this paper, the MRH of an image is adopted as a feature, and then trained using a SVM to detect the splicing operations. Obviously, the criterion of the experimental results is not high, and the best accuracy in the results of the experiment is not higher than 65%. However, the result shows that the score improves with an increase on the size of training image set, especially the average recall. With the MRH's simplicity and efficiency and the use of an SVM tool, the entire experiment's procedure is simple and highly efficient.

Due to the difference between the clone operation and the splicing operation, the prior one is the operation within the same image, and the latter one is the operation between different images, the expectation of each detection method should be different. The clone detection is based on the detection of the existence of a clone region, so the description of the region should be robust; while splicing detection distinguishes authentic images from spliced images, the description of the image should be with more separating capacity. In other words, the features used in clone detection should be more robust, and the feature used in splicing detection should contain more separating capacity. As MRH is a type of robust feature, the use of it in the area of clone detection should be more effective than its use during splicing detection. Our experimental results have proved this.

ACKNOWLEDGMENT

Credit for the use of the Columbia Image Splicing Detection Evaluation Dataset is given to the DVMM Laboratory of Columbia University, CalPhotos Digital Library and the photographers listed in http://www.ee.columbia.edu/ln/dvmm/downloads/AuthSplicedDataSet/photographers.htm. This research was supported by the National Natural Science Foundation of China (Grant No.60803112, Grant No.60873226, and Grant No.60502024); the Electronic Development Fund of Ministry of Information Industry of China (Grant No.[2007]329); the National High Technology Research and Development (863) Program of China (Grant No.2007AA01Z161).

REFERENCES

Chang, C. C., & Lin, C. J. (n.d.). *LIBSVM: A Library for Support Vector Machines*. Retrieved from http://www.csie.ntu.edu.tw/~cjlin/libsvm/index.html

Chen, M., Fridrich, J., Luka, J., & Goljan, M. (2007). *Imaging sensor noise as digital X-ray for revealing forgeries (No. 03029743)*. Berlin: Springer Verlag.

Chen, P.-H., Lin, C.-J., & Scholkopf, B. (2005). A tutorial on v-support vector machines. *Applied Stochastic Models in Business and Industry, 21*(2), 111–136. doi:10.1002/asmb.537

Fridrich, J., Soukal, D., & Lukas, J. (2003). *Detection of copy-move forgery in digital images.* Paper presented at the Digital Forensic Research Workshop, Cleveland, OH.

Gallagher, A. c. (2005). *Detection of linear and cubic interpolation in jpeg compressed images.* Paper presented at the 2nd Canadian Conference Computer and Robot Vision, Victoria, British Columbia, Canada.

Gou, H., Swaminathan, A., & Wu, M. (2007). *Noise features for image tampering detection and steganalysis.* Paper presented at the IEEE International Conference on Image Processing, San Antonio, TX.

Hadjidemetriou, E., Grossberg, M. D., & Nayar, S. K. (2001). Spatial information in multiresolution histograms. In *Proceedings of the 2001 IEEE Computer Society Conference on Computer Vision and Pattern Recognition (CVPR 2001)*, Los Alamitos, CA.

Hadjidemetriou, E., Grossberg, M. D., & Nayar, S. K. (2004). Multiresolution histograms and their use for recognition. *IEEE Transactions on Pattern Analysis and Machine Intelligence, 26*(7), 831–847. doi:10.1109/TPAMI.2004.32

Hsiao, D. Y., & Pei, S. C. (2005). *Detecting digital tampering by blur estimation.* Paper presented at the 1st International Workshop on Systematic Approaches to Digital Forensic Engineering, Taipei, China.

Hsu, Y.-F., & Chang, S.-F. (2006). *Detecting image splicing using geometry invariants and camera characteristics consistency.* Paper presented at the 2006 IEEE International Conference on Multimedia and Expo (ICME 2006), Toronto, ON, Canada.

Huang, H., Guo, W., & Zhang, Y. (2008). *Detection of copy-move forgery in digital images using SIFT algorithm.* Paper presented at the 2008 Pacific-Asia Workshop on Computational Intelligence and Industrial Application (PACIIA 2008), Piscataway, NJ.

Johnson, M. K., & Farid, H. (2005). *Exposing digital forgeries by detecting inconsistencies in lighting*. Paper presented at the ACM Multimedia and Security Workshop, New York.

Johnson, M. K., & Farid, H. (2007). *Exposing digital forgeries through specular highlights on the eye (No. 03029743)*. Berlin: Springer Verlag.

Johnson, M. K., & Farid, H. (2008). *Detecting photographic composites of people (No. 03029743)*. Berlin: Springer Verlag.

Kirchner, M. (2008). Fast and reliable resampling detection by spectral analysis of fixed linear predictor residue. In *Proceedings of the MM and Sec '08 10th ACM Workshop on Multimedia and Security*, Oxford, UK.

Lab, C. D. R. (2004). *Columbia Image Splicing Detection Evaluation Dataset*. Retrieved from http://www.ee.columbia.edu/ln/dvmm/downloads/AuthSplicedDataSet/AuthSplicedDataSet.htm

Li, G., Wu, Q., Tu, D., & Sun, S. (2007). *A sorted neighborhood approach for detecting duplicated regions in image forgeries based on DWT and SVD*. Paper presented at the 2007 International Conference on Multimedia Expo, Piscataway, NJ.

Lin, Z. C., Wang, R. R., Tang, X. O., & Shum, H. Y. (2005). *Detecting doctored images using camera response normality and consistency analysis*. Paper presented at the IEEE Computer Society Conference on Computer Vision and Pattern Recognition, San Diego, CA.

Long, Y. J., & Huang, Y. Z. (2006). *Image based source camera identification using demosaicing*. Paper presented at the 8th Workshop on Multimedia Siganal Processing, Victoria, TX.

Lu, W., Sun, W., Huang, J.-W., & Lu, H.-T. (2008). *Digital image forensics using statistical features and neural network classifier*. Paper presented at the 2008 International Conference on Machine Learning and Cybernetics (ICMLC), Piscataway, NJ.

Lukas, J., Fridrich, J., & Goljan, M. (2006). Digital camera identification from sensor pattern noise. *IEEE Transactions on Information Forensics and Security, 1*(2), 205–214. doi:10.1109/TIFS.2006.873602

Lyu, S., & Farid, H. (2005). How realistic is photorealistic? *IEEE Transactions on Signal Processing, 53*(2), 845–850. doi:10.1109/TSP.2004.839896

Mahdian, B., & Saic, S. (2008). Blind authentication using periodic properties of interpolation. *IEEE Transactions on Information Forensics and Security, 3*(3), 529–538. doi:10.1109/TIFS.2004.924603

Ng, T.-T., Chang, S., & Sun, Q. (2004, May). *Blind Detection of Photomontage Using Higher Order Statistics*. Paper presented at the IEEE International Symposium on Circuits and Systems (ISCAS), Vancouver, Canada.

Popescu, A. C., & Farid, H. (2004). *Exposing Digital Forgeries by Detecting Duplicated Image Regions (Tech. Rep.)*. Hanover, NJ: Dartmouth College, Department of Computer Science.

Popescu, A. C., & Farid, H. (2005). Exposing digital forgeries by detecting traces of re-sampling. *IEEE Transactions on Signal Processing, 53*(2), 758–767. doi:10.1109/TSP.2004.839932

Popescu, A. C., & Farid, H. (2005). Exposing digital forgeries in color filter array interpolated images. *IEEE Transactions on Signal Processing, 53*(10), 3948–3959. doi:10.1109/TSP.2005.855406

Prasad, S., & Ramakrishnan, K. R. (2006). *On resampling detection and its application to image tampering*. Paper presented at the IEEE International Conference Multimedia and Exposition, Toronto, Canada.

Sutcu, Y., Coskun, B., Sencar, H. T., & Memon, N. (2007). Tamper detection based on regularity of wavelet transform coefficients. In *Proceedings of 2007 IEEE International Conference on Image Processing*, San Antonio, TX.

Swaminathan, A., Wu, M., & Liu, K. (2006). *Image tampering identification using blind deconvolution*. Paper presented at the IEEE International Conference on Image Processing, Atlanta.

Tian-Tsong, N., Shih-Fu, C., Jessie, H., Lexing, X., & Mao-Pei, T. (2005). *Physics-motivated features for distinguishing photographic images and computer graphics*. Paper presented at the 13th Annual ACM International Conference on Multimedia, New York.

Zhang, Z., Kang, J., & Ren, Y. (2008). *An effective algorithm of image splicing detection*. Paper presented at the International Conference on Computer Science and Software Engineering (CSSE 2008), Wuhan, Hubei, China.

Zhen, Z., Yukun, B., & Xijian, P. (2008). *Image blind forensics using artificial neural network*. Paper presented at the 2008 International Conference on Computer Science and Software Engineering (CSSE 2008), Piscataway, NJ.

ENDNOTE

[1] Credits for the use of the Columbia Image Splicing Detection Evaluation Dataset are given to the DVMM Laboratory of Columbia University, CalPhotos Digital Library and the photographers listed in http://www.ee.columbia.edu/ln/dvmm/downloads/AuthSplicedDataSet/photographers.htm

This work was previously published in the International Journal of Digital Crime and Forensics, Volume 2, Issue 4, edited by Chang-Tsun Li and Anthony TS Ho, pp. 37-50, copyright 2010 by IGI Publishing (an imprint of IGI Global).

Chapter 12
Digital Image Splicing Using Edges

Jonathan Weir
Queen's University Belfast, UK

Raymond Lau
Queen's University Belfast, UK

WeiQi Yan
Queen's University Belfast, UK

ABSTRACT

In this paper, the authors splice together an image which has been split up on a piece of paper by using duplication detection. The nearest pieces are connected using edge searching and matching and the pieces that have graphics or textures are matched using the edge shape and intersection between the two near pieces. Thus, the initial step is to mark the direction of each piece and put the pieces that have straight edges to the initial position to determine the profile of the whole image. The other image pieces are then fixed into the corresponding position by using the edge information, i.e., shape, residual trace and matching, after duplication or sub-duplication detection. In the following steps, the patches with different edge shapes are searched using edge duplication detection. With the reduction of rest pieces, the montage procedure will become easier and faster.

INTRODUCTION

Image splicing is very similar to jigsaw puzzles which are very widely known and highly popular. Jigsaw puzzles only take shape matching into consideration, the colour and texture information are not fully taken into account. Image splicing is a computational image restoration technique which emphasizes automatic stitching and colour matching.

Image splicing has a very important usage in security. Currently, important documents are split and cut by machines such as shredders. Many of these are only shred into regular shapes, such as identical vertical strips. This presents the possibility of analyzing the strips and potentially reconstructing the original document content. Using automatic image splicing it is possible

DOI: 10.4018/978-1-4666-1758-2.ch012

to solve this problem of shredding, potentially allowing a shredded document to be accurately reconstructed. This provides an opportunity to improve the current splitting and cutting technology which should cut the paper into much smaller sizes. This would encourage the use of cross-shredders within organizations to minimize the risk of information leaking when it comes to document security and destroying certain types of sensitive documentation.

Our proposed scheme is capable of processing a scanned image that has already been segmented into a number of smaller pieces. We use an edge detection algorithm to determine the edges of each of the pieces. Then, based on this edge detection we splice the pieces of the image together to restore the image to its original composition.

The remainder of this paper is set out as follows: Section 2 details the related work; Section 3 outlines our contribution to image splicing; Section 4 presents our experimental results and finally within Section 6 we draw our conclusions.

2 RELATED WORK

One of the most important parts of image splicing and reconstructing images which have been cut into pieces is edge detection. Edge detection techniques proposed by Canny (1986) and Perona and Malik (1990) allow each of the pieces of the split image to be examined. After the edges have been determined, they can be examined and compared. This involves shape and colour matching in order to appropriately reconstruct the image.

Edge detection has been a topic of great discussion, many, including Ziou and Tabbone (1998) have created algorithms and formulas for specific types of edge detection which have varied results depending on the goal of a particular project. Many edge detection algorithms require blurring and differentiating of the image. This makes it difficult to achieve a number of requirements, specifically

for image splicing, where those edges are required to be joined to rebuild the image.

This is where our edge detection software is different from the current tech- techniques, one of which was proposed by Ma and Manjunath (1997). After those edges have been located, they need to be processed in such a way that allows the matching of an edge to its corresponding pair. This is particularly true when it comes to matching colour images which have been split up. Matching the colour edges successfully, previously examined by Mirmehdi and Petrou (2000) and Deng and Manjunath (2001), while correctly splicing the colour image back together is a very important part of our scheme which should require no blurring or altering of the image. This will allow a more accurate reconstruction of the original image.

Ng and Chang (2004) give an account of image splicing. This research area has been taken into account by numerous researchers, however the main focus has been detecting images that have been spliced (Chen et al., 2007; Hsu & Chang, 2006, 2007; Ng et al., 2004; Shi et al., 2007; Zhang et al., 2008) rather than images which have been split up and then trying to reconstruct them using these splicing techniques.

Techniques that are exploited during this splicing detection process are geometry invariants and camera characteristics consistency. These are typically classification problems in which a training set of data is used to guide the detection algorithm in order for it to determine whether an image is an original or whether it has been spliced together. Manual labeling of the image set was required during their tests. This is known as a semi-automatic detection method.

This work presented by Hsu and Chang (2006) places a restriction, such that, an authentic image must originate from a single camera. The technique attempts to find inconsistences which exist between different camera models and therefore make it easier to determine if an image is authentic or not.

Hsu and Chang (2007) then furthered their research by presenting a fully automatic detection method based on consistency checking of camera characteristics among different areas in an image. These different areas are processed and the camera response function is estimated using the geometric invariants from locally planar irradiance points. To classify whether the boundary segment is authentic or spliced, the area intensity features are passed to an SVM classifier, which has an impressive 70% precision and recall statistic.

The most important feature of this scheme is that it is fully passive. No user input or training is required in order to determine the outcome. The results presented show promise in that the classifier is capable of highlighting the image in the correct locations to indicate where its things the image has been spliced.

Ng et al. (2004) illustrate another technique which uses higher order statistics in conjunction with image splicing detection techniques. This technique is also classification based using a Support Vector Machine. The research attempts to examine the properties of biocoherence features on an image set. The results obtained are relatively encouraging and show that using biocoherence feature may be a valid method for detecting image splicing techniques. The accuracy increased in each of the methods presented. However, there are still a few difficulties that appear when using biocoherence. Such as, using a textured image can present problems for the prediction discrepancy features which are less affected by texture.

One of the newest and most up-to-date techniques in splicing detection by Zhang et al. (2008) involves a blind, passive algorithm which effectively detects image splicing. Their proposed technique use multi-size block discrete cosine transformations in combination with image quality metrics which are extracted from a test image. From the results presented, a very high detection rate is achieved using moment features along with image quality metrics. The model that is created is used to extract appropriate features to be used

during the detection process by the algorithm. The key result is that it has a higher detection rate when compared to existing state-of-the-art techniques and it is relatively simple to implement, which is always an important factor.

Different from the previously described work, this paper does not try to detect images which have been spliced together; rather, it attempts to splice the images successfully, in order to reconstruct an original image based on the level of segmentation (Shi & Malik, 2000). This is the main difference between our work and existing techniques. The more highly segmented the image, the harder it is to process. Matching the correct edges can prove to be very challenging when many small pieces of an image are examined. These challenges are outlined in the following sections.

3 CONTRIBUTIONS

Our main contribution within this paper is to successfully reconstruct images which have been split up into smaller pieces. This relies on three main processes, namely accurate edge detection, edge matching and image merging based on edge matching. These processes arrange the pieces in the correct order when it comes to reconstructing the original image. Figure 1 illustrates this process. An explanation of this is presented below.

3.1 Edge Detection

After the system has loaded an image which has already been divided up into a number of pieces, the first thing that must be done is to detect the edges of each of the pieces.

The first problem encountered was how to accurately detect the edges of a black and white image which has been split up unto a number of pieces, specifically textual information. To solve this problem, we used a light blue coloured background, which helped us to differentiate between the correct edges and the background.

Figure 1. Flowchart of the proposed system

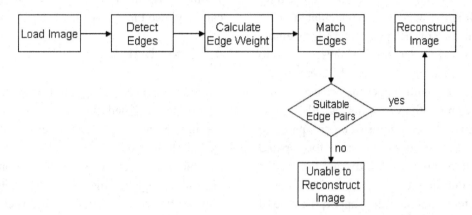

If a white background was used during the edge detection process for a black and white image consisting of text, edge detection becomes problematic. Correctly identifying the white edges of each of the separate pieces of the segmented text is difficult and inefficient. Using this coloured background proved to be more effective.

The same idea was used for colour images. If the edges of the colour pieces contained that same light blue colour, further processing was required. Checks were performed to ensure that any light blue colour found at the edge was actually part of the background. If it wasn't then it should be included as part of the final edge. Figure 2 shows the proposed flowchart for our edge detection.

After the image has been loaded, the background colour is detected. The algorithm scans through the image looking for the longest section of the image which does not contain a light blue

colour. When it finds a section of the image like this, it records its starting point (the upper left hand corner of the section) and processes it vertically to try and obtain the size of the piece. The algorithm then obtains the final bottom right coordinate, which provides the corresponding bounding box for that piece. This bounding box is then recorded in a list and the edges are drawn around this bounding box.

If the entire image has been processed then return all the bounding box coordinates, otherwise go back and process the remainder of the image to get the coordinates of the remaining pieces. Based on these bounding boxes, the side's length of the section is also recorded. We use these boxes and lengths as a measure of the edge weight. The weight for each edge can be calculated by adding all the pixel values together along that edge and then take the average value. So, a number of

Figure 2. Edge detect flowchart

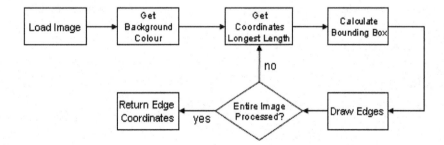

things are taken into consideration when dealing with the weights: edge length (calculated using the bounding box of each piece) and edge weights using the average value. Each of these is used to match corresponding edges from different pieces.

When dealing with images that have been split up digitally and with even splits, calculating the edge weights is very simple when compared to an image which has been physically torn up and scanned into a computer. We discuss these edge weights further in Section 3.2.

Our system does not fully support the type of image reconstruction that involved physically tearing a piece of paper and scanning in those pieces. However uneven digital tears can be detected and spliced using our algorithm. We can successfully detect those uneven digital tears and match those edges correctly. An example of this can be viewed within the results section. The general algorithm can be viewed in Algorithm 1.

3.2 Edge Match

Ordering the pieces is very important. If the pieces cannot be classified and ordered correctly then the image can not be accurately reconstructed by our algorithm.

Once the edges are known, the reconstruction algorithm analyzes the edges in order to place them correctly on the final reconstructed image. The edge matching function takes the edges and compares with other edges of similar size. The highest ranked edges are the ones which belong together and are therefore ordered next to each other. If suitable matches cannot be obtained for

Algorithm 1. The edge detection algorithm

```
Input: Image I with segmented pieces
Output: Image with detected edges I`
begin
    L ← I.getLength();
    W ← I.getWidth();
    B ←I.getBackgroundColour();
    // Locate the first piece and draw BoundingBox;
    for i in L do
        for j in W do
            if I[i,j] != B then
                upperLeft ← I[i,j];
            end
        end
    end
    // Process remainder of located piece; R ← processRemainder(I[i,j], up-
perLeft);
    rL ← R.getLength();
    rW ← R.getWidth();
    lowerRight ← R[rL,rW];
    I`  ← I.drawBBox(upperLeft, lowerRight);
    return I`
end
```

all the edges, the algorithm cannot successfully reconstruct the original image.

It must also be possible to detect each of the corners along with the top, bottom, left and right hand side edges. Typically, pieces of the image which have been split up can be one of three different types. Firstly a corner piece. These pieces will usually have two edges that do not match any other edges. In ideal circumstances, there will be four of these pieces. It is possible to use a corner detection algorithm such as the Harris & Stephen /Plessey corner detection algorithm (Equation 1):

$$S(x,y) = \sum_u \sum_v w(u,v)(I(u,v) - I(u+x,v+y))^2$$

(1)

where I is the image which has been split into a number of pieces, (u,v) is the area of the image and (x,y) are the shift coordinates. S is the weighted sum of square difference between the two coordinates. A corner is characterized by a large variation of S in all directions of the vector $(x\ y)$.

Secondly, there are pieces which will have one edge that has no match. These pieces make up the top, bottom, left, or right side of the image. Finally, there are pieces which will have matches on all four edges, these pieces make up the centre sections of the image and are surrounded by other pieces. Figure 3 illustrates this in the form of a flowchart.

As mentioned previously, we get part of the edge weight from the bounding box of each of the pieces which have been detected. Along with that, the length of each edge can be calculated. After each of these details is calculated we can then compare them against the others.

During the "Compare Pieces" step in Figure 3, depending on how many overall pieces there are that make up the image, many of the pieces can be quickly grouped with their corresponding pieces based purely on the length of their sides. We get this length measurement from the coordinates of that piece's bounding box.

The remaining pieces are then examined based on their edge pixel values and a threshold which can be used to further group the corners, sides and centre pieces. We then count the number of matches which occur and store these matches with each of the pieces. If two side matches occur in a piece then it is a corner piece. Three matches indicate a side or edge piece and four matches would indicate a centre piece. After we obtain this data we can begin the image merge which attempts to splice together all of the pieces based on the retrieved data.

Matches are different from weights in that the weights are used to calculate the number of matches each side has. The matches are then used to assist the placement of the pieces during the image merge process.

Figure 3. Edge match flowchart

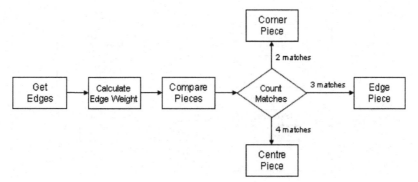

Edge matching can determine correctly, each and every piece it has to deal with. However, it does not take into consideration missing pieces which make up part of a centre piece. The reason for this is that each image has a potentially unknown number of pieces which could be used as a centre piece. Therefore it does not make a note of this type of piece or how many there are. The same applies for side pieces.

The only type of piece the algorithm accounts for is the corner piece. Every image will have at least two corner pieces (for images that have been cut in two) or at most four, which takes into account those images that have been segmented into many pieces.

3.3 Image Merge

After the correct order has been established and it has been determined that suitable edges are available, the pieces of the image are spliced together to re- construct the original image. The process is shown in Figure 4.

Firstly the edge match information is collected. The information is determined by whether the piece corresponds to a corner piece, side piece or centre piece. After each of the corner pieces has been resolved, they can be placed by the algorithm. In this particular case we are not dealing with rotation, therefore each piece will have two unmatched edges. This means placement is very simple. A piece with no top and left edge

match is placed in the upper left hand side of the reconstructed image. This process continues until each of the corner pieces has been placed. If no more pieces remain, then the image has been reconstructed, otherwise continue processing further in order to correctly and accurately place the remaining pieces.

The side edges can be placed next. The placement can be worked out based on the side of the piece which has no match. If more than one piece has the same unmatched edge, then each piece must then be ordered based on its matches with the surrounding pieces. This allows us to correctly arrange the side pieces. If no more side pieces exist, the image is reconstructed.

If more pieces remain, the centre pieces will have to be matched. These matches are based on their edge weight, edge length and a threshold against the other pieces which have already been placed and still have unmatched sides. After this final process the image should be fully reconstructed. Algorithm 2 shows a general overview of what happens during the image merge processing step.

4 RESULTS

Figure 5 highlights the process of loading an image into our application which has been split up into a number of pieces. These pieces then have the edge detection algorithm run on them. After edge detection, the digital image splicing application

Figure 4. Image merge flowchart

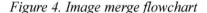

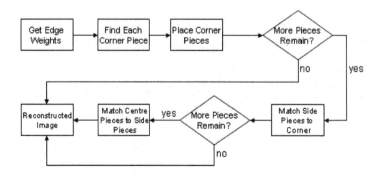

Algorithm 2. The edge merge algorithm

```
Input: Image with weighted edges I
Output: Reconstructed original image I`
    Begin
    // Get array W of coordinates and edge matches of each
    // piece.;
    W ← I.getData();
    for i in W.length() do
        matches ← W[i].getMatches();
        coords ← W[i].getCoords();
        if matches = 2 then
            c ← detectCorners(coords);
            placeCorners(I` , c);
        end
        else if matches = 3 then
            s ← detectSides(coords);
            placeSides(I` , s);
        end
        else
            m ← matchWeights(coords);
            placePieces(I` , m);
        end
    end
    return I`
end
```

can rebuild the original image. The edges are drawn on with a red border. In this simple case, only one edge is required to be matched as the original image has been split into two pieces. More results are presented below with more complex requirements placed upon the reconstruction method.

Figure 6 illustrates the results of the complete process running on a black and white image and a colour image. Detecting the text edges, especially on a black and white image is very challenging. This is due to the fact that after the black and white text has been split, working out the correct boundaries for the text is difficult due to the white background which is typically used to place the pieces onto. A suitable background colour had to be chosen, which helps with the accuracy of the edge detection. In Figure 6(d) the

same colour image is used again, but this time it has been split up into four pieces, this requires more processing and shows that the algorithm is capable of matching many pieces and can correctly splice them together.

Figure 7 shows a completed detection process on the original image which is visible in Figure 6 (d). This image has been split into ten pieces, and illustrates the detection process working on a split image which has all three types of edges that are required to be matched: corner, side and centre. After successful detection, the reconstructed result is identical to that of Figure 6 (d).

Figure 8 depicts the edge detection algorithm working on an uneven digital tear along the top right hand corner of an image. The edges have been marked in red and the process is part of the

Figure 5. The proposed system detecting the edges and splicing the image together

(a) Detect the edges.

(b) Merging progress status.

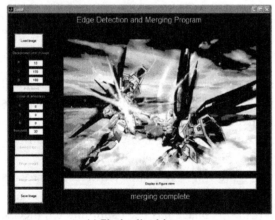

(c) Final spliced image.

way through the final merging process. Currently, only corners of an image which have been torn unevenly can be detected and reconstructed using our system, more experimentation is required in order to fully reconstruct images which have been torn up into many pieces and scanned into the computer. The reason this is more challenging is due to the extra residual marks and paper fragments which are scanned into the computer along with the main body of the document or image after the original document has been torn up.

5 COMPLEXITY ANALYSIS

The complexity of our algorithm can be examined in a number of ways. Each of the steps involved carries its own level of complexity. The ideal algorithm should be as low in complexity as possible. This helps to reduce the overall computation involved in reconstructing the images which have been split.

Our edge detection process is relatively uncomplex and efficient. This is down to the unique background colour which is chosen. Drawing bounding boxes around the edges in order to segment the pieces is a fast procedure. There are many fast edge detection algorithms available, for example, the method pro- posed by Qu et al. (2005) which involve the combination of Zernike moments

with Sobel operators. When given a segmented image, the edge detection step completes almost instantaneously whenever it is invoked. This is also true for the digital tears which were created for the uneven edge detection processing.

The next stage of complexity within our algorithm appears within the edge matching stage. This stage involves a number of steps in order to correctly match each of the pieces that have been segmented via the edge detection step. Each of the edge detected segments are taken and their edge weights are calculated and stored. These edge weights are used to match corresponding edges. Due the way each edge will have its own weight, some complexity exists in that each piece must be checked separately along each edge. This is by far the most complex step in our algorithm.

Firstly, each of the edge weights are calculated and stored for each segmented piece. Then, each

Figure 6. Splicing black and white and colour images

(a) Split text.

(b) Text reconstruction.

(c) Split colour image.

(d) Colour image reconstruction

Figure 7. All three types of edge detection: corner, side and centre

Figure 8. Edge detection and splicing on uneven tears

(a) Detecting uneven edge tears.

(b) Spliced image after detection.

of these weights is checked against the others in order to determine their corresponding pieces (if they exist). Based on the returned data, the corresponding pieces can be correctly arranged and those which do not return any matches along parts of their edges are typically edge pieces in the final reconstructed image. No image merging or joining is done in this step. This step obtains all the relevant data and organizes it. This is why it is the most intensive and complex part of the overall algorithm.

The image merging algorithm takes this relevant data from the edge matching step and processes it. This processing is relatively trivial and can be performed very efficiently on modest hardware. It takes the data and calculates the length and width of the final image and creates a temporary image of this size. The algorithm then goes through each of the data sets and places the pieces according to its order. The algorithm starts from the origin (top left corner of the image) and pastes the corresponding pieces into place. The pieces are placed from left to right, row by row. The overall complexity as stated is low, but processing time increases depending on the size of the final reconstructed image. The images we used in our testing where 651×429 and 535×650 and to reconstruct each of them took less than half a second on a 1.8GHz Celeron processor with 512MB RAM.

Based on the above analysis, it is clear that the most complex and also the most important part of the overall algorithm lies with the edge matching step. This is an area which would require further improvement in terms of processing time. Reducing this algorithm overall complexity while also improving results would be a very worthwhile extension. Adaption should also be considered for dealing with rotation and skewing which occurs when dealing with scanned doc- uments.

6 CONCLUSION

Overall the system performs very well with images that have been chopped up using a digital edge cutting technique. Many more aspects have to be taken into consideration when performing image merging, such as location of the pieces and edge detection information, especially when dealing with simple black and white or colour images.

The reconstruction algorithm works very well as can be seen from the results. However, further work is required in order to make this type of application more useful. Such as being able to detect uneven physical tears that could be made in pieces of paper, or after shredding.

Another area which should also be examined further is alignment. No rotation is required by any of the sample images we have processed in this paper. If someone was to scan in a torn up photograph, rotation of those pieces would definitely be required. Tearing a piece of paper also leads to unmatched colours when reconstruction of the image takes place. Currently the colours are required for matching. Thresholds could therefore be used to improve this scheme further.

As a final thought, when dealing with real pieces of paper which have been torn up and the task of reconstructing them accurately is required, one should think about using image inpainting (Bertalmio et al., 2000) in order to achieve this. Inpainting can help to reduce the noticeable tear marks which will inevitably show up between each section when the original image has been reconstructed. Automatically applying this inpainting process could be achieved when it comes to joining the torn edges together. A white line could be drawn between each of the joined edges, allowing the inpainting algorithm to run on the reconstructed image.

REFERENCES

Bertalmio, M., Sapiro, G., Caselles, V., & Ballester, C. (2000). Image in- painting. In *Proceedings of SIGGRAPH, 00*, 417–424.

Canny, J. (1986). A computational approach to edge detection. *IEEE Transactions on Pattern Analysis and Machine Intelligence, 8*(6), 679–698. doi:10.1109/TPAMI.1986.4767851

Chen, W., Shi, Y. Q., & Su, W. (2007). Image splicing detection using 2-d phase congruency and statistical moments of characteristic function. In *Proceedings of SPIE* (Vol. 6505). Retrieved from http://link.aip.org/link/?PSI/6505/65050R/1

Deng, Y., & Manjunath, B. (2001). Unsupervised segmentation of color-texture regions in images and video. *IEEE Transactions on Pattern Analysis and Machine Intelligence, 23*(8), 800–810. doi:10.1109/34.946985

Hsu, Y.-F., & Chang, S.-F. (2006). Detecting image splicing using geometry in-variants and camera characteristics consistency. In *Proceedings of the IEEE International Conference on Multimedia and Expo* (pp. 549-552).

Hsu, Y.-F., & Chang, S.-F. (2007). Image splicing detection using camera re-sponse function consistency and automatic segmentation. In *Proceedings of the ICME, 07,* 28–31.

Ma, W., & Manjunath, B. (1997). Edge flow: A framework of boundary detection and image segmentation. In *Proceedings of the Computer Vision and Pattern Recognition* (pp. 744-749). Washington, DC: IEEE Computer Society.

Mirmehdi, M., & Petrou, M. (2000). Segmentation of color textures. *IEEE Transactions on Pattern Analysis and Machine Intelligence, 22*(2), 142-159. Ng, T.-T., & Chang, S.-F. (2004). A model for image splicing. In *Proceedings of ICIP '04* (Vol. 2, pp. 1169-1172).

Ng, T.-T., Chang, S.-F., & Sun, Q. (2004). Blind detection of photomontage using higher order statistics. In *Proceedings of the 2004 International Symposium on Circuits and Systems (ISCAS '04)* (Vol. 5, pp. 688-691).

Perona, P., & Malik, J. (1990). Scale-space and edge detection using anisotropic diffusion. *IEEE Transactions on Pattern Analysis and Machine Intelligence, 12*(7), 629–639. doi:10.1109/34.56205

Qu, Y.-D., Cui, C.-S., Chen, S.-B., & Li, J.-Q. (2005). A fast subpixel edge detection method using sobel-zernike moments operator. *Image and Vision Computing, 23*(1), 11–17. Retrieved from http://www.sciencedirect.com/science/article/B6V09-4DH2JHD-4/2/40fc4241382dabeefa9b1576076ae87a. doi:10.1016/j.imavis.2004.07.003

Shi, J., & Malik, J. (2000). Normalized cuts and image segmentation. *IEEE Transactions on Pattern Analysis and Machine Intelligence, 22*(8), 888–905. doi:10.1109/34.868688

Shi, Y. Q., Chen, C., & Chen, W. (2007). A natural image model approach to splicing detection. In *Proceedings of the Workshop on Multimedia & Security '07* (pp. 51-62). New York: ACM.

Zhang, Z., Kang, J., & Ren, Y. (2008). An effective algorithm of image splic- ing detection. In *Proceedings of the International Conference on Computer Science and Software Engineering, 1,* 1035–1039.

Ziou, D., & Tabbone, S. (1998). Edge Detection Techniques-An Overview. *Pattern Recognition & Image Analysis, 8,* 537-559. Retrieved from http://hal.inria.fr/inria-00098446/en/

This work was previously published in the International Journal of Digital Crime and Forensics, Volume 2, Issue 4, edited by Chang-Tsun Li and Anthony TS Ho, pp. 63-75, copyright 2010 by IGI Publishing (an imprint of IGI Global).

Chapter 13
A Biologically Inspired Smart Camera for Use in Surveillance Applications

Kosta Haltis
University of Adelaide, Australia

Matthew Sorell
University of Adelaide, Australia

Russell Brinkworth
University of Adelaide, Australia

ABSTRACT

Biological vision systems are capable of discerning detail as well as detecting objects and motion in a wide range of highly variable lighting conditions that proves challenging to traditional cameras. In this paper, the authors describe the real-time implementation of a biological vision model using a high dynamic range video camera and a General Purpose Graphics Processing Unit. The effectiveness of this implementation is demonstrated in two surveillance applications: dynamic equalization of contrast for improved recognition of scene detail and the use of biologically-inspired motion processing for the detection of small or distant moving objects in a complex scene. A system based on this prototype could improve surveillance capability in any number of difficult situations.

INTRODUCTION

Flying insects have extraordinary visual capabilities that allow them to navigate in cluttered environments without collisions, perform spectacular aerobatic manoeuvres (Land & Collett, 1974) and discriminate the motion of visual targets camou-

flaged within complex background textures (*visual clutter*) (Nordström, Barnett, & O'Carroll, 2006). These are all challenging tasks for artificial vision systems that have attracted substantial attention from scientists and engineers.

One such challenge is discerning detail in scenes with widely varying lighting levels, given that typically only 8-bit (256 level) luminance is usually available in digital imaging despite the

DOI: 10.4018/978-1-4666-1758-2.ch013

huge range of possible luminance levels that natural lighting conditions provide (range in the order of 10⁸) (Brinkworth, Mah, & O'Carroll, 2007). This presents itself as a limitation on the information content, by which we mean, specifically, the ability to distinguish objects within a scene under difficult lighting conditions. Many conventional camera systems tend to have poor performance when capturing images of scenes with complex lighting conditions. As illustrated in Figure 1 traditional camera systems tend to either struggle to capture details in the darkest or brightest parts of the scene, and occasionally in both. The reason for this is that these conventional cameras generally use a relatively simple global adjustment to the luminance on each frame as a whole, in an attempt to improve the final image output quality. However, in some cases the resulting image quality is poor due to a compromise needing to be reached between information in the bright and dark areas.

High dynamic range (HDR) imaging processes allow capture over a much larger luminance range than traditional low dynamic range (LDR or 8-bit), however such images are not supported by the majority of image display and storage media (Seetzen et al., 2004). There are conven-

tional engineering solutions, such as gamma correction and tone mapping (Pattanaik & Yee, 2002; Reinhard, Stark, Shirley, & Ferwerda, 2002), however they tend to be focused on maintaining the psychophysical look of an image to a human observer rather than maximising the information contained within the scene. There are also custom CMOS sensors (Pixim, 2006) that approach the problem differently. By using a different integration time (shutter speed) for every pixel in the image they compress the image before it leaves the camera. This means it is possible to capture information from both the dark and light parts of a scene in a low dynamic range format that is more suitable for transmission, storage and display. While this approach can result in an improvement in the information content in a captured scene it is only part of the solution that exists in biology.

Here we consider a biologically-inspired approach based on photoreceptor cells, whose purpose is precisely luminance range compression (Laughlin & Weckström, 1993) while maintaining information content. As with the custom sensors by Pixim the integration time of each receptor in biological eyes does change (Payne & Howard, 1981) independently of the global illumination

Figure 1. Images captured with a conventional camera using different exposure settings and global gain adjustments. Left) short exposure time which lets the bright background be seen but misses the darker foreground. Right) long exposure time which over-exposes the background saturating it and resulting in a loss of information, however more foreground detail is present. Traditionally camera operators had to decide which one of these modes they would operate in due to the limitations of the image capturing and processing technology.

(Matic & Laughlin, 1981); a large number of cascaded non-linear adaptive processes also occur in order to maximise the information content and reduce the bandwidth of the signal (de Ruyter van Steveninck & Laughlin, 1996; Laughlin, de Ruyter van Steveninck, & Anderson, 1998).

In a previous paper we have shown how such a bioinspired model of image processing can be constructed in analogue hardware by building a single pixel demonstration (Mah, Brinkworth, & O'Carroll, 2008). This paper follows on by presenting a system, based on digital software, which allows for a biomimetic model of the photoreceptor processing operations to be carried out on images captured by a HDR video camera. While the photoreceptor model is well suited to parallel computation it is computationally expensive in a conventional serial computing environment. The model has therefore been implemented on a General Purpose computing Graphics Processing Unit (GPGPU). This allows the model to be applied to HDR images and the resulting images displayed in real-time (25-30 frames/s).

A user study has been performed to explore the performance of the photoreceptor HDR compression technique against typical linear scaling of the luminance range and subsequent gamma adjustment for display. This study concluded that the photoreceptor model is consistently able to retain equal or greater information content of scene through the biologically inspired range compression technique, and is particularly useful under complex lighting conditions.

This system has the potential for application within military and consumer imaging systems including surveillance, target detection, security monitoring, and face and text recognition software.

SPATIAL AND TEMPORAL IMAGE PROCESSING

Spatial image processing is a form of processing performed on each pixel based on surrounding pixels of the same image. For HDR images, some spatial processing techniques that are used include tone mapping and gamma correction.

"Tone mapping" is a technique that is used to map a set of colours to another set. This is useful when attempting to perform dynamic range compression (Ashikhmin, 2002) because it allows us to map a larger dynamic range of colours to a standard 8-bit range of colours, effectively reducing the dynamic range of the image. Tone mapping comes in two main types: global and local. Global processing is faster, as the same non-linear scaling is applied to all pixels, but has limited success in reproducing subtle contrast boundaries between objects. Local processing is better at maintaining contrast boundaries, by applying a form of edge enhancement or high-pass filtering, but often at the expense of global contrast.

"Gamma Correction" is a nonlinear operation used to increase the dynamic range of the luminance of pixels within an image (Sato, 2006). A simple format of a gamma correction encoding is power encoding, which takes the form shown in Equation 1. This function is generally used with a gamma value 2 - 2.4 for gamma correction prior to displaying images on a computer monitor.

$$V_{out} = V_{in}^{1/\gamma} \qquad (1)$$

The results of post captured image stitching with spatial processing applied on a couple of image can be seen in Figure 2. The stitching and image processing was applied using a software package called QTPFSGUI (http://qtpfsgui. sourceforge.net/). Using an algorithm similar to that proposed by Debevec and Malik (1997) this program generated a HDR image by combining the data from the two LDR images (left of Figure 2) based on the exposure values of these images and correcting for the non-linear performance of the camera. Once this was done, some simple gamma correction and tone mapping was performed using

Figure 2. A high dynamic range image created by stitching together two low dynamic range images (left) together and then gamma correcting and tone mapping to create an image with an improved 8-bit representation (right). The reconstructed high dynamic range image allows more detail to be seen in the foreground and background than either of the individual images on the left.

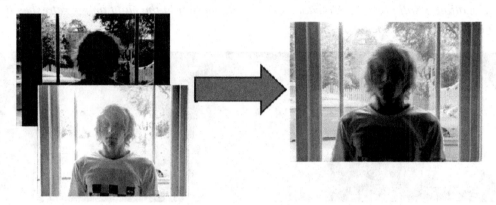

this same software package to improve the 8-bit representation of the image on the display medium.

In terms of image quality, spatial image processing performs very well for images with both moving and stationary scenes. However, it requires largely iterative, and sometimes complex, calculations that depend on all surrounding pixels within the frame. This would make it difficult to perform real-time image processing on video footage using these techniques, especially if the frame resolution is large.

Temporal processing is the action of processing a pixel's new data value based on its previous states in time (that is, previous frames of a video sequence). Pure temporal image processing requires no knowledge of the surrounding pixels, and utilises the temporal characteristics for moving images for the processing.

The issue with temporal systems that utilise some form of high-pass filtering is that if there is no movement of an object within an image the object will slowly fade to become less distinguishable from surrounding objects. Hence, the only way to constantly see detail in stationary objects is to continuously move the camera, as seen in Figure 3. In biological eyes this constant motion is called micro-saccades and is the reason stationary objects can be seen. However in the context

of security the relative amplification of moving objects is a form of salience enhancement, as non-moving objects are less likely to be relevant or contain new information.

BIO-INSPIRED IMAGE PROCESSING

While biological vision systems vary in complexity and capability, our interest is in insect vision, which can be modelled in three primary stages - Photoreceptors, Lamina Monopolar Cells, and Motion Processing.

Photoreceptors receive light through the optical system of the eye, applying non-linear dynamic range compression to achieve a high dynamic range of optical luminance. Each photoreceptor is equivalent to a single pixel in the image and they act independently (temporal processing only) (Matic & Laughlin, 1981; Payne & Howard, 1981) as discussed in more detail below.

Lamina Monopolar Cells in insects remove redundancy in both space and time in an optimal way based on the local light level (van Hateren, 1992). Processing steps include variable and relaxed high-pass filtering (some DC component still included in signal) in both space and time depending on light levels (Juusola, Uusitalo, &

Figure 3. Left) raw, unprocessed image. Middle) snapshot in time after the camera had been stationary for several seconds. Right) snapshot in time during slow movement of the camera. The raw image has a section of pixels that are saturated, hence no identification of the cards is possible. The relaxed high-pass filtering of the temporal processing has caused the detail in the stationary scene to be reduced but card identification is still possible. Constant small-scale motion in the right image refreshes the detail making it easier to resolve the details in the scene.

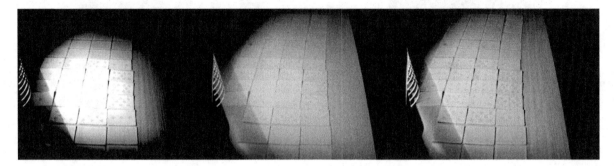

Weckstrom, 1995), signal amplification and a saturating non-linearity. The end result, as seen in Figure 4, highlights edges and areas of relative movement.

Motion Processing is used to calculate the motion of every pixel relative to the camera. This is modelled by the so-called Hassenstein-Reichardt Correlator (Hassenstein & Reichardt, 1956), which compares a pixel with a delayed signal from other surrounding pixels. This is done via a non-linear multiplicative interaction between the two channels. This motion calculation relative to

Figure 4. Left) single frame after simulated photoreceptor processing, notice how information is retained in both the bright (outside the window) and dark (foreground) sections of the scene. Right) output of simulated lamina monopolar cell stage processing, which highlights the contrasting boundaries between objects in the scene. The scene was rapidly moved slightly left and right to simulate micro-saccades normally present in biological eyes.

the visual system can then be used to perform velocity estimation of object within the field of view.

Photoreceptors

The photoreceptors provide the first stage of processing for the biological visual system. They are responsible for dynamic range reduction of the input images. In an attempt to improve the information content of the output photoreceptors utilise non-linear adaptation in order to encode a much larger dynamic range than could be done with a linear system (Mah et al., 2008). Photoreceptors dynamically adjust the dark and bright areas of the images independently through temporal pixelwise operations. The dark pixels are brightened and the bright pixels are darkened to equalize the luminance throughout the whole image, hence reducing the dynamic range of the image.

A model for biological photoreceptors, which can be seen in Figure 5, was proposed by Mah et al. (2008) as an extended version of the model by van Hateren and Snippe (2001). This photoreceptor model has been shown to closely resemble the system response of the fly's visual system and has good results on improving the information content of images under realistic operating conditions (Brinkworth, Mah, Gray, & O'Carroll, 2008). The model can be broken down into 4 individual stages:

- **Stage 1** is a low-pass filter (LPF) with variable gain and corner frequency, to model varying adaptation speeds in different lighting conditions, acting to increase the

Figure 5. Photoreceptor model block diagram and typical step responses of the model. Computation of each stage as per text. Impulse responses became larger and slower (longer time constant) as the background illumination decreased, much like the response of a traditional camera but independent for every pixel. The step responses show the difference between a biologically recorded neuron (Brinkworth et al., 2008) and the model with the two main stages of adaptation, short and mid-term, clearly present. The log-linear response of the system over a number of decades of luminance together with the soft saturation is also the same as seen in biology (Mah et al., 2008).

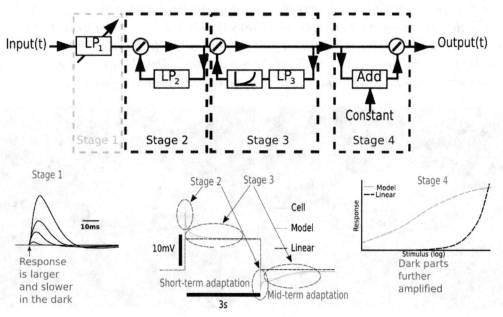

information captured over a wide range of light intensities by reducing the gain, and increasing the corner frequency, as intensity increases.

- **Stage 2** is a non-linear divisive feedback via a LPF, providing rapid short-term adaptation of the photoreceptor response to variations in light intensity through logarithmic compression of the input. The temporal properties cause a form of relaxed high-pass filtering where changes in intensity are amplified.

- **Stage 3** is an exponential divisive feedback loop via a LPF. This stage is responsible for shifting the operating range of the model. The LPF in this stage provides slow adaptation for longer-term adaptation of the system to variations in light intensities.

- **Stage 4** is a Naka-Rushton transformation, where a constant is added to the input and the result used in a divisive feed forward operation. This stage provides a final non-linear static gain control for further amplification to the darker parts of the image.

The result of the full photoreceptor system is to compress the image from high dynamic range to a low dynamic range, by way of independent pixel gain control. This compression system also enhances the useful information capture in the process.

The full system effectively provides an approximate form of relaxed high-pass filtering. The effect is that areas of change are emphasised with greater detail, while temporally stationary objects, such as background regions, fade as the variable gain of the system reaches steady state. Hence, the system is effective in scenes of temporal variations such as local or object movement, or through the use of saccadic like motion of the image capture device.

This temporal processing of the photoreceptors has useful advantages over processing that is only spatial as the photoreceptors makes use of frame history to further improve images. Some improvements include reducing noise and filling in data that may be missing in any one frame of the image stream. An example of the output of the photoreceptor model from a real-world implementation can be seen in Figure 6.

Figure 6. Left) raw image and Right) improved detail after photoreceptor processing. Images were captured at night by a high dynamic range camera from the backseat of a moving car with a spot-light trained to illuminate the scene. The raw image had a global gain selected that caused the mean value (after gamma correction) to be in the middle of the output range. Details of the car number plate are saturated in the raw view however identification is much easier if photoreceptor processing is applied.

IMPLEMENTATION

The key opportunity for implementation of the proposed biologically-inspired vision system was the recognition that pixel-wise image processing could be computed in parallel using a parallel processing system designed for such graphics applications. The objective was to achieve real-time processing at the full image resolution (640 by 480 pixels) at full frame rate (25 or 30 full frames per second).

High Dynamic Range Camera

HDR images can be created using a technique called "image stitching" or through Analogue-to-Digital Conversion (ADC) techniques. State-of-the-art High Dynamic Range cameras incorporate true 12-bit sensor with a 12-bit linear AD convertor, providing a dynamic range of 4096:1 (72dB) from a single shot. There are also many cheaper cameras that state that they have an image sensor that can capture greater than 8-bit, however, many of the additional captured bits contain significant amounts of noise; hence the true useful dynamic range of the sensor may be lower than stated (Motion-Video-Products, 2009).

Image Stitching involves using multiple images of ideally the same frame at different exposure settings to generate a higher dynamic range for all pixels within the image. This technique uses these multiple images to generate HDR layers. Stitching may be performed on the images taken at different shutter speeds with software after transferring them to a computer system, or in some cases within the camera's firmware. For image stitching to be possible with a video camera, the camera must be able to capture two or more frames at different exposure settings per actual high dynamic range frame, and hence must be capable of considerably high frame rates.

The camera used in this work was the A601f-HDR (Basler). This camera was able to capture multiply images at different shutter speeds, combine them in the camera and produce high quality 16-bit HDR images through image stitching on-chip post capture at a rate of 25 frames/s and a resolution of 656x491 pixels. This visual information was then transferred via FireWire (IEEE1394a) to a computer in uncompressed format for software capture and post-processing.

General Purpose Graphics Processing Unit

A General Purpose computing Graphics Processing Unit (GPGPU) is a multi-processing core unit designed for computing many parallel, pipelined and often identical processes on very large segmented data sets. As the photoreceptor model fits this description precisely, it was an obvious candidate for GPGPU implementation, especially as the software-only implementation on a dual-core Pentium processor only achieved frame rates in the order of 10 frames per second.

A GeForce 8800 GT (NVIDIA) processor was used for all GPU related processing requirements in our work, although any compatible GPGPU could be substituted (NVIDIA, 2008). These processing cards are now quite cheap and are widely used for graphics-intensive applications such as video game play.

The GPGPU supported 14 multiprocessor blocks, each with 8 cores, representing a total of 112 processing cores. Each core was clocked at 600MHz, had local access to cache memory and registers and global access to 512MB of memory. The global memory was accessible by the host CPU and has a transfer bandwidth of 57.6Gbit/s, more than sufficient to hold temporary frame data for real-time processing. The GPGPU operated as a co-processor, allowing parallel CPU management of data processing while the GPGPU implemented the photoreceptor model in parallel.

Software Design, Implementation and Bottlenecks

The chosen design approach for this software was to optimize it as a multi-threaded application to ensure maximum parallel processing performance. This ensured that, provided there was enough processing capacity to execute all threads, the frame-rate performance of the system was limited by the thread which took the longest to complete processing each frame.

The software used a production-line approach with each stage on the production line serving a specific purpose, and executing independently from each other. The threads and their order of execution on an image can be seen in Figure 7. In addition to these threads, there was the menu thread which runs along independently to handle all user input throughout the setup and processing. And lastly, there was a single main thread which controlled the execution of all other threads.

To handle streaming footage, image buffers were used between all adjacent threads to provide a means of allowing continuous operation of threads with minimal jitter. The buffer sizes were kept large enough to allow jitter free operation but not too large so the end-to-end delay of the images, from capture to display, was not too unreasonable. For this reason, buffers would only hold at most 2 frames for live camera streaming footage and 5 frames for pre-recorded footage. The end-to-end delay of the software on our test system was typically less than 60ms (including overheads) if Sobel Edge Detection (basic approximation of lamina monopolar cell processing in space) was disabled. With all threads enabled, end-to-end delay increased to <130ms (including overheads). The frame-rate was limited only by the slowest thread. This translated to more than 55fps if only the GPGPU-based photoreceptor model was implemented, or approximately 12fps with CPU-based Sobel Edge Detection enabled. Note that on our dual-core system, there was still

Figure 7. The software thread design and implementation that was used to allow multi-threaded optimized execution. The circles represent the independent threads and their typical execution time per frame is under the thread name within the circle. The arrows represent the direction that frame data travels between threads via the use of frame buffers. Processed Edge refers to optional Sobel edge detection on either the raw or (photoreceptor) processed images.

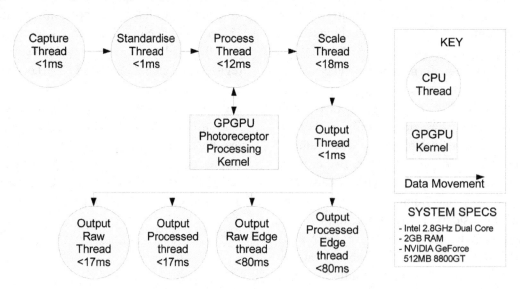

CPU processing capacity to spare. This indicated that additional threads could be implemented and executed in parallel with existing threads, with the possibility of maintaining or even improving the overall frame rate performance.

Applications and Performance Evaluation

Although there are many metrics of the efficacy of a surveillance camera, system or network, the ability to recognize objects and detail, and the ability to automatically detect motion are of particular interest and relevance in the case of surveillance applications of the described visual processing system. We therefore conducted an objective test to demonstrate the effectiveness of the photoreceptor-based processing for detail recognition, and a demonstration of the full model for motion detection of small objects in the field of view.

The first demonstration has direct applications in such areas as number plate pre-processing for automatic or manual character recognition and the identification of other objects under complex lighting conditions; the second demonstrates the ability to pick out moving objects such as aircraft in the sky or people walking across a cluttered background.

Object and Detail Recognition

A test was conceived to compare the effectiveness of an 8-bit representation of an unprocessed video stream (except for global brightness control) with the photoreceptor based processing model for the application of detail recognition through the use of playing cards. Under complex lighting conditions of bright and dark areas with various levels of reflection, it is often difficult to determine the suit and the number of objects on a card, making cards a suitable basis for testing.

Five image streams were captured using these playing cards. Each contained a different set up in terms of lighting conditions, the types of cards used, and the way in which they were displayed. The true configuration of the experiment was noted separately for comparison purposes.

Both the conventionally processed and the photoreceptor-processed image streams were saved as 8-bit JPG images and compiled into 10 individual tests (5 for each processing method). These images were then shown to a variety of people on different days, where they were asked to write down the card numbers and suits in the order that they were displayed in the images. These results were quantified to provide a measure of the efficacy of the processing for detail recognition.

Of the five sets, two resulted in 100% recognition under both unprocessed and processed conditions, and so were discarded. The fifth test included cards that were too far away to clearly identify the faces even under optimal lighting conditions due to the low resolution of the card features, and so are also not considered here. Of the two tests with meaningful results, Test 1 consisted of 20 trials and Test 2 of 40 trials, namely the identification of the correct suit and number of 20 cards as in Figure 8.

As the images were available as a sequence of frames, subjects were permitted to work back and forth through the frame set to find the best possible representation of each card. If users were unable to identify the card they were to leave the answer blank. It can be seen from the test results in Figure 9 that the amount of useful information that was obtained by the test participants varies depending on the lighting situation.

Tests 1 and 2 consisted of a bright beam on the cards, causing luminance saturation on the faces of the cards. It appears as if the bio-inspired processing model has performed very well with a dramatic improvement in the number of correct readings. We conclude that under the appropriate resolution conditions, photoreceptor processing can lead to improved visibility of object artefacts in surveillance vision.

Figure 8. Test configurations for visual comparison. Test 1 is above, Test 2 below. To the left are the unprocessed frames; to the right are frames after photoreceptor processing. Note that if a single global gain control were used either the central cards would be saturated (as shown), or the outlying cards would be too dark.

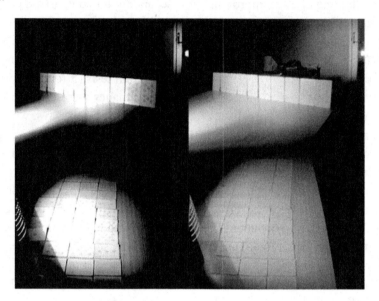

Motion Detection

Security surveillance relies on seeing as much information as possible within the cameras' fields of view. These camera systems would reduce issues with seeing details in shadowed or excessively bright areas within the fields of view at various times of the day; especially if the area under surveillance is exposed to direct sunlight.

Security surveillance could also benefit significantly from the additional stages of the biological vision model (the laminar monopolar cell and motion detection stages). Figure 10 shows a side-by-side comparison of the outputs of the bio-inspired

Figure 9. Quality performance test results for both subjective recognition tests. In the raw images the no-response (blank) rate is high but drops to near zero after processing. The correct response rate after processing exceeds 95% (that is one or two errors) in each case. The average correct identification improved by 88% in Test 1 and by 51% in Test 2. Error bars represent one standard deviation.

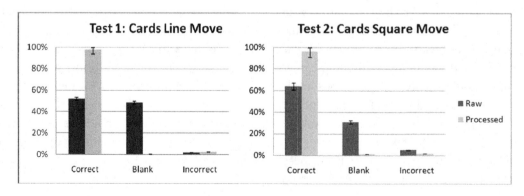

camera system prototypes at each stage of the biological vision model. This image demonstrates how small moving objects can be monitored with ease. After photoreceptor luminance normalisation (top right), it is possible to see objects both in the sky and on the ground simultaneously. The bottom left image shows highlighting of edges of objects with some movement within a scene. The bottom right corner shows motion detection within the scene. The intensity and colour of these pixels represents the velocity of the moving objects relative to the image capture device.

Second (laminar monopolar cell) and third (motion detection) level processing would still be useful on images retrieved from standard camera systems, however, for best results a HDR camera with the first level processing (photoreceptor stage) will be needed as it is impossible to recover information lost when a linear global gain-controlled system is used. The complete system will ensure that useful information is maximised and the most accurate target detection

and tracking will be possible. In the example shown in Figure 10 if the first level processing was skipped, the objects may not have been detected due to them travelling in either the darkest or brightest areas of the image. These areas are where the conventional camera system is more likely to fail in this application.

CONCLUSION AND FUTURE WORK

We have demonstrated that it is possible to implement the photoreceptor stage of the biologically-inspired vision processing system using inexpensive off-the-shelf consumer graphics processing hardware, and provided some details of the surveillance applications of the proposed approach. There is sufficient processing capability in current GPGPUs for the implementation of Lamina Monopolar Cell and Motion processing (2nd and 3rd stage biological processing) elements to be added within the GPGPU environment, com-

Figure 10. Direct comparison of motion processing from each stage of a Bio-Inspired Camera System. Top left) unprocessed image what it is difficult, or impossible to identify either the airplane or the two people walking by the river. Top right) the photoreceptor model normalizes the luminance range making it possible to detect most items within the scene. Bottom left) the laminar monopolar cell processing further enhances the salient objects and suppresses the background making identification easier. Bottom right) motion processing removes the stationary background and provides simultaneous position and velocity information about objects within the scene.

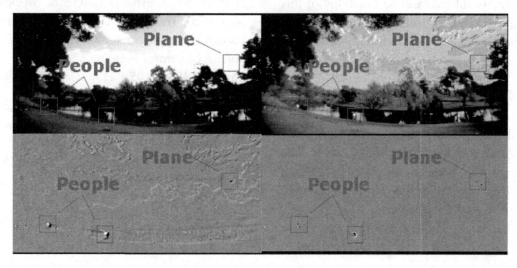

pleting the implementation using commercially-available hardware. In addition to the bio-inspired processing model, other process intensive areas of the software can potentially be implemented on the GPGPU too for systems where the GPGPU processing capacity permits.

High dynamic range cameras are not currently used in surveillance applications due to their relatively high cost, although there are emerging double-photodiode pixel based imaging sensors being developed according to Yamada (Yamada, 2006) which would see a reduction in cost due to economies of scale.

The current software has been set-up to only function correctly with high dynamic range cameras that are DCAM compliant (IEEE1394 cameras) and using limited image formats that aren't widely accepted and used. The case is similar for GPGPU processing as the systems has only been developed to execute correctly on NVIDIA CUDA 1.1 compatible devices and software, however there are several versions of CUDA available and are other GPGPU architectures that will also allow execution on compatible ATI graphics cards. The compatibility of the system with alternate hardware, software and image formats will allow for greater compatibility among computer systems and potentially even with specialised hardware.

Through further development and reduction in pricing of this specialised off-the-shelf hardware, this would increase the feasibility of this bio-inspired visual system in mainstream system surveillance and automated vision systems.

ACKNOWLEDGMENT

The authors wish to acknowledge the contribution of Lee Andersson in assisting with the early code generation. This work was supported by research grants from the Australian Research Council (LP0667744 and DP0986683).

REFERENCES

Ashikhmin, M. (2002). *A tone mapping algorithm for high contrast images*. Paper presented at the 13th Eurographics workshop on Rendering.

Brinkworth, R. S. A., Mah, E. L., Gray, J. P., & O'Carroll, D. C. (2008). Photoreceptor Processing Improves Salience Facilitating Small Target Detection In Cluttered Scenes. *Journal of Vision (Charlottesville, Va.)*, *11*(8), 1–17.

Brinkworth, R. S. A., Mah, E. L., & O'Carroll, D. C. (2007). *Bioinspired Pixel-Wise Adaptive Imaging*. Paper presented at the Smart Structures, Devices, and Systems III.

de Ruyter van Steveninck, R. R., & Laughlin, S. B. (1996). The rate of information transfer at graded-potential synapses. *Nature*, *379*(6566), 642–645. doi:10.1038/379642a0

Debevec, P. E., & Malik, J. (1997). *Recovering High Dynamic Range Radiance Maps from Photographs*. Paper presented at the SIGGRAPH 97, Los Angeles, CA.

Hassenstein, B., & Reichardt, W. (1956). System-theoretische analyse der Zeit-, Reihenfolgen-, und Vorseichenauswertung bei der Berwegungsperzeption des Rüsselkäfers Chlorophanus. *Zeitschrift für Naturforschung*, *11b*, 513–524.

Juusola, M., Uusitalo, R. O., & Weckstrom, M. (1995). Transfer of Graded Potentials at the Photoreceptor Interneuron Synapse. *The Journal of General Physiology*, *105*(1), 117–148. doi:10.1085/jgp.105.1.117

Land, M. F., & Collett, T. S. (1974). Chasing behaviour of houseflies. *Journal of Comparative Physiology. A, Neuroethology, Sensory, Neural, and Behavioral Physiology*, *156*(4), 525–538. doi:10.1007/BF00613976

Laughlin, S. B., de Ruyter van Steveninck, R. R., & Anderson, J. C. (1998). The metabolic cost of neural information. *Nature Neuroscience, 1*, 36–41. doi:10.1038/236

Laughlin, S. B., & Weckström, M. (1993). Fast and slow photoreceptors - a comparative study of the functional diversity of coding and conductances in the Diptera. *Journal of Comparative Physiology. A, Neuroethology, Sensory, Neural, and Behavioral Physiology, 172*, 593–609. doi:10.1007/BF00213682

Mah, E. L., Brinkworth, R. S. A., & O'Carroll, D. C. (2008). Implementation of an elaborated neuromorphic model of a biological photoreceptor. *Biological Cybernetics, 98*, 357–369. doi:10.1007/s00422-008-0222-4

Matic, T., & Laughlin, S. B. (1981). Changes in the intensity-response function of an insect's photoreceptors due to light adaptation. *Journal of Comparative Physiology. A, Neuroethology, Sensory, Neural, and Behavioral Physiology, 145*, 169–177. doi:10.1007/BF00605031

Motion-Video-Products. (2009). *SNR & Dynamic Range, What does it really mean?* San Diego, CA: Motion-Video-Products.

Nordström, K., Barnett, P. D., & O'Carroll, D. C. (2006). Insect detection of small targets moving in visual clutter. *PLoS Biology, 4*(3), 378–386. doi:10.1371/journal.pbio.0040054

NVIDIA. (2008). *What is CUDA*. Retrieved June 2008, from http://www.nvidia.com/object/cuda_what_is.html

Pattanaik, S. N., & Yee, H. (2002). *Adaptive Gain Control For High Dynamic Range Image Display.* Paper presented at the SCCG, Budmerice, Slovakia.

Payne, R., & Howard, J. (1981). Response of an insect photoreceptor: a simple log-normal model. *Nature, 290*(5805), 415–416. doi:10.1038/290415a0

Pixim. (2006). *Digital Pixel System Technology.* Retrieved from http://www.pixim.com/index.html

Reinhard, E., Stark, M., Shirley, P., & Ferwerda, J. (2002). *Photographic Tone Reproduction for Digital Images.* Paper presented at the ACM Transactions on Graphics (SIGGRAPH), San Antonio, TX.

Sato, K. (2006). Image-Processing Algorithms. In Nakamura, J. (Ed.), *Image Sensors and Signal Processing for Digital Still Cameras* (pp. 223–254). Boca Raton, FL: Taylor & Francis Group.

Seetzen, H., Heidrich, W., Stuerzlinger, W., Ward, G., Whitehead, L., Trentacoste, M., et al. (2004). *High Dynamic Range Display Systems.* Paper presented at the ACM Transactions on Graphics (Siggraph).

van Hateren, J. H. (1992). A theory of maximizing sensory information. *Biological Cybernetics, 68*, 68–70.

van Hateren, J. H., & Snippe, H. P. (2001). Information Theoretical Evaluation of Parametric Models of Gain Control in Blowfly Photoreceptor Cells. *Vision Research, 41*, 1851–1865. doi:10.1016/S0042-6989(01)00052-9

Yamada, T. (2006). Image Sensors. In Nakamura, J. (Ed.), *Image Sensors and Signal Processing for Digital Still Cameras* (pp. 95–142). Boca Raton, FL: Taylor & Francis Group.

This work was previously published in the International Journal of Digital Crime and Forensics, Volume 2, Issue 3, edited by Chang-Tsun Li and Anthony TS Ho, pp. 1-14, copyright 2010 by IGI Publishing (an imprint of IGI Global).

Chapter 14
Palmprint Recognition Based on Subspace Analysis of Gabor Filter Bank

Moussadek Laadjel
Algerian National Centre for Research and Development, Algeria

Ahmed Bouridane
Northumbria University, UK

Fatih Kurugollu
Queen's University Belfast, UK

WeiQi Yan
Queen's University Belfast, UK

ABSTRACT

This paper introduces a new technique for palmprint recognition based on Fisher Linear Discriminant Analysis (FLDA) and Gabor filter bank. This method involves convolving a palmprint image with a bank of Gabor filters at different scales and rotations for robust palmprint features extraction. Once these features are extracted, FLDA is applied for dimensionality reduction and class separability. Since the palmprint features are derived from the principal lines, wrinkles and texture along the palm area. One should carefully consider this fact when selecting the appropriate palm region for the feature extraction process in order to enhance recognition accuracy. To address this problem, an improved region of interest (ROI) extraction algorithm is introduced. This algorithm allows for an efficient extraction of the whole palm area by ignoring all the undesirable parts, such as the fingers and background. Experiments have shown that the proposed method yields attractive performances as evidenced by an Equal Error Rate (EER) of 0.03%.

DOI: 10.4018/978-1-4666-1758-2.ch014

INTRODUCTION

As one of the most successful applications of image analysis and understanding, palmprint recognition has recently received a significant attention, especially during the last ten years. This is due to its patterns' richness of the principal lines, wrinkles and texture spread along the palm area (Jing & Zhang, 2004; Zhao, Huang, & Jia, 2007; Ribaric & Fratric, 2005). These patterns have been found stable and unique (Kong, Zhang, & Lu, 2006) and can be efficiently used for person's recognition. However, the difficulty of palm's principal lines extraction and their similarity among different individuals make them insufficient to indicate difference between palmprint images with an appropriate accuracy. For this reason, we believe that by exploiting the palm texture one will add extra discriminating power to the system since the texture provides the dominant visual features for palmprint images with a low resolution (i.e., of 75dpi).

Gabor filtering is one of the most attractive tool for texture analysis in both spatial and frequency domains (Kumar & Zhang, 2004; Kong, Zhang, & Kamel, 2006; Pan & Ruan, 2009). Typically, a Gabor filter can be applied to the whole image through a filtering process in order to break down the image contents into different scales and orientations to obtain a significant feature set with a view to maximize the image classes' separability. However, the resulting dimensionality of the feature vector is usually very high when a bank of Gabor filters are used to filter the image. In the literature, there exist a number of subspace-based approaches that can be used for dimensionality reduction and the two fundamental linear subspace techniques are: eigenpalms (Duta, Jain, & Mardia, 2001) and fisherpalms (Wu, Zhang, & Wang, 2003) which can be used to convert a high dimensional data set into a lower dimensional space that still captures its most discriminant features. Eigenpalms are a set of eigenvectors obtained when applying Principal Component Analy- sis (PCA) to a set of training images in the spatial domain to approximate the original data by a linear projection onto the leading eigenvectors. However, PCA seeks projections that are optimal for image reconstruction from a low dimen- sional basis and it may not be optimal for classification purposes. Compared with PCA, FLDA is a well-known technique for feature extraction and dimensionality reduction which seeks projections that are also efficient for data classification.

In this paper, we propose a new palmprint feature extraction technique which combines Gabor filter and the FLDA technique. This involves the extraction of robust features from palmprint images using a bank of Gabor filters deployed at different scales and orientations and projecting the palmprint image at hand into a Gabor Fisher Subspace (GFS) before recognition can be performed. The main contributions of this work are to: (i) propose an improved ROI algorithm which can extract the palm's area with all the palm information, (ii) show that a Gabor filter bank can be combined with FLDA for efficient palmprint recognition and (iii) investigate and compare the performance of two types of Gabor filters: Gabor wavelet filter bank (GWFB) and log-Gabor wavelet filter bank (LGWFB), respectively.

The remainder of this paper is organized as follows: the improved ROI ex- traction is detailed in section 2. A review of GWFB and LGWFB is described in section 3 and the mathematical model of the FLDA is given in section 4. The proposed palmprint recognition system is described in detail in section 5. Section 6 presents and discusses experimental results. Finally, conclusions are drawn in section 7.

2 REGION OF INTEREST EXTRACTION

The first step of a palmprint recognition process is usually related to the localization and segmentation of the palmprint ROI. A ROI should include the most significant and discriminative patterns which are extracted from complete principal lines, wrinkles and texture. Although, many techniques for segment- ing palmprint ROI have been proposed (Han, Chengb, Linb, & Fanb, 2003; Zhang, Kong, You, & Wong, 2003; Kumar, Wang, Shen, & Jain, 2003), the technique proposed by Zhang, Kong, You, and Wong (2003) is the most widely discussed in the literature. Typically, this method operates on a fixed square region inside the palm. However, this region is not proportional to the palm size and is thus unsuitable to extract all necessary palmprint information from complete lines and wrinkles. To address this prob- lem, an improved ROI extraction technique is proposed in this paper and which can be described as follows:

- *Image binarization*: the palmprint is smoothed using a Gaussian low pass filter and binarized using the Otsu thresholding method (Otsu, 1979). In addition, mor- pho- logical operations are applied to correct the binary image distortion by filling the holes inside the binary image and cleaning the background by eliminating the small blobs as shown in Figure 1 (b).
- *Image alignment*: To ensure that the extracted ROI has minimal rotation and translation errors, two robust key points B1 and B2 are computed using the local minima of the extracted palmprint contour. The line passing through them (B1, B2) and the Y-axis sharing point B1 are used to determine the rotation angle used to align the palmprint image (see Figure 1 (c)).
- *ROI extraction*: Early steps are described in Zhang Kong, You, and Wong (2003). Our contribution is to determine the ROI such that most distinctive palmprint information remains inside it while removing the background pixels. A natural question to ask is how one can determine the limits/boundaries of an effective ROI of a given palmprint? In this work, we automatically determine the

points A_1, A_2, A_3 and A_4 depending on the input palmprint image as follows (see Figure 1 (f)): (i) project the binary palmprint rows onto the Y-axis and detect the first and the last maximum points A_1 and A_2 where the curve changes its direction abruptly (Figure 1 (d)), (ii) project the palmprint columns onto the X-axis and detect the first and last maximum points A_3 and A_4 where the curve changes its direction abruptly (Figure 1 (e)), (iii) once all the coordinates of the above four points are determined the ROI is easily localized as shown in Figure 1 (f).

To demonstrate the efficiency of the improved ROI algorithm, Figure 2 shows a sample of ROIs extracted using our method and Zhang's method in which it can be clearly seen that our algorithm is able to extract ROIs with more palm patterns (complete lines) when compared with Zhang's algorithm which fails to include some part of lines and texture.

3 GABOR FILTERS OVERVIEW

To appreciate Gabor filter as an attractive tool for palm's texture analysis and understanding, the following section provides a theoretical review of two widely used Gabor filters for use in pattern recognition problems: GWFB and LGWFB.

3.1 Gabor Wavelet Filter Bank

A general 2-D Gabor function $g(x, y)$ is defined as:

$$g(x,y) = \frac{1}{2\pi\sigma_x\sigma_y} \exp\left[-\frac{1}{2}\left(\frac{x^2}{\sigma_x^2} + \frac{v^2}{\sigma_y^2}\right) + j2\pi Wx\right]$$

(1)

where the spatial coordinates (x, y) denote the centroid localization of an elliptical Gaussian window and W is the frequency of a sinusoidal plane wave along the X-axis. The parameters σ_x

Figure 1. ROI extraction steps. (a) Original image. (b) Image binarization and distortion correction. (c) Boundary extraction and key points location (B1 and B2). (d) Y-axis projection and (A1 , A2) determination. (e) X-axis projection and (A3 , A4) determina- tion. (f) Image alignment and ROI localization.

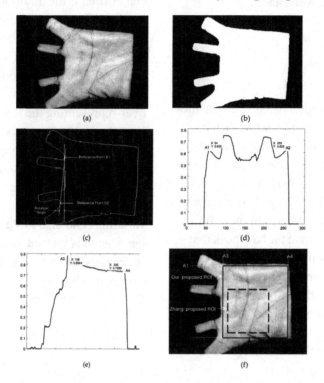

and σ_y are the space constants of the Gaussian envelop along x and y axes, respectively. The Fourier transform $G(u,v)$ of the Gabor function $g(x,y)$ can be written as:

$$G(u,v) = \exp\left\{-\frac{1}{2}\left[\frac{(u-f)^2}{\sigma_u^2} + \frac{v^2}{\sigma_v^2}\right]\right\} \quad (2)$$

where f represents the frequency of the sinusoidal plane along the horizontal axis and the frequency components in the x and y direction are denoted by the pair (u,v), while $\sigma_u = 1/2\pi\sigma_x$ and $\sigma_v = 1/2\pi\sigma_y$. By considering a non-orthogonal basis set formed by Gabor functions, a localized frequency description can be obtained by expanding a signal with this basis. Self-similar class functions, known as Gabor Wavelets, can be generated by dilations and rotations of the mother wavelet $g(x,y)$ through the generating function:

Figure 2. Samples of localized ROI, red squares using our method and green squares using Zhang's method.

$$g_{mn} = a^{-m}g(x',y'), \, a > 1 \quad (3)$$

by considering $m = 1, ..., L$ and $n = 1, ..., K$. L and K denote the total number of dilations and orientations, respectively, and:

$$x' = a^{-m}(x \cos \theta + y \sin \theta)$$
$$y' = a^{-m}(-x \sin \theta + y \cos \theta)$$

(4)

where $\theta = n\pi$ is the angle. To ensure that the energy is independent of m, a scale factor a^m is introduced. By considering the redundant information presented in the filtered images due to the non-orthogonality of the Gabor wavelets, Man-junath (Manjunath & Ma, 1996) designed a strategy to reduce the redundancy of the GWFB. This strategy aims to maintain the half-peak magnitude of the filter responses touches each other in the frequency spectrum.

Let U_l and U_h denote the lower and the upper center frequencies of interest, respectively. The design strategy results in the following equations for computing the filter parameters σ_u and σ_v (Manjunath & Ma, 1996).

$$a = \left(\frac{U_h}{U_l}\right)^{\frac{-1}{S-1}}$$

(5)

$$\sigma_u = \frac{(a-1)U_h}{(a+1)\sqrt{2 \ln 2}}$$

(6)

$$\sigma_v = \tan\left(\frac{\pi}{2k}\right)\left[U_h - 2\ln\left(\frac{\sigma_u^2}{U_h}\right)\right]\left[2\ln 2 - \frac{2\ln 2^2 \sigma_u^2}{U_h^2}\right]^{\frac{-1}{2}}$$

(7)

where $f = U_h$. In order to eliminate the sensitivity of filter response to absolute intensity vales the real components of 2D Gabor filters are biased by adding a constant to make them with zero mean.

3.2 Log-Gabor Filter Bank

Gabor filter is the traditional choice for obtaining localized frequency informa- tion since they offer the best simultaneous localization of spatial and frequency information (Manjunath & Ma, 1996). However, one cannot construct a Gabor function with an arbi- trarily wide bandwidth without over-representing the low frequencies. This will, in essence, produce a correlated and redundant response to the low frequencies. Alternatively, *Field* (Field, 1987) proposed a new version of Gabor filter termed log-Gabor filter which has no DC offset that makes it robust to illumination variations and also has a response that is Gauss-ian when it is viewed on a logarithmic frequency scale, thus allowing for more information to be captured. The Log-Gabor filter is given in the frequency domain by:

$$G(r, \theta) = \exp\left(-\frac{\left[\log\left(r/f_0\right)\right]^2}{2\sigma_r^2}\right) \cdot \exp\left(-\frac{(\theta - \theta_0)^2}{2\sigma_\theta^2}\right)$$

(8)

where (r, θ) represents the polar coordinates, f_0 is the center frequency of the filter, θ_0 is the orien-tation angle of the filter, σ_r determines the scale bandwidth and σ_θ indicates the angular bandwidth (Kovesi, 2006).

4 FISHER LINEAR DISCRIMINANT ANALYSIS

When the training set data is labeled, supervised subspace techniques offer a good description of palmprint images in terms of discriminative features than a unsupervised learning counterpart method. FLDA is relatively more robust for illu-mination variations compared to PCA. However, it suffers from the SSS prob- lem (Belhumeur,

Hespanha, & Kriegman, 1997) which is due to the singularity of the *within-class* scatter matrix since the dimension of the palmprint image vector exceeds, in general, the number of data points. To tackle this problem, the derived feature vectors $[x \mid x_1, x_2, ..., x_n]$ should be first projected into a lower dimensional space by PCA so that the resulting *within-class* scatter matrix is nonsingular. Then, a standard FLDA is employed to process the projected samples. This method, which has been used efficiently in face recognition (Belhumeur, Hespanha, & Kriegman, 1997), is described as follows:

Let us consider a feature vector corresponding to the set of training images as a set of n samples $[x \mid x_1, x_2, ..., x_n]$ taking values in an d-dimensional space, and let us assume that each feature vector belongs to one of c classes $[X_1, X_2, ..., X_c]$.

(i) compute the transformation matrix of PCA transformation W_{pca}:

$$W_{pca} = \arg \min_{W} \left| W^T S W \right| = \left[w_1, w_2, ..., w_m \right]$$

$$(9)$$

where $[w_i \mid i = 1, 2, ..., m(m < n)]$ is the set of eigenvector of S corresponding to the nonzero eigenvalues, T means matrix transpose and S is the total scatter matrix defined as:

$$S = \sum_{k=1}^{N} (x_k - \mu)(x_k - \mu)^T$$

$$(10)$$

μ is the mean image of all samples.

(ii) compute the transformed within-classscatter matrix S' and the transformed between-class scatter matrix S' as fol- lows:

$$S'_W = W^T_{pca} S_W W_{pca}$$

$$(11)$$

$$S'_B = W^T_{pca} S_W W_{pca}$$

$$(12)$$

where:

$$S_B = \sum_{i=1}^{c} N_i (\mu_i - \mu)(\mu_i - \mu)^T$$

$$(13)$$

and:

$$S_W = \sum_{i=1}^{c} \sum_{x_k \in X_i} (x_k - \mu_i)(x_k - \mu_i)^T$$

$$(14)$$

where μ_i is the mean image of class X_i and N_i is the number of samples in class X_i.

(iii) employ a standard FLDA method to process the projected samples:

$$W_{flda} = \arg \max_{W} \frac{\left| W^T W^T_{pca} S_B W_{pca} W \right|}{\left| W^T W^T_{pca} S_W W_{pca} W \right|}$$

$$(15)$$

(iv) compute the optimal projection matrix W_{opt}:

$$W_{opt} = W_{flda} * W_{pca}$$

$$(16)$$

The projection of x in the FLDA space is given by:

$$Y = W^T_{opt} x$$

$$(17)$$

The columns of $[W_{opt} \mid w_1, w_2, ...w_m]$, ($m < c-1$) are the set of the generalized eigenvectors of S_B and S_W corresponding to the m largest eigenvalues $[\lambda_i \mid i = 1, 2...m]$ of the following equation $S_B W = \lambda S_W W$.

5 PROPOSED SYSTEM

5.1 Gabor Feature Extraction

The Gabor representation of a palmprint image $i(x, y)$ can be obtained by con- volving the image with the family of Gabor filter as follows:

$$I_{m,n}(x, y) = \int \int i(x, y) g_{mn}^*(x - x_0, y - y_0) dx_0 dy_0 \tag{18}$$

where $I_{m,n}(x, y)$ denotes the result corresponding to the Gabor filter at scale L and orientation K and * indicate the complex conjugate. Figure 3 (a) and Figure 3 (b) show the magnitude of the convolution result of a random palmprint image with GWFB and LGWFB, respectively. The filters' sittings are shown in the same figures in which four scales and six orientations have been used to generate a series of Gabor responses. As a result, a palmprint image can be represented by a set of 24 (4x6) Gabor sub-images $(I_{m,n}(x, y), m = 0, ..., 3; n = 0, ..., 5)$. The orientation of Gabor features shown in Figure 3 and Figure 4 vary along the horizontal axis, while their scales very along the vertical axis. The white blobs represent the palmprint energy in the corresponding orientation and scale. The resultant Gabor feature vector can be obtained by concatenating all Gabor sub- images $(I_{m,n}(x, y), m = 0, ..., 3; n = 0, ..., 5)$ into a single vector v as follows $(v = I^{1 \times 16384}_{0,0}, I^{1 \times 16384}_{0,1}, ..., I^{1 \times 16384}_{3,5})$.

For instance, a palmprint image with a size of 128x128 pixels convolved by a bank of Gabor filters with 4 scales and 6 orientations results in a feature vector of 393216 (128x128x4x6). The dimension of the derived feature vector x is too high thus requiring a high computational effort.

5.2 Downsampling

Due to the high dimension of the extracted Gabor feature vector v, the com- putational cost associated with learning the FLDA subspace projection matrix is consequentially very high. Therefore, a prior dimensionality reduction is re- quired to speed up the recognition process. A bilinear down-sampling operation with a factor of 8 has been used to reduce the size of Gabor sub-images from 128x128 to 16x16. The down-sampling process results in a feature vector of 6144 (16x16x4x6) elements instead of feature vector of 393216 which is very easy for processing.

Figure 3. Responses of Gabor wavelet filter bank (Magnitudes) for S = 4 and K =6 with $U_l = 0.05$ and $U_h = 0.4$ using an image of 128 × 128

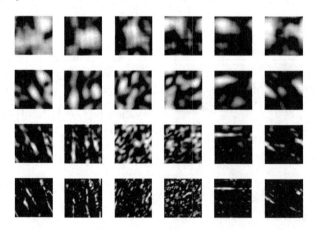

Figure 4. Responses of log-Gabor filter bank (Magnitudes) for S = 4 and K = 6 with f_0 = 1/3 and σ_r = 0.2 using an image of 128 × 128

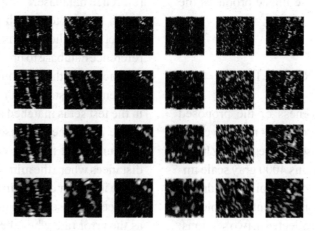

Figure 5. Diagrams showing the steps of the recognition process

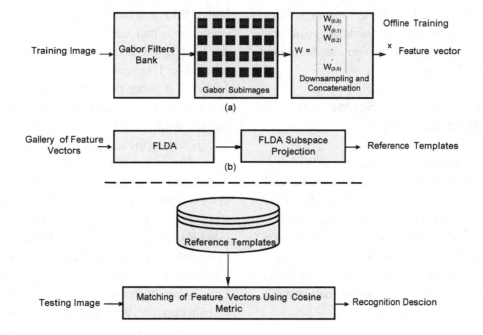

5.3 System Description

Figure 5 shows a block diagrams demonstrating the use of Gabor features and FLDA (Belhumeur, Hespanha, & Kriegman, 1997) for palmprint recognition. Initially, a Gabor filter bank is used to extract the palmprint features as described in previous section (see Figure 5 (a)). Then, the Gabor feature vectors extracted from a set of training im-

ages are used to learn the Fisher Gabor Subspace (FGS), which is represented by the projection matrix W_{opt} given in (Belhumeur, Hespanha, & Kriegman, 1997) as can be seen in Figure 5 (b). To identify a person, Gabor feature vector of the palmprint image is extracted, concatenated into a vector, projected to the learned FGS and finally compared with the reference templates in the database as illustrated in Figure 5 (c). After comparison using Cosine distance, the person is identified as the one whose image produces the smallest distance.

6 EXPERIMENTAL RESULTS

To assessed the effectiveness of the proposed method, the Hong Kong Polytech- nic University (PolyU) palmprint database has been used (Zhang, 2004). The database contains 4000 gray scale images having a resolution of 75 dpi and is drawn from 200 different persons. Twenty samples of each person's palm were collected in two sessions: ten (10) samples were captured in the first session and the other ten (10) in the second. The average interval between the first and the second collection was two months. Illuminations and positions, including translations and rotations, are the major distortions of this database.

6.1 Gabor Filter Bank Scales and Orientations Selection

The first experiment has been conducted to determine the appropriate number of orientations and scales that can be used for GWFB and LGWFB to achieve the best performance. The first 5 palmprint images of the first session have been used for training while the remaining 15 palmprint have been used for test. The cosine distance has been used as the similarity measure between the

Table 1. EER of GWFB and LGWFB for different scales and orientations

scale * orientation	GWFB EER (%)	LGWFB EER (%)
2 * 4	0.81	0.16
2 * 6	0.71	0.10
3 * 4	0.40	0.06
3 * 6	0.16	0.05
4 * 4	0.10	0.03
4 * 6	0.03	0.03
3 * 8	0.03	0.03

test palmprint images and their counterpart in the reference database.

To run the test, each palmprint image in the test set is matched against its five templates in the reference database to produce five genuine cosine distances with the minimum value considered to be the genuine distance score. Similarly, a palmprint in the test set is matched against all the templates in the reference database to produce $5 * c$ (c is the number of training classes) imposter cosine distances where the minimum value is considered as the imposter cosine distance. The performance has been assessed using the EER which is defined as the error rate when the False Acceptance Rate (FAR) and the False Rejection Rate (FRR) are equal. Table 1 summarized the EERs obtained for both GWFB and LGWFB for a varied number of orientations and scales, respectively. The lower the EER is, the better the system performances are. Table 1 suggests that the performance of LGWFB is better than all of that of GWFB for all orientations and scales settings, showing that the worst EER of 0.16% for LGWFB has been obtained using the setting of 2 scales and 4 orientations. The same ERR (0.16%) has been obtained in the setting of 3 scales and 6 orientations for GWFB thereby resulting in added complexity to the system. The performance of LGWFB over GWFB is due to its structure which allows more information to be captured and provides a good coverage of the frequency components of interest. For a better illustration, the genuine and imposter distributions of GWFB and LGWFB with a setting of 4 scales and 4 orientations are drawn in Figure 6 (a) and Figure 6 (b), respectively. The genuine and imposter distributions are generated by 3000 correct and 597000 incorrect recognition cosine distances, respectively. The decidability index is a good measure of how well the genuine and imposter distributions are separated (Daugman, 1993). Let μ_G and μ_I be the means of the genuine and the imposter distributions, respectively. Let σ_G and σ_I be their corresponding standard deviations. The decidability index d is given by:

Figure 6. Genuine and imposter distributions of (a) GWFB test, (b) LGWFB test

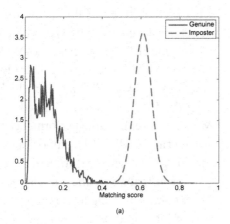 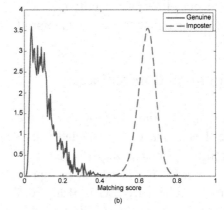

$$d = \frac{\left| \mu_G - \mu_I \right|}{\sqrt{\left(\sigma_G^2 + \sigma_I^2 \right)/2}} \tag{19}$$

The higher the decidability index, the greater the separation of genuine and imposter distributions. The decidability index and all the statistical values (i.e., means and standard deviations) are summarized in Table 2. The decidability index values indicate that LGWFB produces better separability between genuine and imposter users.

6.2 Effect of the Number of Training images on the System

Performance

The second experiment is dedicated to investigate the effect of the number of the training images on the proposed system performance. The tests have been conducted in a similar way as the last experiment by varying the number of the training

Table 2. The statistical values and decidability index of the genuine and imposter distributions

Filter type	μ_G	σ_G	μ_I	σ_I	d
GWFB	0.1217	0.0746	0.6109	0.0446	7.9665
LGWFB	0.1091	0.0691	0.6400	0.0468	8.9980

palmprint images from 2 to 5 using only LGWFB with 4 scales and 4 orientations since it has shown better performance compared to GWFB.

The Receiver Operating Characteristic (ROC) Curves which are the plot of the variations of the FAR against the FRR of all the tests are graphically shown in Figure 7. From this figure, it is clear that when the number of the training images increase the system performance increase as well. An ERRs of 0.36%, 0.19%, 0.13% and 0.03% have been obtained using 2, 3, 4 and 5 training

Figure 7. ROC curves show the performance of LGWFB for different number of training palmprint images.

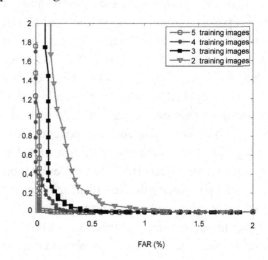

palmprint images, respectively. These results show that our system can efficiently identify individuals even when using only two training palmprint images each.

6.3 Performance Comparisons

To emphasize the discriminating power of the improved ROI area and the ex- tracted Gabor feature vector, the comparative performance of direct PCA, direct FLDA on the raw palmprint images and the combination of LGWFB and PCA are reported in Table 3 in terms of EER. Note that the Euclidean distance has been used in the case of raw palmprint since it has given better results compared to the Cosine distance. One can see that the combination of Gabor feature vec- tor with PCA or FLDA has improved the performance of PCA and FLDA if they applied directly on a raw palmprint images. The Gabor feature combined with PCA has given an EER of 1.75% which is much lower than that of PCA implemented on the raw palmprint images of 15.25%. A 4.7% improvement is observed for FLDA when it is combined with Gabor feature. This implies that the augmented Gabor feature vectors carry more discriminating power than the original images do. The reason of the improvement is due to the robustness of LGWFB features and the large area of the extracted ROI.

To further demonstrate the effectiveness of our proposed combined Gabor filter and FLDA technique, a comparison with the combination of wavelet decomposition and the FLDA for palmprint feature extraction has been carried out. Three-level wavelet transform is adopted to decompose a palmprint image into different subbands with different frequency components. Only the high frequency subbands are concatenated in one vector and subjected to FLDA representation in order to: (i) reducing the redundant or irrelevant information contained in wavelet coefficients, (ii) recover the underlying features which has more discrim- inative power. Many wavelet filters have

been tested and their performance in terms of the EER are reported in Table 4, the lowest EER of 3.74% has been given by Daubechie filter (db4). The resulted EERs from using the Daubechies (db), Coiflets (coif) and Biorthogonal (bior) wavelets filters are between 3% and 5% which are higher than the EER of 0.03% obtained by using LG-WFB. This remarkable performance between the wavelet and LGWFB decompositions is due to the lack of good characterization of the discriminant palmprint feature by the wavelet transform. For a clear understanding to the wavelet limitation in palmprint feature extraction, a comparison with two existing methods have been carried out. The first method combines a wavelet decomposition and two- dimensional PCA (2DPCA) and has been used to obtain the most discriminant infor- mation contained in the low-frequency band of a palmprint image as claimed by the authors (Lu, Zhang, Kang, Xue, & Chen, 2006). In the second method, a dual-tree complex wavelet transform and support vector machines are used for a reliable palmprint classification (Chen, Bui, & Krzyzak, 2006). The performances are compared in terms of Genuine Acceptance Rate (GAR). The authors have reported a GAR of 97% in both techniques (Lu, Zhang, Kang, Xue, & Chen, 2006; Chen, Bui, & Krzyzak, 2006) using the same database but with less samples (only 100 person with 6 samples each). A GAR of 99.97% has been ob- tained using our proposed system in database of 4000 palmprint images which clearly outperforms the result reported in Lu, Zhang, Kang, Xue, and Chen (2006), and Chen, Bui, and Krzyzak (2006). The performance of LGWFB using a wavelet decomposition is due to the fact that the use of multiple filters with different scales and orientations generate more discriminating features since wavelet decomposition captures only the palmprint information in the horizontal, vertical and diagonal directions. In fact, palmprint texture information is random and spread along different directions. It is also worth to mention that our proposed technique is comparable with

Table 3. Recognition performance using similar methods

Method	Feature vector dimension	EER (%)	distance
PCA FLDA	200	15.25	Euclidean
PCA + LGWFB	199	4.73	Euclidean
FLDA + LG-WFB	200	1.75	ean Cosine
	199	0.03	Cosine

Table 4. Recognition performance wavelet decomposition

Wavelet filters	EER (%)	Wavelet filters	EER (%)
db1 db4 db8	4.63	db2 db6 db10	4.64
coif1 coif3 coif5	3.74	coif2 coif4	3.95
bior2.2	4.34	bior1.1 bior3.7	4.36
	4.36		3.79
	3.81		3.82
	4.32		4.63
	4.55		4.65

the PalmCode algorithm (Zhang, Kong, You, & Wong, 2003); one of the popular coding-based approaches in which an EER of 0.77% has been reported.

7 CONCLUSION

This paper has described a new technique for palmprint recognition based on the combination of Gabor filter bank and Fisher Linear Discriminant Analysis. The proposed technique starts first by extracting the palm's ROI which generates the most discriminating palm information, then a Gabor filter bank is used to extract a set of robust features which can be used subsequently by FLDA for dimensionality reduction and class separability. The experimental results have demonstrated the effectiveness of the augmented method since by using multiple filters with different scales and orientations more discriminating features are gen- erated. Testing PCA and FLDA using the raw features and the extracted Gabor feature vector respectively, has shown that the Gabor feature vector yields a sig- nificantly more discriminative representation of the palmprint than the original images.

REFERENCES

Belhumeur, P. N., Hespanha, J. P., & Kriegman, D. J. (1997). Eigenfaces vs. Fisherfaces: Recognition using class specific linear projection. *IEEE Transactions on Pattern Analysis and Machine Intelligence, 19*(7), 711–720. doi:10.1109/34.598228

Chen, G. Y., Bui, T. D., & Krzyzak, A. (2006, October). Palmprint classification using dual-tree complex wavelets. In *Proceedings of the IEEE Inter. Conf. on Image Processing* (pp. 2645-2648).

Daugman, J. G. (1993). High confidence visual recognition of persons by a test of statistical independence. *IEEE Transactions on Pattern Analysis and Machine Intelligence, 15*(11), 1148–1161. doi:10.1109/34.244676

Duta, N., Jain, A. K., & Mardia, K. V. (2001). Palmprint recognition using eigenpalms features. *Pattern Recognition Letters, 32*(4), 477–485.

Field, D. J. (1987). Relations between the statistics of natural images and the response properties of cortical cells. *Journal of the Optical Society of America. A, Optics and Image Science, 4*, 2379–2394. doi:10.1364/JOSAA.4.002379

Han, C.-C., Chengb, H.-L., Linb, C.-L., & Fanb, K.-C. (2003). Personal authentication using palmprint features. *Pattern Recognition Letters, 36*(2), 371–381.

Jing, X. Y., & Zhang, D. (2004, December). A face and palmprint recognition approach based on discriminant DCT feature extraction. *IEEE Transactions on Systems, Man, and Cybernetics, 34*, 2405–2415. doi:10.1109/TSMCB.2004.837586

Kong, A., Zhang, D., & Kamel, M. (2006). Palmprint identification using feature-level fusion. *Pattern Recognition Letters, 39*(3), 478–487.

Kong, A., Zhang, D., & Lu, G. (2006). A study of identical twins' palmprints for personal verification. *Pattern Recognition Letters, 39*(11), 2149–2156.

Kovesi, D. P. (2006). *What are log-gabor filters and why are they good?* Retrieved from http://www.csse.uwa.edu.au/~pk/Research/MatlabFns/PhaseCongruency/Docs/convexpl.html

Kumar, A., & Zhang, D. (2004). Integrating shape and texture for hand verification. In *Proceedings of the 3rd Inter. Conf. on Image and Graphics* (pp. 222-225).

Kumar, A. J., Wong, D. C. M., Shen, H. C., & Jain, A. K. (2003). *Personal verification using palmprint and hand geometry biometric* (pp. 668–678). LNCS.

Lu, J., Zhang, E., Kang, X., Xue, Y., & Chen, Y. (2006, June). Palmprint recognition using wavelet decomposition and 2D principal component analysis. In

Manjunath, B. S., & Ma, W. Y. (1996). Texture features for browsing and retrieval of image data. *IEEE Transactions on Pattern Analysis and Machine Intelligence, 18*(8), 837–842. doi:10.1109/34.531803

Otsu, N. (1979). A threshold selection method from gray level histograms. *IEEE Transactions on Systems, Man, and Cybernetics, 9*.

Pan, X., & Ruan, Q.-Q. (2009). Palmprint recognition using gabor-based local invariant features. *Neurocomput., 72*(7-9), 2040–2045. doi:10.1016/j.neucom.2008.11.019

Proceedings of the. 2006 Inter. Conf. on Communications, Circuits and Systems *(Vol. 3)*.

Ribaric, S., & Fratric, I. (2005). A biometric identification system based on eigenpalm and eigenfinger features. *IEEE Transactions on Pattern Analysis and Machine Intelligence, 24*, 1698–1709. doi:10.1109/TPAMI.2005.209

Wu, X., Zhang, D., & Wang, K. (2003). Fisherpalms based palmprint recognition. *Pattern Recognition Letters, 24*(15), 2829–2838. doi:10.1016/S0167-8655(03)00141-7

Zhang, D. (2004). *Polyu palmprint database.* Retrieved from http://www.comp.polyu.edu.hk/biometrics/

Zhang, D., Kong, W.-K., You, J., & Wong, M. (2003). Online palmprint identification. *IEEE Transactions on Pattern Analysis and Machine Intelligence, 25*(9), 1041–1050. doi:10.1109/TPAMI.2003.1227981

Zhao, Z.-Q., Huang, D.-S., & Jia, W. (2007). Palmprint recognition with 2DPCA+PCA based on modular neural networks. *Neurocomput., 71*(1-3), 448–454. doi:10.1016/j.neucom.2007.07.010

This work was previously published in the International Journal of Digital Crime and Forensics, Volume 2, Issue 4, edited by Chang-Tsun Li and Anthony TS Ho, pp. 1-15, copyright 2010 by IGI Publishing (an imprint of IGI Global).

Section 5
Digital Evidence

Chapter 15
Suspect Sciences?
Evidentiary Problems with Emerging Technologies

Gary Edmond
University of New South Wales, Australia

ABSTRACT

This article examines the standards governing the admission of new types of expert evidence. Based on the rules of evidence and procedure in Australia, it explains how judges have been largely uninterested in the reliability of expert opinion evidence. Focused on the use of CCTV images and covert sound recordings for the purposes of identification, but relevant to other forensic sciences, the article explains the need for interest in the reliability of incriminating expert opinion evidence. It also explains why many of the traditional trial safeguards may not be particularly useful for identifying or explaining problems and complexities with scientific and technical evidence. In closing, the article argues that those developing new types of evidence and new techniques, whether identification-based or derived from IT, camera or computer forensics, need to be able to explain why it is that the court can have confidence in any opinions expressed.

1. INTRODUCTION

This article uses recent developments surrounding the admission of expert evidence derived from images and sound recordings to critically examine the response to new forms of incriminating expert opinion evidence in Australia. The article argues that forensic sciences, biometrics and other forms of expert identification and comparison evidence,

along with incriminating expert opinion evidence more generally, should all be demonstrably reliable before they are relied upon by the state in criminal proceedings.

The article begins with a succinct introduction to rules regulating the admissibility of expert evidence in Australia and then considers several cases exemplifying the ways courts have responded to new and emerging forms of expert opinion evidence in order to explain some of the problems with contemporary jurisprudence and practice.

DOI: 10.4018/978-1-4666-1758-2.ch015

2. THE AUSTRALIAN ADMISSIBILITY FRAMEWORK

How have new forms of expert identification evidence been received in Australian courtrooms? To understand recent developments we need to review the rules of admissibility prescribed by the Uniform Evidence Law (UEL) and the common law.[1] Here, it is useful to explain that there are basically two systems governing the admissibility of expert opinion evidence in Australia. The most recent, the UEL, is a statutory regime based on a series of substantially similar evidence acts applicable in New South Wales (NSW), Tasmania, the Australian Capital Territory, and the Federal Court. Significantly, it will soon operate in Victoria. The alternative system is the common law (and several parochial acts), applicable in Queensland, Western Australia, South Australia, the Northern Territory and Victoria (in the interim).

According to the UEL, to be admissible all evidence must be *relevant*:

56 Relevant evidence to be admissible

    (1)   Except as otherwise provided by this Act, evidence that is relevant in a proceeding is admissible in the proceeding.

    (2)   Evidence that is not relevant in the proceeding is not admissible.

Evidence is relevant if it has *probative value*. The UEL *Dictionary* explains that the "probative value of evidence means the extent to which the evidence could rationally affect the assessment of the probability of the existence of a fact in issue." Consequently,

55 Relevant evidence

    (1)   The evidence that is relevant in a proceeding is evidence that, if it were accepted, could rationally affect (directly or indirectly) the assessment of the probability of the existence of a fact in issue in the proceeding. ...

Normally, even if relevant, opinions are presumptively inadmissible. Under the UEL the *opinion rule* (section 76) states that "evidence of an opinion" is not admissible "to prove the existence of a fact about the existence of which the opinion was expressed". This means that witnesses cannot usually express their opinions about issues relevant to facts in dispute during proceedings. There are, however, several exceptions to the exclusionary impact of the opinion rule.[2] Although it does not attempt to codify the common law, section 79(1) provides the major exception for expert opinion evidence. It reads:

79 Exception: opinions based on specialised knowledge

    (1)   If a person has specialised knowledge based on the person's training, study or experience, the opinion rule does not apply to evidence of an opinion of that person that is wholly or substantially based on the knowledge.

Provided an "opinion" is "wholly or substantially" *based* on "specialised knowledge" which is *based* on "training, study or experience" it is not caught by the exclusionary opinion rule.[3] Where these conditions are satisfied, a witness can proffer relevant opinions about facts in issue, subject only to the exclusionary discretions and the requirement that the trial be substantially fair. In criminal proceedings, incriminating evidence is to be excluded if its probative value is outweighed by the danger of unfair prejudice to the accused (section 137).[4] In all proceedings, the probative value of the evidence should also be weighed against the danger that it is misleading, confusing, or an undue waste of time (sections 135 and 136) (Edmond, 2008).

At common law a witness is usually prevented from expressing an opinion unless they are an "expert" in a recognisable "field of knowledge" (which is legally relevant to the facts in issue). This means that the witness must possess some formal qualification and/or experience in a profession or area recognised by the court as a "field of knowledge". Historically, those from fields with formal training and accreditation, such as medical specialists, raised few problems. In practice, common law judges developed quite liberal approaches to their interpretation of "expert" and "field". Several of the early cases revolve around the admissibility of the opinions of mechanics and truck drivers in the aftermath of motor vehicle accidents.[5]

In addition, judges applying the common law often considered the *basis* of the expert's opinion—particularly in civil cases.[6] Interest in the basis of—or the reasoning behind—the opinion has been carried over into the interpretation of section 79(1) of the *Evidence Act*.[7] Unremarkably, practice in both the UEL jurisdictions and the remaining states tends to be relatively uniform.

3. THE ADMISSIBILITY OF IDENTIFICATION EVIDENCE DERIVED FROM IMAGES AND SOUNDS

We can observe the very generous ways in which judges, under the UEL and the common law, have responded to the admission of new forms of incriminating expert evidence by focusing on the jurisprudence regulating expert opinions about identity derived from recordings of sounds and images.[8] A series of exemplary judgments provides a usefully introduction to the ways in which Australian judges have allowed a range of experts and non-experts (such as police officers and other investigators) to proffer incriminating *identification* evidence.

A. Identification from Images

Our discussion of images begins with the influential case of *R v Tang* (2006). *Tang* was an appeal to the NSW Court of Criminal Appeal (CCA)

concerned with the admissibility of *facial mapping* and *body mapping* evidence. "Facial mapping" involves the comparison of a person of interest using anthropometric and/or morphological analysis of the face. It usually entails quantitative and/or qualitative comparisons of images of an unknown person—usually from security and surveillance cameras such as CCTV—with images of a known person—usually the prime suspect. "Body mapping" involves a similar set of processes extended to the body and gait.

In *Tang* an anatomist called by the prosecution opined that the person of interest in security images from an armed robbery was Hien Puoc Tang. From her comparison of the security images—which were of such poor quality that the CCA was of the opinion that they "could not be left for the jury"—and a set of high quality forensic procedure (i.e. police) images of Tang, Dr. Sutisno was convinced that the two persons were the same and testified to that effect. This positive identification evidence was admitted over objection and its admissibility became the principal ground of appeal.

In reviewing the admissibility of this evidence under the UEL, Spigelman CJ (with Simpson and Adams JJ agreeing) directed his attention to section 79, and explained its operation:

Section 79 has two limbs. Under the first limb, it is necessary to identify "specialised knowledge", derived from one of the three matters identified, i.e. "training, study or experience". Under the second limb, it is necessary that the opinion be "wholly or substantially based on that knowledge". Accordingly, it is a requirement of admissibility that the opinion be demonstrated to be based on the specialised knowledge. (Tang, 2006, [134])

Applying this construction of the *Evidence Act 1995* (NSW) to the evidence, the Court concluded that facial mapping was not "specialised knowledge" that would enable Dr. Sutisno to give her opinion about the identity of the unknown person in the security images: "Facial mapping, let alone body mapping, was not shown, on the evidence in the trial, to constitute 'specialised knowledge' of a character which can support an opinion of identity" (*Tang*, 2006, [146]). Dr. Sutisno's opinions about the identity of the person of interest were characterised by the Court, somewhat pejoratively, as *ipse dixit* (*Tang*, 2006, [154], [140]-[141]).[9] Chief Justice Spigelman was concerned that the reasoning process (i.e. the basis) employed by Dr. Sutisno was inadequately explained. Facial mapping and body mapping were, therefore, incapable of supporting opinions about identity and should not have been admitted.

Things did not end there, however. Dr. Sutisno's training in anatomy combined with the fact that she had repeatedly compared the security images with the police photographs led Spigelman CJ to qualify her as an *ad hoc expert* (Edmond & San Roque, 2009). This common law exception to the general prohibition on opinion evidence was used—in an UEL jurisdiction—to enable Dr. Sutisno to testify about similarities and (at least in theory) differences between the person(s) in the images. Even though Dr. Sutisno was not giving opinion evidence based on "specialised knowledge", the Court was willing to allow this expert to testify about similarities between the two sets of photographs in a future trial. She would be allowed (as a legally qualified anatomist) to give opinion evidence about similarities but would be prevented from positively identifying the accused as she had done during the first trial. According to Spigelman CJ, any weaknesses or limitations with Dr. Sutisno's techniques and opinions were for cross-examination. It would be for a jury to determine the reliability and weight of her similarity evidence.

Perhaps the most disconcerting aspect of *Tang* is the attitude expressed by the Court toward the reliability of Dr. Sutisno's opinion evidence. Adopting what might be considered a very narrow reading of the text of section 79, Spigelman CJ explained that: "The focus must be on the words

'specialised knowledge', not on the introduction of an extraneous idea such as 'reliability'" (*Tang*, 2006, [137]). In consequence, the CCA dismissed the need to consider reliability when determining the admissibility of incriminating expert opinion evidence. Instead, emphasis was placed on the more amorphous idea of "specialised knowledge". And, Dr. Sutisno's opinions were admitted even though there was no "specialised knowledge" and no explanation of how her anatomical training (or study of the images) would provide a basis for drawing inferences about identity that were not merely "speculative" or "subjective" (*Tang*, 2006, [138]).

In the months following the appeal in *Tang*, judges in the Supreme and District Courts of NSW began to accept facial mapping as "specialised knowledge" and admitted the opinions of *experts* in *R v Jung* (2006), *R v Kaliyanda* (2006) and *R v Alrekabi* (2007). Interestingly, despite this legal recognition, there was no new evidence supporting the reliability of this evidence, or the existence of a "field" of facial mapping, and the restraints on positive identification remained. (We might wonder what, if anything, had changed since *Tang*?)

Similar results were obtained at common law in *R v Murdoch* (2005, 2007). In 2005, in the Supreme Court of the Northern Territory, Bradley John Murdoch was convicted of the murder of Peter Falconio and the abduction of Joanne Lees. During the trial, prosecutors adduced and relied upon Dr. Sutisno's morphological assessment of images to help implicate Murdoch (*Murdoch*, 2005, [82]).[10] The circumstantial prosecution case included poorly resolved images of a person and vehicle of interest at a truck stop in the relevant vicinity at a time proximate to the murder and abduction (see Figure 1). The images, described by the court as "enhanced", were of such poor quality that the number plate of the vehicle, adjacent to where the person of interest was standing in some of the images, could not be resolved (*Murdoch*, 2005, [10], [11], [12], [18], [20], esp. [15]-[55]).[11]

Figure 1. Person of interest (identified as Murdoch) entering the truck stop. Courtesy of the Northern Territory Police.

Notwithstanding these limitations, at trial Dr. Sutisno testified, based on comparisons of the video images taken at the truck stop and reference images of Murdoch, that in her opinion it was Murdoch at the truck stop. Considering the admissibility of this opinion evidence, Martin CJ explained:

Dr. Sutisno was an impressive witness. She is highly qualified and experienced in her field. ... Applying both morphological analysis and photographic superimposition, Dr. Sutisno concluded that the person depicted in the image taken from the security film was the accused. She was unable to identify any differences of significance. (Murdoch, 2005, [95]: italics added)

Martin CJ was satisfied that "the principles underlying the work of Dr. Sutisno can be readily understood" (*Murdoch*, 2005, [112]).[12]

At the end of 2006 Murdoch appealed his conviction to the Northern Territory Court of Criminal Appeal. Among the grounds of appeal was the admissibility of Dr. Sutisno's facial mapping evidence. Though applying common law criteria, the Court basically reiterated the approach to facial mapping evidence proposed by the NSW CCA in *Tang*.

This Court has found that the technique employed by Dr. Sutisno did not have a sufficient basis to render the results arrived at by that means part of a field of knowledge which is a proper subject of expert evidence. However the evidence given by Dr. Sutisno was capable of assisting the jury in terms of similarities between the person depicted in the truck stop footage and the appellant. It was evidence that related to, and was admissible as, demonstrating similarities but was not admissible as to positive identity. Dr. Sutisno was not qualified to give evidence, as she did, based on "face and body mapping" as to whether the two men were, indeed, the same man. Her evidence in this regard should not have been received. (Murdoch, 2007, [300]: italics added)

The Northern Territory CCA concluded that while Dr. Sutisno should not have been permitted to give positive identification evidence, the admission of her testimony did not warrant a re-trial.[13]

The other important decision affecting the admissibility of opinions based on incriminating images was *Smith v The Queen* (2001).[14] The appeal to the High Court focused on whether police officers could testify that they *recognised* Mundarra Smith in the images recorded by a bank's security system during a robbery. Two police officers, apparently acting independently, both purported to recognise one of the robbers in the security photographs as Smith. They were allowed, over objection, to express these opinions during the trial. These police officers had each had about half a dozen encounters with Smith, including several "brief (under five minute) conversations", in the months leading up to the robbery (Biber, 2007).

In the High Court a majority comprised of Gleeson CJ, Gaudron, Gummow and Hayne JJ, concluded that the police officers "were in no better position to make a comparison between the person in the photographs than the jurors" and consequently their evidence was deemed irrelevant (*Smith*, 2001, [8]-[11]). (Irrelevant evidence is not admissible and so there was no role for exceptions to the opinion rule.)

Significantly, the decision in *Smith* did not mean that police officers would be permanently prevented from testifying about the identity of persons in images associated with criminal acts. The majority provided examples of the kinds of circumstances in which the (opinion) evidence of police officers might yet prove relevant (if not necessarily admissible):

In other cases, the evidence of identification will be relevant because it goes to an issue about the presence or absence of some identifying feature other than one apparent from observing the accused on trial and the photograph which is said to depict the accused. Thus, if it is suggested that the appearance of the accused, at trial, differs in some significant way from the accused's appearance at the time of the offence, evidence from someone who knew how the accused looked at the time of the offence, that the picture depicted the accused as he or she appeared at that time, would not be irrelevant. Or if it is suggested that there is some distinctive feature revealed by the photographs (as, for example, a manner of walking) which would not be apparent to the jury in court, evidence both of that fact and the witness's conclusion of identity would not be irrelevant. (Smith, 2001, [15]: italics added)

In the aftermath of *Smith*, police and prosecutors were obliged to re-orient the presentation of evidence based on images. The *Smith* decision explains recourse, in Australia, to those with some kind of pre-existing *expertise* to provide facial mapping evidence.[15] It also helps us to understand the scope afforded to investigators, to express opinions about identity, where they possess some, albeit limited, familiarity with the accused that is not available to the jury.

B. Identifications from Recorded Sounds

Interestingly enough, things are less restrictive when it comes to the identification of voices from sound recordings (Edmond & San Roque, 2009).

A good example is the case of *Li v The Queen* (2003). Here, the NSW CCA declared that positive voice identification evidence was properly admitted by the trial judge. The Court was satisfied that interpreters—who had listened to the voice recordings in order to make a transcript—as well as a linguist could express their opinions about the identity of the speakers on a tape, and the jury was well positioned to evaluate any weaknesses in this evidence exposed during the course of the proceedings.

In *Li*, voice comparisons and positive identifications were made by an interpreter (Stephen Chan), a police officer (Sergeant Lee) and a senior lecturer in linguistics from the University of Sydney (Dr Gibbons). Each had been asked to express an opinion as to whether a person speaking Cantonese on a surveillance tape (referred to as "tape 6") was the voice of the appellant. Tape 6 recorded one side of an incriminating telephone conversation. The defence argued, in relation to the opinions of Chan, Lee and Dr Gibbons, that the evidence purporting to identify the voice on the tape as that of the appellant should not have been admitted and, further, that the trial judge had not given an adequate warning about the dangers of voice identification and voice similarity evidence.

In the CCA the primary issue was whether Chan—an experienced and highly accredited interpreter and translator, working between English, Cantonese and Mandarin—could express his opinion about the identity of the speaker. In July 1998 Chan had been given a number of surveillance tapes which included tape 6. He was asked to transcribe and translate conversations on the tapes; which were primarily in Cantonese. Chan listened to the tapes several times and isolated a number of different speakers.[16] He designated a voice on tape 6 as "M1" and opined that the voice of M1 appeared on all five of the tapes supplied to him. About a year later Chan was asked to listen to part of the audio recording of the appellant's police interview. It is not clear from the judgment, but it appears that the police interview was conducted in English. Chan was asked to give his opinion as to whether the voice he had identified as M1 was that of the appellant. Having listened to the original, though perhaps "only once", Chan identified M1 as Alan Siu Lun Li (*Li*, 2003, [36]). The trial judge concluded that Chan's opinion about the identity of the speakers was relevant and admissible.

The appellant identified ten problems with the voice identification evidence. They included: that Chan "was not a voice recognition expert" and gave "an ordinary man's opinion" as to the similarity between the voices on the tapes; that he "would not say there were any special features of the voice"; (he agreed) that "people speaking on a telephone have a different type of speech from people speaking face to face"; and that he had "no training, knowledge or experience in comparing voices speaking in English with those speaking in Cantonese" (*Li*, 2003, [45], [77]). According to the defence, the combined effect of these (and other) weaknesses meant that the identification evidence ought to have been excluded under section 137 of the *Evidence Act* because its probative value was outweighed by the danger of unfair prejudice to the accused. Somewhat inconsistently, the defence also argued, following *Smith v The Queen* (2001), that the comparison was one that could have been conducted by the jury and was thus irrelevant (according to sections 55 and 56).

Writing for the CCA, Ipp JA (Whealy and Howie JJ agreeing) dismissed these concerns. First, Ipp JA explained that the evidence was relevant because Chan was able to bring to the comparison of the tapes something more than the jury. He was able to understand the words spoken on the tapes (*Li*, 2003, [43]). Second, he had listened to the tapes multiple times, and had

thereby acquired a "familiarity" with the voice of M1 that qualified him as an ad hoc expert able to give an opinion about the identity of the voice on tape 6.[17] Finally, the contention that Chan ought to possess expertise in "voice recognition" was unequivocally rejected:

The very many hours that Mr Chan spent listening to and working on the five tapes with a view to identifying the words spoken by M1 qualified him as an ad hoc expert in the characteristics of M1's voice. ... Mr Chan did not have to become a voice recognition expert to become an ad hoc expert within the meaning of R v Leung. In any event, his years of practicing as an interpreter and translator would have been of great assistance to him as it meant he had considerable familiarity with the language spoken and with voices speaking Cantonese and English. (Li, 2003, [42], [48], [51])

Weaknesses in this incriminating opinion evidence were characterised as issues for the jury. Justice Ipp was not persuaded that there were fundamental problems with Chan's opinion evidence. He saw "no reason why the cross-lingual element in the comparison that Mr Chan was required to undertake detracted significantly from his ability to express a *reliable* opinion" (*Li*, 2003, [56]: italics added).

The arguments rehearsed in relation to Chan were extended to cover the opinions of the two other witnesses who also identified the voice on tape 6 as that of Li. Sergeant Lee, a police officer fluent in Cantonese, Mandarin and English, with some experience in Cantonese to English translation, initially heard the incriminating speech via audio surveillance. At that time Lee transcribed and translated the words recorded on the tapes. He subsequently listened to two tapes which contained short passages of the appellant speaking in both Mandarin and Cantonese, had access to the incriminating conversation from tape 6, and reached the conclusion that the voice on tape 6 was that of Li. There is no indication of the number of times that Lee listened to any of these tapes, nor how long he spent transcribing and translating the original conversation. Once again, the CCA doubted that weaknesses in the identification evidence gave rise to any unfair prejudice to the appellant.

The third prosecution witness, the linguist Dr Gibbons, listened to the audio recording of the accused's police interview. This became his base or comparison tape. Dr Gibbons identified a number of specific characteristics of the accused's voice on the base tape, and then compared the base tape (in English) with the surveillance tapes, including tape 6 (where the voices were speaking both Mandarin and Cantonese). He identified the voice on tape 6 as that of Li, based on "general voice properties" as well as the presence of several allegedly distinctive characteristics. In cross-examination Dr Gibbons conceded that he had no specific expertise in either Cantonese or Mandarin and that he was not an expert in cross-lingual comparisons. He also conceded that he had no statistical information about the frequency and distribution amongst Cantonese speakers of the features that he had suggested were distinctive—particularly a feature known as "eshing". Again the CCA explained that any problems went merely to the weight of the evidence and that Dr Gibbons was properly qualified to give expert opinion evidence identifying the voice of the accused on the relevant tapes.

Dr Gibbons did not appear to apply scientific methodology in the sense of using machines or measuring (or other) equipment, and although he relied only on his experience, knowledge and hearing, that did not detract from the inherent expert quality of his evidence and I consider that his evidence was properly admitted as being expert in nature. (Li, 2003, [85]: italics added)

Judicial receptiveness to incriminating opinions about identity derived from voice comparison is exemplified in other recent cases. Later in 2003

the NSW CCA heard another appeal in relation to the identification evidence of an interpreter. In *Regina v Riscuta and Niga* (2003) the admissibility of the incriminating opinion evidence of Clarice Kandic was upheld.

In 1994 Kandic translated a series of covert recordings from Romanian into English. Eighteen months earlier, in 1993, she had been requested by the New South Wales Crime Commission to attend a short interview with Mariana Niga; in case her translation skills were required. They were not; the 15-20 minute interview proceeded in English. In 2001, just before the prosecution associated with the translations was about to commence, Kandic identified the voice on the tapes as that of the woman she had observed being interviewed in English at the Crime Commission in 1993. This was the first time Kandic openly identified the voice on the tape as belonging to Mariana Niga. While Kandic suggested that she could recall distinctive features of one of the female voices on the covert recordings, she testified that she recalled no "unusual" features in the voice from the Crime Commission (from 1993). She was, however, told by the investigating police, before making the identification in 2001, that they believed the person on the surveillance tapes was the woman she had seen interviewed in English at the Crime Commission and that the recordings she transcribed in 1994 were from Niga's phone. It was in this context that Kandic purported to identify Mariana Niga as the voice of "Mariana" on the covert recordings.

The trial judge thought that Kandic's voice identification evidence was properly admitted. For the CCA the main problem with the conduct of the trial was the failure to adequately warn the jury about particular dangers associated with voice identification evidence (according to sections 116 and 165 of the UEL).[18] Notwithstanding some obvious dangers and inadequate warnings, in what was characterised as a compelling circumstantial case, the CCA thought Kandic's identification evidence was properly admitted and dismissed the appeal.

Niga and Riscuta is revealing because it demonstrates inconsistency and the lack of principle surrounding the treatment of opinion evidence associated with identification. Remarkably, and in the context of this article revealingly, in a prosecution and appeal where the admissibility of the identification evidence was robustly challenged, the NSW CCA (Heydon JA with Hulme J and Carruthers AJ agreeing) did not mention the fact that Kandic was expressing an opinion or consider whether the opinion was based on "specialised knowledge".[19] The relevance and, more problematically, the admissibility of her opinion evidence were simply taken for granted.[20]

A similar approach to the opinion of an interpreter was followed in *R v El-Kheir* (2004). During an investigation into the importation of narcotics, the interpreter, Dr Gamal, listened to covert recordings "again and again and again" in order to prepare a transcript and identify the speakers. Once again, the NSW CCA did not concern itself with the interpreter's opinions about identity even though: the sound recording was "very poor" (rated at 2 on a scale from 0 to 10); there was considerable background noise, "extended breaks where nothing could be heard", where "words could be heard but not understood", "bits and pieces were missing" and "at times insufficient detail in the quality of the soundtrack to form a definite opinion as to who was speaking to whom" (*El-Kheir*, 2004, [97]-[98]).[21] In relation to one of the allegedly incriminating statements Dr Gamal "accepted that there was a 50% chance that the statement he attributed to M2 [i.e. identified as El-Kheir] was attributable to M1" but was "adamant that either M1 or M2 ... made the statement" (*El-Kheir*, 2004, [103]).[22]

Referring to *Li*, the Court of Criminal Appeal (Tobias JA with Hoeben J and Smart AJ agreeing) suggested that "the admission of voice identification evidence was a matter for judicial discretion" (*El-Kheir*, 2004, [96], [105]). Without troubling

themselves with the opinion rule or the exception for "specialised knowledge" (or even referring to ad hoc expertise), the CCA took the admissibility of the voice identification evidence for granted, in circumstances where there were real doubts about its independence, probative value or necessity. *Niga and Riscuta* and *El-Kheir* exemplify an enthusiasm for the reception of incriminating identification evidence and indifference to boundaries between translation and identification.

This generally permissive trend was reinforced by *R v Madigan* (2005). In *Madigan* the investigating police officers spent a total of "maybe 50 hours, maybe more" listening to covert recordings. They replayed "some tracks up to 20 times in an attempt to make out the words". On the basis of this repeated listening they made transcripts and gave voice identification evidence (*Madigan*, 2005, [96]-[97]). Justice Wood (with Grove and Hoeben JJ agreeing) concluded, on the basis that the accused and others identified themselves in the incriminating recordings, that there was little risk that the jury might misuse or improperly value the voice identification evidence of the investigating police officers.

The most remarkable feature of the *Madigan* decision was the exclusion of the evidence of an expert witness called by the defence. Madigan sought to rely on a linguist (Elliott) to describe alternative and apparently more rigorous approaches to forensic voice comparison than those employed by the investigating police. According to the Court of Criminal Appeal:

It does not however follow that the defence should have been permitted to call Ms Elliot to give her expert opinion on the "methodology". All that she was able to offer was to describe an approach to voice identification that differed from the method of identification by a person who had the opportunity of listening to the tapes and having some familiarity with the voices of the speakers, either as direct evidence or as ad hoc expert evidence, which has been accepted by the courts: see R v

Leung (1999) 47 NSWLR 405 where it was held that s 79 of the Evidence Act was sufficiently wide to accommodate the idea of an ad hoc expert witness, and see also R v Gao [2003] NSWCCA 390 at [23].

She had not undertaken any acoustic analysis herself and was not in a position to offer an opinion as to whether the speakers were the Appellant, Woods and Ms Walker. ... The defining point for the rejection of her evidence was that it did no more than identify an alternative method of voice identification that was dependent upon acoustic analysis, without placing in issue that which was led by the Crown. (Madigan, 2005, [107]-[109])

Challenging, directly or implicitly, the expertise of the police officers was not enough. To the extent that the defence were able to point to the existence of qualified experts from an established field of research, able to testify about emerging scientific techniques and notorious problems, this response seems difficult to reconcile with an accusatorial system interested in fairness or accuracy.

Whether under the UEL or at common law, the approach to the admissibility of *expert* voice identification evidence is similar. Perhaps the main difference is that in NSW, following the introduction of the UEL, judges have effectively abandoned their common law rules—concerned with the distinctiveness and clarity of the voice, the length of exposure and degree of familiarity—regulating the use of voice *identification* evidence.[23]

C. Ad Hoc Experts

Many of the cases discussed above involve experts and non-experts expressing opinions in areas where they possess limited, if any, "training, study or experience". In some cases, such as facial mapping, the existence of a "field" or "specialised knowledge" is contestable and there appear to be few, if any, standardised techniques

or validated studies (Kemp, 2008). This, curiously enough, has not prevented judges from allowing these experts (in anatomy, translation, linguistics and physical anthropology—if not face, body and voice comparison) and non-experts (such as police officers) to express their opinions about identity in serious criminal proceedings. Often, at common law and even more prominently under the UEL, the category of ad hoc expertise is invoked to support the admission of incriminating opinion evidence (Edmond & San Roque, 2009). But what is ad hoc expertise and on what basis does it circumvent statutory rules—in UEL jurisdictions—requiring opinion evidence to be based on "specialised knowledge"?

The idea of ad hoc expertise emerged in New Zealand when, in *R v Menzies* (1982, 48), the Court of Appeal held that a transcript, prepared by a detective who had repeatedly listened to lengthy low quality voice recordings, was admissible as an aid to the jury. This approach, allowing the jury to be assisted in their interpretation of sounds by a transcript prepared by a police officer or interpreter, was followed in Australia in the common law case of *Butera v Director of Public Prosecutions for the State of Victoria* (1987). During the last decade, however, things have become rather messy. For, as we have seen, judges in NSW began to allow persons who listened repeatedly to the tape to compare the voices with other recordings in order to *identify* the unknown speakers. This rather large conceptual leap—from *translating* words (and possibly differentiating among speakers) to *identifying* the speakers—passed without judicial comment.

This leap was all the more remarkable because section 48 of the recently enacted UEL made transcripts potentially admissible, not merely as aids for the jury but, as evidence of the content of the tapes.[24] That is, the jury could consider a transcript as evidence of what was recorded on the tapes. This surpassed the possibilities available at common law (from *Menzies* and *Butera*) and practically eliminated the need for ad hoc expertise in UEL jurisdictions. Curiously then, the expansion of ad hoc expertise proceeded against the explicit text of the UEL. (There are no references to ad hoc expertise in any of the Acts.) Section 76 proscribes opinion evidence and the UEL provides a series of exceptions; including the exception for opinions based on "specialised knowledge". Through the invocation and expansion of the concept of the ad hoc expert the judges of NSW were re-defining and expanding pre-*Evidence Act* categories in ways that undermined the Act.

The judges of NSW have expanded the concept of the ad hoc expert to enable investigators and experts (sometimes from marginally relevant domains and/or with very limited "experience") to express opinions about identity on the basis of exposure to sound recordings and/or images. The fact that there is no "specialised knowledge" as in *Tang* or "field of expertise" as in *Murdoch* seems to make little difference. Even where there are comparison techniques emerging from scientific research traditions, judges seem content to admit the opinions of investigators (such as police and interpreters) rather than require the prosecution to retain the services of properly trained linguists (or psychologists or statisticians) using experimentally validated techniques with known rates of error.

D. Explaining the Reasoning Behind the Opinion

As previously mentioned, there is at common law and under the UEL, an expectation that expert witnesses will explain the *basis* for their opinions. This is sometimes described as the *basis rule*.[25] In theory, an explanation of techniques and methods relied upon, and the reasoning behind them, affords the fact finder an opportunity to evaluate opinion evidence.

Grounded in the influential Scottish case of *Davie v Lord Provost, Magistrates and Counsellors of the City of Edinburgh* (1953) judges operating

under common law have affirmed the need for experts to explain the grounds of their opinions.

Expert witnesses, however skilled or eminent, can give no more than evidence. They cannot usurp the functions of the jury or Judge sitting as a jury, any more than a technical assessor can substitute his advice for the judgment of the Court. ... Their duty is to furnish the Judge or jury with the necessary scientific criteria for testing the accuracy of their conclusions, so as to enable the Judge or jury to form their own independent judgment by the application of these criteria to the facts proved in evidence. The scientific opinion evidence, if intelligible, convincing and tested, becomes a factor (and often an important factor) for consideration along with the whole other evidence in the case, but the decision is for the Judge or jury. In particular the bare ipse dixit of a scientist, however eminent, upon the issue in controversy, will normally carry little weight, for it cannot be tested by cross-examination nor independently appraised, and the parties have invoked the decision of a judicial tribunal and not an oracular pronouncement by an expert. (Davie, 1953, 39-40)

This principle from *Davie* has also found support in UEL jurisdictions; most prominently in *Makita (Australia) Pty Ltd v Sprowles* (2001).

We only need to consider the response to facial mapping evidence in the Supreme Court of NSW, just a few months after the CCA determined that facial mapping was not "specialised knowledge" in *Tang*, to appreciate the perfunctory way in which judges often approach the reasoning behind *expert* opinion. Considering the admissibility of Dr. Sutisno's *identification* evidence in *R v Jung* (2006), Hall J referred to her academic qualifications, recent practice as a forensic anatomist and "practical experience in facial identification" (*Jung*, 2006, [51]). The question of whether the opinion expressed by Dr. Sutisno was wholly or substantially based on her specialised knowledge was answered in the affirmative (*Jung*, 2006, [59]). Justice Hall drew support from *Davie* and *Makita*:

However adequate or inadequate the photographic materials utilised by Sutisno for the purpose of her analysis, the evidence on the voir dire does not establish that she has failed to disclose the factual material she has utilised (the photographic images), the nature of the methodology that she has employed and the type of analysis described in her reports (morphological analysis). I have carefully reviewed the reports and her evidence in order to determine whether it may properly be said that, having regard to the specific principles governing admissibility of expert evidence as identified by Heydon JA in Makita and as summarised above, Dr. Sutisno's evidence complies with the requirements for admissibility. (Jung, 2006, [62]-[65])

Dr. Sutisno explained how she compared police photographs of the accused with poorly resolved images of the person of interest recorded by an ATM camera. Her PhD in anatomy and the comparison of the images, rather than information about the validity and accuracy of her qualitative morphological approach, rendered the Crown's highly incriminating (but highly prejudicial) expert opinion evidence admissible.

This example, along with those discussed in previous sections, illustrate how judges often treat the reasoning behind an opinion in a rather superficial manner. The fact that an expert has used a comprehensible process, regardless of how valid, accurate or rigorous that process actually is, seems to be the main concern.

E. Common Knowledge and the Ultimate Issue (Section 80)

It is also worth noting that at common law there are rules regulating the expression of expert opinions on ultimate issues and subjects perceived to be within the experience of the jury. While section 80 of the UEL (and modern common law jurisprudence) modified the severity of the common law in a way that makes opinions on ultimate issues and common knowledge potentially admissible, sensitivity to the dangers of opinions on ultimate issues, like the identity of persons of interest in incriminating sound recordings or images, should continue. Research from experimental psychology would seem to provide good grounds for believing that popular beliefs about identification and similarity evidence is often mistaken (Wells & Quinlivan, 2009).

In *R v GK* (2001, [40]) the President of the NSW Court of Appeal observed that: "judges should exercise particular scrutiny when experts move close to the ultimate issue, lest they arrogate expertise outside their field or express views unsupported by disclosed and testable assumptions." This is an important consideration and one that applies with even greater force to the opinions of ad hoc experts and those whose expertise might not be entirely germane to their opinion.

F. The Exclusionary Discretions

It might have been thought that the statutory incarnation of *Christie*, a common law discretion empowering the trial judge to exclude otherwise admissible evidence where the probative value of that evidence is outweighed by the danger of unfair prejudice to the accused, would provide a practical means of excluding incriminating expert opinion evidence of unknown reliability.[26] This, however, has not been the case.

Sections 135 and 137 (of the UEL) embody the statutory response to the *Christie* discretion.[27] Here we focus on section 137 because it is mandatory, exclusively concerned with evidence adduced by the prosecutor in criminal proceedings, and imposes the most demanding threshold.

137 Exclusion of prejudicial evidence in criminal proceedings

In a criminal proceeding, the court must refuse to admit evidence adduced by the prosecutor if its probative value is outweighed by the danger of unfair prejudice to the defendant.

The "probative value" of evidence is its ability to rationally affect the probability of the existence of a fact in issue. "Unfair prejudice" is the danger that the evidence might be improperly valued or misused by the fact finder (Australian Law Reform Commission, 1985, [957]).[28] In effect, the trial judge is required to balance the ability of the evidence to rationally influence the assessment of the facts in issue against real dangers that the evidence may be misused by the jury. If the danger outweighs the probative value then the judge must exclude the evidence.

In practice section 137 does not afford much protection for defendants. On its face section 137 would appear to provide the means of excluding incriminating opinion evidence that is not particularly probative and/or is prejudicial in some unfair way. Indeed, section 137 might appear to offer a viable means of excluding evidence that is either of low or unknown probative value, especially where there is a very real chance that the jury might attach considerable weight to it and certainly more weight than it can credibly sustain.

Unfortunately, judges are reluctant to determine the reliability of expert identification or comparison evidence when applying section 137 (and section 135 and the *Christie* discretion at common law). Rather than actually gauging the probative value of the opinion evidence and balancing it against real dangers of unfair prejudice to the accused, judges take the probative value of the identification evidence *at its highest*.[29] The trial judge balances the risk of unfair prejudice against the maximum value that the opinion evidence could, *if accepted*, sustain.[30] This means that the trial judge assumes that the evidence *is reliable* without knowing whether *expert* witnesses can actually do what they claim—because a jury

might—and then considers dangers associated with the evidence on the basis of that assumption.

This approach is structurally oblivious to the most serious prejudice associated with the admission of any opinion evidence. It ignores the very real danger that the jury might rely upon unreliable *identification* and similarity evidence (though here presented by an investigator or highly-credentialed expert).

G. Overview

Australian judges have actively developed the UEL and the common law to allow investigators and experts—though not necessarily experts from the relevant domain or possessed of the most appropriate expertise—to proffer their incriminating opinions in court.

In practice, section 79(1) is not applied particularly strictly—at least not to the evidence adduced by the prosecution in criminal proceedings. Rather than focus on whether opinions are based "wholly or substantially" on "specialised knowledge" that is based on an individual's "training, study or experience", in the criminal sphere judges have a tendency to privilege formal training and recognisable forms of expertise. Sometimes formal training, in established fields like medicine, anatomy or biology, enables a witness to testify about matters that are not based on "knowledge" (let alone "specialised knowledge") and not based in their actual training, study or experience. There is a tendency to allow trained professionals to testify in areas beyond (or adjacent to) their actual expertise or beyond the demonstrated ability of any recognisable field or identifiable sub-discipline. There can be considerable *slippage* between an expert's "training, study or experience" and the bases and knowledge purportedly grounding what becomes admissible *expert* opinion evidence.

Similar results obtain when we consider the common law and its traditional concern with expertise in an established field. Judges operating in both systems evince a willingness to admit incriminating opinions even where the proponent does not have relevant qualifications, has not tested their technique or opinions, and even where the proponent is a police officer involved in the investigation.

There is, in addition, an unexplicated inconsistency in the approach to expert identification evidence. In relation to images, those with training in anatomy, physical anthropology and photography are prohibited from positively identifying the accused. Their opinions are limited to describing similarities (and differences) between images of varying resolution. In contrast, police officers and investigators who may have some familiarity with a suspect, such as knowledge of their gait or posture, are allowed to proffer positive identification evidence. This holds even where the familiarity is quite limited and the features may not, whether individually or in combination, be very discriminating.

There are also inconsistencies when it comes to the identification of voices. Interestingly, police officers, interpreters and linguists with no formal training in voice comparisons are allowed to interpret recordings and give positive identification evidence on the basis of repeated exposure (i.e. listening over and over). This permissive approach also extends to positive identifications based on cross-lingual comparisons.

The lack of principle is compounded if we include judicial responses to attempts by defence counsel to introduce expert evidence or to argue for a more restrained approach. Attempts to use rebuttal experts to respond to the opinions of *experts* conjured by the prosecution have on occasion been unsuccessful. Judges routinely allow incriminating evidence from ad hoc experts but have prevented an accused person from adducing evidence from rebuttal witnesses actually qualified in an ostensibly relevant field—such as acoustics, linguistics, psychology, statistics or image interpretation.

Unfortunately, the problems go much deeper than mere inconsistency and cannot be repaired

by restricting incriminating expert evidence to opinions about similarity (rather than identity).

4. EVIDENTIARY AND PROCEDURAL PROBLEMS

Prosecutorial and judicial indifference to the reliability of expert evidence is difficult to comprehend. In this section it is my intention to discuss some of the problems with expert identification evidence. Perhaps the most remarkable aspect is the fact that our judges have been reluctant to exclude incriminating expert opinion evidence of unknown reliability. Overwhelmingly their preference has been to admit the testimony and leave it to the trial and the jury.

A. Validity and Reliability Problems with Voice and Image Comparisons

The most serious problem with most forms of *identification* (and comparison) evidence is the fact that the techniques have not been adequately tested and the evidence is often obtained in circumstances that accentuate bias and the risks of error. We do not know whether police officers, investigators and even *experts* can reliably produce the kinds of *identifications* that courts allow them to make. We do not know if their techniques are valid or reliable. We do not know the rates of error involved. Remarkably, our judges have conscientiously developed the admissibility rules to facilitate the admission of incriminating identification and comparison evidence in circumstances where the techniques and opinions are of *unknown reliability* (Edmond, 2008). That is, where the probative value of the evidence is unknown (even if many of the epistemological limitations and risks to the accused are).

It is important to stress that the range of techniques associated with voice and visual identification, which primarily rely upon different kinds of comparison and repeated exposure, could be tested but have not been (National Research Council, 2009). It would not be difficult to formally test the ability of police, interpreters, linguists and anatomists. The need for testing is forcefully advocated by Saks and Faigman. Having characterised the forensic identification sciences—i.e. voice identification, bite marks, tool marks, tyre prints, shoe prints, fingerprints and handwriting evidence—as the "nonscience forensic sciences". They continue:

The nonscience forensic sciences, as the paradoxical phrase suggests, are those fields within forensic science that have little or no basis in actual science. They neither borrow from established science nor systematically test their hypotheses. Their primary claims for validity rest on anecdotal experience and proclamations of success over time. Hypothesis and supposition are typically considered sufficient. ... [They rely] on unspecified, unsystematic "experience" coupled with plausible-sounding arguments as the nearly exclusive bases for their hypotheses. (Saks & Faigman, 2008, 150; Saks & Koehler, 2005)

In the absence of testing, the confidence of the expert witness is largely irrelevant, as are formal qualifications, many forms of experience, and even claims about the existence of a "field".

At this point it is my intention to briefly discuss some of the problems with expert identification and comparison evidence (Edmond et al, 2009). The first problem with the interpretation of images (with some obvious analogies to the interpretation of sound recordings) concerns quality. Not infrequently the images associated with a criminal act are very poorly resolved (e.g. *Li, Tang, Murdoch* and *Jung*). In most situations there is very limited scope to improve or enhance the images. The poor quality of the images is often a result of inexpensive cameras (especially lenses), the type of lens (frequently wide angle), the angle and distance from the camera, the amount of information recorded, as well as the available lighting, background noise, and so on.

Conventionally, forensic scientists use strict controls to assure that images are suited to forensic examination and comparisons. They are particularly concerned with obtaining clearly resolved and well lit images free of rectilinear distortion (Horswell, 2004). Though standard for most forensic photographic applications, these pre-requisites are rarely satisfied by the images obtained from CCTV systems, surveillance cameras, ATMs and mobile phones.

In addition, in order to obtain images for comparison, police, forensic scientists and anatomists often cherry-pick frames from videos or among photographs. That is, they may spend hours carefully scrutinising video recordings in search of frames displaying features that appear *similar* to those exhibited in forensic procedure photographs of the prime suspect. This is not a desirable process, especially when the *experts* are often police officers or within the sphere of the investigation. Methodologically, indifference to the many images which do not provide similarities is not adequately explained. Why should images that *appear* to present similarities be preferred over those which suggest dissimilarity or are considered insufficiently resolved? Revealingly, analytical and statistical techniques are not employed to explain the prejudicial selections.

Another serious problem with the interpretation of images concerns the analyst's response to image perspective (Porter, 2008, 2007). Image perspective is an effect produced by the conversion of three-dimensional objects into two-dimensional images (see Figure 2). It can compress or expand visual space and can also change the size relationship between objects represented within an image. In conjunction with the effects caused by lenses, angles, lighting, level of resolution and noise, image perspective can create serious difficulties for those trying to overcome distortion in order to compare or identify strangers. It is notable that there is no discussion of image perspective in any

Figure 2. Note how the relative size and form of facial features and the relationships between facial features change depending upon the distance between the subject and the camera ('u' distance). The question here, and the question confronting all of those trying to interpret incriminating images (almost always of much lower quality and from less desirable angles) is what does the face of the person of interest actually look like. Photographs courtesy of Glenn Porter.

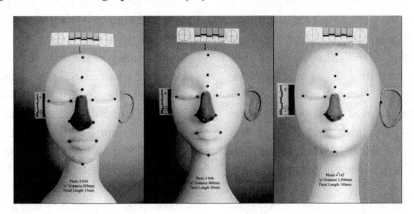

of the reported decisions. More importantly, training in anatomy or physical anthropology, along with possession of a technical vocabulary, does not allow experts to somehow transcend distortion and image artefacts.

Training in anatomy, for example, does not enable a person to see things that are not available from the image or intuitively overcome problems created by the way images are obtained, stored and displayed. Currently, there are no simple operational methods for transcending the problems plaguing many of the incriminating images associated with crimes. Nevertheless, anatomists and investigators have been allowed to comment on *apparent* similarities between a distorted, poorly resolved image (or images) and high quality police reference photos of the accused. In many cases, the fact that similarities may be artefacts, epiphenomena or coincidence seems to be ignored.

Similarity evidence suffers from many, and frequently all, of the problems with positive identifications. However, where *identification* is not based on clearly visible features capable of supporting individualisation (e.g. observation of some types of highly unusual scarring and/or blemishes and/or deformity), it is really only comparison

evidence. Almost always, there is no information about the frequency of any features purportedly observed or heard. Yet, legitimate use of most types of comparison evidence requires information about the frequency of somatic features (along with clothing, mannerisms and so on) and, where there are more than two features, there is a need for information about any relationship between the observed features (Saks & Koehler, 2008).[31]

In a recent trial in the District Court of NSW, experts called by the prosecution (Professor Maciej Henneberg, Department of Anatomy, University of Adelaide) and defence (Dr Richard Kemp, Department of Psychology, UNSW) agreed on Dr Kemp's written response to a jury question about the interpretation of CCTV images. Dr Kemp explained:

We do not know the frequency with which these characteristics [e.g. head and nose shape (under a balaclava), right-handedness and somatatype—which were all contested] occur within the Australian population. Furthermore, we do not know whether the characteristic noted are independent of each other.

The issue of independence is critical. If two features are statistically independent of each other, then the observation that an individual possesses one feature tells us nothing about the likelihood that this individual will also poses the second feature. In contrast, if two features are not independent of each other then they are said to be correlated and the observation that an individual possesses one feature will affect the probability that they also possess the second. For example, we know that in the Australia population earnings and gender are correlated, so the probability than a man earns more than $100,000 is much higher than the probability that a woman earns this much.

In order to estimate what proportion of the population would share a particular set of features we need to know both the frequency with which each feature occurs in the population and the degree of correlation between all possible pairs of features. We do not know either of these things and therefore it is not possible to make a valid estimate of the proportion of the population who will share a particular set of features. In the absence of this information it would be very dangerous to attempt such an estimate, because even quite low correlations between features could have a large effect on our estimate. (R v Morgan, 2009, Exhibit 77)

Anatomists have been allowed to testify about similarities between the accused and a person of interest in incriminating images. These experts—in anatomy, if not the comparison of persons in poor quality two-dimensional images—have tended to select a small number of attributes *apparent* in the incriminating image(s) and link them to features of the accused in high quality reference photos. Ears, lips, chin, nose and general morphology of the head and body have been particularly noteworthy in this regard. Though, as the previous extract explains, in the absence of detailed information about the frequency of particular features in the general population (and even sub-populations) and the interrelationships

(and independence) between different facial (and body) features, apparent similarities may not be particularly revealing (Mardia et al, 1996, 658; Aronson, 2007; Saks & Koehler, 2008). The failure to obtain population samples and actually test the various identification techniques means that these problems do not feature as prominently as they should. It also means that we have no idea of the actual rate of error (Saks & Faigman, 2008).[32]

Further, limiting opinions to comments on similarities and differences does not somehow sanitise incriminating opinion evidence (contra *Tang* and *Murdoch*). Where *experts* (and ad hoc experts) are not able to make reliable identifications because of problems with the images and unproven techniques, they will not necessarily be able to undertake useful comparisons. If the images are poorly resolved or there are no credible means of overcoming artefactual impediments, such as image perspective and other distortions, then allowing experts to opine about similarities and differences is as undesirable as positive identification evidence. Apparent similarities and opinions about similarities may be no more or less reliable than positive identification evidence.

There are no accepted (or standardised) methods for making reliable identifications from CCTV and other surveillance images (Edmond et al, 2009; compare Porter & Doran, 2000). This, it is important to emphasise, is not because forensic scientists, engineers, information technology specialists, professional photographers, psychologists and others have no interest in the subject matter. Rather, the identification of strangers from images has proven surprisingly difficult for humans and machines (Kemp et al, 1997). To allow police, anatomists and physical anthropologists to proffer opinions, even considered opinions, in the absence of demonstrated ability and in the absence of techniques accepted by relevant professional communities, is to treat ongoing scientific and commercial research and development, and the magnitude of the difficulties, with contempt. Indeed, it is because some of the world's leading forensic scientific agencies and IT professionals have been unable to produce reliable techniques that judges and prosecutors should proceed with great caution. As things stand investigators, prosecutors and judges have created an admissibility pathway for untested and potentially unreliable opinions because relevant experts—such as research scientists and engineers—are unwilling or unable to testify.

Many analogous difficulties apply with respect to voice identification evidence even if they are not always quite as obvious (Gonzales-Rodriguez et al, 2007; Ormerod, 2000). How, for example, does the type of microphone, its position and proximity to those speaking, the amount of background noise and so on influence the quality and interpretation of the recording (e.g. *El-Kheir*)?[33] What roles do the type of recorder, the storage medium, and the reproduction system play? For interpretation: can different voices appear similar to those who are unfamiliar with the speaker(s)? Do families and those exposed to long processes of socialisation and interaction influence both the sound of the voice and the kinds of things spoken about? What about accents, disguises, jargon and context? How should we approach cross-lingual comparisons and identifications, especially when the languages have radically divergent genealogies and sounds (e.g. *Regina v Korgbara*, 2007)? How common are distinctive words and phrases or characteristics like speech impediments, unusual pronunciations and accents (e.g. *Li*)? Do voices remain stable over time? Can we meaningfully compare a voice speaking calmly on a phone with a voice screaming during an armed robbery? Even though judges do not seem to have fully appreciated the fact, the lack of information about the distribution of linguistic features (such as accents and eshing) constitutes a serious problem. There is, once again, a very grave danger of equating (apparent) similarity or similarities with identity (Shannon, 1984, 39).

In addition, the interpretation of sound recordings often introduces ambiguities. Even where the identity of the speaker is not controversial the inculpatory dimensions of any words or phrases may be. In consequence, there may be debate about the significance of certain words and phrases that have a range of different meanings and valencies.[34] Both sounds and images are susceptible to radically divergent interpretations (Goodwin, 1994; Good, 2006).

These are not hypothetical or trivial problems and should not be casually abandoned to weight. Prosecutors and judges (as well as police and forensic scientists) should want to know how they are addressed when considering relevance, admissibility and the exercise of discretions.

B. Production Problems (And the Lack of Method)

As things stand, judges have exhibited little interest in the ways in which some forms of identification and comparison evidence are developed. Repeated exposure to sound and visual images provides police and a range of experts with access to the courtroom and the jury. Yet the way in which police and experts are introduced to images or voice recordings may have serious implications for the independence and reliability of any identification or similarity evidence. Concerns about the way that procedures can limit the choices open to the expert, as well as the conclusions, become particularly significant when we consider how expert witnesses are enlisted and the manner in which information from the investigation is presented to them (Risinger et al, 2002; Wells & Quinlivan, 2009).

The way experts, like formally qualified anatomists, are enlisted to provide *evidence* about identity provides a useful illustration. It is not uncommon for an anatomist to be sent an envelope containing just two sets of images (or for the identity of the suspect to be disclosed by investigators).[35] One set is made up of high quality police reference photographs of the main suspect and the other set is composed of images associated with a crime which includes the person of interest. The expert is usually asked to compare the two sets of images. Often this comparison occurs at a relatively late stage in the investigation. Curiously, this process resembles widely discredited approaches to photographic arrays, confrontations and dock identifications.[36] For, the process is ripe with suggestion. Without a publicly validated method the anatomist sets about comparing two sets of images in circumstances where they know that the investigating police officers believe the two sets of images are of the same person. This process is disconcerting regardless of whether the expert witness is a state employed forensic scientist or *independent* consultant retained by the police or prosecution.

Equally troubling, at trial the opinions of *identification experts* are routinely treated as independent and corroborative evidence of guilt. If we return to the example in the previous paragraph we can see how this approach, and the treatment of any resulting identification or similarity evidence as an independent piece of evidence in a circumstantial case, may be misleading. First, the actual process of enrolment may undermine the independence and value of the opinion evidence. Where, for example, an interpreter, police officer or expert (such as an anatomist or linguist) identifies the prime suspect, knowing who the prime suspect is, this evidence is not independent and should not be used for corroboration. For, if the actual suspicion in mistaken and there are no effective methods to control the *identification* (or similarity) evidence or to determine its accuracy then there is a real danger that this evidence will simply compound the mistaken suspicion. Significantly, recent studies of experienced fingerprint examiners suggest that even in circumstances where there are established protocols, trained professionals may have their opinions altered by what should be extraneous information—such as the suspicions of investigating police officers (Dror et al, 2006; Dror & Rosenthal, 2008).

Second, it is not uncommon for investigators to have informal contact with police officers and to know about other dimensions of the investigation. An expert witness might be apprised of the fact, for example, that the police recovered the accused's fingerprint from stolen merchandise or know that friends of the accused (implicitly accomplices) confessed and even implicated him (e.g. *Tang*). Police officers (and others) making identifications are almost always involved in the investigation (as in *Li* and *Madigan*) and so, necessarily, have a great deal of supplementary—though often unsubstantiated—information when they undertake their visual and aural *identification* work.

C. Cross-Racial and Cross-Lingual Comparisons

A recurring feature of expert evidence, in voice and image *identification* cases, is the reliance on opinions based on cross-lingual or cross-racial comparisons and the reluctance of the courts to exercise any form of discretionary control over the admission of this evidence. This runs parallel to the general reluctance to consider, in a systematic way, the different methods that might be used to make the process of cross-cultural comparisons more reliable. Cross-cultural identifications based on voices and images are notoriously unreliable (Scheck et al, 2000; Garrett & Neufeld, 2009). They compound the normal problems with identification experienced by lay persons and experts alike. To the extent that images and sounds are poorly resolved, fleeting or foreign, the likelihood that resulting opinions are unreliable (or carry a substantial risk or error) is considerable (Wells & Quinlivan, 2009).

D. Residual "Safeguards": Cross-Examination, Defence Experts and Warnings

Judges who admit *expert* identification and similarity evidence based on voices and images tend to place confidence in the restorative potential of cross-examination, defence (or rebuttal) experts and judicial warnings (sections 116 and 165 under the UEL).[37] The effectiveness of these purported safeguards, on closer examination, seems to be more of an article of faith than any kind of rational response to the very real risks to the accused. There is little empirical evidence suggesting that cross-examination, rebuttal experts and directions are effective at consistently and fairly exposing problems with expert opinion evidence.

Cross-examination and rebuttal expertise provide means of challenging expert *identification* evidence and exposing some of its weaknesses. Though, in practice, effective cross-examination and rebuttal experts are often just possibilities. Proponents assume that the defence is in a good position to challenge the opinion of senior police or experienced interpreters and forensic scientists retained by the prosecution. Confidence in cross-examination and the restorative potential of defence experts assumes that: defence lawyers are conversant with the technical detail and limitations with identification and comparison *expertise*; will be capable of effectively conveying limitations to a lay jury (and judge); and have the resources to undertake the task. It also assumes that rebuttal experts can be identified and funded, will agree to participate, and will be admitted. None of these are guaranteed.

Even where the defence secures highly competent counsel and the services of professionally competent experts there is no guarantee that they will perform as well or effectively convey the weaknesses in the *expert* identification evidence adduced by the prosecution. Ordinarily, the defence will be contesting the opinions of an experienced police officer or forensic scientist along with pervasive assumptions about the sensory prowess of experienced investigators. In the absence of standardised techniques in established fields, challenges to incriminating *expertise* will often appear to be *ad hominem*. It will be the opinion of an experienced investigator or scientist, carefully

integrated into an incriminating narrative, against cross-examination or the opinion of a critical expert engaged by the defence. Often, the *expert witness*—such as the anatomist in *Tang* and the interpreters in *Li*—will have no apparent stake in the case and may have even given evidence in similar circumstances to which they can advert. Defence lawyers and rebuttal experts, in contrast, appear to have conspicuous biases regardless of their independence or the quality of their evidence and performance.

In addition, judicial directions and warnings seem to have limited potential in combating problems with expertise and identification. Virtually all of the experimental studies and empirical research suggests that judicial directions and instructions are either incomprehensible or difficult to follow, especially when presented seriatim at the end of the trial.[38] Judges can warn the jury about some of the dangers with expert identification and similarity evidence but if they are willing to admit unreliable forms of expert evidence then there may be genuine questions about their ability to appreciate the magnitude of the dangers as well as effectively convey them to a jury (Findley, 2008).

None of this should be understood to suggest that cross-examination and rebuttal experts cannot, on occasion, be highly effective (Jasanoff, 1995; Lynch, 1998). Similarly, judicial instructions might occasionally inform jury decision making. This, however, does not provide adequate grounds for making them the primary protection against the opinions of investigators (and others in their "camp") masquerading as "specialised knowledge". As protections, cross-examination, rebuttal experts and directions are deceptive. They tend to be inconsistent in operation and their value is frequently exaggerated. They provide rhetorical grounds for allowing incriminating *expert* opinion evidence to go before the jury rather than effective protections for the accused. In addition, they privilege the state by allowing the prosecution to adduce unfairly prejudicial *identification* evidence and then require the defence to somehow negate it. This represents improper burden shifting. Why should the defence be obliged to demonstrate unreliability instead of the state being required to establish that incriminating opinion evidence is reliable?

I do not doubt the ability of juries to approach conflicting expert evidence in a considered fashion (Edmond & Mercer 1999). Jury competence, however, is not the main issue here. The primary issue is whether conflicts of *expert* opinion and substantial criticism of identification and similarity evidence should be left for the jury to resolve. The absence of principle simply compounds the problems. Some juries are confronted with positive identifications from police officers and interpreters—*qua* ad hoc experts—whereas others receive only *de facto* identifications, couched in the language of similarity, from forensic scientists and distinguished anatomists.

The jury's fundamental constitutional role is not undermined by the exclusion of unreliable evidence or evidence of unknown reliability or putting the prosecution to proof.

E. Empirical Research

It is unfortunate that Australian courts have been largely indifferent to relevant scholarly research on the subject of identification.[39] Put simply, most of the empirical and experimental research suggests that interpreting voices and images is quite complex and certainly more complex than many expert witnesses would have us believe (Wells & Quinlivan, 2009; Saks & Koehler 2005; Edmond et al, 2009; Costigan 2007). There is also little evidence supporting the contention that experts, whether anatomists, interpreters, artists, police officers or psychologists, perform particularly well when asked to compare the images and voices of strangers. The accuracy of identification evidence tends to decline: as the comparisons become more complex; where there is considerable time between recordings; where the persons of interest are wearing different clothing, have different hair

styles or facial expressions or appear at different angles; where the persons are featured in different lighting; where the voices speak in different languages or in different styles and tones (e.g. demands made during a bank robbery as opposed to speech with a friend on a telephone); where the amount of background noise or distortion is high, the quality of the recoding low and the duration of the recording short. Interestingly, experimental research suggests that even high quality images and sound recordings do not always dramatically improve the ability of persons to accurately identify strangers (Burton et al, 1999; Davis & Valentine, 2009). Further, there is no empirical evidence that experts can overcome problems with images and sounds through experience, intuition or simply by "taking them into account".

Legal practitioners and judges should not disregard standardised research methods and empirically-predicated research. They should not forget the lessons from the controversy over the development of DNA technologies and population statistics (Aronson, 2007; Lynch et al, 2008). Furthermore, the so-called "experience of judges" should always be tempered by rigorous published experimental research (Beecher-Monas, 2006; National Research Council, 2009).

5. INTERNATIONAL TRENDS (IN NORTH AMERICA, AT LEAST)

At this point, sensitive to the many limitations, I want to emphasise the importance of making *expert* opinion evidence based on sounds and images *more reliable*. Our admissibility jurisprudence can assist this goal by insisting on *reliability* as a pre-condition to the admissibility of this incriminating expert opinion evidence.[40]

There is support for reading "reliability" into "specialised *knowledge*". In *Tang*, notwithstanding its apparent indifference to the reliability of the expert opinion evidence, the CCA purported to place a premium on "knowledge". These judges recognised that knowledge "connotes more than subjective belief or unsupported speculation". The Chief Justice even accepted that the word "applies to any body of known facts or to any body of ideas inferred from such facts *on good grounds*" (*Tang*, 2006, [153]-[154]).

This definition was taken from *Daubert v Merrell Dow Pharmaceuticals, Inc.* (1993), a decision of the Supreme Court of the United States. In attempting to define Rule 702 of the *Federal Rules of Evidence* (1975)—which influenced the drafting of section 79 of the UEL—the Supreme Court insisted on the need for evidentiary reliability when parsing the phrase "scientific, technical or other *specialized knowledge*". The *Daubert* decision requires trial judges to act as gatekeepers (*Daubert*, 1993, 589). In so doing, the majority presented a set of criteria that might assist trial judges to gauge *legal reliability*. These criteria included whether the technique had been tested, published, peer reviewed, whether it was generally accepted as well as information about the rate of error (consider Edmond, 2008a, 120-130). That approach was affirmed and extended to "technical and other specialised knowledge" in *Kumho Tire Co. v Carmichael* (1999).[41]

In 2000, the US *Federal Rules of Evidence* were revised. Rule 702 now states:

If scientific, technical, or other specialized knowledge will assist the trier of fact to understand the evidence or to determine a fact in issue, a witness qualified as an expert by knowledge, skill, experience, training, or education, may testify thereto in the form of an opinion or otherwise, if (1) the testimony is based upon sufficient facts or data, (2) the testimony is the product of reliable principles and methods, and (3) the witness has applied the principles and methods reliably to the facts of the case.

In the wake of *Daubert*, *Kumho* and the revision to the FRE, federal and most state courts in the United States now require evidence of reli-

ability as a basis for the admissibility of all expert opinion evidence.

In recent years the Canadian Supreme Court and several of the provincial courts of appeal have also placed increasing emphasis on the reliability of incriminating expert opinion evidence. At least since the Supreme Court handed down *R v Mohan*, the exclusionary discretions provided a loose framework for these developments (1994). More recent decisions, such as *R v DD* (2000), *R v J-LJ* (2000) and *Re Truscott* (2007), have brought the need for reliable expert opinion evidence to centre stage. This trend is perhaps most clearly expressed in a decision by Deschamp J. Writing for the majority in *R v Trochym* (2007, [27]) she explained:

Reliability is an essential component of admissibility. Whereas the degree of reliability required by courts may vary depending on the circumstances, evidence that is not sufficiently reliable is likely to undermine the fundamental fairness of the criminal process. (italics added)

In a recent inquiry into the quality of paediatric forensic pathology evidence in Ontario, Justice Goudge (2008, 496) recommended that:

In determining the threshold reliability [i.e. admissibility] of expert scientific evidence, the trial judge should assess the reliability of the proposed witness, the field of science, and the opinion offered in the particular case. In doing so, the trial judge should have regard to the tools and questions that are most germane to the task in the particular case.

6. "RELIABILITY" IN AUSTRALIAN EVIDENCE JURISPRUDENCE?

At this point, one of the many things to wonder about is the parochial aversion to *reliability*. The idea of *reliability* has not been central to common law jurisprudence (in Australia or England) concerned with expert opinion evidence, nor opinion based upon "specialised knowledge" under the UEL. We can, perhaps, appreciate that many judges are not skilled or experienced in assessing the reliability of different forms of expertise. Reticence and the difficulty of the task should not, however, deflect them from this important civic responsibility. If our criminal justice system aspires to be rational and fair, and not committed to convicting the innocent, then reliability needs to take a more central position in our admissibility jurisprudence and institutionalised forensic science practice (National Research Council, 2009; Saks & Faigman, 2008; Beecher-Monas, 2006).

The word "reliability" does not feature in sections 79, 135 or 137 of the UEL. Notwithstanding this omission, there have been a few occasions where senior members of our judiciary have indicated that section 79, and its common law equivalents, might actually require some assessment of *reliability*. Several High Court judges have explicitly recognised such a need. Part of the South Australian common law, requiring "a body of knowledge or experience which is sufficiently organised or recognised to be accepted as a reliable body of knowledge or experience" was endorsed by Gaudron and Gummow JJ in *Osland v The Queen* (1998, [53], [164]-[169]). Subsequently, in *HG v The Queen* (1999, [58]), Gaudron J indicated that this passage may be relevant to section 79. That suggestion was reiterated in *Velevski v The Queen* (2002, [82]). Further references to reliability can be found in a series of prominent common law cases from state and territory courts of appeal. These include *R v Gilmore* (1977), *R v Carroll* (1985), *R v Lewis* (1987), as well as *R v Bonython* (1984).

At common law, the need for reliable expert opinion evidence, particularly forensic scientific evidence, has occasionally been quite prominent. This has been most conspicuous in the aftermath of notorious miscarriages of justice.[42] The appeal in *R v Lewis* (1987), delivered in the wake of the

Morling Royal Commission into the Chamberlain convictions, affords a useful illustration of the potential of a reliability threshold. The trial and appeal featured the testimony of some of the expert odontologists involved in the original Chamberlain prosecution. Like facial mappers, these experts made positive identifications on the basis of non-standardised techniques and limited information about the distribution of the odontological features relied upon (Beecher-Monas, 2009).

In the *Lewis* appeal Maurice J explained that there was a need for the "Crown ... to carefully lay the ground for the reception of the opinions expressed by [the dental experts]. *It could only do this by proving the scientific reliability of the exercise they carried out*" (*Lewis*, 1987, 122: italics added). Instead, at trial the Crown "chose to rely on the witness' qualifications and experience in the field of forensic dentistry generally, and, in particular, upon the impressive curriculum vitae" (*Lewis*, 1987, 122). Significantly, "[n]o experimental research was pointed to nor other studies which demonstrated the reliability of the deduction made by these witnesses" (*Lewis*, 1987, 122-123). Maurice J continued:

Forensic evidence, especially if it goes to a vital issue implicating an accused person in the commission of an offence, may often have a prejudicial effect on the minds of a jury which far outweighs its probative value. ...

For my part I think that whenever the Crown wishes to rely upon forensic evidence the prosecutor has a clear duty, not just to his client, the Crown, but to the trial judge and the jury to acquaint them, in ordinary language, through the evidence he leads, with those aspects of the expert's discipline and methods necessary to put them in a position to make some sort of evaluation of the opinions he expresses. Where the evidence is of a comparatively novel kind, the duty resting on the Crown is even higher: it should demonstrate its scientific reliability. It is not an answer to considerations that dictate these things be done to say the defence may draw it out in cross-examination; that is an abdication of the Crown's primary function in a criminal prosecution. (Lewis, 1987, 123-124)

The *Lewis* decision emphasised the need for the Crown to "demonstrate" the "scientific reliability" of novel expert opinion evidence.[43] Surrogates, such as credentials, confidence and experience in court, cannot substitute for studies demonstrating the reliability of the techniques or the process of deduction. Similarly, leaving the issue for weight and cross-examination represents "an abdication of the Crown's primary function".

Another important and illuminating set of examples concerned with *reliability* are the common law decisions structuring the admissibility of DNA typing evidence.[44] Most of these refractory decisions revolved around novel techniques and the development of population statistics associated with early DNA testing. These decisions have obvious parallels with identification and comparison evidence associated with voice recordings and images, particularly with respect to novelty, issues of standardisation, the meaning of population statistics (i.e. distribution of, and relation between, features), and the rapid proliferation of the respective technologies. Responses to DNA evidence are instructive because many Australian judges adopted critical stances even though DNA techniques and evidence were firmly grounded in mainstream biological research fields (e.g. molecular genetics) and supported by extensive research into population genetics.

In cases such as *R v Elliott* (1990), *Tran* (1990), *R v Lucas* (1992), *Regina v Green* (1993), and *Pantoja* (1996), senior judges excluded the prosecution's incriminating DNA evidence. These judges, interestingly, did not refer to the common law *tradition* of taking the evidence "at its highest" and did not, on principle, accept the evidence as reliable simply because a jury might. Similarly, the possibility of cross-examination, rebuttal experts, and directions did not prevent the exclusion of incriminating expert

evidence even in circumstances where the overall case was considered strong. Rather, these judges deemed expert evidence adduced by the prosecution inadmissible because they were concerned about its reliability, the capability of the jury to meaningfully assess it, along with the danger of unfair prejudice to the accused.

These cautionary approaches seem to have been abandoned in recent years. This is unfortunate because the exclusion of incriminating expert opinion evidence—particularly in the US and England, but also in Australia—contributed to the refinement of DNA typing techniques, stimulated research into population genetics, and improved the way the evidence was presented (Aronson, 2007; Lynch et al, 2008). Requiring the state to demonstrate reliability can actually change institutional behaviour, encourage further study, and improve the reliability and probative value of techniques and opinions.

Authority, international trends, the parochial need for "specialised *knowledge*", the experience with DNA evidence, and the desire for fair trials should all encourage Australian judges to read "reliability" into section 79(1) of the Uniform Evidence Law and the common law equivalents. Where incriminating expert identification evidence is involved, *demonstrable reliability* should be a pre-requisite to admissibility.[45] This would not only raise the quality of expert opinion evidence and reduce the number of wrongful convictions, but simultaneously enhance the professionalism of our forensic science institutions and personnel.

7. CONCLUSION: *DEMONSTRABLE RELIABILITY* AND RESTRAINT

A. Taking "Specialised Knowledge" and "Probative Value" More Seriously

There would seem to be no particular reason, when it comes to incriminating opinion evidence based on specialised knowledge, why the UEL and common law could not support a *reliability threshold*.[46] Notwithstanding the marginalisation of "reliability" by the CCA in *Tang*, in a rational system of justice it is not desirable to interpret "knowledge" and certainly "specialised knowledge" without incorporating some notion of reliability.

"Reliability" tends to engender an expectation of trustworthiness. Consequently, judges should consider whether there has been any attempt (by the expert or her peers) to validate or even assess the techniques and underlying assumptions. While there may be disagreements over the adequacy, independence and significance of validation studies—obviously large scale testing, testing undertaken at arm's-length, and testing where the results are published in reputable peer reviewed journals, will generally be preferable—the failure to validate techniques or credibly respond to obvious limitations should ordinarily be damning (National Research Council, 2009; consider Collins 1992).

Where a type of evidence, technique or procedure, whether DNA typing or identification based on sound recordings, CCTV or security images, is likely to be used repeatedly there is an even greater need for the state (or prosecution) to test the techniques and demonstrate their reliability. *Ipse dixit,* and even educated guesses, are not appropriate when it comes to opinions based on ubiquitous and proliferating forms of evidence. To be admissible, the techniques supporting an expert's opinions must be able to consistently and accurately do what is claimed for them. The prosecution should be able to satisfy the court, using evidence, that this is so.

Where we can actually measure validity and error rates, or determine that they have not been ascertained or even considered, it makes little sense to allow (or require) them to be determined by a jury on the basis of in-court conflict, or transform a lay person into an ad hoc expert. Such an approach cannot be considered fair or efficient. Where vital information—such as the frequency

and distribution of face and body features or the frequency of certain sounds and accents—is not available, deference to the jury is inappropriate. The jury should be responsible for resolving disagreements around expert opinion evidence once the prosecution has demonstrated that the incriminating expert opinion evidence satisfies a reliability threshold. This balances meaningful jury participation with the accused's right to a fair trial.

Regardless of what judges do with "specialised knowledge" the time has come to change the way they apply section 137 (section 135 and, for common law judges, the *Christie* discretion). Trial judges should draw principled distinctions between lay evidence and expert opinion evidence. They must be willing to make an assessment of the probative value of expert opinion evidence adduced by the prosecution. That is, trial judges should be attentive to the actual reliability of techniques so they can meaningfully assess "the extent to which the evidence *could rationally affect* the assessment of the probability of the existence of a fact in issue." Once the probative value of the expert opinion evidence adduced by the prosecution has been determined a more meaningful balancing exercise can be undertaken. If the techniques and opinions are not demonstrably reliable then there will always be a very substantial risk that the jury will overvalue or misuse opinion evidence proffered by experts, police and investigators (Cole & Dioso-Villa, 2009).

B. Abandoning Ad Hoc *Expertise*

In passing, it seems appropriate to make a few remarks about the expansion of the idea of the ad hoc expert. Even though section 79 would seem to cover the field, since 1995 judges in UEL jurisdictions—most prominently in NSW—have expanded the common law concept of the *ad hoc expert* (Edmond & San Roque, 2009; Munday, 1995). They have allowed investigators and experts from peripheral realms to express their opinions about identity on the basis of repeated exposure to sounds and images.

The expansion is curious because section 48 of the *Evidence Act* allows transcripts prepared from recordings to be used as evidence of a tape's contents. And, in NSW the exclusionary opinion rule appears to cover the field. That is, opinion evidence is not admissible unless there is a statutory exception. Nevertheless, as *Tang* illustrates, the concept of the ad hoc expert has been invoked to enable highly credentialed individuals, lacking relevant "specialised knowledge", to proffer incriminating opinion evidence about the identity of a person associated with a criminal act.

Significantly, recourse to ad hoc expertise is only ever used to admit incriminating opinion evidence—usually where the witness is not appropriately qualified to give an opinion or the opinion is not from a recognisable "field" or based on "specialised knowledge".[47] Perhaps predictably, where judges create or feel compelled to develop exceptions to the opinion rule which are not to be found in the UEL or credibly grounded in common law authority, they almost never refer to sections 137 and 135 (or the *Christie* discretion) to address the very real danger of unfair prejudice to the accused.

Recourse to ad hoc expertise should stop and the category should be abandoned. Judges should not be creating exceptions to the opinion rule (or expanding the common law) to enable the prosecution to adduce opinion evidence of unknown reliability in circumstances not permitted by section 79.

C. Emulating DNA

In its recent survey of forensic sciences, the National Research Council (NRC), of the National Academies of Science (US), concluded:

With the exception of nuclear DNA analysis, however, no forensic method has been rigorously shown to have the capacity to consistently, and *with a high degree of certainty, demonstrate a connection between evidence and a specific individual or source. (NRC, 2009, 5)*

The NRC (2009, 7) raised an institutionally awkward question, for law and the forensic sciences, "of whether—and to what extent—there is science in any given forensic science discipline".

Experts with techniques and tools of relevance to the legal system should be determining the reliability of their evidence. Ideally, those involved in identification, comparison and biometrics should be aiming to emulate DNA (Gonzales-Rodriguez et al, 2007; Rose, 2002; Porter, 2008). This means they should be aiming to develop sound probabilistic bases to their comparisons predicated upon population databases and rigorous testing. This is particularly important if the evidence is to be relied upon by the prosecution in criminal proceedings.

The standards required of opinion evidence may be lower in civil contexts but this should not encourage lax attitudes to the production of evidence and the assessment of techniques and methods. Those presenting themselves as experts should be aiming to produce the most reliable evidence possible, to know about limitations and weaknesses in their approaches, to be familiar with opposing perspectives and approaches, and to disclose them to opposing parties and the court. They should also testify clearly and cautiously. Anything else is disingenuous and inappropriately partisan.

Further, experts should not enter courts hoping to hide behind intellectual property laws so that they do not need to explain how their techniques and equipment actually work or how accurate they are.

"Emulating DNA" will be a slow, demanding and expensive process, but there are few credible alternatives. Those manufacturing biometric systems and those involved in *identification* whether through their own observations and/ or algorithms, should be generating population databases, reference populations and calculating errors and probabilities in statistically credible ways. Alternatively, if there are other ways of satisfying *legal reliability* then these should be demonstrated to the court.

D. Professional Regulation, Professional Restraint and the Future

This article has provided a critical overview of the main rules governing the admissibility of expert *identification* evidence (and biometric evidence) in Australia.

As for the future, the international trend is for courts to require expert evidence to be relevant *and reliable*. The United States and Canada have moved decisively in this direction, England (Law Commission, 2009) appears set to consider a reliability standard and it is hard—though, perhaps not impossible—to imagine Australian judges resisting the trend.[48] Increasingly, judges from common law jurisdictions will be attentive to the evidence supporting theories and techniques underpinning expert identification evidence. Even if Australian judges do not impose these kinds of standards—that is, those required in a rational and fair system of justice—expert witnesses will need to be wary of rising awareness among lawyers—prosecutors as much as the defence bar. Heightened critical consciousness among lawyers may make it harder for those with credentials to enter courts and opine about a range of issues at the margins or beyond their actual abilities. Those engaged as experts should expect to have their methods and techniques scrutinised.

Further, emerging fields and disciplines should be thinking about forms of *self-regulation* that are scientifically legitimate. (They should NOT expect judges to develop lists of certified experts or set out standards and protocols. Judges, on average, are poorly positioned to undertake such tasks.) While self-regulation may involve sanctions and exclusion, perhaps the better approach is to develop and maintain consensus statements about techniques and processes that have been tested (and the results), along with the kinds of practices and methods that are best avoided. To the extent that such statements are grounded in experimental research, developed in conjunction with scientists and experts from other fields, and widely accepted, they will provide practitioners as well as lawyers and judges with genuine assistance.

What those engaged in biometrics, e-forensics and expert identification and comparison should avoid is simply embracing the very lax standards currently favoured by Australian judges. They should not (selectively) disregard validity and reliability issues. It is important to emphasise that notwithstanding the very low thresholds that Australian courts have imposed on experts—and particularly experts called by prosecutors in criminal proceedings—experts should not testify unless their methods and techniques have been formally validated (or draw upon some kind of credible surrogate). Experts should strive for accuracy and not give evidence in criminal proceedings where their techniques, methods and conclusions are of unknown reliability.

In a very recent public inquiry in Canada the former chief forensic pathologist for Ontario apologised to one of the individuals he had helped to wrongfully convict. Based on pathological evidence that he was not competent to give, Dr Charles Smith testified that a young girl, the niece of the accused, had been sodomised and suffocated. William Mullins-Johnson was subsequently convicted and spent twelve years in protective custody before the mistake was serendipitously exposed. The following salutary exchange took place at the inquiry before the assembled public and media.

Dr Smith: *Could you stand, sir?*

[32 second pause]

Dr Smith: *Sir, I don't expect that you forgive me, but I do want to make it – I'm sorry. I do want to make it very clear to you that I am profoundly* *sorry for the role that I played in the ultimate decision that affected you. I am sorry.*

Mr Mullins-Johnson*: For my healing, I'll forgive you but I'll never forget what you did to me. You put me in an environment where I could have been killed any day for something that never happened. You destroyed my family, my brother's relationship with me and my niece that's still left and my nephew that's still living. They hate me because of what you did to me.*[49] *(Goudge, 2008, 15)*

List of Cases

Adam v The Queen (2001) 207 CLR 96.

Alexander v The Queen (1981) 145 CLR 395.

Alphapharm Pty Ltd v H Lundbeck A/S [2008] FCA 559.

ASIC v Rich (2005) 53 ACSR 623.

Atkins v The Queen [2009] EWCA 1876.

BD (1997) 94 A Crim R 131.

Brownlowe (1986) 7 NSWLR 461.

Bulejcik v The Queen (1996) 185 CLR 375.

Butera v Director of Public Prosecutions for the State of Victoria (1987) 164 CLR 180.

Clark v Ryan (1960) 103 CLR 486.

Commissioner for Government Transport v Adamcik (1961) 106 CLR 292.

Daubert v Merrell Dow Pharmaceuticals, Inc. 509 US 579 (1993).

Davie v Lord Provost, Magistrates and Counsellors of the City of Edinburgh (1953) SC 34.

Domican v The Queen (1991) 173 CLR 555.

Driscoll v The Queen (1977) 137 CLR 517.

Evans v The Queen [2007] HCA 59.

GK (2001) 52 NSWLR 317.

HG v The Queen (1999) 197 CLR 414.

Irani v R [2008] NSWCCA 217.

Keller v R [2006] NSWCCA 204.

Kumho Tire Co. v Carmichael 526 US 137 at 148 (1999).

Li v The Queen (2003) 139 A Crim R 281.

Makita (Australia) Pty Ltd v Sprowles [2001] NSWCA 305.

Murdoch v The Queen [2007] NTCCA 1.

Nguyen v R [2007] NSWCCA 249.

Osland v The Queen (1998) 197 CLR 316.

Pantoja (1996) 88 A Crim R 554.

People v Collins 68 Cal. 2d 319 (1968).

R v Alrekabi [2007] NSWDC 110.

R v Bartle [2003] NSWCCA 329.

R v Bonython (1984) 38 SASR 45.

R v Brotherton (1992) 29 NSWLR 95.

R v Camilleri [2001] NSWCCA 527.

R v Cannings [2004] EWCA Crim 1.

R v Carroll (1985) 19 A Crim R 410.

R v Carusi (1997) 92 A Crim R 52.

Regina v Cassar and Sleiman [1999] NSWSC 436.

R v Christie [1914] AC 545.

R v Clark [2003] EWCA Crim 1020.

R v Colebrook [1999] NSWCCA 262.

R v Corke (1989) 41 A Crim R 292.

R v Cornwell [2003] NSWSC 97.

R v Cornwell [2003] NSWSC 657.

R v DD [2000] 2 SCR 275.

R v EJ Smith (1987) 7 NSWLR 444.

R v El-Kheir [2004] NSWCCA 461.

R v Elliott (1990) NSWSC (unreported BC9003196).

R v Festa [2001] HCA 72.

R v Gallagher (2001) NSWSC 462

R v Gao [2003] NSWCCA 390.

R v Gilmore [1977] 2 NSWLR 935.

Regina v Green (1993) NSWCCA (unreported BC9303689).

Regina v Hall [2001] NSWSC 827.

Regina v Korgbara [2007] NSWCCA 84.

R v J-LJ [2000] 2 SCR 600.

R v Jung [2006] NSWSC 658.

R v Kaliyanda (17 October 2006) NSWSC.

R v Karger [2001] SASC 64.

R v Lam [2002] NSWCCA 377.

R v Lewis (1987) 88 FLR 104.

R v Leung and Wong [1999] NSWCCA 287.

R v Lucas [1992] 2 VR 109.

R v Madigan [2005] NSWCCA 170.

R v Menzies [1982] 1 NZLR 41.

R v Mohan (1994) 2 SCR 9.

R v Morgan (2009) NSWDC (June 2009).

R v Murrell [2001] NSWCCA 179.

R v Niga and Riscuta [2003] NSWCCA 6.

R v Robb (1991) 93 Cr App R 161.

R v Shamouil [2006] NSWCCA 112.

R v Stockwell (1993) 97 Cr App R 260.

R v Tang [2006] NSWCCA 167.

R v Trochym [2007] 1 SCR 239.

R v Watson [1999] NSWCCA 417.

Ramsay v Watson (1961) 108 CLR 642;

Re Truscott [2007] ONCA 575.

Smith v The Queen [2001] HCA 50.

Sydneywide Distributors Pty Ltd v Red Bull Australia Pty Ltd [2002] FCAFC 157.

The Queen v Hoey [2007] NICC 49.

The Queen v Murdoch (No 4) [2005] NTSC 78.

Tran (1990) 50 A Crim R 233.

Velevski v The Queen (2002) 187 ALR 233.

Winmar v The State of Western Australia (2007) 35 WAR 159.

ACKNOWLEDGMENT

Thanks to Kath Biber, Richard Kemp, Mehera San Roque, Glenn Porter, Matthew Sorrel and Nigel Wilson for comments and feedback. A draft of this article was presented as the keynote lecture at the e-Forensics International Workshop, Adelaide, January 2009. The work was, in part, supported by the Australian Research Council grants DP0772770 and FT0992041 and draws upon Edmond (2008), Edmond, Biber, Kemp & Porter (2009) and Edmond & San Roque (2009).

REFERENCES

Aronson, J. (2007). *Genetic witness: Science, law, and controversy in the making of DNA profiling.* New Bunswick, NJ: Rutgers University Press.

Australian Law Reform Commission. (1985). *Evidence* (Interim Report ALRC 26). Canberra, Australia: AGPS.

Beecher-Monas, E. (2006). *Evaluating scientific evidence.* Cambridge, UK: Cambridge University Press.

Beecher-Monas, E. (2009). Reality bites: The illusion of science in bite-mark evidence. *Cardozo Law Review, 30,* 1369–1410.

Biber, K. (2007). *Captive images: Race, crime, photography.* London: Routledge.

Burton, A. M., Wilson, S., Cowan, M., & Bruce, V. (1999). Face recognition in poor-quality video: Evidence from security surveillance. *Psychological Science, 10,* 243–248. doi:10.1111/1467-9280.00144

Cole, S., & Dioso-Villa, R. (2009). Investigating the 'CSI effect': Media and litigation crisis in criminal law. *Stanford Law Review, 61,* 1335–1374.

Collins, H. (1992). *Changing order: Replication and induction in scientific practice.* Chicago: University of Chicago Press.

Costigan, R. (2007). Identification from CCTV: The risk of injustice. *Criminal Law Review (London, England),* 591–608.

Davis, J., & Valentine, T. (2009). CCTV on trial: Matching video images with the defendant in the Dock. *Applied Cognitive Psychology, 23,* 482–505. doi:10.1002/acp.1490

Dror, I., Charlton, D., & Peron, A. (2006). Contextual information renders experts vulnerable to making erroneous identifications. *Forensic Science International, 156,* 74–78. doi:10.1016/j.forsciint.2005.10.017

Dror, I., & Rosenthal, R. (2008). Meta-analytically quantifying the reliability and biasability of forensic experts. *Journal of Forensic Sciences, 53,* 900–903. doi:10.1111/j.1556-4029.2008.00762.x

Edmond, G. (2008). Specialised knowledge, the exclusionary discretions and reliability: Reassessing incriminating opinion evidence. *The University of New South Wales Law Journal, 31*, 1–55.

Edmond, G. (2008a). Pathological science: Demonstrable reliability and expert forensic pathology evidence. In K. Roach (Ed.), *Pediatric forensic pathology and the justice system* (pp. 91-149). Toronto, Ontario, Canada: Queens Printer for Ontario.

Edmond, G., Biber, K., Kemp, R., & Porter, G. (2009). Law's looking glass: Expert identification evidence derived from photographic and video images. *Current Issues in Criminal Justice, 20*, 337–377.

Edmond, G., & Mercer, D. (1997). Scientific literacy and the jury. *Public Understanding of Science (Bristol, England), 6*, 329–359. doi:10.1088/0963-6625/6/4/003

Edmond, G., & San Roque, M. (2009). *Quasi-*justice: Ad hoc expertise and identification evidence. *Criminal Law Journal, 33*, 8–33.

Findley, K. (2008). Innocents at risk: Adversary imbalance, forensic science, and the search for the truth. *Seton Hall Law Review, 38*, 893–974.

Garrett, B., & Neufeld, P. (2009). Invalid forensic science testimony and wrongful convictions. *Virginia Law Review, 95*, 1–97.

Gonzales-Rodriguez, J., Rose, P., Ramos, D., Toledano, D. T., & Ortega-Garcia, J. (2007). Emulating DNA: Rigorous quantification of evidential weight in transparent and testable forensic speaker recognition. *IEEE Transactions on Audio, speech and Language Processing, 15*, 2104-2115.

Good, A. (2006). *Anthropology and expertise in the asylum courts*. Cambridge, UK: Cambridge University Press.

Goodwin, C. (1994). Professional vision. *American Anthropologist, 96*, 606–633. doi:10.1525/aa.1994.96.3.02a00100

Goudge, S. (2008). *Inquiry into pediatric forensic pathology in Ontario*. Toronto, Ontario, Canada: Queens Printer for Ontario.

Horswell, J. (Ed.). (2004). *The practice of crime scene investigation*. Boca Raton, FL: CRC Press.

Jasanoff, S. (1995). *Science at the bar*. Cambridge, MA: Harvard University Press.

Kemp, R., & Coulson, K. (2008). *Facial mapping and forensic photographic comparison: An international survey* (in press).

Kemp, R., Towell, N., & Pike, G. (1997). When seeing should not be believing: Photographs, credit cards and fraud. *Applied Cognitive Psychology, 11*, 211–222. doi:10.1002/(SICI)1099-0720(199706)11:3<211::AID-ACP430>3.0.CO;2-O

Law Commission. (2009). *The admissibility of expert evidence in criminal proceedings in England and Wales: A new approach to the determination of evidentiary reliability* (Consultation Paper 190). Norwich, UK: TSO.

Lynch, M. (1998). The discursive production of uncertainty: The OJ Simpson "dream team" and the sociology of knowledge machine. *Social Studies of Science, 28*, 829–868. doi:10.1177/030631298028005007

Lynch, M., Cole, S., McNally, R., & Jordan, K. (2008). *Truth machine: The contentious history of DNA fingerprinting*. Chicago: University of Chicago Press.

Mardia, K., Coombes, A., Kirkbride, J., Linney, A., & Bowie, J. L. (1996). On statistical problems with face identification from photographs. *Journal of Applied Statistics, 23*, 655–675. doi:10.1080/02664769624008

Munday, R. (1995). Videotape evidence and the advent of the expert ad hoc. *Justice of the Peace, 159*, 547.

National Research Council (NRC). (2009). *Strengthening the forensic sciences in the US: The path forward.* Washington, DC: National Academies Press.

Ormerod, D. (2000). Sounds familiar. *Criminal Law Review (London, England),* 595–623.

Porter, G. (2007). Visual culture in forensic science. *The Australian Journal of Forensic Sciences, 39*, 81–91. doi:10.1080/00450610701650054

Porter, G. (2008). CCTV images as evidence. *The Australian Journal of Forensic Sciences, 41*, 1–15.

Porter, G., & Doran, G. (2000). An anatomical and photographic technique for forensic facial identification. *Forensic Facial Identification, 114*, 97–105.

Redmayne, M. (2001). *Expert evidence and criminal justice.* Oxford, UK: Oxford University Press.

Risinger, M., Saks, M., Thompson, W., & Rosenthal, R. (2002). The Daubert/Kumho implications of observer effects in forensic science: Hidden problems of expectation and suggestion. *California Law Review, 90*, 1–56. doi:10.2307/3481305

Roberts, A. (2008). Drawing on expertise: Legal decision making and the reception of expert evidence. *Criminal Law Review (London, England),* 443–462.

Rose, P. (2002). *Forensic speaker identification.* London: Taylor & Francis.

Saks, M., & Faigman, D. (2008). Failed forensics: How forensic science lost its way and how it might yet find it. *Annual Review of Law & Social Science, 4*, 149–171. doi:10.1146/annurev.lawsocsci.4.110707.172303

Saks, M., & Koehler, J. (2005). The coming paradigm shift in forensic identification science. *Science, 309*, 892–895. doi:10.1126/science.1111565

Saks, M., & Koehler, J. (2008). The individualization fallacy in forensic science evidence. *Vanderbilt Law Review, 61*, 199–219.

Scheck, B., Neufeld, P., & Dwyer, J. (2000). *Actual innocence.* New York: Doubleday.

Shannon, C. (1984). *Royal Commission report concerning the conviction of Edward Charles Splatt.* Adelaide, UK: Government Printer.

Wells, G., & Quinlivan, D. (2009). Suggestive eyewitness identification procedures and the Supreme Court's reliability test in light of eyewitness science: 30 years later. *Law and Human Behavior, 33*, 1–24. doi:10.1007/s10979-008-9130-3

ENDNOTES

[1] The *Evidence Act 1995* (NSW) is part of the UEL. All references to legislation are to this Act.

[2] Other exceptions to the opinion rule, such as sections 77 and 78, are not applicable to this discussion.

[3] See, for example, *HG v The Queen* (1999, [39]).

[4] The judicial discretion based around weighing "probative value" against "unfair prejudice" is sometimes referred to as the *Christie* discretion, after *R v Christie* (1914).

[5] *Clark v Ryan* (1960); *Ramsay v Watson* (1961); *Commissioner for Government Transport v Adamcik* (1961); *R v Bonython* (1984, 46-47). For England, see *R v Robb* (1991) and *Atkins v The Queen* (2009).

[6] *Davie v Lord Provost, Magistrates and Counsellors of the City of Edinburgh* (1953).

[7] *Makita (Australia) Pty Ltd v Sprowles* (2001); *ASIC v Rich* (2005, [249]-[259]).

8 The UEL says nothing about voice identification but Part 3.9 deals with 'picture identification evidence'. This is concerned with those who perceived the matter or event and as such does not apply to remote viewers or the analysis of images and sounds. This has not, though, prevented judges in NSW from selectively invoking or ignoring the common law around images and particularly sounds to admit incriminating opinion evidence (Edmond & San Roque, 2009).

9 According to the OED, *ipse dixit* is a "dogmatic statement resting merely on the speaker's authority".

10 Dr. Sutisno was described, by the court, as a "forensic anatomist" who had gained "anthropological experience".

11 Apparently, the digital images were converted to analogue and then re-converted to digital and enhanced.

12 In *Murdoch*, Dr. Sutisno did not rely upon anthropometrical techniques and evidence.

13 The prosecution also relied upon low copy number (LCN) DNA evidence in *Murdoch*. This, as appeals in the UK suggest, seems to have its own reliability problems. See *The Queen v Hoey* (2007, [64]-[65]).

14 See also *Evans v The Queen* (2007).

15 Throughout this article I sometimes use an italicised form of *expert* to draw attention to the fact that some witnesses who are allowed to give opinion evidence, have no (or arguably no) relevant qualifications, even though some have extensive training and experience in adjacent fields and disciplines.

16 See also *R v Leung and Wong* (1999).

17 Like *Tang*, this case involved the invocation of this common law concept in a UEL jurisdiction.

18 Section 116 of the UEL does not seem to apply to *displaced* voice identification evidence.

19 Another decision, *R v Gao* (2003, [20]-[24]), decided a month after *Niga and Riscuta*,

upheld the admissibility of Detective Lee's opinion that the voice he heard briefly during a police interview—where the accused indicated that he did not want to answer any further questions—was the same voice he had heard during telephone interceptions of Cantonese speakers.

20 See also *Irani v R* (2008). In *R v Camilleri* (2001) the CCA upheld an appeal concerning the (in)adequacy of the warnings about the problems with a police officer's identification evidence without any apparent consideration of the basis for the admissibility of the police officer's opinion.

21 The clearest parts of the recording (apparently) enabled the interpreter to distinguish between the respective abilities in Arabic of the two speakers, nevertheless: "the quality of the utterances and terms of recording were poor and … at times the language was such as to be either inaudible or indecipherable. At times there was corruption in the phonemic structure of the speech that made it difficult to understand" (*El-Kheir*, 2004, [98]).

22 Dr Gamal seems to have been told by investigating police that there were only two males present in the house at the time of the recordings.

23 *R v Gilmore* (1977); *R v EJ Smith* (1987); *Brownlowe* (1986); *R v Corke* (1989); *R v Brotherton* (1992); *R v Colebrook* (1999); *Bulejcik v The Queen* (1996).

24 *Regina v Cassar and Sleiman* (1999).

25 Although, the basis rule most often refers to the question of whether the facts (or assumptions) underlying an expert opinion need to be proven for any opinion (derived from them) to be admissible. A decade-long dispute, following *Makita Pty Ltd v Sprowles* (2001), seems to have been resolved in favour of the proposition that the status of the underlying (or assumed) facts may influence the weight afforded to the expert opinion evidence rather than its admissibility *per*

se: see *Sydneywide Distributors Pty Ltd v Red Bull Australia Pty Ltd* (2002, [9], [87]) and *Alphapharm Pty Ltd v H Lundbeck A/S* (2009, [758]).

26 *R v Christie* (1914, 559); *Driscoll v The Queen* (1977, 541).

27 Section 135 provides a general discretion to exclude evidence where the probative value of the evidence is 'substantially outweighed' by a series of dangers.

28 *BD* (1997, 151); *GK* (2001, [30]).

29 *R v Carusi* (1997, 65-66); *R v Shamouil* (2006).

30 *Adam v The Queen* (2001, [59]-[61]).

31 The existence of such features may be contested. Though, judges should be wary of simply allowing such disagreements to go before the jury, especially where the resolution is poor and the expert claiming to be able to see some feature has not explained the method employed to overcome image quality problems.

32 Interestingly, the two main experts used by the prosecution in NSW—Dr. Sutisno and Professor Henneberg—publicly disagreed over whether salacious photographs published in several Australian newspapers depicted a notorious former politician (Pauline Hanson) as a young adult. Although, Henneberg was quoted as expressing the (curious) belief that the photos "were '99.2 per cent sure' to be of Ms Hanson", the newspaper that first revealed the images subsequently printed a retraction, apparently accepting that the images were not of Ms Hanson. Nick Leys, *The Daily Telegraph* (22 March 2009).

33 *Regina v Hall* (2001, [39]). See also *R v Watson* (1999) and *R v Murrell* (2001).

34 See, for example: *Nguyen v R* (2007); *R v Lam* (2002, [69]-[82]); *Keller v R* (2006); *R v Cornwell* (2003); *R v Cornwell* (2003); *R v Bartle* (2003).

35 On the single occasion, that I know of, where *foils* seem to have been used in relation to the interpretation of images (of an armed robbery): the two "foils" were quite different in body shape and appearance to the prime suspect (who was an Australian Aborigine). They were not, for example, indigenous, or endomorphs, and seem to have been confederates of the main suspect. Furthermore, the investigating police were present while the expert (Professor Maciej Henneberg) undertook his comparison and no contemporaneous notes were recorded: *R v Morgan* (2009). Compare *Atkins v The Queen* (2009).

36 *R v Festa* (2001).

37 For example, *Alexander v The Queen* (1981); *Domican v The Queen* (1991).

38 Even when the directions are considered inadequate or insufficient, as in *Niga and Riscuta*, Courts of Appeal often downplay their significance.

39 A conspicuous exception is *Winmar v The State of Western Australia* (2007).

40 For England, consider: Redmayne (2001); Roberts (2008); Law Commission (2009).

41 In *Kumho* the Court explained that in *Daubert*: "the Court specified that it is the Rule's word 'knowledge,' not the words (like 'scientific') that modify that word, that 'establishes a standard of evidentiary reliability.'"

42 Prominent Australian examples include Lindy and Michael Chamberlain (the Morling Royal Commission) and Edward Charles Splatt (the Shannon Royal Commission).

43 Though, in principle, there is no reason why the obligation to demonstrate "scientific reliability" should not be ongoing. If fresh doubts about a technique or approach emerge then the prosecution should be obliged to dispel them.

44 Many of the DNA decisions are pre-UEL.

45   Consider the response to admissibility challenges to DNA evidence in *R v Karger* (2001) and *R v Gallagher* (2001, [36], [62], [72], [114], [140]). In *Gallagher,* for example, Barr J ruled that DNA typing was admissible under s 79 on the basis that the system was properly validated, reliable and accurate.

46   *HG v The Queen* (1999, [41]), *Makita* (2001, [85]) and *Tang* (2006, [134], [150]-[152]) all employ the language of "demonstration", though not in relation to "reliability".

47   Ad hoc experts are not required to abide by rules and codes governing the performance of expert witnesses, used especially in civil litigation. Consider the NSW *Uniform Civil Procedure Rules* (2005), Schedule 7.

48   Although recent jurisprudence, as in *Atkins v The Queen* (2009), perpetuates the disinterest in reliability expressed in *R v Robb* (1991) and *R v Stockwell* (1993).

49   See also *R v Clark* (2003) and *R v Cannings* (2004).

This work was previously published in the International Journal of Digital Crime and Forensics, Volume 2, Issue 1, edited by Chang-Tsun Li and Anthony TS Ho, pp. 40-72, copyright 2010 by IGI Publishing (an imprint of IGI Global).

Chapter 16
Mobile Phone Forensic Analysis

Kevin Curran
University of Ulster, UK

Andrew Robinson
University of Ulster, UK

Stephen Peacocke
University of Ulster, UK

Sean Cassidy
University of Ulster, UK

ABSTRACT

During the past decade, technological advances in mobile phones and the development of smart phones have led to increased use and dependence on the mobile phone. The explosion of its use has led to problems such as fraud, criminal use and identity theft, which have led to the need for mobile phone forensic analysis. In this regard, the authors discuss mobile phone forensic analysis, what it means, who avails of it and the software tools used.

1. INTRODUCTION

Forensic Science is the use of forensic techniques and values to provide evidence to legal or related investigations (Jansen, 2008). Issues such as deoxyribonucleic acid (DNA) typing or the identification of drugs are obvious topics within this field. These involve the use of specialised scientific apparatus. Mobile phone forensic analysis is the science of recovering digital evidence from a mobile phone under forensically sound conditions using accepted methods. Digital forensics

has grown rapidly due in part to the increase in mobile devices (Harrill, 2007). The phone no longer simply connects us vocally with another, instead it stores our activities, dates, private numbers, experiences – written, visual or audio-visual; and it allows access to the internet where we send private and public messages. We no longer laugh, cry and love face to face; instead, all is recorded on our 'Smartphone'. As we transfer our experiences from the active, interpersonal world, to the digital; nothing remains private. Whispered conversations, clandestine notes, and mental images are transferred and recorded by phone instead. Although it may defy the ICT novice,

DOI: 10.4018/978-1-4666-1758-2.ch016

deletion has never really meant deletion. Forensic investigators commonly start with phone numbers dialled, answered, received or missed; stored phone numbers of people whom the mobile phone user may know and text messages sent, received or deleted (Punja, 2008). Mobile phone capabilities increase in performance, storage capacity and multimedia functionality turning phones into data reservoirs that can hold a broad range of personal information. From an investigative perspective, digital evidence recovered from a cell phone can provide a wealth of information about the user, and each technical advance in capabilities offers greater opportunity for recovery of additional information (Jansen, 2008). Mobile phone forensics is a challenge as there is yet no de facto mobile phone operating system.

There are two important points to remember when about to analyse a mobile phone. If the device is found switched on, DO NOT switch it off and if the device is found switched off, DO NOT switch it on. Pay as you go mobile phones are seen as 'disposable' in the criminal world. They are a means of communication that is not traceable, because there is no signed contract with the network provider for the authorities to trace. However if the phone is seized from the criminal then a number of forensic tests can be carried out and will reveal the entire call history and messaging history of the criminals in question. Another place where mobile phone forensic analysis plays a very large role is in domestic disputes. For example in the case of an abusive person who has been ordered by the court to stay away from their spouse but returns to the family home to harass the other. Here the police can have a cell site analysis carried out and determine where the abusive partner's mobile phone was at the time of the alleged incident. Mobile phone forensics can also play a vital role in road traffic collisions. The mobile phone can be taken and call records and logs checked to see if the accused was using the phone when the accident occurred.

Access to recovered information from mobile devices must be kept stable and unchanged, if it is to stand up in court. The integrity of the recovered data must therefore be kept intact. This is a vulnerable process, but as the years pass, advancements have been made to literally copy the information as fixed images, and thus unchanged, and unchangeable. Data saved on phones is stored as flash electronically erasable programmable (EEPROM) read-only memory (ROM)).

Mobile phone forensic analysis involves either manual or automatic extraction of data to be carried out by the mobile phone forensic examiners. Automatic extraction is used when the device is compatible with one or more pieces of forensic software and manual extraction is necessary when no compatible software is present. Automatic reading of a SIM Card is used when the mobile phone is supported by one or more pieces of forensic software. A manual verification is then required to confirm the extracted data is complete and correct. Manual reading of SIM card is used when the mobile phone is not supported by any forensic software, or the support offered is limited to such a degree that very little data is capable of being extracted. This method of analysis requires a forensics examiner to manually traverse a handset and digitally record each of the screens. This will include the recording of audio and videos in a format playable by the OIC. All images taken will be produced as a paper based report. Forensic analysis of a mobile device using either manual or automatic techniques can produce some or all of the following data: Make and model of the mobile handset; Mobile Station International Subscriber Directory Number (MSISDN); Integrated circuit card ID (ICCID) - The SIM cards serial number service provider name (SPN); Abbreviated dialling numbers; Last numbers received; Last numbers dialled; Missed calls; Short messages (SMS); Calendar entries; Photographs stored in handset; Video stored in handset; Smart media/compact flash; MMS Messages; Sim card link integrated circuit card ID (ICCID); International mobile subscriber identity (IMSI); Mobile country code (MCC); Mobile network code (MNC); Mobile subscriber identification number (MSIN); Mobile subscriber international ISDN number (MSISDN) and SMS messages. It is also possible to use AT on devices which have modem support to extract information from the operating system without affecting other aspects of the system state.

This paper is structured as follows: section 2 provides an overview of forensic guidelines drafted by the association of chief police officers, section looks at the extraction of data from the Subscriber Identity Module (SIM) and phone, section 4 highlights some popular mobile forensics applications and section 5 provides a conclusion.

2. FORENSIC GUIDELINES

The UK Association of Chief Police Officers (ACPO) has developed a guide for computer based electronic evidence which contains rules for handling such evidence. The guidelines recommend that the mobile phone must be isolated from the network by either turning the device off or placing it in a shielded secure container so that undesirable changes do not occur, which may jeopardise important information. Delays may be encountered if personnel try to regain access to such a device when a Personal Identification Number (PIN) is required. A shielded room should be used for examining a mobile phone. There are portable solutions to this problem in the form of a "Faraday Tent" but this option is less secure and cables going to and from the tent may act as aerials for the device. Devices also need to be fully charged before any form of examination, so as to preserve any vital information found. For instance, it is worth noting that there will be a strain on the battery, reducing power as it tries to re-connect to a local network.

The examination process needs to be well planned in order to prevent important data being lost, which may be relevant and crucial to a court case. For example, the removal of the SIM card often requires the removal of the battery beforehand. Therefore the date and time on the device may be lost. This would also be the case if the battery was allowed to fully discharge its power. The insertion of a different SIM card into the device must be avoided as such a process may result in a loss of information such as the call registers (received calls, dialled numbers, rejected calls, missed calls). It will often be the case that manual examination will have to be carried out on such a device as it may not be supported by analysis tools and therefore this would be the only option available for examination. This procedure should be carried out even if the device is supported by analysis tools so as to validate results gathered previously and ensure that the information download has completed successfully. Personnel carrying out such an examination should familiarise themselves with that particular type of device/phone model in order that mistakes are not made. User manuals can be downloaded from the manufacturer's website on the internet. If familiarisation is not carried out mistakes such as, the deletion of data through pressing the wrong button could occur.

For instance, an access card must be inserted into the device to imitate the original SIM card and therefore blocking further network access and destruction of important information. This allows personnel to examine safely, such a device as a mobile phone, at different locations. Furthermore, intervention from the service provider can be requested so as to disconnect or block the device/phone from the network. However, this is not recommended as the effects of such intervention are unknown, for example the voicemail recorded on the mobile phone account may be lost. It is recommended that specially designed software be used for examining such a device as a mobile phone. If non forensic tools are used, there should be a 'dummy-run' carried out with the same model type as the device to be tested in order to rule out damage to important information. Such non forensic tools should be used as a last resort during the examination process. The connection with the device must be secure so as to reduce the possibility of a loss of information. Cable is the recommended interface, followed by infra-red, Bluetooth and WiFi. Any of the interfaces after cable are considered to be very insecure and come with risks such as viruses.

Figure 1 details the actions taken by personnel involved in the forensic analysis of a mobile device. This is precise work which needs to be carried out professionally so as to preserve the information collected. Other forensic evidence such as DNA, fingerprints, firearms and narcotics should also be considered so as to protect evidence. The order in which forensic examinations take place is crucial, for example the examining of a mobile phone for fingerprints may result in that particular handset

being inoperative. Careful consideration must be taken so as not to destroy important fingerprint or DNA evidence found on the device. The personnel involved with the seizure of the device must ensure that they acquire everything involved with the device. This includes cables, chargers, memory cards, boxes and network account bills. These items may help the inquiry considerably as the original packaging may contain helpful pieces of data such as the PIN/PUK details. PC equipment must also be seized as the device in question may have been connected with such a system at some stage. The PC may contain relevant software that was used to transfer files, music, calendar dates, etc to and from the mobile phone. It must be taken into account that some devices may have a clearance or 'housekeeping' feature

Figure 1. Recommended actions for phone analysis (adapted from ACPO, 2009)

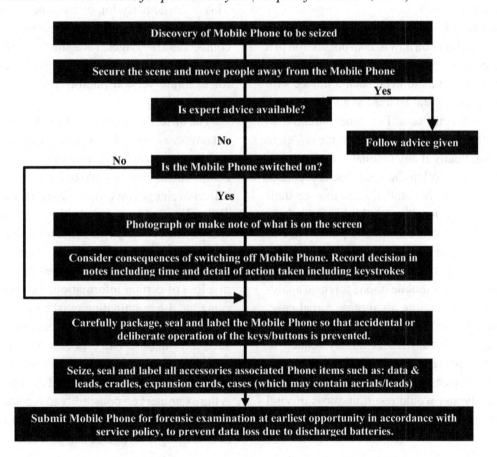

which carries out data wiping at a set time. For example, call logs may be deleted after a default period of thirty days (ACPO, 2009).

Care needs to be taken when encountering access codes such as PINs/passwords in order to avoid permanent damage and loss of information from a device/mobile phone. The number of remaining password or Personal Unblocking Key (PUK) attempts allowed on a SIM card should be verified. Subsequently, if the information on the device/mobile phone is needed urgently, it would be appropriate to try the default PIN as set by the device's service provider so that delays may be avoided. It should be noted that only three attempts can be made to enter the correct PIN. Nevertheless, one attempt should always be reserved in case the device owner provides the required PIN or it is found elsewhere. Guessing the PUK should never be attempted as the data found on the SIM card is lost forever once ten PUK attempts are made (ACPO, 2009).

Personnel who seize such devices should be trained extensively on how to take possession of a device appropriately and they should have relevant packaging materials to keep such a device safe and secure, as it could be used as a vital piece of evidence in a court case. Personnel should also be aware that some devices may remove/delete data automatically if any manual examination is carried out. It is often the case that computers/PCs may have tools installed so as to keep their information private, although this kind of behaviour is on the increase in mobile phones due to their development over the past number of years. Personnel should be fully trained in the tools and techniques used in mobile phone forensic analysis/examination. Before attempting a real case, experience in such fields of expertise should be previously obtained. This is mainly related to the use of non-forensic tools which may connect or join the device and PC either through cables or wirelessly and would result in a loss of vital information/evidence (ACPO, 2009).

It is recommended that personnel involved with the examining of a device or mobile phone, make suitable use of photography and video equipment so as to record or document the state of the device during various stages within the examining processes. The scene from which the device was acquired should also be given the same level of detail in recording or documenting the status of that area. The status of the device at the point of seizure needs to be recorded and photographed carefully, especially any on-screen data. A log of actions must be maintained and accompanied with the device when the device is seized and during the processes involved with examination. During such an examination, the log of actions must be updated, for example if messages are received, this must be documented. Such information as this must be documented in a way that is fitting to be incorporated into the final report. Photographs and video may be used as forms of documentation. This is particularly important when it comes to the recording of important information such as contacts and messages. Yet again the analysis tools or software used have to be detailed extensively, for example version number and add-ons used (ACPO, 2009).

The officer in charge must ensure that personnel involved with the seizure of such devices/mobile phones are suitably trained. An effective communication line should be created between the officer in charge (investigating) and the examiner of the device in question. It is only the officer in charge who can fully realise the important aspects of the data held on the device. In rare cases the process used to examine the device may result in a loss of certain information. The person carrying out the examination must be guided by the officer in charge so as to grasp the importance of such information. The officer in charge and the examiner need to relate to one another so as to preserve vital information found on the device. It is the examiners responsibility to recommend the examination approach used relating it to the type of case being investigated and give an explanation for the use of such an approach to the officer in charge. As a standard process, forensic analysis tools should recover mobile phone data such as SIM card details and whatever can be viewed by the user of such a device via the handset. Other relevant information can also be recovered from the SIM card which includes previously deleted messages. At an intermediate level an analysis technique such as 'flash dump' may be used to retrieve previously deleted material but this type of work is extremely specialised and requires certain skills and hardware. At the most advanced level, very specialist skills and hardware is often used to remove memory chips, if possible. This is an important part of forensic analysis as this particular level of expertise may result in data being retrieved which is necessary as evidence (ACPO, 2009).

3. SUBSCRIBER IDENTITY MODULE ANALYSIS

The Subscriber Identity Module (SIM) card is a smart card that is used in all mobile phones. It stores both user and network data, the latter is used to authenticate and identify subscribers on the Network. A mobile phone cannot be used without accessing the SIM. To access the SIM a personal identification number (PIN) is required. This is a four digit code that must be entered when the phone is turned on. If a user fails to enter the correct PIN after three attempts, the SIM card is blocked and the only way to undo this is to enter the eight digit PUK (Personal Unblocking Key) code. The SIM allows ten attempts to be made if all entries are incorrect then the SIM card becomes permanently blocked. The types of information that can be retrieved from a SIM card include the date, time and phone numbers of calls made from the mobile; date time and phone numbers of calls received from the mobile; SMS messages sent and received from the mobile and other data such as address / phone book details, pictures and videos

that have been saved to the SIM card. There are a number of different types of SIM cards available:

- **USIM:** Universal Subscriber Identity Module. This type of SIM card has an application running on it to allow Universal Mobile Telecommunications System (UMTS) mobile telephone, which is the technology behind 3G. This type of card holds the subscribers information, authentication information, and has 128KB of dedicated storage for contacts.

- **ISIM:** IP Multimedia Services Identity Module. This application is for use with a 3G mobile phone which is operating on the IMS type network. It contains information for authenticating the user as well as identifying them.

- **W-SIM:** Willcom SIM. This type of SIM has all the basic functions of any normal SIM card, however it also has the core components which make up a mobile phone transmitter and receiver already built into the card.

- **RUIM:** Re-Usable Identification Module. This type of SIM is a removable smart card which is designed to run in phones that work on the Code Division Multiple Access (CDMA) networks.

- **HCSIM:** High Capacity SIM. This type of SIM has all the same functions and features as that of a standard SIM, but with a greater storage capacity.

- **MSIM:** MegaSIM. The MegaSIM type of SIM comes equipped with Flash storage of between 64MB to 1GB. It also comes with its own dedicated processing power and a high speed interface.

These SIMs can be protected from access by a Personal Identification Number (PIN) (also known as Chip Holder Verification (CHV) and in many cases the SIMs have two PINs and these can be enabled or disabled by the user and changed to suit their needs. The PINs are normally referred to as PIN1 and PIN2. Whenever a SIM card is to be analysed it is important to prevent it from connecting to the mobile phone network as this could allow it to overwrite important data contained on the SIM which may be very valuable to a case. To prevent this from happening an image or a copy of the SIM card is made. Firstly the suspect SIM card is placed into a special holder to allow it to fit into the copying machine, next the SIM card is copied onto a new blank SIM card. The machine prevents the SIM card from connecting to the network as well as copying the contents of the SIM. The analysis will then be carried out on the new copied SIM so that no 'contamination' of data can occur on the original SIM. Logical analysis is carried out via a PC and involves the handset communicating with the forensic tool. What actually happens is that the forensic tool being used requests data from the phone, to which the phone responds and returns the requested data when it is available. The data that this approach can extract varies with make and individual handset, but will usually include, SMS, MMS, call registers, videos, pictures, audio files and calendar entries and tasks. Physical analysis is generally a little more difficult requiring specialist hardware and the forensics examiner must be trained in the correct techniques. A physical analysis involves making an image of the complete memory of the phone, which does not include any expandable memory, for example memory cards. Physical acquisition implies a bit-by-bit copy of an entire physical store while logical acquisition implies a bit-by-bit copy of logical storage objects that reside on a logical store. The difference lies in the distinction between memory as seen by a process through the operating system facilities (i.e., a logical view), versus memory as seen in raw form by the processor and other related hardware components (i.e., a physical view). Physical acquisition allows deleted files and unallocated memory or file system space to be examined this is not the case with a logical acquisition (National institute of standards and technology, 2007).

There are a number of methods available to the analyst to recover data from the phone. The primary method is to physically access the phone circuit board and remove the memory chip and retrieve the data directly. The secondary method is to use JTAG test points which are found on the printed circuit board. However these are not always available on every circuit board and so on occasion this method is unavailable to the analyst. The third method is to use unlock and reprogramming boxes. Whichever technique is used, a binary file will always be obtained or as it is known a PM file or Permanent Memory file. This file must then be translated into a format that is easier recognised and is readable and true. This process not only recovers the viewable data but also any deleted data that may be on the phone. The different types of analysis that is carried out on the SIM card are as follows:

- **Integrated Circuit Card ID (ICCID):** Each SIM card is internationally identified via its ICCID. This 18 or 19 digit number is stored on the SIM. This number tells the analyst where internationally the SIM card is from.
- **International Mobile Subscriber Identity (IMSI):** This number identifies the individual operator network, which is the network the SIM card works on, for example 3. The network provider communicates with the SIM card via this number and it is used for connect mobile phone calls to the SIM from the network.
- **Mobile Country Code (MCC):** This three digit number is used to identify which country the SIM card originated from. These codes are also required to be dialled when making an international phone call from a mobile phone. The MCC for the UK is 234.

- **Mobile Network Code (MNC):** This code is used in conjunction with the above MCC to identify the Network provider to which the SIM card belongs e.g. in the UK the 3 network has a MNC of 20.
- **Mobile Station International Subscriber Directory Number (MSISDN):** This is a 15 digit number which uniquely identifies the subscription in either a UTMS or GSM network.
- **Abbreviated Dialing Numbers (ADN):** This is a list of numbers that the user of the SIM card has stored to allow easy access to the numbers to dial. This is simply the user's contacts. From looking at these numbers the analyst is able to see who the user has contact details for as well as the incoming and outgoing calls to these numbers. The time and date of any calls made or received by the SIM can also be recovered.
- **Short Message Services (SMS):** More commonly known as text messages these are short messages which the user can send to another user. From looking at these the analyst is able to not only see who the user was communicating with but also read the messages that were sent and received by them. The time and date on which the message was sent is also stored on the SIM along with any deleted messages.

The SIM card is read using a smart card reader and because files can be read directly from the smart card operating system, it is possible to retrieve deleted information. When a message is deleted from the SIM only the status byte is set to 0. Deleted text-messages can be recovered except for the status byte as long as the slot has not been overwritten by a new message. Recovery is done by interpreting bytes 2-176 of the stored message (Willassebb, 2003). Removable storage devices are not dependent on a continuous power so they can be removed from the phone and are capable of

holding their data. They use the same formatting as found on a hard drive, typically File Allocation Table 32 (FAT32) and so can be treated the same way for analysis.

4. MOBILE FORENSIC TOOLS

Data can be retrieved from a mobile device by using forensic software and being able to connect to the mobile device either by a cable, Bluetooth or an infrared connection. Examples of such software are Oxygen Forensic Suite, SIMIS and data doctor phone inspector. One type of software may produce a more detailed and precise report in a specific area but may lack detail in another. Another method a forensic analyst could use is to access information directly from the mobile by the use of the keypad if possible but this is a risky method and should be used as a last resort as there is a high chance of data being modified if a wrong button is pressed. The number one objective is to extract as much data as possible without altering any data in the process. The analyst must also be careful not to lose any information e.g., some phones store data on missed and received calls on the SIM card. Another factor that must be addressed when carrying out a forensic analysis on a mobile phone is to keep it out of electromagnetic contact as even in an idle state a mobile is constantly trying to communicate with a network. What may happen is new data is sent to the mobile that may overwrite existing data for example this new contact with the network could have destroyed potential evidence such as a SMS message or a missed call. It is very important that no data is manipulated during the process of removing data if the data is to be used as evidence. So during a procedure to extract data from a mobile phone to a computer a log file is created which records all communication between the computer and the phone so that it can be satisfactorily demonstrated that no data has been written to the phone during the extraction process (Forensic Science Service, 2003).

Some of the important pieces of evidence for forensics are the *address book* which can contain various types of data from numbers to pictures and the *call history* of the phone as well as the message history and other forms of media that is stored on the phone. Much of these items can be retrieved with little need for sophisticated tools however when it comes to the other identifying items such as deleted contacts and erased history – then dedicated software is needed. Many of the leading forensics tools are usually licensed from specialists that have developed their own bespoke version of forensic software. Forensic software will retrieve the information from the phone either by targeting a physical aspect of the phone or a logical aspect. A physical aspect of a mobile would be the SIM as this is an independent storage device and can be separated from the phone, as well as possibly a memory card such as a MicroSD card. A logical aspect is the directories or files residing on the phone. Both physical and logical aspects are key areas for forensic investigation. When deciding what type of software to use, it is also important to take into consideration the type of network the phone is on as well as the actual software OS. There are different types of software some specializing for instance on smart phones and others on Symbian devices.

The software applications for mobile forensics available today are not 100% *forensically sound*. The reason is that they use command and response protocols that provide indirect access to memory (McCarthy, 2005; McCarthy & Slay, 2006). This means that the forensic software does not have direct access or low level access to data within the phone's memory as it depends on the mobile phone's operating system based command to retrieve data in the memory. Therefore in querying the operating system, the device could be creating changes to the memory of the device. Some command based mobile forensics software was not originally developed for forensic purposes and therefore they could unexpectedly write to the mobile phone device's memory (Horenbeeck, 2007).

Sometimes forensic software such as *MOBLedit Forensic*[1] requires the user to install additional software on the mobile phone being examined. This is in direct violation of the principles of electronic evidence as published by the UK's Association of Chief Police Officers (ACPO) Good Practice Guide for Computer based Electronic Evidence (ACPO, 2009) which states that "No action taken by law enforcement agencies or their agents should change data held on a computer or storage media which may subsequently be relied upon in court."

There are alternative methods to gain direct access to data held on mobile phones which do not breach best practice guidelines. Flasher boxes for instance can provide this direct access to data held on mobile phones without the need of resorting to operating system software or hardware command and response protocols. Flashers are a combination of software, hardware and drivers. Flasher boxes do not require any software to be installed on the mobile being examined. In theory, this should ensure that they do not manipulate any data that may be used as evidence. However, because they are not usually documented, there are no easy methods of determining if they do actually preserve evidence in the phones memory and there is no guarantee that the flashers will work in a consistent manner (Gratzer et al., 2006). It must be noted that mobile phone companies have not approved or tested flasher boxes on their products nor have they been tested or approved for forensic use.

The Cellebrite UFED System[2] (Universal Forensic Extraction Device) is a mobile hardware device which accepts SIM cards. It will also allow access to the phonebook, text messages, call history (received, dialed, missed), deleted text messages from SIM/USIM, audio recordings, video, pictures and images and more.

PDA Seizure[3] facilitates accessing information on a PALM or Blackberry PDA. It also allows the retrieval of information on the physical and logical parts of the PDA device. This software is windows based.

Device Seizure[4] is similar to PDA seizure but more comprehensive in provided features. It allows deleted data recovery, full data dumps of certain cell phone models, logical and physical acquisitions of PDAs, data cable access, and advanced reporting. It provides access to phones via IrDA and Bluetooth.

Some approaches rely on the AT command system developed in the late 1970s to initialize modems to ask the phone specific questions about the information it may be storing. However, not all mobiles respond to modem-style commands with for instance Nokia phones being particularly hard to crack. It must be remembered that in the U.S. alone there are over 2,000 models of phones and even within one model range there may be a dozen phones using different codes for each function (Hylton, 2007).

The initial preservation stage should secure the evidence and to record and document in its current state so as to prevent tampering with the evidence. Documents for the scene including photographs of the phone undisturbed should be included. When handling and moving the device one point is to keep it away from harmful elements such as high temperatures and any large magnetic sources that may affect the device. There also needs to be great care taken to preserve the DNA evidence that could be on the phone including finger prints or saliva. All accessories for the phone should be acquired if possible and taken as part of the evidence for testing. Another aspect of preservation is to note whether or not the phone was on when found, for this reason the phone should be turned off so as to stop any further interaction with radio waves that may cause some data on the phone to overwritten. The acquisition stage is where a copy of the data from the phone is made. This should be a mirror image of the SIM data and relevant memory cards. This process will usually happen in a lab however there can be problems due to battery damage or excess damage to the phone. This stage is when forensic tools are used most. Currently there is no one tool that can be used on all phones so there would be a range of software used in order to acquire the data. Here it may be common to encounter problems when trying to acquire the data through items such as pin protection. Fortunately, contacting the network providers can solve many of these problems as many networks will have a backdoor way to access the data on the device. The analysis stage is where the data is examined. This part of the process needs to be done carefully so as not to miss anything that may be relevant to the case. The examiner ideally should be familiar with the work that has gone on prior to the examination. Finally, the reporting stage is where the evidence is summarized so as to be presented in court as evidence (Jansen & Ayers, 2007).

A number of companies provide the service of mobile phone forensic analysis. These include Inta Forensics[5], Mobile Phone Forensics[6], Integrity Forensics[7], Sector Forensics[8] and CY4OR[9]. Whilst all these companies offer a similar services and follow similar analysis techniques different report application software is used to present the retrieved data.

As with many of the other mobile phone forensic analysis providers, Inta Forensics uses their own in house software application called ART (Automatic Report Tool) (see Figure 2). This application allows mobile phone forensic examiners to capture images (via a camera) of mobile devices and subsequently produce a Microsoft Word document. ART is supplied by www.IntaForensics.com for free to registered users conducting Mobile Phone Forensic Analysis.

The main benefits of using ART is that it allows its users to capture images from USB camera and then store these images under appropriately named folders and then publish a customizable report containing the captured images of the mobile device (see Figure 3). ART's only requirements include a USB or external Camera with Microsoft Windows Driver installed

Figure 2. Information on each exhibit in ART

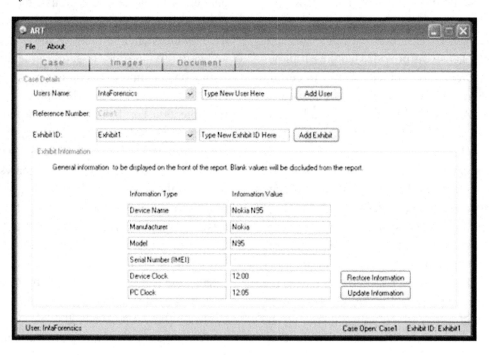

along with Microsoft Word installed for the generation of a device report. ART allows for the management of multiple cases containing large amounts of visual evidence. These cases can be accessed at any time so to allow the capture of additional images or to generate further reports. All images that are captured are saved to folders reflecting the location of the photographed object for easy reference by the user and easy report generation. ART design also allows for basic formatting of the report prior to printing in both the document and header sections.

5. CONCLUSION

Mobile phone forensics analysis involves the technical examination of mobile phones and the retrieval of data from these devices. Data for analysis can be obtained from SIM cards, memory cards and from the phone handset itself. Forensic analysis of mobile phones can be carried out on various forms of data, including textual (SMS Mes-

sages), Graphic (Images), Audio Visual (Videos) and Audio (Sound recordings) (Inta Forensics, 2009). Rapid advancements in mobile phone technology and the introduction of smart phones to the market by companies such as Apple and Blackberry providing large storage capacities has meant that increasingly, larger amounts of personal information is now being stored on these devices. Individuals are now becoming increasing reliant on their mobile phones as part of their daily lives. The variety of applications and facilities these devices provide including Internet, Wi-Fi, email, document viewing and editing software along with the more common mobile phone features of phonebook, call history, text messaging, voice mail, built in camera and audio facilities have seen it overlap with computer technology.

The existing generation of mobile phones are sophisticated and increasingly difficult to examine however they can ultimately provide valuable evidence in prosecuting individuals. Quite often the information obtained from a phone, after intensive analysis techniques proves to be adequate for a

Figure 3. Folder structure of captured data in ART

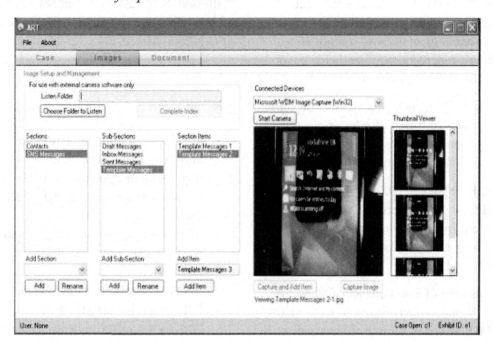

conviction of a criminal by detectives involved with the case. Internal memory and external memory as well as the call and text records can all be analysed to gain an insight into the activities of the mobiles owner as well as who they have been speaking or exchanging messages with. The area is ever expanding and allows for cutting edge technology to be used to keep up with the ever growing array of mobile phones on the market today and the ever increasing feature list of these phones. Mobile forensic analysis will continue to be a specialised field while technology progresses rapidly with the sheer number of phones to be examined posing a challenge for the police.

REFERENCES

ACPO. (2009). *Practice Guide for Computer-Based Electronic Evidence*. Retrieved from www. acpo.police.uk/asp/policies/Data/ACPO%20 Guidelines%20v18.pdf

Gratzer, V., Naccache, D., & Znaty, D. (2006, March 13-17). Law Enforcement, Forensics and Mobile Communications. In *Proceedings of the PerCom Workshop*, Pisa, Italy (pp. 256-260).

Harrill, D. C., & Mislan, R. P. (2007). A Small Scale Digital Device Forensics ontology. *Small Scale Digital Device Forensics journal, 1*(1).

Hylton, H. (2007, August 15). What Your Cell Knows About You. *Time Magazine*. http://www.time.com/time/health/article/0,8599,1653267,00.html?xid=rss-health

Inta Forensics. (2009). *Mobile Phone Forensics*. Retrieved from www.intaforensics.com/pdf/mobile-phone-forensics.pdf

Jansen, W., & Ayers, R. (2007). *Guidelines on Cell Phone Forensics*. Gaithersburg, MD: National Institute of Standards and Technology. Retrieved from http://csrc.nist.gov/publications/nistpubs/800-101/SP800-101.pdf

Jansen, W., Delaitre, A., & Moenner, L. (2008). Overcoming Impediments to Cell Phone Forensics. In *Proceedings of the 41st Annual Hawaii International Conference on System Sciences* (pp. 483-483). ISBN: 978-0-7695-3075-8

McCarthy, P. (2005). *Forensic Analysis of Mobile Phones*. Retrieved from http://esm.cis.unisa. edu.au/new_esml/resources/publications/forensic%20analysis%20of%20mobile%20phones.pdf

McCarthy, P., & Slay, J. (2006). Mobile phones: admissibility of current forensic procedures for acquiring data. In *Proceedings of the Second IFIP WG 11.9 International Conference on Digital Forensics*.

National Institute of Standards and Technology. (2007). *Guidelines on cell phone forensics*. Gaithersburg, MD: National Institute of Standards and Technology. Retrieved from http://csrc.nist.gov/publications/nistpubs/800-101/SP800-101.pdf

Punja, S., & Mislan, R. (2008). Mobile Device Analysis. *Small scale digital device forensics journal, 2*(1), 1-16. ISSN 1941-6164

Willassen, S. Y. (2003). Forensics and the GSM mobile telephone system. *International Journal of Digital Evidence, 2*(1), 12–24.

ENDNOTES

[1] http://www.mobiledit.com/forensic
[2] http://www.cellebrite.com
[3] http://www.softpedia.com/get/System/Back-Up-and-Recovery/PDA-Seizure.shtml
[4] http://www.digitalintelligence.com/software/parabenforensictools/deviceseizure/
[5] http://www.intaforensics.com
[6] http://www.mobilephoneforensics.com
[7] http://www.integrityforensics.co.uk
[8] http://www.sectorforensics.co.uk
[9] http://www.cy40r.co.uk

This work was previously published in the International Journal of Digital Crime and Forensics, Volume 2, Issue 3, edited by Chang-Tsun Li and Anthony TS Ho, pp. 15-27, copyright 2010 by IGI Publishing (an imprint of IGI Global).

Chapter 17
Grey Areas:
The Legal Dimensions of Cloud Computing

Michael Davis
Adelta Legal, Adelaide, Australia

Alice Sedsman
Adelta Legal, Adelaide, Australia

ABSTRACT

Cloud computing has been heralded as a new era in the evolution of information and communications technologies. ICT giants have invested heavily in developing technologies and mega server facilities, which allow end users to access web-based software applications and store their data off-site. Businesses using cloud computing services will benefit from reduced operating costs as they cut back on ICT infrastructure and personnel. Individuals will no longer need to buy and install software and will have universal access to their data through any internet-ready device. Yet, hidden amongst the host of benefits are inherent legal risks. The global nature of cloud computing raises questions about privacy, security, confidentiality and access to data. Current terms of use do not adequately address the multitude of legal issues unique to cloud computing. In the face of this legal uncertainty, end users should be educated about the risks involved in entering the cloud.

INTRODUCTION

The term 'cloud computing' is used in this article to refer to the general system of centralised storage and maintenance of end user data by internet servers. For the purposes of this article, no distinction is made between those cloud computing services which offer software as a service and those that offer mass data storage facilities. Throughout this article, the corporations that offer cloud computing services are referred to as 'hosts'.

The phrase 'cloud computing' originates from standard ICT industry practice, where the internet is graphically represented as a 2D stencil of a cloud (Ranger, 2008). As hosts offer their services online, the basic premise of cloud computing is that end

DOI: 10.4018/978-1-4666-1758-2.ch017

users transfer all their data from their personal computers into cyberspace (Lyons, 2008a). End users simply upload data, such as photographs or insert text and other data onto host software applications that function online. Once end user data is uploaded to a host, it is sent through cyberspace to purpose-built mega storage facilities filled with masses of hard drives (Corey, 2008). These facilities are located in various regions around the world and end user data may be divided across several of these super computer stores (Marshall, 2008). The host retrieves and dispatches the data from the storage facility whenever an end user requests access. The personal computer of the end user becomes little more than an access point and display screen for the data (Princeton University [PU], 2008a).

To date, the most successful cloud computing services have been online collaboration models targeted at private consumers, such as Facebook, Gmail and Hotmail (Ranger, 2008). However, the new wave of cloud computing is capturing the business market by providing software as a service (Hoover, Martin, & Hall, 2008). Small and big business alike is being drawn to cloud computing services by promises of reduced ICT expenditure. The centralised service delivery and storage model of cloud computing reduces, if not eliminates, the need for end users to purchase and maintain their own servers, individual software licenses, ICT support staff, and floor space for hard drive storage (Arnold, E., 2008). Power costs are also cut down as fewer computers and cooling systems are required to be maintained in house (IBM, 2008a).

With the world moving online, e-commerce is set to experience a new boom which will outpace current internet regulation laws.

THE GROWING CLOUD

Sceptics have denounced cloud computing as the next 'dot.com bubble burst', but since the emergence of Amazon Web Services, Google Apps, Microsoft Office Live and IBM Blue Cloud, cloud computing appears to have become a significant and sustainable force in the ICT Sector.

The uptake of cloud computing services by major corporations such as Coca Cola Enterprises, Nokia and The New York Times has given credence to the permanency of cloud computing (Arnold, E., 2008; Lyons, 2008a; Fitzgerald, 2008).

Cloud computing is reaching into the world hubs of software development. IBM is developing its latest cloud computing facility in the software development region of Wuxi, China. For a subscription fee, software developers will be able to use IBM's open access source code to collaborate, design, develop and test their software (IBM, 2008b).

The high uptake of cloud computing services can be attributed to clever marketing campaigns that promise end users low charges for data storage facilities and unrivalled access to computer programs such as word processing, bookkeeping and collaborative networking (Microsoft Corporation [Microsoft], 2008a). The centralised series of host servers that supports cloud computing, enables end users to carry out their everyday ICT tasks without in house software, downloads, storage space and support services (Otey, 2008). Cloud computing hosts are further reducing end user costs by assuming managerial control for the running and maintenance of ICT services. However, the decline of end user responsibility and control over ICT management has consequences for possession rights and ultimate accountability.

The implications for end users who place data into the cloud without properly understanding the inherent legal risks can be serious.

PAYMENT MODELS

Currently, cloud computing hosts are offering their services on either a flat subscription rate or a usage fee basis. The flexibility of these payment models makes programs that were previously beyond the budgets of small and medium sized business affordable. However, the portability of end user data held by a host is yet to be tested and there is a corresponding concern that end users will find themselves locked in to a particular service (PU, 2008b). If end users are locked in, cloud computing hosts will have considerable market power.

'FREE' CLOUD SERVICES

Cloud computing hosts are also trialling free versions of their services (with limited capabilities) to domestic consumers (Microsoft, 2008b). Experience has shown that whenever the word 'free' is used in marketing, consumers should beware. Surprising conditions are often couched in rarely-read terms of use. One well publicised example is that of Google's free Gmail account service. On its publicly accessible website, Google advises end users that the contents of their emails are scanned by Google's computer systems which could be used to deliver targeted advertising to the end user (Google Inc. [Google], 2008a).

ACCESS TO DATA

One of the greatest conveniences of cloud computing is its worldwide accessibility. Being internet based, cloud computing allows end users to access and modify their data from any suitable device capable of connecting to the internet (Lyons, 2008b). Access is available from any location where internet connection is available with a high enough bandwidth.

The universal accessibility of data stored on cloud computing servers eliminates the need to copy or email data from one computer to another. Corporations will no longer have to set-up remote access to their internal servers in order for their employees to work after hours or off-site. The potential for workplace collaboration is also enhanced, with account administrators being able to invite multiple individuals to access and modify uploaded data (Microsoft, 2008c). Document merging will no longer have to be manually executed.

However, such benefits of cloud computing services should be weighed against the risk that access to end user applications is denied and data is lost during system outages. Businesses can make alternative arrangements when outages are scheduled for in-house system maintenance and upgrades, but when an internet server goes down without warning, all access to critical applications and data could be lost for the duration of the outage. Even large cloud computing hosts experience unscheduled outages from time-to-time. In February 2008, Amazon suffered an outage that lasted for four hours (Brynko, 2008). End users of Google, Yahoo! and Apple cloud services were similarly hit by outages in 2008 (Arnold, E., 2008).

At best, an outage might cause a minor disruption to business. At worst, it may mean a huge loss of business, missing of deadlines and permanent loss of data (Arnold, E., 2008). Last year MobileMe, a cloud computing initiative of Apple designed to synchronise data stored in Macbooks, iPhones and iPods, crashed. A small percentage of MobileMe end users who had paid for the service instantly lost every email they had ever sent or received (Arnold, E., 2008; Brynko, 2008). The thought that business records could similarly be lost is alarming, especially when most contractual terms of use for cloud computing systems exclude or limit liability for loss of business in such circumstances (Google, 2008b). Of further concern is the general inadequacy of technical support offered by host companies. When cloud computing systems glitch, end users are often unable to do anything but wait for the functionality of the systems to be restored.

Direct technician support is commonly made available to end users for a premium, but considering the enormity of cloud computing systems, this support may be inadequate in practice. If all end users of a cloud computing service lost access simultaneously, support lines would probably be overwhelmed. Other limitations of host support services are evident in Google's cloud computing offering: Google Apps Premium Edition. While the Premium Edition promises 24/7 telephone support for its end users, end users are only connected to a technician if their problem is deemed a 'critical issue' (Google, 2007a). Until Google recognises the problem as critical, end users must rely on self-help pages and chat rooms hosted on the server (Google, 2008c).

There remain many questions about end users ability to access data stored by cloud computing hosts (Brodkin, 2008). For example, there are obvious risks if all of a person's information stored on a remote server is damaged or destroyed by terrorist activity, fire, flood or some other unforeseen event (Brynko, 2008). Most terms of use assure end users that recovery plans are in place for such disasters, but the timeframe and costs for recovery are uncertain.

It is also doubtful whether the end user will be able to transfer his or her information to other hosts at will and without charge. Similarly, questions arise about what happens to end user data in the event that the host goes out of business. The terms of use for Google Apps Premier Edition provide for the return of end users' data on request (Google, 2008b). However, no timeframe or cost basis is established for this process and there is no guarantee that the returned information will be in a portable format.

End users who pay for cloud computing services face uncertainties relating to the failure to pay their accounts within time (Brynko, 2008). Google and Microsoft warn that in such circumstances use of the services will be suspended (Google, 2008b). If the account remains unpaid, the end user's access to the services will eventually be terminated (Google, 2008f). Termination is in itself problematical. For instance, on termination the end user may lose all control over his or her data and have that data permanently deleted by the host.

Most standard forms of agreement for cloud computing services currently fail to address these issues. Until these scenarios are adequately addressed in standard forms of agreement end users should think twice about placing mission critical information into the cloud.

CENTRALISED SERVICE

Cloud computing heralds a return to a central storage and management system. Under the cloud computing model, all ICT needs are met and managed by the third party host; cloud computing hosts assume the burden of general trouble shooting, and the installation of software, updates, firewall protection and security screens as part of their services (Ranger, 2008).

Having industry expert hosts like Google and Microsoft manage end user data and ICT systems has its advantages, but it is not without its risks. The old adage: 'possession is nine-tenths of the law' is a pertinent warning to end users who place their data in the physical possession of cloud computing hosts.

Domestic end users rarely appreciate the consequences of losing control of their personal data (Horrigan, 2008). The fact that in 2008 a reported 45 million customer records were stored by unknown third parties demonstrates a popular lack of awareness about the importance of protecting personal data (Arnold, S., 2008).

Trusting a third party with personal or business information carries risks, especially when that third party has interests that compete with the interests of end users. The ICT industry is currently under-regulated and under-monitored, and the potential for misuse of sensitive information looms large.

PRIVACY ISSUES

Cloud computing hosts exercise ultimate control over the data that end users place on their networks.

It is the hosts that will either grant or deny access by third parties to this data. Concerns have been expressed that, without scrutiny, hosts may be tempted to covertly sell end user personal information to market and consumer profiling corporations (Desloge, 1998). Most governments around the world have instituted some form of privacy law to regulate dealings with the personal information of customers. However, the effectiveness of these laws becomes more diluted the further from home the information is stored.

Under privacy laws there are generally two categories of information that are protected: personal and sensitive information (*Privacy Act 1988* (Cth); *Data Protection Act 1998* (UK)). Personal information is that which can be used, either independently or accumulatively, to identify an individual (The Office of the Privacy Commissioner [OPC], 2008). Sensitive information is a further category of personal information which receives additional protection under most privacy laws. Sensitive information is information that could be used to discriminate against an individual, such as information about an individual's racial or ethnic origin, political affiliations, religious affiliations, philosophical beliefs, sexual preferences or practices, criminal record or health (OPC, 2008).

Privacy laws generally require prior notice to be given to individuals before their personal or sensitive information is collected and used by a third party. However, experience has shown that the requirement of prior notice is often only loosely fulfilled, especially when such notice is given through links on an organisation's website homepage. The surveillance by Google of sensitive information under its Gmail service is a prime example. In its Privacy Policy Google states:

...maintains and processes your Gmail account and its contents to provide the Gmail service to you and to improve our services. The Gmail service includes relevant advertising and related links based on the IP address, content of messages and other information related to your use of Gmail.

Google's computers process the information in your messages for various purposes, including formatting and displaying the information to you, delivering advertisements and related links, preventing unsolicited bulk email (spam), backing up your messages, and other purposes relating to offering you Gmail. (Google, 2008d)

End users are therefore informed that Google provides targeted advertising "based on the ... content of messages and other information related to your use of Gmail". Privacy protection legislation is aimed at ensuring that individuals make informed consent to the collection of their personal and sensitive information. Google relies on the public availability of its Privacy Policies to provide notice of collection to individual users of its sites, but in reality few people will ever read these policies.

In our commercial world we have come to accept the term "caveat emptor" (buyer beware) as good policy. However, it is a term that should not be given application in a field as critical as personal privacy rights. Some uses and collection of personal and sensitive information clearly need to be prohibited, no matter whether constructive or actual notice has been given to individuals. Getting users to actively 'opt in' to individual terms of use that affect their privacy should also be considered as a protective measure.

It has been argued that there is no risk to privacy when data collection is automated by computer programs (Google, 2008a). However, it is improbable that such system could operate without any form of human intervention. Some form of human monitoring is likely to be involved. An additional concern is that other unauthorised employees may have access to the storage or collection systems (Brodkin, 2008). Furthermore, in an age where identity theft is on the increase, the risk of the professional hacker looms large (Newville, 2001).

Human and system errors can also result in the accidental leaking of personal information. In 2001, pharmaceutical company Eli Lilly accidentally disclosed the email addresses of 669 Prozac users (Federal Trade Commission (United States of America), 2002).

As cloud computing continues to attract clients in the banking, telecommunications, government, education and health industries, the need for vigilance over personal information of end users increases (M2 Press Wire, 2008). In developing countries the number of industries turning to cloud computing as an affordable alternative to in house ICT infrastructure is growing exponentially and includes organisations that maintain sensitive personal records ("The Long Nimbus", 2008).

The protection and enforcement of individual rights to privacy is complicated by the trans-border flow of data that is at the heart of cloud computing. Every time an end user inputs data into the cloud, information is transmitted from that end user's home State. Every time end users log into their accounts, their information may pass through any number of unknown States as it is retrieved and transmitted back to the end user's computer. In most instances end users will never know where their personal information is stored, let alone which State's privacy laws apply and how to invoke them.

A State's privacy laws may apply transnationally. This is the case in Australia, where under the Privacy Act any organisation, no matter its location, must comply with Australian privacy laws whenever it collects or holds the personal information of Australian citizens (*Privacy Act 1988* (Cth) Schedule 3). Yet the ability of the Australian government to effectively monitor such collection and enforce compliance is questionable, especially when the information flow occurs beyond country borders.

There is evidence to suggest that even within its own borders the Australian government is failing to properly protect its citizens' rights to privacy. The Australian Law Reform Commission ('ALRC') recently reviewed Australia's privacy laws and reported that some businesses (namely database operators, detective agencies and provid-

ers of telecommunications goods and services) pose a high risk to the confidentiality of personal information (Australian Law Reform Commission [ALRC], 2007). These businesses generally hold vast quantities of information (often sensitive in nature) about individuals and routinely carry out privacy intrusive activities.

In Australia, approximately 94% of businesses were exempt from the application of the Privacy Act in 2007 (ALRC, 2007). The ALRC is recommending changes that would see all businesses subject to uniform privacy laws (ALRC, 2008).

The trans-border nature of cloud computing complicates jurisdictional issues. For instance, if an end user resides in Australia but his or her information is stored in America and China, the governments of both those countries may monitor the contents of that end user's cloud computing account. In such circumstances, the non-national end user is unlikely to be informed of, let alone oppose, such privacy intrusions. Many cloud computing terms of use compound jurisdictional problems by remaining silent on the issue of how long an end user's information will be stored for and how it can be destroyed or de-identified (see Google, 2008e).

In its terms of use, Google endeavours to make reasonable attempts to contact the end user when a third party attempts to access end user data (Google, 2008f). However, sometimes it will fall on the cloud computing host to resist the proposed incursions of privacy on behalf of the end user.

To its credit, Google recently resisted an attempt by the FBI to access millions of Google end user logs by subpoena (McCullagh, 2008). This attempt to access end user records highlights the dangers of storing sensitive information in another legal jurisdiction.

International uniformity of privacy laws, incorporating commitments to cooperate in the monitoring and prosecution of offenders must be achieved in order to protect the personal and sensitive information of end users.

SECURITY

The importance of securing end user data is reaffirmed daily, with the ever escalating rate of cyber crime (Newville, 2001). Corporate espionage costs business millions of dollars every year (Chickowski, 2007).

It is now common practice for businesses to ban their employees from using live cloud computing networking applications such as Facebook in order to reduce the risk of employees leaking confidential company information ("The long nimbus", 2008).

Businesses that use cloud computing services trust hosts to protect their critical data from identity theft, corporate espionage and accidental leaking. Yet there remains the potential for employees of cloud computing hosts to sell the confidential information, intellectual property and trade secrets of end users (Otey, 2008). This is especially true of cloud computing networks that host the data of rival businesses. If an employee were to leak critical information, disclosure of the leak would be against the interests of the employer host.

End users of cloud computing services do not know which employees have access to their data or whether any security certification or external system audits of the services are conducted (Google, 2008b).

The central housing of end user data in mega storage facilities presents perhaps the biggest threat to the security of cloud computing systems. Computer hackers and terrorists will be attracted to concentrate their efforts towards infiltrating or destroying these storage facilities. Cloud computing hosts may ensure that encryption is available at all stages of data transfer and implement state of the art security checks, but it is highly unlikely that a computer system will ever be entirely impervious to infiltration (Australian Broadcasting Corporation, 2008).

TERMS OF USE: SOME CAUSE FOR CONCERN

In addition to wider concerns about privacy, security and access to data, end users of cloud computing systems should beware terms of use that limit or remove their usual legal rights, particularly those terms that pertain to intellectual property and choice of law.

INTELLECTUAL PROPERTY

When end users upload their data to cloud computing hosts, they generally expect to retain the copyright and other intellectual property rights in that data. However, in some instances, cloud computing hosts have undermined these expectations by issuing end user terms of use that grant the host a licence to use end user data without charge. There have been incidences of cloud computing hosts claiming full intellectual property rights over any and all end user data entered into cloud computing networks.

In 2008, Google experienced customer backlash when a drafting oversight resulted in clauses, which granted Google intellectual property rights over all data uploaded by end users, being inserted into the end user license agreement for its new internet browser, Google Chrome (Fried, 2008). Google said the clause was an accidental replication of the terms of use of its standard services (Fried, 2008). Google altered the offending clause within 24 hours and Google Chrome end users now enjoy retention of their intellectual property rights (Google, 2008g). However, under the current terms of use of Google's cloud computing service, Google Docs, end users grant Google a worldwide irrevocable license to use their intellectual property to display, distribute and promote the service (Google, 2007b).

JURISDICTION FOR DISPUTES

It is common for cloud computing hosts to insert jurisdiction and choice of law clauses into their end user licence agreements. These clauses usually purport to be a binding nomination of a specific court in a specific place to hear any dispute that may arise out of provision of the services. The nominated court is usually selected for its proximity to the operations of the company that drafted the contract.

For Australian users of Microsoft Office Live, the courts of Singapore have jurisdiction (Microsoft, 2008d). For users of Google Apps, the courts of Santa Clara, California are given jurisdiction (Google, 2007b). The laws to be applied are those of Singapore and Santa Clara County respectively.

Choice of law terms aim to override domestic laws that grant citizens specific contractual rights. Cloud computing hosts can protect their own interests by electing the most sympathetic forum to determine claims. The consequences for end users are clear: the application of foreign laws and the hearing of matters in foreign territories seriously impede the ability of end users to bring or defend claims against cloud computing hosts. The legal and ethical accountability and responsibility of the hosts is thereby diminished.

While choice of law clauses are not always upheld by courts, they are persuasive. In Europe, the countries of the European Union are bound by two international treaties: the Brussels Convention and the Rome Convention. The Brussels Convention provides for 'prorogation of jurisdiction' which allows the parties to a contract to pre-determine which courts are to have jurisdiction in event of a dispute (Chicago-Kent College of Law [CKCL], 2007). The Rome Convention also provides that the law chosen by the parties to a contract should govern that contract (CKCL, 2007). However, both Conventions provide that a choice-of-law clause cannot deprive a private consumer of the protection of any mandatory consumer protection laws in the consumer's own country (CKCL, 2007). It

is therefore likely, despite choice of law clauses, that any disputes between cloud computing hosts and private European end users will be heard and determined in European courts.

In the United States, the courts may decide to deny jurisdiction if they believe that factors make it unreasonable for a party to appear in a US court (CKCL, 2000). The US courts have indicated that they will only consider upholding choice-of-law clauses when they are made between two commercial entities (CKCL, 2000).

Most courts in Canada require a party to have a 'real and substantial connection' with the jurisdiction asserted before they will grant jurisdiction (Gates, 2008). Canadian courts consider matters such as: the physical location of the parties; witnesses and evidence; the coordination of legal systems; the justice of the end result and the protection of agreed conditions, in balancing the interests of the parties to determine if jurisdiction should be granted (Gates, 2008).

Businesses that opt to use cloud computing services that impose choice of forum and choice of law terms on the end user could end up facing significant jurisdictional issues in the event that they need to resort to litigation.

CONCLUSION

Cloud computing may be cutting edge technology, but it is still a service in its infancy.

This article has only touched on some of the legal issues that are likely to affect this developing sector of the online industry. Our aim in this article was to educate end users and industry players so that they can make informed choices about the applications for which cloud computing is an appropriate platform. The protection of end users is particularly important when cloud computing end user licence agreements give small players little or no opportunity to negotiate the terms.

Cloud computing illustrates that as the world moves online, there is greater need for the laws that apply to these new activities to become more adaptive to international realities.

REFERENCES

M2 PressWire. (2008). *IBM: Cloud computing spreads in emerging countries*. Retrieved December 4, 2008, from http://www.m2.com

Arnold, E. (2008). Get your head out of the clouds. *Searcher, 16*. Retrieved from http://www.infotoday.com/

Arnold, S. E. (2008). *A risky cloud approach?* Retrieved from http://www.kmworld.com

Australian Broadcasting Corporation. (2008). Microsoft releases emergency patch for IE. *ABC News*. Retrieved January 4, 2009, from http://www.abc.net.au/news/

Australian Law Reform Commission. (2007). *Review of Australian privacy law* (Discussion Paper No. 72).

Australian Law Reform Commission. (2008). *For your information* (Report No. 108).

Brodkin, J. (2008, February 7). Gartner: Seven cloud-computing security risks. *Network World*. Retrieved January 2, 2009, from http://www.networkworld.com/news/

Brynko, B. (2008). *Cloud computing: Knowing the ground rules*. Retrieved from http://www.infotoday.com/IT/nov08/index.shtml

Chicago-Kent College of Law. (2000). *An overview of the law of personal (adjudicatory) jurisdiction: The United States perspective*. Retrieved from http://www.kentlaw.edu/cyberlaw/docs/rfc/usview.html

Chicago-Kent College of Law. (2007). *Jurisdiction on the internet – the European perspective: An analysis of conventions, statutes and case law*. Retrieved from http://www.kentlaw.edu/cyberlaw/docs/rfc/euview.html

Chickowski, E. (2007, February 16). $400 million corporate espionage incident at Du Pont. *SC Magazine*. Retrieved from http://www.scmagazineus.com/400-million-corporate-espionage-incident-at-DuPont/article/34633/

Correy, S. (Producer). (2008, September 14). ABC Radio National: Background briefing. *Cloud Computing*. Podcast retrieved from http://www.abc.net.au/rn/backgroundbriefing/stories/2008/2359128.htm

Desloge, R. (1998, October 16). State makes $500,000 a year selling personal information. *St. Louis Business Journal*. Retrieved from http://stlouis.bizjournals.com/stlouis/stories/1998/10/19/newscolumn1.html

Federal Trade Commission. (2002). *Eli Lilly settles FTC charges concerning security breach*. Retrieved January 6, 2009, from http://www.ftc.gov/

Fitzgerald, M. (2008). Microsoft puts its head in the cloud. *Fast Company, 130*. Retrieved from http://www.fastcompany.com/magazine/130/microsoft-puts-its-head-in-the-cloud.html

Fried, I. (2008, September 3). Google backtracks on Chrome license terms. *CNet News*. Retrieved from http://news.cnet.com/8301-13860_3-10031703-56.html?tag=newsEditorsPicksArea.0

Gates, A. (2008). *Canadian law on jurisdiction in cyberspace*. Chicago: Chicago-Kent College of Law. Retrieved January 7, 2009, from http://www.kentlaw.edu/cyberlaw/docs/rfc/canadaview.html

Google Inc. (2007a). *Google introduces new business version of popular hosted applications*. Retrieved December 4, 2008, from http://www.google.com/intl/en/press/pressrel/google_apps.html>

Google Inc. (2007b). *Google terms of service*. Retrieved January 7, 2009, from http://www.google.com/accounts/TOS?hl=en

Google Inc. (2008a). *About Gmail: More on Gmail and privacy*. Retrieved January 3, 2009, from http://mail.google.com/mail/help/about_privacy.html

Google Inc. (2008b). *Google Apps Premier Edition agreement*. Retrieved December 4, 2008, from http://www.google.com/apps/intl/en/terms/premier_terms.html

Google Inc. (2008c). *Google Apps for business: Find answers to your questions*. Retrieved December 4, 2008, from http://www.google.com/apps/intl/en/business/support.html

Google Inc. (2008d). *Gmail privacy notice*. Retrieved January 1, 2009, from http://mail.google.com/mail/help/intl/en/privacy.html

Google Inc. (2008e). *Google Apps admin help: Privacy policy; your choices*. Retrieved January 2, 2009, from http://www.google.com/support/a/bin/answer.py?hl=el&answer=33926

Google Inc. (2008f). *Google Apps Standard Edition agreement*. Retrieved January 7, 2009, from http://www.google.com/apps/intl/en/terms/standard_terms.html

Google Inc. (2008g). *Google Chrome terms of service*. Retrieved December 27, 2008, from http://www.google.com/chrome/intl/en/eula_text.html

Hoover, J., Martin, R., & Paul, F. (2008, January 19) Demystifying the cloud. *InformationWeek*. Retrieved from http://www.informationweek.com/news/

IBM. (2008a). *IBM debuts new enterprise data center specialty for business partners*. Retrieved December 4, 2008, from http://www-03.ibm.com/press/us/en/index.wss

IBM. (2008b). *Made in IBM Labs: IBM to build first cloud computing centre in China*. Retrieved December 4, 2008, from http://www-03.ibm.com/press/us/en/pressrelease/23426.wss

Lyons, D. (2008a). Today's forecast: Cloudy; people are going to be putting their information not into some device but into some service that lives in the sky. *Newsweek, 152*. Retrieved December 9, 2008, from http://www.newsweek.com/id/166818

Lyons, D. (2008b, November 4). A mostly cloudy computing forecast. *The Washington Post*. Retrieved from http://www.encyclopedia.com/doc/1P2-19537475.html

Marshall, R. (2008). Cloud computing: The dark and stormy side. *TechNewsWorld*. Retrieved December 4, 2008, from http://www.technewsworld.com/rsstory/64831.html

McCullagh, D. (2006, February 17). Google to feds: Back off. *CNet*. Retrieved from http://news.cnet.com/Google-to-feds-Back-off/2100-1030_3-6041113.html

Microsoft Corporation. (2008a). *Microsoft Office Live*. Retrieved January 5, 2009, from http://office.microsoft.com/en-au/office_live/FX101754491033.aspx?pid=CL101750181033&ofcresset=1

Microsoft Corporation. (2008b). *Office Live Workspace: Frequently asked questions*. Retrieved December 8, 2008, from http://workspace.officelive.com/FAQ#1

Microsoft Corporation. (2008c). *Microsoft Office Live Small Business: Shared online workspace*. Retrieved December 8, 2008, from http://small-business.officelive.com/Manage/WorkSpaces

Microsoft Corporation. (2008d). *Microsoft service agreement*. Retrieved December 4, 2008, from http://help.live.com/help.aspx?mkt=en-au&project=touat

Newville, L. (2001). Cyber crime and the courts – investigating and supervising the information age offender. [Retrieved from http://www.uscourts.gov/library/fpcontents.html]. *Federal Probation, 65*.

Otey, M. (2008). Up in the air over cloud computing. *SQL Magazine, 10*. Retrieved from http://www.sqlmag.com/articles/index.cfm?articleid=100580

Princeton University (Producer). (2008a, January 14-15). UChannel: Princeton University's Centre for Information Technology Policy. *Computing in the cloud: Panel 1*. Podcast retrieved from http://uc.princeton.edu/main/index.php?option=com_content&task=view&id=2589&Itemid=1

Princeton University (Producer). (2008b, January 14-15). UChannel: Princeton University's Centre for Information Technology Policy. *Computing in the cloud: Panel 2*. Podcast retrieved from http://uc.princeton.edu/main/index.php?option=com_content&task=view&id=2589&Itemid=1

Ranger, S. (2008). Behind the cloud. [Retrieved from http://www.director.co.uk]. *Director (Cincinnati, Ohio), 62*.

The Economist (London). (2008). *The long nimbus*. Retrieved December 4, 2008, from http://www.economist.com/specialreports/

The Office of the Privacy Commissioner. (2001). *Guidelines to the national privacy principles*. Retrieved December 8, 2008, from http://www.privacy.gov.au/publications/

This work was previously published in the International Journal of Digital Crime and Forensics, Volume 2, Issue 1, edited by Chang-Tsun Li and Anthony TS Ho, pp. 30-39, copyright 2010 by IGI Publishing (an imprint of IGI Global).

Chapter 18
A Conceptual Methodology for Dealing with Terrorism "Narratives"

Gian Piero Zarri
University Paris Est/Créteil/Val de Marne (UPEC), France

ABSTRACT

This paper concerns the use of in-depth analytical/conceptual techniques pertaining to the Artificial Intelligence domain to deal with narrative information (or "narratives") in the terrorism- and crime-related areas. More precisely, the authors supply details about NKRL (Narrative Knowledge Representation Language), a representation and querying/inferencing environment especially created for an advanced exploitation of all types of narrative information. This description will be integrated with concrete examples that illustrate the use of NKRL tools in two recent 'defence' applications, the first dealing with a corpus of "Southern Philippines terrorism" news stories used in an R&D European project, the second, carried out in collaboration with the French "Délégation Générale pour l'Armement" (DGA, Central Bureau for Armament), which handles news stories about Afghanistan's war.

INTRODUCTION

'Narrative' information concerns in general the account of some real-life or fictional story (a "narrative") involving concrete or imaginary 'characters': these try to attain a specific result, experience particular situations, manipulate concrete or abstract materials, send or receive mes-

sages, buy, sell, deliver etc. Narratives are formed of *temporally ordered sequences of 'elementary events'*, and this diachronic aspect represents one of their most important characteristics. Some important properties of narratives/elementary events are listed below – see Zarri (2009, pp. 2-13) for more details:

- Each elementary event of the stream corresponds to (is recognized through) the

DOI: 10.4018/978-1-4666-1758-2.ch018

presence of a single 'predicate' ("buy", "kill", "send"…) in the natural language (NL) description of the narrative under examination. According to the so-called 'neo-Davidsonian approach' – see, e.g., Higginbotham (1985, 2000), Parson (1990), etc. – a 'predicate' may correspond here not only to verbs in general but also to adjectives, nouns and preposition when they have a 'predicative' function.

- Besides time, 'space' is also very important from a narrative point of view, given that the elementary events of the stream occur generally in well-defined 'locations', real or imaginary ones. The connected events that make up a narrative are then both temporally and spatially bounded. Bakhtin (1982) speaks about "chronotopes" when drawing attention on the fact that time and spaces in narratives are strictly interrelated.

- As already stated, the elementary/monadic events of the stream must be logically correlated: this means that simple chronological successions of elementary events that take place in given locations cannot be defined as a unique 'narrative' without some sort of 'semantic coherence' and 'uniqueness of the theme' that characterise the different events of the stream. If this logical coherence is lacking, the events pertain to different complex events/narratives: a narrative can also be represented by a single elementary event.

- When the constitutive elementary events of the narrative are verbalized in NL terms, their logical/semantic coherence is normally expressed through syntactic constructions like causality, goal, indirect speech, co-ordination and subordination, etc. In this paper, we will systematically make use of the terms '*connectivity phenomena*' to denote the existence of this sort of clues, i.e., to denote what, in a stream of events, i) leads to a 'global meaning' that goes beyond the simple addition of the 'meanings' conveyed by a single elementary event; ii) defines the influence of the context in which a particular event is used on the meaning of this individual event, or part of it.

- The characters involved in the elementary events/narratives are not necessarily human beings; we can have elementary events/narratives concerning, e.g., the vicissitudes in the journey of a nuclear submarine (the 'actor', 'character' etc.), the various avatars in the life of a commercial product, the transition of a given industrial machine from an 'idle' to a 'running' state, etc.

- Eventually, even if the narratives are often included within natural language (NL) texts, this is *not* necessarily true. A photo representing a situation that, verbalized, could be expressed as "The US President is addressing the Congress" is not an NL document, yet it surely represents a narrative.

A common differentiation carried out in the narrative domain concerns the separation between *fictional* and *non-fictional* narrative, see, e.g., Jahn (2005). 'Fictional' narratives have principally an entertainment value, and represent a narrator's account of a story that happened in an imaginary world: a novel is a typical example of fictional narrative. 'Non-fictional' narratives have, very often, some sort of intrinsic economic value, which means in practice that people could be willing to pay for a system able to process in an 'intelligent' way this sort of information and/or for the results of the processing. This sort of narratives are embodied, in fact, into corporate memory documents (memos, policy statements, reports, minutes etc.), news stories, normative and legal texts, medical records, many intelligence messages, surveillance videos, actuality photos for newspapers and magazines, material (text, image, video, sound…) for eLearning, Cultural

Heritage material, etc. Dealing with non-fictional narrative material is of paramount importance, in particular, for the analysis and management of any sort of crisis situation and, more in general, for enhancing the ability to fight terrorism and other crimes. For example, six critical mission areas have been identified in the "National Strategy for Homeland Security" report (2002). Of these, at least two, "Intelligence and Warning" and "Domestic Counter-terrorism" are based on the processing of non-fictional narrative information in order, e.g., to "… find cooperative relationships between criminals and their interactive patterns". Managing non-fictional narrative information must then be considered as an essential component of the emerging science of "Intelligence and Security Informatics" (ISI) see, e.g., Chen and Wang (2005), Chen (2006), Yang et al. (2008).

In this paper, we will present NKRL ("Narrative Knowledge Representation Language"), an Intelligent Information Retrieval (IIR) tool based on a conceptual and Artificial Intelligence approach. NKRL, see Zarri (2003, 2005a, 2009) is, at the same time:

- A knowledge representation system for describing in some detail the essential content (the 'meaning') of complex (non-fictional) narratives;
- A system of reasoning (inference) procedures that, thanks to the richness of the representation system, is able to automatically establish 'interesting' relationships among the represented data;
- An implemented software environment.

The paper will be illustrated by examples concerning two recent 'defence' applications of NKRL, the first dealing with a corpus of "Southern Philippines terrorism" news stories used in an R&D European project, the second, carried out in collaboration with the French "*Délégation Générale pour l'Armement*" (DGA, Central Bureau for Armament), which handles news stories about Afghanistan. After having introduced the main principles underpinning the 'conceptual' representation of narrative documents, we will supply some technical details about NKRL and its inference procedures. A short "Conclusion" will end the paper.

Representing Narrative Documents

The current semantic and ontological applications make normally use of languages, like RDF(S) and OWL – see (Manola & Miller, 2004; McGuinnes & van Harmelen, 2004; W3C OWL Working Group, 2009) – where the *properties* are strictly limited to a *binary relationship linking two individuals or an individual and a value*. This inhibits us, in practice, from making use of these 'binary' languages when the situations to be represented are characterised, as in the narratives, by a high level of complexity. If we consider, in fact, a very simple narrative like "John gives a book to Mary", "give" corresponds now to a *ternary relationship*. This last, to be represented in a complete and unambiguous way, asks for the use of a complex, '*n-ary*' syntax where the arguments of the predicate "give", i.e., "John", "book" and "Mary", cannot be directly associated with this predicate but must be introduced by functional relations ('roles') in the style of, e.g., "agent of give", "object of give" and "beneficiary of give" respectively. For representing the 'meaning' of narrative documents, the notion of '*role*' must then be added to the traditional (binary) 'generic/specific' and 'property/value' representational principles in order to specify the exact function of the different components of an event within the general description of this event – see also Mizoguchi et al. (2007) in this context. A detailed discussion about the '*n*-ary problem' can be found in Zarri (2005b, 2009, pp. 14-22).

NKRL makes use of a well-formed and complete solution to the n-*ary* problem, based on the use of both the 'conceptual predicate' and 'functional role' notions. Returning then to the "John gives a book…" example above, a representation that captures all the 'meaning' of this elementary narrative amounts to:

- Defining JOHN_, MARY_ and BOOK_1 as 'individuals', instances of general 'concepts' like human_being and information_ support. Concepts and individuals are, as usual, collected into a standard 'binary' ontology.

- Defining an *n*-ary structure organized around a predicate like GIVE or PHYSICAL_TRANSFER, and associating the above individuals with the predicate through the use of functional roles that specify their 'function' within the global narrative. JOHN_ will then be introduced by an AGENT (or SUBJECT) role, BOOK_1 by an OBJECT (or PATIENT) role, MARY_ by a BENEFICIARY_ role.

Formally, an *n*-ary structure defined as above can be described as:

$$(L_i (P_j (R_1 \ a_1) (R_2 \ a_2) \ … \ (R_n \ a_n))), \qquad (1)$$

where L_i is the symbolic label identifying the particular *n*-ary structure (e.g., that corresponding to the "John gives a book…" example), P_j is the conceptual predicate, R_k is the generic role and a_k the corresponding argument (the individuals JOHN_, MARY_ etc.).

The whole, *n*-ary conceptual structure denoted by Equation 1 must be considered *globally*, and corresponds to the formal representation of a single elementary event: see below with respect to the representation of those 'connectivity phenomena' – like causality, goal, indirect speech, co-ordination and subordination etc. – introduced in the previous Section.

A General Survey of NKRL

We will now enter into some details about NKRL, to show how this tool could be used for applications to be likened to crisis management and 'standard' defence tasks.

ONTOLOGIES AND NKRL

To deal with narratives in a sufficiently complete way, NKRL innovates by adding to the usual '*ontologies of concepts*' – the frame-oriented ones, see, e.g., Noy et al. (2000), or those inspired by the Semantic Web research, see Bechhofer *et al.* (2004), Horridge (2004), etc. – an '*ontology of events*', i.e., a new sort of hierarchical organization where the nodes correspond to *n*-ary structures called 'templates'. This new hierarchy is called HTemp (hierarchy of templates).

Note that, in the NKRL environment, an 'ontology of concepts' not only exists, but it represents in fact an essential component for assuring the correct functioning of the whole environment. This 'standard' ontology is called HClass (hierarchy of classes): structurally and functionally, HClass is not fundamentally different from a frame-oriented or semantic-web oriented ontology. An (extremely reduced) representation of HClass is given in Figure 1 – note that HClass includes presently (November 2009) more than 7,500 concepts. See Zarri (2009, pp. 123-138) for a discussion about concepts like non_sortal_concept (the specialisations of this concept, i.e., its subsumed concepts like substance_ cannot be endowed with direct instances), sortal_concept etc.

Instead of using the traditional binary attribute – value structure, see the discussion in the previous Section, templates correspond to the general schema represented by Equation 1 above, i.e., they are generated by the *n*-ary association of quadruples following the *symbolic label – predicate – role – argument* organization. More precisely, predicates pertain to the set {BEHAVE,

Figure 1. Fragment of the 'standard' ontology of concepts (HClass)

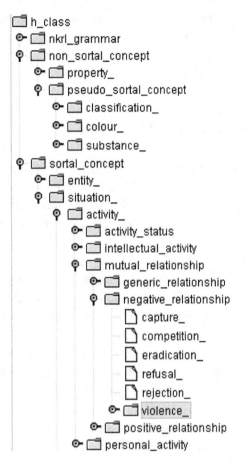

EXIST, EXPERIENCE, MOVE, OWN, PRODUCE, RECEIVE}, and roles to the set {SUBJ(ect), OBJ(ect), SOURCE, BEN(e)F(iciary), MODAL(ity), TOPIC, CONTEXT}; predicates and roles are then 'primitives'. An argument a_k of the predicate, see Equation 1, denotes through a 'variable' (see below Table 1) either a simple concept of the standard (HClass) ontology of concepts or a structured association ('expansion') of several HClass concepts. Figure 2 reproduces a fragment of the 'external' organization of HTemp – see Table 1 below for the 'internal' structure of a template – that includes, in particular, some offsprings of the general Produce: template (this template with all its offsprings

are characterized by the presence of the PRODUCE conceptual predicate, P_j).

Templates represent then formally generic classes of elementary events like "move a physical object", "be present in a place", "send/receive a message", "carry out violence on someone/something", etc., see Zarri (2003, 2009). More than 150 templates are permanently inserted into HTemp; HTemp corresponds then to a sort of 'catalogue' of narrative formal structures, very easy to enrich and customize. This approach is particularly advantageous for practical applications, and it implies that: i) a system-builder does not have to create himself the structural knowledge needed to describe a large class of narratives; ii) it becomes easier to secure the reproduction and sharing of previous results.

When a particular event pertaining to one of these general classes must be represented, the corresponding template is 'instantiated' to produce what, in the NKRL's jargon, is called a *'predicative occurrence'*. To represent then, in a DGA application context, a simple narrative like: "On November 17, 2003, in an unspecified location, an armed group of people shot dead a woman", we must select firstly in HTemp the template corresponding to 'killing of human being', see Figure 2 and Table 1a below.

In a template, as already stated, the arguments of the predicate (the a_k terms in Equation 1) are represented by variables with associated constraints. When deriving a predicative occurrence like afga0404.c6 in Table 1b, the role fillers in the occurrence must conform to the constraints of the father-template. For example, WOMAN_2 (the BEN(e)F(iciary) of the action of killing) and INDIVIDUAL_PERSON_84 (the unknown *group* – see (SPECIF cardinality_several_) – of people corresponding to the actor, initiator etc. of this action) are both 'individuals', instances of the HClass concept individual_person. This last is a specialization of human_being_or_social_body, see, in Table 1a, the constraint on the variables *var1* and *var6*. Note that, in the occur-

Table 1. Building up and querying predicative occurrences

---

a)

name: Produce:HumanBeingKilling
father: Produce:Violence
position: 6. 492
NL description: 'Killing the Filler (Human Being) of the BEN(e)F(iciary) Role'

PRODUCE SUBJ *var1*: [(*var2*)]
OBJ *var3*
    [SOURCE *var4*: [(*var5*)]]
    BENF *var6*: [(*var7*)]
    [MODAL *var8*]
    [TOPIC *var9*]
    [CONTEXT *var10*]
    { [modulators], ≠abs }

var1 = human_being_or_social_body
var3 = human_being_killing
var4 = human_being_or_social_body
var6 = human_being
var8 = criminality/violence_related_tool, machine_tool, small_portable_equipment, weapon_
var9 = h_class
var10 = situation_, symbolic_label
var2, var5, var7 = geographical_ocation

b)

afga0404.c6) PRODUCE SUBJ (SPECIF INDIVIDUAL_PERSON_84 weapon_wearing (SPECIF cardinality_several_)):
(GEOGRAPHICAL_LOCATION_6)
OBJ HUMAN_BEING_KILLING_1
BENF WOMAN_2
MODAL TERRORIST_SHOOTING_ATTACK_1
date-1: 17/11/2003
date-2:

Produce:HumanBeingKilling (6.351)

On November 17, 2003, in an unspecified location, an armed group of people shot dead a woman.

c)

PRODUCE
SUBJ: human_being
OBJ: human_being_killing
BENF: woman_
date-1: 1/11/2003
date-2: 31/12/2003

Is there any information in the system concerning women killing in November 2003?

rences, we make (systematically) use as fillers of 'individuals' (represented in upper case) like WOMAN_2 instead of 'concepts' (in lower case) when the corresponding entities – the specific woman killed in this case – must be mentioned in several, different occurrences (co-reference).

The 'attributive operator', SPECIF(ication), of Table 1b, is one of the four operators used for the set up of 'structured arguments' ('expansions'). The SPECIF lists, with syntax (SPECIF e_i p_1 … p_n), are used to represent the properties or attributes that can be asserted about the first

Figure 2. Produce: Branch of HTemp, the 'ontology of events'

- ○ ☐ Experience:
- ○ ☐ Own:
- ○ ☐ Produce:
  - ○ ☐ Produce:Acceptance/Refusal
  - ○ ☐ Produce:RelationInvolvement
  - ○ ☐ Produce:Entity
  - ○ ☐ Produce:PerformTask/Activity
    - ☐ Produce:Assessment/Trial
    - ☐ Produce:BeautyCareProcess/Activity
    - ☐ Produce:R/DActivity
    - ☐ Produce:Numerical/StatisticalProcess
    - ☐ Produce:Services
    - ☐ Produce:Didactic/OrganizationalActivities/Events
    - ☐ Produce:IndustrialProcess
    - ○ ☐ Produce:EconomicInterestActivity
    - ○ ☐ Produce:Violence
      - ☐ Produce:HumanBeingInjuring
      - ☐ Produce:HumanBeingKilling
    - ○ ☐ Produce:CreateCondition/Result
      - ☐ Produce:NegativeCondition/Result
      - ☐ Produce:PositiveCondition/Result
    - ○ ☐ Produce:Increment/Decrement
- ○ ☐ Exist:
- ○ ☐ Receive:
- ○ ☐ Behave:

element e_i, concept (cardinality_) or individual (INDIVIDUAL_PERSON_84), of the list. The residual three operators are ALTERN(ative), ENUM(eration) and COORD(ination). More details about structured arguments can be found in Zarri (2003, 2009, pp. 69-70).

The 'location attributes', represented in the predicative occurrences as lists, are linked with the arguments of the predicate by using, see the individual GEOGRAPHICAL_LOCATION_6 in Table 1b, the 'colon' operator, ':'. In the occurrences, the two operators date-1, date-2 materialize the temporal interval normally associated with narrative events, see again Table 1b. The representation of temporal information constitutes one of the 'strong points' of NKRL. Based on the notions of 'category of dating' to represent the duration of an event on the time axis, and of that of 'perspective of dating' to represent the accuracy according to which a given timestamp can

be located on this axis, this sort of representation is, at the same time, simple, powerful and elegant, and compares favourably with particularly convoluted systems like TimeML (Pustejovsky et al., 2005). A detailed description of the methodology for representing temporal data in NKRL can be found in Zarri (1998, 2009, pp. 76-86).

Until now, we have evoked the NKRL solutions to the problem of representing *elementary events*. To deal with the *'connectivity phenomena'*, NKRL makes use of *second order structures* created through *reification* of the conceptual labels (like afga0404.c6 in Table 1) of the predicative occurrences. These second order structures take the name of *'completive construction'* and *'binding occurrences'*: in particular, binding occurrences make use of lists of conceptual labels identified by specific binding operators like GOAL, COND(ition), CAUSE etc. see, for a detailed description and some examples, Zarri (2003, 2009, pp. 86-98).

As an informal example, let us suppose we are dealing with the representation of a 'Southern Philippines terrorism' narrative like: "On November 20, 1999, in an unspecified village, an armed group of people has kidnapped Robustiniano Hablo *in order to* ask his family for a ransom". The first part (elementary event) of the narrative is represented by a predicative occurrence derived from the Produce:Violence template, see Zarri (2005a) for a complete description of the corresponding NKRL code: let us name this occurrence, describing then to the kidnapping action, mod3.c5. The second part of the narrative, "the unknown individuals will ask for a ransom" corresponds to a new predicative occurrence (a new elementary event), e.g., mod3.c7, derived from the Receive:Information template and having Robustiniano Hablo's family as SUBJ(ect). To represent the narrative completely, we must add to the two previous predicative occurrences a *binding occurrence*, e.g., mod3.c8, to link together the conceptual labels mod3.c5 (corresponding to the kidnapping occurrence) and mod3.c7 (that describes the intended result, i.e., asking for a ransom). mod3.c8 will have then the form: "mod3.c8) (GOAL mod3.c5 mod3.c7)"; its meaning can be paraphrased as: "the activity described in mod3.c5 is focalised towards (GOAL) the realization of mod3.c7".

INFERENCE PROCEDURES

First Level of Inference Procedures

The basic building block for all the NKRL querying and inference procedures is called *Fum*, '*Filtering Unification Module*'. It takes as input specific NKRL data structures called '*search patterns*'.

Search patterns can be considered as the NKRL counterparts of natural language queries; they offer then the possibility of querying directly an NKRL knowledge base of conceptual annotations. Formally, the search patterns correspond to specialized/partially instantiated HTemp templates, where the 'explicit variables' that characterize the templates (*var$_i$*, see Table 1a) have been replaced by concepts/individuals compatible with the constraints originally imposed on these variables.

All the (HClass) concepts inserted into a search pattern p_i, are then used as '*implicit variables*'. When trying to unify a search pattern, as a formal query, with the predicative occurrences of the knowledge base, a concept p_i can then match the individuals representing its own instances in these occurrences, and all its subsumed HClass concepts with their own instances. The set of predicative occurrences unified by a search pattern constitutes the answer to the query represented by the pattern. Note all the terms used to build up a search pattern must be explicitly found in the matched occurrences, either in an identical form (e.g., predicate and roles), or as subsumed concepts or instances of the implicit variables. Additional terms – roles, fillers and part of fillers – with respect to those explicitly declared in the pattern can be freely found in the occurrences.

A simple example of search pattern, translating the query: "There is there any information in the system concerning women killing in November 2003?" is given in Table 1c, producing the occurrence afga0404.c6 (Table 1b) as one of the possible answers. We can also note that the two timestamps, *date1* and *date2* associated with the pattern, see Table 1c, constitute now the 'search interval' used to limit the search for unification to the slice of time that the user considers as appropriate to explore, see (Zarri, 1998).

NKRL search patterns correspond roughly to the formal queries proper to the SPARQL query language used in an RDF context, see (Prud'hommeaux & Seaborne, 2008). Apart from the syntactic differences – SPARQL is heavily SQL-based – NKRL and SPARQL queries are fundamentally different with respect to the power of the matching/unification operations that, in NKRL, take into account the ontological information (HClass) whilst in SPARQL are purely syntactically-based.

The high-level inference operations correspond mainly to the use of two classes of inference rules, 'hypotheses' and 'transformations'. Execution of both requires employing a complex *InferenceEngine*, having *Fum* as its core mechanism.

Transformation Rules

These rules try to '*adapt*', from a semantic point of view, a search pattern p_i that '*failed*' (that was unable to find an unification within the knowledge base) to the real contents of this base making use of a sort of '*analogical reasoning*'. The original pattern (query) is then transformed into one or more different patterns that are not strictly 'equivalent' but only 'semantically close' to the original one.

Suppose, e.g., we ask, in a "Southern Philippines terrorism" context: "Search for the existence of some links between ObL (a well known international 'terrorist') and Abubakar Abdurajak Janjalani, the leader of the Abu Sayyaf group" – this group is one of the Muslim independence movements in Southern Philippines. In the absence of a direct answer, the query can be transformed into: "Search for the attestation of the transfer of economic/financial items between the two", which could lead to retrieve: "During 1998/1999, Abubakar Abdurajak Janjalani has received an undetermined amount of money from ObL through an intermediate agent".

From a formal point of view, transformation rules are made up of a left-hand side, the '*antecedent*' – i.e. the formulation, in search pattern format, of the 'query' to be transformed – and one or more right-hand sides, the '*consequent(s)*' – the representation(s) of one or more queries that must be substituted for the given one. A transformation rule can be expressed as: A (antecedent, left-hand side) $\Rightarrow B_i$ (consequent(s), right-hand side). The 'transformation arrow', '$\Rightarrow$', has a double meaning:

- Operationally speaking, the arrow indicates the direction of the transformation: the left-hand side A (the original search pattern) is removed and replaced by the right-hand side B_i (one or more consequents corresponding to new search patterns);
- The 'semantic' meaning of the arrow is that information obtained through consequent(s) B_i implies (in a weak sense) the information we should have obtained from antecedent A.

Some formal details can be found in Zarri (2009, pp. 212-216). A representation of the previous 'economic/financial transfer' transformation is given in Table 2. Note that the left-hand side (antecedent) of this transformation corresponds to a partial instantiation of the template Behave:FavourableConcreteMutual that is routinely used to represent into NKRL format a (positive) mutual behaviour among two or more entities.

Many of the transformation rules used in NKRL are characterized by the very simply format of Table 2 implying then only one 'consequent' schema. An informal example of 'multi-consequent' transformation is given by this specific 'Terrorism in Southern Philippines' rule: "In a context of ransom kidnapping, the certification that a given character is wealthy or has a professional role can be substituted by the certification that i) this character has a tight kinship link with another person (first consequent schema, *consequent1*), and ii) this second person is a wealthy person or a professional people (second consequent schema, *consequent2*)". Let us suppose that, during the search for all the possible information associated with Robustiniano Hablo's kidnapping (see above), we ask to the system whether Robustiano Hablo is wealthy. In the absence of a direct answer, the system will automatically 'transform' the original query using the above 'kinship' rule. The result is given in Figure 3: we do not know if Robustiano Hablo is wealthy, but we can say that his father is a wealthy businessperson.

Table 2. A simple example of 'transformation' rule

'economic/financial transfer' transformation:
t1) BEHAVE SUBJ (COORD1 *var1 var2*) $\Rightarrow$ RECEIVE SUBJ *var2*   OBJ (COORD1 *var1 var2*) OBJ *var3* SOURCE *var1*   MODAL *var4*   *var1* = human_being_or_social_body   *var2* = human_being_or_social_body   *var3* = economic/financial_entity   *var4* = business_agreement, mutual_relationship

To verify the existence of a relationship or of a business agreement between two (or more) persons, try to verify if one of these persons has received a 'financial entity' (e.g., money) from the other.

Figure 3. InferenceEngine results corresponding to the application of the 'kinship' transformation to the query about Robustiniano Hablo's status. (© Springer's Journal of Data Semantics IV, used with permission).

To conclude about transformations, we can note they have been massively used in the context of the DGA experiment mentioned in the "Introduction" – an important set of transformation rules is reproduced, e.g., in the report (Dourlens & Zarri, 2007). For example, let us suppose we would like to know whether, within a given time span, there have been some anti-US demonstrations in Afghanistan, see Table 3.

In the DGA experiment, we have used a knowledge base derived from the simple accu-mulation of (unedited and randomly stored) news stories: under these conditions, it can be very difficult to get a *direct answer* to a quite general

Table 3. NKRL query (search pattern) in the context of a recent 'defence' experiment

EXIST *SUBJ*: mass_demonstration: (AFGHANISTAN_) *TOPIC*: (SPECIF rejection_ US_) *date-1*: 1/1/2002 *date-2*: 31/12/2003

Table 4. An example of (DGA) 'multi-consequent' transformation

'explicit hostility' transformation:	
antecedent EXIST SUBJ *var1*: (*var2*) TOPIC (SPECIF negative_relationship *var3*) *var1* = mass_demonstration *var2* = country_ *var3* = country_ *var2* ≠ *var3* **consequent1** EXIST SUBJ *var1*: (*var4*) *var4* = city_ **consequent2** EXIST SUBJ (SPECIF *var4* (SPECIF *var5 var2*)) *var5* = geographical_location **consequent3** PRODUCE SUBJ human_being: (*var4*) OBJ (SPECIF *var6 var3*) CONTEXT *var1*	
var6 = violence_	

query like that of Table 3. It is then necessary to resort to transformation rules like that reproduced in Table 4 in order to make use of 'local' events that will allow us to *infer* some sort of *indirect answer* to the original question. The transformation of Table 4 is 'multi-consequent' – like the previous one, the 'wealthy businessperson' transformation. This means that three different steps

of reasoning must be *simultaneously satisfied* to produce the (analogy-reasoning based) answer.

After unification of the antecedent with the original query, variable *var2* is bound to AFGHANISTAN_ and variable *var3* to USA_. *consequent1* is used to retrieve, in the knowledge base, all the cities known by the system (*var4*) where some mass_demonstration (*var1*) occurred. This allow us to retrieve, among many other occurrences, occurrence afga0314.c4 evoking the fact that a MASS_DEMONSTRATION_1 against the Second Gulf War has taken place in the city of MEHTARLAN_ on March 24, 2003 – i.e., within the time span specified by the original query. *consequent2* consents to us to select, among all the possible cities bound to *var4* where some demonstration occurred, those that are really located in Afghanistan: Mehtarlan satisfies this constraint given that another occurrence, afga0314.c6, informs us that this city corresponds really to a geographical_location (*var5*) of (SPECIF) Afghanistan (*var2*). Eventually, *consequent3* supplies, through a new predicative occurrence, afga0314.c8, the expected relationship between MASS_DEMONSTRATION_1 and USA_, see Table 5: the demonstration of March 24, 2003, in Mehtarlan, can then be considered as a protest against the US given that the protesters have set fire to the US flag.

Hypothesis Rules

With respect now to the *hypothesis rules*, these allow us to build up automatically a sort of *'causal*

Table 5. Details about an anti-western manifestation in Afghanistan

afga0314.c8) PRODUCE SUBJ (SPECIF INDIVIDUAL_PERSON_90 (SPECIF cardinality_ several_) (SPECIF approximate_amount 10000)): (MEHTARLAN_) OBJ (SPECIF flag_burning UK_ USA_ ALLIED_COALITION) CONTEXT MASS_DEMONSTRATION_1 date-1: 24/3/2003 date-2:

Produce: Violence (6.35) The protesters have burnt some flags of the United Kingdom, of the US and of the countries pertaining to the Western coalition.

explanation/context' for a narrative (a predicative occurrence c_j) originally retrieved within a NKRL knowledge base using *Fum* and a search-pattern in a querying-answering mode. The theoretical fundaments of hypotheses are expounded in detail in Zarri (2005a, 2009, pp. 205-212).

Very in short, the first move in a hypothesis context consists in checking whether the 'premise' of the rule (corresponding, in a way, to the 'antecedent' part of a transformation rule) can really unify the starting occurrence c_j – this means, among other things, that the rule is able, at least in principle, to supply a causal explanation/context for occurrence c_j. We try then to validate a series of 'reasoning steps' s_i – called 'condition schemata' and corresponding, once again, to partially instantiated templates – by deriving, from each of them, some well-formed search pattern p_i and by checking whether at least one of them is able to find a successful unification with the occurrences of the base. If all the reasoning steps s_i can be really satisfied, then *the corresponding sequence of $c_1, c_2 \ldots c_n$ predicative occurrences (retrieved by Fum) can be interpreted as a causal explanation/context of the original occurrence c_j.*

As an informal example, let us suppose we want to find a 'plausible explanation' for the narrative corresponding to the occurrence afga0404. c6 above, see Table 1b, i.e., "On November 17, 2003, in an unspecified location, an armed group of people shot dead a woman". We can make use for this of two 'parallel' hypothesis rules, where the 'common sense rule' underpinning the first says that: "The Taliban (we are in a DGA/Afghanistan context) do not like to see women working", and the second says: "The Taliban dislike people working for the UN agencies". In the two cases, the first reasoning step consists then in verifying that the Taliban are effectively at the origin of the murder. After this, in the first case we must prove, directly (or indirectly through transformations, see next Section) that the Taliban are against the employment of women; the third step will, therefore, consist in proving that the killed woman was

a UN regular employee – more precisely, we will discover that she was an employee of UNHCR (the UN Agency for the Refugees). In the second case, the intermediate reasoning steps consists in verifying – one again directly or indirectly – that the Taliban dislike the UN agencies like UNHCR; the last step is then identical to that to be verified for the first hypothesis. A detailed description of the use of the two hypotheses for this specific case is supplied in (Dourlens et Zarri, 2007).

RECENT DEVELOPMENTS

The application on terrorism in Southern Philippines has allowed us to attain a very important (theoretical and practical) result: this has concerned *the possibility of running hypotheses and transformations in an 'integrated' way to get the best from the high-level modelling capabilities of NKRL.* Integrating these two inference modes corresponds to:

- From a very practical point of view, transformations can now be used to try to find some useful answers when the search patterns derived directly from a condition schema (one of the reasoning steps s_i) of a hypothesis fail. A hypothesis deemed to fall short could then, on the contrary, continue successfully until its normal end. For example, returning to an example of the previous Section, in the absence of direct information about the hostility of the Taliban vis-à-vis of UN agencies we can retrieve, by transformation, an indirect information relating that the Taliban have battered UNHCR's employees or have burnt their trucks.

- From a more general point of view, transformations can be used to modify in an *a priori* unpredictable way the condition schemata (the reasoning steps s_i) to be executed within a 'hypothesis' context, independently from the fact that these steps have been successful or not. This is equivalent to 'break' the predefined scenarios proper to the hypothesis rules, and to augment then the possibility of discovering 'implicit information' within the knowledge base.

A very detailed description on the principles of the integration procedures can be found in Zarri (2005a). We will limit ourselves to supply here some general information and an informal example.

Let us suppose that, as one of the possible answers to a question concerning the kidnapping events in Southern Philippine during 1999, we have retrieved the information: "Lieven de la Paille and Eric Brown have been kidnapped by a group of people on June 13, 1999". Making use of a hypothesis rule like that described in an informal way in Table 6 in order to 'explain' this kidnapping as a more precise 'kidnapping for ransom' will give rise to a failure because of the impossibility of satisfying directly the 'intermediate' steps Cond1, Cond2 and Cond3 of the hypothesis, i.e., of founding *direct matches* for the search patterns p_i derived from these condition schemata with information in the knowledge base.

If we allow now the use of transformations in a hypothesis context, this is equivalent in practice to make use of a hypothesis corresponding to that of Table 6 but having a format potentially equivalent to the format reproduced in Table 7.

Transformations T*n* mentioned in Table 7 can include only one 'consequent' schema, like T2, T6 and the transformation reproduced in Table 2

above, or they can be 'multi-consequent' like T0, T4 and T5 (and the transformation of Table 4).

In the multi-consequent case, all the consequent schemata must be simultaneously satisfied to give rise to a valid transformation, i.e., 'successful' search patterns (search patterns able to find an unification within the knowledge base) must be derived from all of them. We can see, in particular, that there is a whole family of transformations corresponding to the condition schemata Cond2 of Table 6. They correspond to variants of this general scheme: the separatist movement or terrorist organization, or some group or single person affiliated with them, have requested/received money for the hostage's ransom.

For example, the proof that the kidnappers of Lieven de la Paille and Eric Brown are part of a terrorist group or separatist organization can be now obtained *indirectly*, transformation T3, by checking whether they are members of a specific subset of the group or organization. The fragment of listing reproduced in Figure 4 illustrates then the use of T3 to satisfy the requirements of the condition schema Cond1. It is, in fact, impossible to demonstrate directly that the kidnappers (several unknown persons denoted as INDIVIDUAL_PERSON_68 in Figure 4) are part of a separatist movement, but we can retrieve from the knowledge base that they are part of the renegades of the Moro Islamic Liberation Front (MILF) and that, at the moment of the kidnapping, the MILF was probably – see the 'modal modulator' poss(ibility) associated with the occurrence mod57.c17 in Figure 4 – still in control of its renegades.

Table 6. Inference steps in a 'kidnapping for ransom' context

(Cond1) The kidnappers are part of a separatist movement or of a terrorist organization.
(Cond2) This separatist movement or terrorist organization currently practices ransom kidnapping of specific categories of people.
(Cond3) In particular, executives or assimilated categories are concerned (other rules will deal with civil servants, servicemen, members of the clergy etc.).
(Cond4) It can be proven that the kidnapped is really a businessperson or assimilated.

Table 7. Hypothesis 'kidnapping for ransom' in the presence of transformations concerning the intermediary inference steps

(Cond1) The kidnappers are part of a separatist movement or of a terrorist organization.
– (**Rule T3, Consequent1**) *Try to verify whether a given separatist movement or terrorist organization is under the strict control of a specific sub-group and, in this case,*
– (**Rule T3, Consequent2**) *check if the kidnappers are members of this sub-group. We will then assimilate the kidnappers to 'members' of the movement or organization.*
(Cond2) This movement or organization practices ransom kidnapping of given categories of people.
– (**Rule T2, Consequent**) *The family of the kidnapped has received a ransom request from the separatist movement or terrorist organization.*
– (**Rule T4, Consequent1**) *The family of the kidnapped has received a ransom request from a group or an individual person, and*
– (**Rule T4, Consequent2**) *this second group or individual person is part of the separatist movement or terrorist organization.*
– (**Rule T5, Consequent1**) *Try to verify if a particular sub-group of the separatist movement or terrorist organization exists, and*
– (**Rule T5, Consequent2**) *check whether this particular sub-group practices ransom kidnapping of particular categories of people.*
– ...
(Cond3) In particular, executives or assimilated categories are concerned.
– (**Rule T0, Consequent1**) *In a 'ransom kidnapping' context, we can check whether the kidnapped person has a strict kinship relationship with a second person, and*
– (**Rule T0, Consequent2**) *(in the same context) check if this second person is a businessperson or assimilated.*
(Cond4) It can be proven that the kidnapped person is really an executive or assimilated.
– (**Rule T6, Consequent**) *In a 'ransom kidnapping' context, 'personalities' like consultants, physicians, journalists, artists etc. can be assimilated to businesspersons.*

Figure 4. Application of the transformation rule about the 'renegades'

```
*********  the result for condition 1  ****************
*********************************************************************************
***Entering an internal transformation module : internal level 1 ************************
*********************************************************************************
***                     The model to transform
***
***:
***      ] BEHAVE
***      SUBJ(ect)  : INDIVIDUAL_PERSON_68 :
***      MODAL(ity) : part_of
***      TOPIC      : separatist_movement
***      {}
***      date-1     :null
***      date-2     :null
***      is instance of:
***
***          *********  the result for consequent 1  ****************
***mod57.c17:
***      ] OWN
***      SUBJ(ect)  : MORO_ISLAMIC_LIBERATION_FRONT :
***      OBJ(ect)   : control_ :
***      TOPIC      : MORO_ISLAMIC_RENEGADE
***      {poss }
***      date-1     :24/3/1999
***      date-2     :null
***      is instance of:Own:Control
***Natural language description :
***On March 24, 1999, it is possible that the MILF is still in control of its renegades.
***
***          *********  the result for consequent 2  ****************
***mod33.c10:
***      ] BEHAVE
***      SUBJ(ect)  : ( SPECIF INDIVIDUAL_PERSON_68 { SPECIF cardinality_ several_ } ) :
***      MODAL(ity) : part_of
***      TOPIC      : MORO_ISLAMIC_RENEGADE
***      {obs }
***      date-1     :13/6/1999
***      date-2     :null
***      is instance of:Behave:Member
***Natural language description :
***The kidnappers are member of a group of renegades of the Moro Islamic Liberation Front.
```

Figure 5 refers to the application of transformation T4 to satisfy the condition schema Cond2: the ransom kidnapping activity of the Moro National Liberation Front is proved by the fact that some of its members have required a ransom to the family of Wilmarie Ira Furigay; etc.

CONCLUSION

In this paper, we have described the use of symbolic techniques in the 'Intelligent Information Retrieval' (IIR) style to deal with narrative information in the terrorism- and crime-related areas. More precisely, we have supplied some details about NKRL (Narrative Knowledge Representation Language), a representation and querying/ inferencing environment especially created for an advanced exploitation of (non-fictional) narrative information. We recall here that the main innovation of NKRL consists in associating with the traditional ontology's of concepts an 'ontology of events', i.e., a new hierarchical organization where the nodes correspond to *n*-ary structures called 'templates'.

The paper has been illustrated by examples concerning two successful applications of NKRL techniques, the first making use of a corpus of news stories about the "Southern Philippines terrorism" utilized in an R&D European project, see Zarri (2005a), the second making using a corpus of news stories about Afghanistan in the context of a recent project carried out in collaboration with the French "*Délégation Générale pour l'Armement*" (DGA, Central Bureau for Armaments), see Dourlens and Zarri (2007). Other

Figure 5. People related to MILF ask for ransom

```
********** the result for condition 2  ***************
***************************************************************************
***Entering an internal transformation module : internal level 1 ********************
***************************************************************************
***                        The model to transform
***
***:
***     ] PRODUCE
***     SUBJ(ect)  : MORO_ISLAMIC_LIBERATION_FRONT :
***     OBJ(ect)   : ransom_kidnapping :
***     BENF       : human_being :
***     {}
***     date-1     :null
***     date-2     :null
***     is instance of:
***
***          ********** the result for consequent 1  ***************
***mod18.c10:
***     ] PRODUCE
***     SUBJ(ect)  : ( SPECIF INDIVIDUAL_PERSON_67 ( SPECIF cardinality_ several_ ) ) :
***     OBJ(ect)   : RANSOM_DEMAND_1 :
***     BENF       : ( SPECIF family_ WILMARIE_IRA_FURIGAY ) :
***     TOPIC      : ( SPECIF hostage_release WILMARIE_IRA_FURIGAY )
***     { }
***     date-1     :11/8/1999 28/8/1999
***     date-2     :null
***     is instance of:Produce:PerformTask/Activity
***Natural language description :
***In a period included between August 11, 1999, the date of the kidnapping, and August 28, 1999, the
date of the news, the kidnappers have sent a ransom demand to the family of Wilmarie Ira Furigay.
***
***          ********** the result for consequent 2  ***************
***mod18.c7:
***     ] BEHAVE
***     SUBJ(ect)  : ( SPECIF INDIVIDUAL_PERSON_67 ( SPECIF cardinality_ several_ ) ) :
***     MODAL(ity) : part_of
***     TOPIC      : MORO_ISLAMIC_LIBERATION_FRONT
***     {obs }
***     date-1     :11/8/1999
***     date-2     :null
***     is instance of:Behave:Member
***Natural language description :
***The kidnappers were members of the Moro Islamic Liberation Front.
***************************************************************************
```

applications of the NKRL techniques that have been suggested in a (general) digital forensic and crime area concern the protection of the intellectual property, the dismantling of drug traffic networks and the fight against pornography – note that some results concerning the application of NKRL-like techniques in this last domain have already been achieved in the context of an European project, EUFORBIA, see, e.g., Zarri (2009, pp. 234-239).

REFERENCES

W3C OWL Working Group. (2009, October 27). *OWL 2 Web Ontology Language, Document Overview – W3C Recommendation (W3C)*. Retrieved November 16, 2009 from http://www.w3.org/TR/2009/REC-owl2-overview-20091027/

Bakhtin, M. M. (1982). Forms of Time and of Chronotope in the Novel (Trans. K. Bronstom & V. Liaponov). In Holquist, M., & Liapunov, V. (Eds.), *The Dialogic Imagination: Four Essays*. Austin, TX: University of Texas Press.

Chen, H. (2006). *Intelligence and Security Informatics for International Security: Information Sharing and Data Mining*. New York: Springer.

Chen, H., & Wang, F.-Y. (2005). Artificial Intelligence for Homeland Security. *IEEE Intelligent Systems*, *20*(5), 12–16. doi:10.1109/MIS.2005.88

Dourlens, S., & Zarri, G. P. (2007). *Étude et réalisation du logiciel DECISIF, détection de signaux crisogènes faibles – rapport fin de phase 2 (version 1.1)*. Courtabœuf, France: CityPassenger.

Higginbotham, J. (1985). On Semantics. *Linguistic Inquiry*, *16*, 547–593.

Higginbotham, J. (2000). On Events in Linguistic Semantics. In Higginbotham, J., Pianesi, F., & Varzi, A. C. (Eds.), *Speaking of Events*. Oxford, UK: Oxford University Press.

Jahn, M. (2005). *Narratology: A Guide to the Theory of Narrative* (version 1.8). Cologne, Germany: English Department of the University. Retrieved November 16, 2009 from http://www.uni-koeln.de/~ame02/pppn.htm

Manola, F., & Miller, E. (Eds.). (2004, February 10). *RDF Primer – W3C Recommendation (W3C)*. Retrieved November 16, 2009 from http://www.w3.org/TR/rdf-primer/

McGuinness, D. L., & van Harmelen, F. (Eds.). (2004, February 10). *OWL WEB Ontology Language Overview – W3C Recommendation (W3C)*. Retrieved November 16, 2009 from http://www.w3.org/TR/owl-features/

Mizoguchi, R., Sunagawa, E., Kozaki, K., & Kitamura, Y. (2007). The Model of Roles Within an Ontology Development tool: Hozo. *Applied Ontology*, *2*, 159–179.

(2002). *National Strategy for Homeland Security*. Washington, DC: Office of Homeland Security.

Parson, T. (1990). *Events in the Semantics of English*. Cambridge, MA: The MIT Press.

Prud'hommeaux, E., & Seaborne, A. (Eds.). (2008, January 15). *SPARQL Query Language for RDF – W3C Recommendation (W3C)*. Retrieved November 16, 2009 from http://www.w3.org/TR/rdf-sparql-query/

Pustejovsky, J., Ingria, R., Saurí, R., Castaño, J., Littman, J., & Gaizauskas, R. (2005). The Specification Language TimeML. In Mani, I., Pustejovsky, J., & Gaizauskas, R. (Eds.), *The Language of Time: A Reader*. Oxford, UK: Oxford University Press.

Yang, C. C., Chen, H., Chau, M., Chang, K., Lang, S.-D., Chen, P. S., et al. (Eds.). (2008). In *Proceedings of the IEEE Intelligence and Security Informatics International Workshops (PAISI, PACCF, and SOCO 2008)* (LNCS 5075). Berlin: Springer-Verlag.

Zarri, G. P. (1998). Representation of Temporal Knowledge in Events: The Formalism, and Its Potential for Legal Narratives. *Information & Communications Technology Law – Special Issue on Models of Time, Action, and Situations*, *7*, 213–241.

Zarri, G. P. (2003). A Conceptual Model for Representing Narratives. In *Innovations in Knowledge Engineering*. Adelaide, Australia: Advanced Knowledge International.

Zarri, G. P. (2005a). Integrating the Two Main Inference Modes of NKRL, Transformations and Hypotheses. [JoDS]. *Journal on Data Semantics*, *4*, 304–340.

Zarri, G. P. (2005b). An *n*-ary Language for Representing Narrative Information on the Web. In *Proceedings of the Semantic Web Applications and Perspectives (SWAP 2005) the 2nd Italian Semantic Web Workshop* (Vol. 166). Aachen, Germany: Sun SITE Central Europe. Retrieved November 16, 2009 from http://ftp1.de.freebsd.org/Publications/CEUR-WS/Vol-166/63.pdf

Zarri, G. P. (2009). *Representation and Management of Narrative Information – Theoretical Principles and Implementation*. London: Springer. doi:10.1007/978-1-84800-078-0

This work was previously published in the International Journal of Digital Crime and Forensics, Volume 2, Issue 2, edited by Chang-Tsun Li and Anthony TS Ho, pp. 47-63, copyright 2010 by IGI Publishing (an imprint of IGI Global).

Compilation of References

ACPO. (2009). *Practice Guide for Computer-Based Electronic Evidence*. Retrieved from www.acpo.police.uk/asp/policies/Data/ACPO%20Guidelines%20v18.pdf

Ahumada, A. J. Jr, & Peterson, H. A. (1992). Luminance-Model-Based DCT Quantization for Color Image Compression. *Proceedings of the Society for Photo-Instrumentation Engineers, 1666*, 365–374.

Alparone, L., Argenti, F., & Torricelli, G. (2006). MMSE filtering of generalised signal-dependent noise in spatial and shift-invariant wavelet domain. *Signal Process Journal, 86*(8), 2056–2066. doi:10.1016/j.sigpro.2005.10.014

Altman, D. G., & Bland, J. M. (1994). Diagnostic tests - sensitivity and specificity. *BMJ (Clinical Research Ed.), 308*(6943), 1552.

Amano, T., & Misaki, D. (1999). A feature calibration method for watermarking of document images. In *Proceedings of the fifth international conference on document analysis and recognition (ICDAR'99)*, Bangalore, India (pp. 91-94). Washington, DC: IEEE Computer Society.

Amerini, I., Caldelli, R., Cappellini, V., Picchioni, F., & Piva, A. (2010). Estimate of PRNU noise based on different noise models for source camera identification. *International Journal of Digital Crime and Forensics, 2*(2).

Arnold, E. (2008). Get your head out of the clouds. *Searcher, 16*. Retrieved from http://www.infotoday.com/

Arnold, S. E. (2008). *A risky cloud approach?* Retrieved from http://www.kmworld.com

Aronson, J. (2007). *Genetic witness: Science, law, and controversy in the making of DNA profiling*. New Bunswick, NJ: Rutgers University Press.

Ashikhmin, M. (2002). *A tone mapping algorithm for high contrast images*. Paper presented at the 13th Eurographics workshop on Rendering.

Atsawaprecha, C. (1992). Thai input output methods. In *Computer and Thai language*.

Australian Broadcasting Corporation. (2008). Microsoft releases emergency patch for IE. *ABC News*. Retrieved January 4, 2009, from http://www.abc.net.au/news/

Australian Law Reform Commission. (1985). *Evidence* (Interim Report ALRC 26). Canberra, Australia: AGPS.

Australian Law Reform Commission. (2007). *Review of Australian privacy law* (Discussion Paper No. 72).

Australian Law Reform Commission. (2008). *For your information* (Report No. 108).

Backes, M., & Cachin, C. (2005) Public-key steganography with active attacks. In *Proceedings of the Theory of cryptography conference* (LNCS 3378, pp. 210-226). New York: Springer.

Bakhtin, M. M. (1982). Forms of Time and of Chronotope in the Novel (Trans. K. Bronstom & V. Liaponov). In Holquist, M., & Liapunov, V. (Eds.), *The Dialogic Imagination: Four Essays*. Austin, TX: University of Texas Press.

Barba, D., & Callet, P.-L. (2003). A robust quality metric for color image quality assessment. In *Proceedings of the IEEE International Conference on Image Processing (ICIP '03)*, Barcelona, Spain (Vol. 1, pp. 437-440). Washington, DC: IEEE.

Bas, P., & Hurri, J. (2006). Vulnerability of DM watermarking of non-IID host signals to attacks utilising the statistics of independent components. *IEEE Trans. Information Forensics and Security, 153*(3), 127–139.

Bayram, S., Sencar, H. T., & Menon, N. (2006). Identifying Digital Cameras Using CFA Interpolation. In *Proceedings of the International Conference on Digital Forensics* (pp. 289-299).

Bayram, S., Sencar, H. T., & Menon, N. (2005). Source camera identification based on CFA interpolation. In. *Proceedings of IEEE International Conference on Image Processing, 3*, 69–72.

Bayram, S., Sencar, H. T., & Menon, N. (2008). Classification of digital camera-models based on demosaicing artifacts. *Digital Investigation, 5*, 49–59. doi:10.1016/j.diin.2008.06.004

Beecher-Monas, E. (2006). *Evaluating scientific evidence.* Cambridge, UK: Cambridge University Press.

Beecher-Monas, E. (2009). Reality bites: The illusion of science in bite-mark evidence. *Cardozo Law Review, 30*, 1369–1410.

Belhumeur, P. N., Hespanha, J. P., & Kriegman, D. J. (1997). Eigenfaces vs. Fisherfaces: Recognition using class specific linear projection. *IEEE Transactions on Pattern Analysis and Machine Intelligence, 19*(7), 711–720. doi:10.1109/34.598228

Bellare, M., & Namprempre, C. (2008). Authenticated encryption: Relations among notions and analysis of the generic composition paradigm. *Journal of Cryptology, 21*(4), 469–491. doi:10.1007/s00145-008-9026-x

Bender, W., Gruhl, D., Morimoto, N., & Lu, A. (1996). Techniques for data hiding. *IBM Systems Journal, 35*(3-4), 313–336. doi:10.1147/sj.353.0313

Benford, F. (1938). The law of anomalous numbers. *Proceedings of the American Philosophical Society, 78*, 551–572.

Bertalmio, M., Sapiro, G., Caselles, V., & Ballester, C. (2000). Image in- painting. In [New York: ACM Press/ Addison-Wesley Publishing Co.]. *Proceedings of SIGGRAPH, 00*, 417–424.

Biber, K. (2007). *Captive images: Race, crime, photography.* London: Routledge.

Bishop, C. M. (1995). *Neural networks for pattern recognition.* Oxford, UK: Oxford University Press.

Blythe, P., & Fridrich, J. (2004). Secure digital camera. In *Proceedings of Digital Forensic Research Workshop,* Baltimore (pp. 12-47).

Brassil, J. T., Low, S., & Maxemchuk, N. F. (1999). Copyright protection for the electronic distribution of text documents. *Proceedings of the IEEE, 87*(7), 1181–1196. doi:10.1109/5.771071

Brinkworth, R. S. A., Mah, E. L., & O'Carroll, D. C. (2007). *Bioinspired Pixel-Wise Adaptive Imaging.* Paper presented at the Smart Structures, Devices, and Systems III.

Brinkworth, R. S. A., Mah, E. L., Gray, J. P., & O'Carroll, D. C. (2008). Photoreceptor Processing Improves Salience Facilitating Small Target Detection In Cluttered Scenes. *Journal of Vision (Charlottesville, Va.), 11*(8), 1–17.

Brodkin, J. (2008, February 7). Gartner: Seven cloud-computing security risks. *Network World.* Retrieved January 2, 2009, from http://www.networkworld.com/news/

Brynko, B. (2008). *Cloud computing: Knowing the ground rules.* Retrieved from http://www.infotoday.com/IT/nov08/index.shtml

Bunting, S. (2008). *The official EnCase certified examiner guide.* New York: Wiley.

Burton, A. M., Wilson, S., Cowan, M., & Bruce, V. (1999). Face recognition in poor-quality video: Evidence from security surveillance. *Psychological Science, 10*, 243–248. doi:10.1111/1467-9280.00144

Cachin, C. (2004). An information-theoretic model for steganography. *Information and Computation, 192*(1), 41–56. doi:10.1016/j.ic.2004.02.003

Caldelli, R., Amerini, I., & Picchioni, F. (2009). Distinguishing between camera and scanned images by means of frequency analysis. In M. Sorell (Ed.), *Second International Conference, e-Forensics* (pp. 95-101).

Caldelli, R., Amerini, I., & Picchioni, F. (2010). A DFT-Based Analysis to Discern Between Camera and Scanner Images. *International Journal of Digital Crime and Forensics, 2*(1).

Callas, J., et al. (2007, November). *OpenPGP message format*. Menlo Park, CA: PGP Corporation.

Canny, J. (1986). A computational approach to edge detection. *IEEE Transactions on Pattern Analysis and Machine Intelligence, 8*(6), 679–698. doi:10.1109/TPAMI.1986.4767851

Carnec, M., Callet, P.-L., & Barba, D. (2008). Objective quality assessment of color images based on a generic perceptual reduced reference. *Signal Processing Image Communication, 23*(4), 239–256. doi:10.1016/j.image.2008.02.003

Carter, H. (2007). Paedophiles jailed for hatching plot on internet to rape two teenage sisters. *The Guardian*.

Cayre, F., & Bas, P. (2008). Kerchkhoffs-based embedding security classes for WOA data hiding. *IEEE Trans. Information Forensics and Security, 3*(1), 1–15. doi:10.1109/TIFS.2007.916006

Cayre, F., Fontaine, C., & Furon, T. (2005). Watermarking security: Theory and practice. *IEEE Transactions on Signal Processing, 53*(10), 3976–3987. doi:10.1109/TSP.2005.855418

Chandler, D., & Hemami, S. (2007). VSNR: A wavelet-based visual signal-to-noise ratio for natural images. *IEEE Transactions on Image Processing, 16*(9), 2284–2298. doi:10.1109/TIP.2007.901820

Chang, C. C., & Lin, C. J. (n.d.). *LIBSVM: A Library for Support Vector Machines*. Retrieved from http://www.csie.ntu.edu.tw/~cjlin/libsvm/index.html

Chang-Tsun, L. (2009). Source Camera Linking Using Enhanced Sensor Pattern Noise Extracted from Images. In *Proceedings of the 3rd International Conference on Imaging for Crime Detection and Prevention*, London.

Chen, G. Y., Bui, T. D., & Krzyzak, A. (2006, October). Palmprint classification using dual-tree complex wavelets. In *Proceedings of the IEEE Inter. Conf. on Image Processing* (pp. 2645-2648).

Chen, S.-H., & Hsu, C.-T. (2007). Source camera identification based on camera gain histogram. In *Proceedings of the IEEE International Conference on Image Processing* (pp. 429-432).

Chen, W., Shi, Y. Q., & Su, W. (2007). Image splicing detection using 2-d phase congruency and statistical moments of characteristic function. In *Proceedings of SPIE* (Vol. 6505). Retrieved from http://link.aip.org/link/?PSI/6505/65050R/1

Chen, B., & Wornell, G. W. (2001). Quantization index modulation: a class of provably good methods for digital watermarking and information embedding. *IEEE Transactions on Information Theory, 47*(4), 1423–1443. doi:10.1109/18.923725

Chen, H. (2006). *Intelligence and Security Informatics for International Security: Information Sharing and Data Mining*. New York: Springer.

Chen, H., & Wang, F.-Y. (2005). Artificial Intelligence for Homeland Security. *IEEE Intelligent Systems, 20*(5), 12–16. doi:10.1109/MIS.2005.88

Chen, M., Fridrich, J., Goljan, M., & Lukas, J. (2008). Determining Image Origin and Integrity Using Sensor Noise. *IEEE Trans. on Information Forensics and Security, 3*(1), 74–90. doi:10.1109/TIFS.2007.916285

Chen, M., Fridrich, J., Luka, J., & Goljan, M. (2007). *Imaging sensor noise as digital X-ray for revealing forgeries (No. 03029743)*. Berlin: Springer Verlag.

Chen, P.-H., Lin, C.-J., & Scholkopf, B. (2005). A tutorial on v-support vector machines. *Applied Stochastic Models in Business and Industry, 21*(2), 111–136. doi:10.1002/asmb.537

Chicago-Kent College of Law. (2000). *An overview of the law of personal (adjudicatory) jurisdiction: The United States perspective*. Retrieved from http://www.kentlaw.edu/cyberlaw/docs/rfc/usview.html

Chicago-Kent College of Law. (2007). *Jurisdiction on the internet – the European perspective: An analysis of conventions, statutes and case law*. Retrieved from http://www.kentlaw.edu/cyberlaw/docs/rfc/euview.html

Chickowski, E. (2007, February 16). $400 million corporate espionage incident at Du Pont. *SC Magazine*. Retrieved from http://www.scmagazineus.com/400-million-corporate-espionage-incident-at-DuPont/article/34633/

Choi, K. S., Lam, E. Y., & Wong, K. K. Y. (2006). Automatic source camera identification using the intrinsic lens radial distortion. *Optics Express*, *14*(24), 11551–11565. doi:10.1364/OE.14.011551

Cole, S., & Dioso-Villa, R. (2009). Investigating the 'CSI effect': Media and litigation crisis in criminal law. *Stanford Law Review*, *61*, 1335–1374.

Collins, H. (1992). *Changing order: Replication and induction in scientific practice.* Chicago: University of Chicago Press.

Comesaña, P., Pérez-Freire, L., & Pérez-González, F. (2005). An information-theoretic framework for assessing security in practical watermarking and data hiding scenarios. In *Proceedings of the International Workshop on Image Analysis for Multimedia Interactive Services*.

Coria, L., Pickering, M., Nasiopoulos, P., & Ward, R. (2008). A video watermarking scheme based on the dual-tree complex wavelet transform. *IEEE Transactions on Information Forensics and Security*, *3*(3), 466–474. doi:10.1109/TIFS.2008.927421

Correy, S. (Producer). (2008, September 14). ABC Radio National: Background briefing. *Cloud Computing*. Podcast retrieved from http://www.abc.net.au/rn/backgroundbriefing/stories/2008/2359128.htm

Costigan, R. (2007). Identification from CCTV: The risk of injustice. *Criminal Law Review (London, England)*, 591–608.

Cox, I., Killian, J., Leighton, T., & Shamoon, T. (1996). A secure, robust watermark for multimedia. In *Proceedings of the Workshop on Information Hiding* (pp. 175-190).

Craver, S., Memon, N., Yeo, B., & Yeung, M. (1998). Resolv-ing rightful ownerships with invisible watermarking techniques: Limitations, attacks, and implications. *IEEE Journal on Selected Areas in Communications*, *16*(4), 573–586. doi:10.1109/49.668979

Cvejic, N., & Seppänen, T. (2004). Increasing robustness of LSB audio steganography using a novel embedding method. In *Proceedings of the international conference on information technology: Coding and computing (ITCC'04)*, Las Vegas, NV (Vol. 2, pp. 533). Washington, DC: IEEE Computer Society.

Dailey, M., Namprempre, C., & Samphaiboon, N. (2010). *How to do embedding steganography securely*. Retrieved from http:///www.cs.ait.ac.th/~mdailey/papers/DNS-ES-09.pdf

Daly, S. (1998). Engineering observations from spatio velocity and spatiotemporal visual models. *Proceedings of the Society for Photo-Instrumentation Engineers*, *3299*, 180–191.

Damnjanovic, I., & Izquierdo, E. (2006). Perceptual watermarking using just noticeable difference model based on block classification. In *Proceedings of the 2nd international conference on Mobile multimedia communications* (No. 36).

Daugman, J. G. (1993). High confidence visual recognition of persons by a test of statistical independence. *IEEE Transactions on Pattern Analysis and Machine Intelligence*, *15*(11), 1148–1161. doi:10.1109/34.244676

Davis, J., & Valentine, T. (2009). CCTV on trial: Matching video images with the defendant in the Dock. *Applied Cognitive Psychology*, *23*, 482–505. doi:10.1002/acp.1490

de Ruyter van Steveninck, R. R., & Laughlin, S. B. (1996). The rate of information transfer at graded-potential synapses. *Nature*, *379*(6566), 642–645. doi:10.1038/379642a0

Debevec, P. E., & Malik, J. (1997). *Recovering High Dynamic Range Radiance Maps from Photographs*. Paper presented at the SIGGRAPH 97, Los Angeles, CA.

Dehnie, S., Sencar, T., & Memon, N. (2006). Digital Image Forensics for Identifying Computer Generated and Digital Camera Images. In *Proceedings of the International Conference on Image Processing*, Atlanta, GA (pp. 2313-2316).

Deng, Y., & Manjunath, B. (2001). Unsupervised segmentation of color-texture regions in images and video. *IEEE Transactions on Pattern Analysis and Machine Intelligence*, *23*(8), 800–810. doi:10.1109/34.946985

Desloge, R. (1998, October 16). State makes $500,000 a year selling personal information. *St. Louis Business Journal*. Retrieved from http://stlouis.bizjournals.com/stlouis/stories/1998/10/19/newscolumn1.html

Dickson, M. (2006). An examination into AOL Instant Messenger 5.5. *Digital Investigation*, *3*(4), 227–237. doi:10.1016/j.diin.2006.10.004

Dirik, A. E., Sencar, H. T., & Manon, N. (2008). Digital single lens reflex camera identification from traces of sensor dust. *IEEE Transactions on Information Forensics and Security*, *3*(3), 539–552. doi:10.1109/TIFS.2008.926987

Do, M., & Vetterli, M. (2000). Texture Similarity Measurement using Kullback-Leibler Distance on Wavelet Subbands. In *Proceedings of the IEEE International Conference on Image Processing (ICIP '00)*, Vancouver, Canada (Vol. 3, pp. 703-733).

Dodis, Y., Reyzin, L., & Smith, A. (2004). Fuzzy extractors: How to generate strong keys from biometrics and other noisy data. In *Eurocrypt* (LNCS 3027, pp. 523-540).

Doerr, G., & Dugelay, J. L. (2003). A guide tour of video watermarking. *Signal Processing Image Communication*, *18*(4), 263–282. doi:10.1016/S0923-5965(02)00144-3

Dourlens, S., & Zarri, G. P. (2007). *Étude et réalisation du logiciel DECISIF, détection de signaux crisogènes faibles – rapport fin de phase 2 (version 1.1)*. Courtabœuf, France: CityPassenger.

Draper, S., Khistiy, A., Martinianz, E., Vetro, A., & Yedidia, J. (2007, January). Secure storage of fingerprint biometrics using slepian-wolf codes. In *Proceedings of the Information theory and applications workshop*.

Dror, I., Charlton, D., & Peron, A. (2006). Contextual information renders experts vulnerable to making erroneous identifications. *Forensic Science International*, *156*, 74–78. doi:10.1016/j.forsciint.2005.10.017

Dror, I., & Rosenthal, R. (2008). Meta-analytically quantifying the reliability and biasability of forensic experts. *Journal of Forensic Sciences*, *53*, 900–903. doi:10.1111/j.1556-4029.2008.00762.x

Durtschi, C., Hillison, W., & Pacini, C. (2004). The effective use of Benford's Law to assist in detecting fraud in accounting data. *Journal of Forensic Accounting*, *5*, 17–34.

Duta, N., Jain, A. K., & Mardia, K. V. (2001). Palmprint recognition using eigenpalms features. *Pattern Recognition Letters*, *32*(4), 477–485.

Earl, J., & Kingsbury, N. (2003). Spread transform watermarking for video sources. In *Proceedings of the IEEE International Conference on Image Processing (ICIP '03)*, Barcelona, Spain (Vol. 2, pp. 491-494).

Edmond, G. (2008a). Pathological science: Demonstrable reliability and expert forensic pathology evidence. In K. Roach (Ed.), *Pediatric forensic pathology and the justice system* (pp. 91-149). Toronto, Ontario, Canada: Queens Printer for Ontario.

Edmond, G. (2008). Specialised knowledge, the exclusionary discretions and reliability: Re-assessing incriminating opinion evidence. *The University of New South Wales Law Journal*, *31*, 1–55.

Edmond, G., Biber, K., Kemp, R., & Porter, G. (2009). Law's looking glass: Expert identification evidence derived from photographic and video images. *Current Issues in Criminal Justice*, *20*, 337–377.

Edmond, G., & Mercer, D. (1997). Scientific literacy and the jury. *Public Understanding of Science (Bristol, England)*, *6*, 329–359. doi:10.1088/0963-6625/6/4/003

Edmond, G., & San Roque, M. (2009). *Quasi*-justice: Ad hoc expertise and identification evidence. *Criminal Law Journal*, *33*, 8–33.

Fawcett, T. (2006). An introduction to ROC analysis. *Pattern Recognition Letters*, *27*, 861–874. doi:10.1016/j.patrec.2005.10.010

Federal Trade Commission. (2002). *Eli Lilly settles FTC charges concerning security breach*. Retrieved January 6, 2009, from http://www.ftc.gov/

Field, D. J. (1987). Relations between the statistics of natural images and the response properties of cortical cells. *Journal of the Optical Society of America. A, Optics and Image Science*, *4*, 2379–2394. doi:10.1364/JOSAA.4.002379

Filler, T., Fridrich, J., & Goljan, M. (2008). Using sensor pattern noise for camera model identification. In *Proceedings of the International Conference on Image Processing*, San Diego, CA (pp. 1296-1299).

Findley, K. (2008). Innocents at risk: Adversary imbalance, forensic science, and the search for the truth. *Seton Hall Law Review, 38*, 893–974.

Fisher, R. A. (1966). *The design of experiments and statistical estimation* (8th ed.). Edinburgh, UK: Hafner.

Fitzgerald, M. (2008). Microsoft puts its head in the cloud. *Fast Company, 130*. Retrieved from http://www.fastcompany.com/magazine/130/microsoft-puts-its-head-in-the-cloud.html

Fridrich, J., Soukal, D., & Lukas, J. (2003). *Detection of copy-move forgery in digital images*. Paper presented at the Digital Forensic Research Workshop, Cleveland, OH.

Fried, I. (2008, September 3). Google backtracks on Chrome license terms. *CNet News*. Retrieved from http://news.cnet.com/8301-13860_3-10031703-56.html?tag=newsEditorsPicksArea.0

Fu, D., Shi, Y. Q., & Su, Q. (2007). A generalized Benford's law for JPEG coefficients and its applications in image forensics. In *Proceedings of the SPIE Security, Steganography, and Watermarking of Multimedia Contents IX* (Vol. 6505, pp. 1L1-1L11).

Gallagher, A. c. (2005). *Detection of linear and cubic interpolation in jpeg compressed images*. Paper presented at the 2nd Canadian Conference Computer and Robot Vision, Victoria, British Columbia, Canada.

Garrett, B., & Neufeld, P. (2009). Invalid forensic science testimony and wrongful convictions. *Virginia Law Review, 95*, 1–97.

Gates, A. (2008). *Canadian law on jurisdiction in cyberspace*. Chicago: Chicago-Kent College of Law. Retrieved January 7, 2009, from http://www.kentlaw.edu/cyberlaw/docs/rfc/canadaview.html

Ge, R., Arce, G. R., & DiCrescenzo, G. (2006). Approximate message authentication codes for n-ary alphabets. *IEEE Transactions on Information Forensics and Security, 1*(1), 56–67. doi:10.1109/TIFS.2005.863504

Geradts, Z., Bijhold, J., Kieft, M., Kurosawa, K., Kuroki, K., & Saitoh, N. (2001). Methods for identification of images acquired with digital cameras. In. *Proceedings of the Enabling Technologies for Law Enforcement and Security, 4232*, 505–512.

Giakoumaki, A., Pavlopoulos, S., & Koutsouris, D. (2006). *Multiple image watermarking applied to health information management*. IEEE Trans. Information.

Goljan, M., & Fridrich, J. (2008b). Camera Identification from Scaled and Cropped Images. In *Proceedings of the SPIE, Electronic Imaging, Forensics, Security, Steganography, and Watermarking of Multimedia Contents*, San Jose, CA (pp. OE-1-OE-13).

Goljan, M., Fridrich, J., & Lukas, J. (2008a). Camera Identification from Printed Images. In *Proceedings of the SPIE Electronic Imaging, Forensics, Security, Steganography, and Watermarking of Multimedia Contents*, San Jose, CA (pp. OI-1-OI-12).

Gonzales-Rodriguez, J., Rose, P., Ramos, D., Toledano, D. T., & Ortega-Garcia, J. (2007). Emulating DNA: Rigorous quantification of evidential weight in transparent and testable forensic speaker recognition. *IEEE Transactions on Audio, speech and Language Processing, 15*, 2104-2115.

Good, A. (2006). *Anthropology and expertise in the asylum courts*. Cambridge, UK: Cambridge University Press.

Goodwin, C. (1994). Professional vision. *American Anthropologist, 96*, 606–633. doi:10.1525/aa.1994.96.3.02a00100

Google Inc. (2007a). *Google introduces new business version of popular hosted applications*. Retrieved December 4, 2008, from http://www.google.com/intl/en/press/pressrel/google_apps.html>

Google Inc. (2007b). *Google terms of service*. Retrieved January 7, 2009, from http://www.google.com/accounts/TOS?hl=en

Google Inc. (2008a). *About Gmail: More on Gmail and privacy*. Retrieved January 3, 2009, from http://mail.google.com/mail/help/about_privacy.html

Google Inc. (2008b). *Google Apps Premier Edition agreement*. Retrieved December 4, 2008, from http://www.google.com/apps/intl/en/terms/premier_terms.html

Google Inc. (2008c). *Google Apps for business: Find answers to your questions*. Retrieved December 4, 2008, from http://www.google.com/apps/intl/en/business/support.html

Google Inc. (2008d). *Gmail privacy notice.* Retrieved January 1, 2009, from http://mail.google.com/mail/help/intl/en/privacy.html

Google Inc. (2008e). *Google Apps admin help: Privacy policy; your choices.* Retrieved January 2, 2009, from http://www.google.com/support/a/bin/answer.py?hl=el&answer=33926

Google Inc. (2008f). *Google Apps Standard Edition agreement.* Retrieved January 7, 2009, from http://www.google.com/apps/intl/en/terms/standard_terms.html

Google Inc. (2008g). *Google Chrome terms of service.* Retrieved December 27, 2008, from http://www.google.com/chrome/intl/en/eula_text.html

Gou, H., Swaminathan, A., & Wu, M. (2007). *Noise features for image tampering detection and steganalysis.* Paper presented at the IEEE International Conference on Image Processing, San Antonio, TX.

Gou, H., Swaminathan, A., & Wu, M. (2007). Robust scanner identification based on noise features. In E. J. Delp III & P. W. Wong (Eds.), *Security, steganography, and watermarking of multimedia contents IX* (Vol. 6505, pp. 6505). Bellingham, WA: SPIE Press.

Goudge, S. (2008). *Inquiry into pediatric forensic pathology in Ontario.* Toronto, Ontario, Canada: Queens Printer for Ontario.

Gratzer, V., Naccache, D., & Znaty, D. (2006, March 13-17). Law Enforcement, Forensics and Mobile Communications. In *Proceedings of the PerCom Workshop*, Pisa, Italy (pp. 256-260).

Hadjidemetriou, E., Grossberg, M. D., & Nayar, S. K. (2001). Spatial information in multiresolution histograms. In *Proceedings of the 2001 IEEE Computer Society Conference on Computer Vision and Pattern Recognition (CVPR 2001)*, Los Alamitos, CA.

Hadjidemetriou, E., Grossberg, M. D., & Nayar, S. K. (2004). Multiresolution histograms and their use for recognition. *IEEE Transactions on Pattern Analysis and Machine Intelligence*, 26(7), 831–847. doi:10.1109/TPAMI.2004.32

Han, C.-C., Chengb, H.-L., Linb, C.-L., & Fanb, K.-C. (2003). Personal authentication using palm-print features. *Pattern Recognition Letters*, 36(2), 371–381.

Hao, F., Anderson, R., & Daugman, J. (2006). Combining crypto with biometrics effectively. *IEEE Transactions on Computers*, 55(9), 1081–1088. doi:10.1109/TC.2006.138

Harrill, D. C., & Mislan, R. P. (2007). A Small Scale Digital Device Forensics ontology. *Small Scale Digital Device Forensics journal*, 1(1).

Hassenstein, B., & Reichardt, W. (1956). Systemtheoretische analyse der Zeit-, Reihenfolgen-, und Vorseichenauswertung bei der Berwegungsperzeption des Rüsselkäfers Chlorophanus. *Zeitschrift für Naturforschung*, 11b, 513–524.

Hernandez, J., Amado, M., & Perez-Gonzalez, F. (2000). DCT-domain watermarking techniques for still images: Detector performance analysis and a new structure. *IEEE Transactions on Image Processing*, 9(1), 55–68. doi:10.1109/83.817598

Higginbotham, J. (1985). On Semantics. *Linguistic Inquiry*, 16, 547–593.

Higginbotham, J. (2000). On Events in Linguistic Semantics. In Higginbotham, J., Pianesi, F., & Varzi, A. C. (Eds.), *Speaking of Events.* Oxford, UK: Oxford University Press.

Hill, T. P. (1995). The significant-Digit Phenomenon. *The American Mathematical Monthly*, 102, 322–327. doi:10.2307/2974952

Holliman, M., Memon, N., & Yeung, M. (1999). Watermark estimation through local pixel correlation. In *Proceedings of the SPIE Security and watermarking of multimedia content I, 3675*, 134-146.

Hoover, J., Martin, R., & Paul, F. (2008, January 19) Demystifying the cloud. *InformationWeek.* Retrieved from http://www.informationweek.com/news/

Hopper, N. J., Langford, J., & von Ahn, L. (2002). Provably secure steganography. In *Proceedings of the 22nd annual international cryptology conference on advances in cryptology*, Santa Barbara, CA (pp. 77-92). New York: Springer.

Horswell, J. (Ed.). (2004). *The practice of crime scene investigation.* Boca Raton, FL: CRC Press.

Hsiao, D. Y., & Pei, S. C. (2005). *Detecting digital tampering by blur estimation.* Paper presented at the 1st International Workshop on Systematic Approaches to Digital Forensic Engineering, Taipei, China.

Hsu, Y.-F., & Chang, S.-F. (2006). Detecting image splicing using geometry in-variants and camera characteristics consistency. In *Proceedings of the IEEE International Conference on Multimedia and Expo* (pp. 549-552).

Hsu, Y.-F., & Chang, S.-F. (2007). Image splicing detection using camera re-sponse function consistency and automatic segmentation. In. *Proceedings of the ICME, 07*, 28–31.

Huang, H., Guo, W., & Zhang, Y. (2008). *Detection of copy-move forgery in digital images using SIFT algorithm.* Paper presented at the 2008 Pacific-Asia Workshop on Computational Intelligence and Industrial Application (PACIIA 2008), Piscataway, NJ.

Huang, D., & Yan, H. (2001). Interword distance changes represented by sine waves for watermarking text images. *IEEE Transactions on Circuits and Systems for Video Technology, 11*(12), 1237–1245. doi:10.1109/76.974678

Huang, J., Shi, Y. Q., & Shi, Y. (1998). Adaptive image watermarking scheme based on visual masking. *Electronics Letters, 34*, 748–750. doi:10.1049/el:19980545

Hylton, H. (2007, August 15). What Your Cell Knows About You. *Time Magazine.* http://www.time.com/time/health/article/0,8599,1653267,00.html?xid=rss-health

IBM. (2008a). *IBM debuts new enterprise data center specialty for business partners.* Retrieved December 4, 2008, from http://www-03.ibm.com/press/us/en/index.wss

IBM. (2008b). *Made in IBM Labs: IBM to build first cloud computing centre in China.* Retrieved December 4, 2008, from http://www-03.ibm.com/press/us/en/press-release/23426.wss

Inta Forensics. (2009). *Mobile Phone Forensics.* Retrieved from www.intaforensics.com/pdf/mobile-phone-forensics.pdf

Jahn, M. (2005). *Narratology: A Guide to the Theory of Narrative* (version 1.8). Cologne, Germany: English Department of the University. Retrieved November 16, 2009 from http://www.uni-koeln.de/~ame02/pppn.htm

Jain, A. K. (1989). *Fundamentals of Digital Image Processing.* Upper Saddle River, NJ: Prentice Hall.

Janesick, J. R. (2001). *Scientific Charged-Coupled Devices (Vol. PM83).* Bellingham, WA: SPIE. doi:10.1117/3.374903

Jansen, W., & Ayers, R. (2007). *Guidelines on Cell Phone Forensics.* Gaithersburg, MD: National Institute of Standards and Technology. Retrieved from http://csrc.nist.gov/publications/nistpubs/800-101/SP800-101.pdf

Jansen, W., Delaitre, A., & Moenner, L. (2008). Overcoming Impediments to Cell Phone Forensics. In *Proceedings of the 41st Annual Hawaii International Conference on System Sciences* (pp. 483-483). ISBN: 978-0-7695-3075-8

Jasanoff, S. (1995). *Science at the bar.* Cambridge, MA: Harvard University Press.

Jia, Y., Lin, W., & Kassim, A. A. (2006). Estimating justnoticeable distortion for video. *IEEE Transactions on Circuits and Systems for Video Technology, 16*(7), 820–829. doi:10.1109/TCSVT.2006.877397

Jing, X. Y., & Zhang, D. (2004, December). A face and palmprint recognition approach based on discriminant DCT feature extraction. *IEEE Transactions on Systems, Man, and Cybernetics, 34*, 2405–2415. doi:10.1109/TSMCB.2004.837586

Johnson, M. K., & Farid, H. (2005). *Exposing digital forgeries by detecting inconsistencies in lighting.* Paper presented at the ACM Multimedia and Security Workshop, New York.

Johnson, M. K., & Farid, H. (2007). *Exposing digital forgeries through specular highlights on the eye (No. 03029743).* Berlin: Springer Verlag.

Johnson, M. K., & Farid, H. (2008). *Detecting photographic composites of people (No. 03029743).* Berlin: Springer Verlag.

Jolion, J. M. (2001). Images and Benford's Law. *Journal of Mathematical Imaging and Vision, 14*, 73–81. doi:10.1023/A:1008363415314

Juusola, M., Uusitalo, R. O., & Weckstrom, M. (1995). Transfer of Graded Potentials at the Photoreceptor Interneuron Synapse. *The Journal of General Physiology, 105*(1), 117–148. doi:10.1085/jgp.105.1.117

Kalker, T. (2001). Considerations on watermarking security. In *Proceedings of the Multimedia Signal Processing, IEEE Fourth Workshop on* (pp. 201-206).

Kankanhalli, M. S., & Ramakrishnan, K. R. (1998). Content based watermarking of images. In *Proceedings of the sixth ACM international conference on Multimedia* (pp. 61-70).

Karoonboonyanan, T. (1999). Standardization and implementation of Thai language. In *National electronics and computer technology center*, Bangkok, Thailand.

Kay, S. (1989). Asymptotically optimal detection in incompletely characterized non-Gaussian noise. *IEEE Transactions on Acoustics, Speech, and Signal Processing, 37*(5), 627–633. doi:10.1109/29.17554

Kay, S. (1998). *Fundamentals of Statistical Signal Processing: Detection Theory (Vol. 2)*. Upper Saddle River, NJ: Prentice-Hall.

Kelly, D. H. (1979). Motion and vision. II. Stabilized spatio-temporal threshold surface. *J. opt. Sot. Am., 69*, 1340–1349.

Kemp, R., & Coulson, K. (2008). *Facial mapping and forensic photographic comparison: An international survey* (in press).

Kemp, R., Towell, N., & Pike, G. (1997). When seeing should not be believing: Photographs, credit cards and fraud. *Applied Cognitive Psychology, 11*, 211–222. doi:10.1002/(SICI)1099-0720(199706)11:3<211::AID-ACP430>3.0.CO;2-O

Khanna, N., Chiu, G. T.-C., Allebach, J. P., & Delp, E. J. (2008). Forensic techniques for classifying scanner, computer generated and digital camera images. In *Proceedings of the IEEE International Conference on Acoustics, Speech and Signal Processing, 2008 (ICASSP 2008)* (Vol. 6, pp. 1653-1656).

Khanna, N., Mikkilineni, A. K., Chiu, G. T.-C., Allebach, J. P., & Delp, E. J. (2007). Scanner identification using sensor pattern noise. In E. J. Delp III & P. W. Wong (Eds.), *Security, steganography, and watermarking of multimedia contents IX* (Vol. 6505, pp. 6505- 65051K). Bellingham, WA: SPIE Press.

Kiayias, A., Raekow, Y., & Russell, A. (2005). Efficient steganography with provable security guarantees. In *Proceedings of the 7th international workshop on information hiding (IH'05)*, Barcelona, Spain (LNCS 3727, pp. 118-130). New York: Springer.

Kim, Y.-W., Moon, K.-A., & Oh, I.-S. (2003). A text watermarking algorithm based on word classification and inter-word space statistics. In *Proceedings of the seventh international conference on document analysis and recognition (ICDAR'03)*, Edinburgh, Scotland (pp. 775-779). Washington, DC: IEEE Computer Society.

Kimbrough, J. R., Moody, J. D., Bell, P. M., & Landen, O. L. (2004). Characterization of the series 1000 camera system. *The Review of Scientific Instruments, 75*(10), 4060–4062. doi:10.1063/1.1789261

Kim, Y.-W., & Oh, I.-S. (2004). Watermarking text document images using edge direction histograms. *Pattern Recognition Letters, 25*(11), 1243–1251. doi:10.1016/j.patrec.2004.04.002

Kingsbury, N. (1998). The Dual-Tree Complex Wavelet Transform: A new Technique for Shift-Invariance and Directional Filters. In *Proceedings of the 8th IEEE DSP Workshop*, Bryce Canyon, UT (pp. 9-12).

Kingsbury, N. (2001). Complex Wavelets for Shift-Invariant Analysis and Filtering of Signals. *Journal of Applied Computational Harmonic Analysis, 10*(3), 234–253. doi:10.1006/acha.2000.0343

Kirchner, M. (2008). Fast and reliable resampling detection by spectral analysis of fixed linear predictor residue. In *Proceedings of the MM and Sec'08 10th ACM Workshop on Multimedia and Security*, Oxford, UK.

Knight, S., Moschou, S., & Sorell, M. (2009). Analysis of Sensor Photo Response Non-Uniformity in RAW Images. In *Proceedings of e-Forensics (Vol. 8*, pp. 130–141). Lecture Notes of the Institute for Computer Sciences, Social Informatics and Telecommunications Engineering.

Koanantakool, T. (1991). The keyboard layouts and input method of the Thai language. In *Information processing institute for education and development Thammasat university*, Bangkok, Thailand.

Kong, A., Zhang, D., & Kamel, M. (2006). Palmprint identification using feature-level fusion. *Pattern Recognition Letters, 39*(3), 478–487.

Kong, A., Zhang, D., & Lu, G. (2006). A study of identical twins' palmprints for personal verification. *Pattern Recognition Letters, 39*(11), 2149–2156.

Kovesi, D. P. (2006).*What are log-gabor filters and why are they good?.* Retrieved from http://www.csse.uwa.edu.au/_pk/Research/MatlabFns/PhaseCongruency/ Docs/convexpl.html

Kumar, A., & Zhang, D. (2004). Integrating shape and texture for hand verification. In *Proceedings of the 3rd Inter. Conf. on Image and Graphics* (pp. 222-225).

Kumar, A. J., Wong, D. C. M., Shen, H. C., & Jain, A. K. (2003). *Personal verification using palmprint and hand geometry biometric* (pp. 668–678). LNCS.

Kumaran, T., & Thangavel, P. (2008). Genetic algorithm based watermarking in double-density dual-tree DWT. In *Proceedings of the International Conference on Wavelet Analysis and Pattern Recognition (ICWAPR '08)* (pp. 585-590).

Kundur, D., & Hatzinakos, D. (1999). Digital watermarking for telltale tamper proofing and authentication. *Proceedings of the IEEE, 87*(7), 1167–1180. doi:10.1109/5.771070

Kurosawa, K., Kuroki, K., & Saitoh, N. (1999). CCD fingerprint method – identification of a video camera from videotaped images. In *Proceedings of the International Conference on Image Processing*, Kobe, Japan (pp. 537-540).

Kutter, M., Voloshynovskiy, S., & Herrigel, A. (2000). The watermark copy attack. In *Proceedings of the SPIE, security and watermarking of multimedia contents II* (Vol. 3971).

Lab, C. D. R. (2004). *Columbia Image Splicing Detection Evaluation Dataset*. Retrieved from http://www.ee.columbia.edu/ln/dvmm/downloads/AuthSplicedDataSet/AuthSplicedDataSet.htm

Laird, J., Rosen, M., Pelz, J., Montag, E., & Daly, S. (2006). Spatio-velocity CSF as a function of retinal velocity using unstabilized stimuli. *Proceedings of the Society for Photo-Instrumentation Engineers, 6057*, 32–43.

Land, M. F., & Collett, T. S. (1974). Chasing behaviour of houseflies. *Journal of Comparative Physiology. A, Neuroethology, Sensory, Neural, and Behavioral Physiology, 156*(4), 525–538. doi:10.1007/BF00613976

Langelaar, G. C., & Lagendijk, R. L. (2001). Optimal differential energy watermarking of DCT encoded images and video. *IEEE Transactions on Image Processing, 10*(1), 148–158. doi:10.1109/83.892451

Lanh, T. V., Chong, K. S., Emmanuel, S., & Kankanhalli, M. S. (2007). A Survey on Digital Camera Image Forensic Methods. In *Proceedings of the IEEE International Conference on Multimedia and Expo* (pp.16-19).

Laughlin, S. B., de Ruyter van Steveninck, R. R., & Anderson, J. C. (1998). The metabolic cost of neural information. *Nature Neuroscience, 1*, 36–41. doi:10.1038/236

Laughlin, S. B., & Weckström, M. (1993). Fast and slow photoreceptors - a comparative study of the functional diversity of coding and conductances in the Diptera. *Journal of Comparative Physiology. A, Neuroethology, Sensory, Neural, and Behavioral Physiology, 172*, 593–609. doi:10.1007/BF00213682

Law Commission. (2009). *The admissibility of expert evidence in criminal proceedings in England and Wales: A new approach to the determination of evidentiary reliability* (Consultation Paper 190). Norwich, UK: TSO.

Legge, G. E. (1981). A power law for contrast discrimination. *Vision Research, 21*, 457–467. doi:10.1016/0042-6989(81)90092-4

Li, G., Wu, Q., Tu, D., & Sun, S. (2007). *A sorted neighborhood approach for detecting duplicated regions in image forgeries based on DWT and SVD*. Paper presented at the 2007 International Conference on Multimedia Expo, Piscataway, NJ.

Li, Q., & Chang, E.-C. (2006). Robust, short and sensitive authentication tags using secure sketch. In *Proceedings of the ACM multimedia and security workshop*.

Lin, C. Y., & Chang, S. F. (2000). Semi-fragile watermarking for authenticating JPEG visual content. *In Proceedings of the SPIE Security and Watermarking of Multimedia Contents II EI '00*.

Lin, E. T., Podilchuk, C. I., & Delp, J. (2000). Detection of image alterations using semi-fragile watermarks. *In Proceedings of the SPIE International Conference on Security and Watermarking of Multimedia Contents II* (Vol. 3971, No. 14).

Lin, L., Doërr, G. J., Cox, I. J., & Miller, M. L. (2005). An efficient algorithm for informed embedding of dirty-paper trellis codes for watermarking. In *Proceedings of the ICIP (1)* (pp. 697-700).

Lin, Z. C., Wang, R. R., Tang, X. O., & Shum, H. Y. (2005). *Detecting doctored images using camera response normality and consistency analysis.* Paper presented at the IEEE Computer Society Conference on Computer Vision and Pattern Recognition, San Diego, CA.

Ling, H. F., Lu, Z. D., & Zou, F. H. (2004). Improved Differential Energy Watermarking (IDEW) Algorithm for DCT-Encoded Imaged and Video. In *Proceedings of the Seventh International Conference on Signal Processing (ICSP'2004)* (pp. 2326-2329).

Ling, H. F., Lu, Z. D., Zou, F. H., & Li, R. X. (2006). An Energy Modulated Watermarking Algorithm Based on Watson Perceptual Model. *Journal of Software, 17*(5), 1124–1132. doi:10.1360/jos171124

Long, Y. J., & Huang, Y. Z. (2006). *Image based source camera identification using demosaicing.* Paper presented at the 8th Workshop on Multimedia Siganal Processing, Victoria, TX.

Loo, P. (2002). *Digital Watermarking with Complex Wavelets.* PhD thesis, University of Cambridge, UK.

Loo, P., & Kingsbury, N. (2000). Digital watermarking using complex wavelets. In *Proceedings of the IEEE International Conference on Image Processing (ICIP '00)*, Vancouver, Canada (Vol. 3, pp. 29-32).

Lou, D.-C., & Liu, J.-L. (2002). Steganographic method for secure communications. *Computers & Security, 21*(5), 449–460. doi:10.1016/S0167-4048(02)00515-1

Lu, J., Zhang, E., Kang, X., Xue, Y., & Chen, Y. (2006, June). Palmprint recognition using wavelet decomposition and 2D principal component analysis. In

Lu, W., Sun, W., Huang, J.-W., & Lu, H.-T. (2008). *Digital image forensics using statistical features and neural network classifier.* Paper presented at the 2008 International Conference on Machine Learning and Cybernetics (ICMLC), Piscataway, NJ.

Lukas, J., Fridrich, J., & Goljan, M. (2005). Determining Digital Image Origin Using Sensor Imperfections. In *Proceedings of the SPIE Electronic Imaging, Image and Video Communication and Processing*, San Jose, CA (pp. 249-260).

Lukas, J., Fridrich, J., & Goljan, M. (2006). Digital Camera Identification from Sensor Pattern Noise. *IEEE Trans. on Information Forensics and Security, 1*(2), 205–214. doi:10.1109/TIFS.2006.873602

Lynch, M., Cole, S., McNally, R., & Jordan, K. (2008). *Truth machine: The contentious history of DNA fingerprinting.* Chicago: University of Chicago Press.

Lynch, M. (1998). The discursive production of uncertainty: The OJ Simpson "dream team" and the sociology of knowledge machine. *Social Studies of Science, 28*, 829–868. doi:10.1177/030631298028005007

Lyons, D. (2008a). Today's forecast: Cloudy; people are going to be putting their information not into some device but into some service that lives in the sky. *Newsweek, 152*. Retrieved December 9, 2008, from http://www.newsweek.com/id/166818

Lyons, D. (2008b, November 4). A mostly cloudy computing forecast. *The Washington Post.* Retrieved from http://www.encyclopedia.com/doc/1P2-19537475.html

Lyu, S., & Farid, H. (2005). How realistic is photorealistic? *IEEE Transactions on Signal Processing, 53*(2), 845–850. doi:10.1109/TSP.2004.839896

M2 Press Wire. (2008). *IBM: Cloud computing spreads in emerging countries.* Retrieved December 4, 2008, from http://www.m2.com

Ma, W., & Manjunath, B. (1997). Edge flow: A framework of boundary detection and image segmentation. In *Proceedings of the Computer Vision and Pattern Recognition* (pp. 744-749). Washington, DC: IEEE Computer Society.

Mabtoul, S., Elhaj, E., & Aboutajdine, D. (2007). Robust color image watermarking based on singular value decomposition and dual tree complex wavelet transform. In *Proceedings of the 14th IEEE International Conference on Electronics, Circuits and Systems (ICECS '07)* (pp. 534-537). Washington, DC: IEEE.

Mabtoul, S., Elhaj, E., & Aboutajdine, D. (2009). Robust Semi-Blind Digital Image Watermarking Technique in DT-CWT Domain. *International Journal of Computer Science*, 4(1), 8–12.

MacKay, D., & Neal, R. (1997). Near Shannon limit performance of low density parity check codes. *Electronics Letters*, 33(6), 457–458. doi:10.1049/el:19970362

Mahdian, B., & Saic, S. (2008). Blind authentication using periodic properties of interpolation. *IEEE Transactions on Information Forensics and Security*, 3(3), 529–538. doi:10.1109/TIFS.2004.924603

Mah, E. L., Brinkworth, R. S. A., & O'Carroll, D. C. (2008). Implementation of an elaborated neuromorphic model of a biological photoreceptor. *Biological Cybernetics*, 98, 357–369. doi:10.1007/s00422-008-0222-4

Malvar, H., & Florencio, D. (2003). Improved spread spectrum: A new modulation technique for robust watermarking. *IEEE Transactions on Signal Processing*, 51(4), 898–905. doi:10.1109/TSP.2003.809385

Manjunath, B. S., & Ma, W. Y. (1996). Texture features for browsing and retrieval of image data. *IEEE Transactions on Pattern Analysis and Machine Intelligence*, 18(8), 837–842. doi:10.1109/34.531803

Manola, F., & Miller, E. (Eds.). (2004, February 10). *RDF Primer – W3C Recommendation (W3C)*. Retrieved November 16, 2009 from http://www.w3.org/TR/rdf-primer/

Mardia, K., Coombes, A., Kirkbride, J., Linney, A., & Bowie, J. L. (1996). On statistical problems with face identification from photographs. *Journal of Applied Statistics*, 23, 655–675. doi:10.1080/02664769624008

Marini, E., Autrusseau, F., Callet, P.-L., & Campisi, P. (2007). Evaluation of standard watermarking techniques. In *Proceedings of SPIE, Security, Steganography and Watermarking of Multimedia Contents IX*, San Jose, CA (Vol. 6505).

Marshall, R. (2008). Cloud computing: The dark and stormy side. *TechNewsWorld*. Retrieved December 4, 2008, from http://www.technewsworld.com/rss-story/64831.html

Martinian, E., Yekhanin, S., & Yedidia, J. (2005). Secure biometrics via syndromes. In *Proceedings of the Allerton conference on communications, control, and computing*.

Matam, B. R., & Lowe, D. (2009a). Exploiting sensitivity of nonorthogonal joint diagonalisation as a security mechanism in steganography. In *Proceedings of the Int. Conf. Digital Signal Processing* (pp. 532-538).

Matam, B. R., & Lowe, D. (2009b). Watermarking: How secure is the DM-QIM watermarking technique? In *Proceedings of the Int. Conf. Digital Signal Processing*, (pp. 401-408).

Matic, T., & Laughlin, S. B. (1981). Changes in the intensity-response function of an insect's photoreceptors due to light adaptation. *Journal of Comparative Physiology. A, Neuroethology, Sensory, Neural, and Behavioral Physiology*, 145, 169–177. doi:10.1007/BF00605031

McCarthy, P. (2005). *Forensic Analysis of Mobile Phones*. Retrieved from http://esm.cis.unisa.edu.au/new_esml/resources/publications/forensic%20analysis%20of%20mobile%20phones.pdf

McCarthy, P., & Slay, J. (2006). Mobile phones: admissibility of current forensic procedures for acquiring data. In *Proceedings of the Second IFIP WG 11.9 International Conference on Digital Forensics*.

McCullagh, D. (2006, February 17). Google to feds: Back off. *CNet*. Retrieved from http://news.cnet.com/Google-to-feds-Back-off/2100-1030_3-6041113.html

McGuinness, D. L., & van Harmelen, F. (Eds.). (2004, February 10). *OWL WEB Ontology Language Overview – W3C Recommendation (W3C)*. Retrieved November 16, 2009 from http://www.w3.org/TR/owl-features/

McKay, D. (2002). *Information theory, inference and learning algorithms*. Cambridge, MA: Cambridge University Press.

Microsoft Corporation. (2008a). *Microsoft Office Live*. Retrieved January 5, 2009, from http://office.microsoft.com/en-au/office_live/FX101754491033.aspx?pid=CL101750181033&ofcresset=1

Microsoft Corporation. (2008b). *Office Live Workspace: Frequently asked questions.* Retrieved December 8, 2008, from http://workspace.officelive.com/FAQ#1

Microsoft Corporation. (2008c). *Microsoft Office Live Small Business: Shared online workspace.* Retrieved December 8, 2008, from http://smallbusiness.officelive.com/Manage/WorkSpaces

Microsoft Corporation. (2008d). *Microsoft service agreement.* Retrieved December 4, 2008, from http://help.live.com/help.aspx?mkt=en-au&project=touat

Mihcak, M. K., Kozintsev, I., & Ramchandran, K. (1999). Spatially adaptive statistical modeling of wavelet image coefficients and its application to denoising. In *Proceedings of the IEEE International Conference on Acoustics, Speech and Signal Processing, 2008 (ICASSP 2008)* (Vol. 6, pp. 3253-3256).

Mihcak, M., & Venkatesan, R. (2001). A perceptual audio hashing algorithm: A tool for robust audio identification and information hiding. In *Proceedings of the Information hiding workshop* (Vol. 2137, pp. 51-65).

Mihcak, M. K., Kozintsev, I., & Ramchandran, K. (1999). Spatially Adaptive Statistical Modeling of Wavelet Image Coefficients and its Application to Denoising. In. *Proceedings of the IEEE ICASSP, 6,* 3253–3256.

Mirmehdi, M., & Petrou, M. (2000). Segmentation of color textures. *IEEE Transactions on Pattern Analysis and Machine Intelligence, 22*(2), 142-159. Ng, T.-T., & Chang, S.-F. (2004). A model for image splicing. In *Proceedings of ICIP '04* (Vol. 2, pp. 1169-1172).

MIT Vision and Modeling Group. (n.d.). *VisTeX* (Online). Retrieved May 13, 2009 from http://vismod.media.mit.edu

Mittelholzer, T. (2000). An information-theoretic approach to steganography and watermarking. In *Proceedings of the 3rd international workshop on information hiding (IH'99)*, Dresden, Germany (LNCS 1768, pp. 1-16). Berlin: Springer.

Miyahara, M. (1998). Objective picture quality scale (PQS) for image coding. *IEEE Transactions on Communications, 46*(9), 1215–1226. doi:10.1109/26.718563

Mizoguchi, R., Sunagawa, E., Kozaki, K., & Kitamura, Y. (2007). The Model of Roles Within an Ontology Development tool: Hozo. *Applied Ontology, 2,* 159–179.

Mondaini, N., Caldelli, R., Piva, A., Barni, M., & Cappellini, V. (2007). Detection of malevolent changes in digital video for forensic applications. In E. J. Delp III & P. W. Wong (Eds.), *Security, steganography, and watermarking of multimedia contents IX* (Vol. 6505, 65050T1-65050T12). Bellingham, WA: SPIE Press.

Motion-Video-Products. (2009). *SNR & Dynamic Range, What does it really mean?* San Diego, CA: Motion-Video-Products.

Moulin, P., & O'Sullivan, J. (1999). Information-theoretic analysis of information hiding. *IEEE Transactions on Information Theory, 49,* 563–593. doi:10.1109/TIT.2002.808134

Muhammad, H., Rahman, S., & Shakil, A. (2009). Synonym based Malay linguistic text steganography. In *Proceedings of the Innovative technologies in intelligent systems and industrial applications (CITISIA'09)*, Sunway Campus, Malaysia (pp. 423-427). Washington, DC: IEEE.

Munday, R. (1995). Videotape evidence and the advent of the expert ad hoc. *Justice of the Peace, 159,* 547.

Nabney, I. T. (2002). *Netlab, algorithms for pattern recognition.* New York: Springer.

Nadarajah, S. (2005). A generalized normal distribution. *Journal of Applied Statistics, 32*(7), 685–694. doi:10.1080/02664760500079464

Narkundkar, S., & Priestly, L. (2004). *Assessment of evaluation methods for binary classification modelling.* Paper presented at DSI 2004.

National Institute of Standards and Technology. (2007). *Guidelines on cell phone forensics.* Gaithersburg, MD: National Institute of Standards and Technology. Retrieved from http://csrc.nist.gov/publications/nistpubs/800-101/SP800-101.pdf

National Research Council (NRC). (2009). *Strengthening the forensic sciences in the US: The path forward.* Washington, DC: National Academies Press.

Newville, L. (2001). Cyber crime and the courts – investigating and supervising the information age offender. [Retrieved from http://www.uscourts.gov/library/fpcontents.html]. *Federal Probation, 65.*

Ng, T.-T., Chang, S.-F., & Sun, Q. (2004). Blind detection of photomontage using higher order statistics. In *Proceedings of the 2004 International Symposium on Circuits and Systems (ISCAS '04)* (Vol. 5, pp. 688-691).

Nigrini, M. J. (1999, May). I've got your number. *Journal of Accountancy*.

Nikolaidis, A., & Pitas, I. (2003). Asymptotically optimal detection for additive watermarking in the DCT and DWT domains. *IEEE Transactions on Image Processing, 12*(5), 563–571. doi:10.1109/TIP.2003.810586

Niu, Y. Q., Liu, J. B., Krishnan, S., & Zhang, Q. (2009). Spatio-Temporal Just Noticeable Distortion Model Guided Video Watermarking. In *Proceedings of the 2009 IEEE Pacific-Rim Conference on Multimedia (PCM 2009)*.

Niu, Y. Q., Zhang, Y., Krishnan, S., & Zhang, Q. (2009). A Video-Driven Just Noticeable Distortion Profile for Watermarking. In *Proceedings of the 2009 International Conference on Engineering Management and Service Sciences (EMS 2009)*.

Nordström, K., Barnett, P. D., & O'Carroll, D. C. (2006). Insect detection of small targets moving in visual clutter. *PLoS Biology, 4*(3), 378–386. doi:10.1371/journal.pbio.0040054

NVIDIA. (2008). *What is CUDA*. Retrieved June 2008, from http://www.nvidia.com/object/cuda_what_is.html

Ormerod, D. (2000). Sounds familiar. *Criminal Law Review (London, England)*, 595–623.

Otey, M. (2008). Up in the air over cloud computing. *SQL Magazine, 10*. Retrieved from http://www.sqlmag.com/articles/index.cfm?articleid=100580

Otsu, N. (1979). A threshold selection method from gray level histograms. *IEEE Transactions on Systems, Man, and Cybernetics, 9*.

Pan, X., & Ruan, Q.-Q. (2009). Palmprint recognition using gabor-based local invariant features. *Neurocomput., 72*(7-9), 2040–2045. doi:10.1016/j.neucom.2008.11.019

Parson, T. (1990). *Events in the Semantics of English*. Cambridge, MA: The MIT Press.

Pattanaik, S. N., & Yee, H. (2002). *Adaptive Gain Control For High Dynamic Range Image Display*. Paper presented at the SCCG, Budmerice, Slovakia.

Payne, R., & Howard, J. (1981). Response of an insect photoreceptor: a simple log-normal model. *Nature, 290*(5805), 415–416. doi:10.1038/290415a0

Pérez-Freire, L., & Pérez-González, F. (2007). Exploiting security holes in lattice data hiding. In *Proceedings of the 9th International Workshop on Information Hiding* (pp. 159-173).

Pérez-Freire, L., Pérez-González, F., Furon, T., & Comesaña, P. (2006). Security of lattice-based data hiding against the known message attack. *IEEE Trans. Information Forensics and Security, 1*(4), 421–439. doi:10.1109/TIFS.2006.885029

Perez-Gonzalez, F., Heileman, G. L., & Abdallah, C. T. (2007). Benford's Law in image processing. In. *Proceedings of the IEEE International Conference on Image Processing, 1*, 405–408.

Perona, P., & Malik, J. (1990). Scale-space and edge detection using anisotropic diffusion. *IEEE Transactions on Pattern Analysis and Machine Intelligence, 12*(7), 629–639. doi:10.1109/34.56205

Pixim. (2006). *Digital Pixel System Technology*. Retrieved from http://www.pixim.com/index.html

Podilchuk, C. I., & Zeng, W. (1998). Image-adaptive watermarking using visual models. *Proceedings of the IEEE, 16*, 525–539.

Popescu, A. C., & Farid, H. (2004). *Exposing Digital Forgeries by Detecting Duplicated Image Regions (Tech. Rep.)*. Hanover, NJ: Dartmouth College, Department of Computer Science.

Popescu, A. C., & Farid, H. (2005). Exposing digital forgeries by detecting traces of re-sampling. *IEEE Transactions on Signal Processing, 53*(2), 758–767. doi:10.1109/TSP.2004.839932

Popescu, A. C., & Farid, H. (2005). Exposing digital forgeries in color filter array interpolated images. *IEEE Transactions on Signal Processing, 53*(10), 3948–3959. doi:10.1109/TSP.2005.855406

Porter, G. (2007). Visual culture in forensic science. *The Australian Journal of Forensic Sciences*, *39*, 81–91. doi:10.1080/00450610701650054

Porter, G. (2008). CCTV images as evidence. *The Australian Journal of Forensic Sciences*, *41*, 1–15.

Porter, G., & Doran, G. (2000). An anatomical and photographic technique for forensic facial identification. *Forensic Facial Identification*, *114*, 97–105.

Prasad, S., & Ramakrishnan, K. R. (2006). *On resampling detection and its application to image tampering*. Paper presented at the IEEE International Conference Multimedia and Exposition, Toronto, Canada.

Princeton University (Producer). (2008a, January 14-15). UChannel: Princeton University's Centre for Information Technology Policy. *Computing in the cloud: Panel 1*. Podcast retrieved from http://uc.princeton.edu/main/index.php?option=com_content&task=view&id=2589&Itemid=1

Princeton University (Producer). (2008b, January 14-15). UChannel: Princeton University's Centre for Information Technology Policy. *Computing in the cloud: Panel 2*. Podcast retrieved from http://uc.princeton.edu/main/index.php?option=com_content&task=view&id=2589&Itemid=1

Prud'hommeaux, E., & Seaborne, A. (Eds.). (2008, January 15). *SPARQL Query Language for RDF – W3C Recommendation (W3C)*. Retrieved November 16, 2009 from http://www.w3.org/TR/rdf-sparql-query/

Punja, S., & Mislan, R. (2008). Mobile Device Analysis. *Small scale digital device forensics journal*, *2*(1), 1–16. ISSN 1941-6164

Pustejovsky, J., Ingria, R., Saurí, R., Castaño, J., Littman, J., & Gaizauskas, R. (2005). The Specification Language TimeML. In Mani, I., Pustejovsky, J., & Gaizauskas, R. (Eds.), *The Language of Time: A Reader*. Oxford, UK: Oxford University Press.

Qu, Y.-D., Cui, C.-S., Chen, S.-B., & Li, J.-Q. (2005). A fast subpixel edge detection method using sobel-zernike moments operator. *Image and Vision Computing*, *23*(1), 11–17. Retrieved from http://www.sciencedirect.com/science/article/B6V09-4DH2JHD-4/2/40fc4241382dabeefa9b1576076ae87a. doi:10.1016/j.imavis.2004.07.003

Ranger, S. (2008). Behind the cloud. [Retrieved from http://www.director.co.uk]. *Director (Cincinnati, Ohio)*, *62*.

Reddy, T. (2005). *Murder will out - Irish murder cases*. Park West, Ireland: Gill & Macmillan.

Redmayne, M. (2001). *Expert evidence and criminal justice*. Oxford, UK: Oxford University Press.

Reinhard, E., Stark, M., Shirley, P., & Ferwerda, J. (2002). *Photographic Tone Reproduction for Digital Images*. Paper presented at the ACM Transactions on Graphics (SIGGRAPH), San Antonio, TX.

Ribaric, S., & Fratric, I. (2005). A biometric identification system based on eigenpalm and eigenfinger features. *IEEE Transactions on Pattern Analysis and Machine Intelligence*, *24*, 1698–1709. doi:10.1109/TPAMI.2005.209

Risinger, M., Saks, M., Thompson, W., & Rosenthal, R. (2002). The Daubert/Kumho implications of observer effects in forensic science: Hidden problems of expectation and suggestion. *California Law Review*, *90*, 1–56. doi:10.2307/3481305

Roberts, A. (2008). Drawing on expertise: Legal decision making and the reception of expert evidence. *Criminal Law Review (London, England)*, 443–462.

Rogaway, P., Bellare, M., & Black, J. (2003). OCB: A block-cipher mode of operation for efficient authenticated encryption. *ACM Transactions on Information and System Security*, *6*(3), 365–403. doi:10.1145/937527.937529

Rose, P. (2002). *Forensic speaker identification*. London: Taylor & Francis.

Ryder, J. (2004). Steganography may increase learning everywhere. *Journal of Computing Sciences in Colleges*, *19*(5), 154–162.

Saks, M., & Faigman, D. (2008). Failed forensics: How forensic science lost its way and how it might yet find it. *Annual Review of Law & Social Science*, *4*, 149–171. doi:10.1146/annurev.lawsocsci.4.110707.172303

Saks, M., & Koehler, J. (2005). The coming paradigm shift in forensic identification science. *Science*, *309*, 892–895. doi:10.1126/science.1111565

Saks, M., & Koehler, J. (2008). The individualization fallacy in forensic science evidence. *Vanderbilt Law Review, 61*, 199–219.

Samphaiboon, N. (in press). Steganography via running short text messages. *Multimedia Tools and Applications*.

Sato, K. (2006). Image-Processing Algorithms. In Nakamura, J. (Ed.), *Image Sensors and Signal Processing for Digital Still Cameras* (pp. 223–254). Boca Raton, FL: Taylor & Francis Group.

Schaefer, G., & Stich, M. (2004). UCID - an uncompressed colour image database. In *Proceedings of the SPIE, Storage and Retrieval Methods and Applications for Multimedia* (pp. 472-480).

Scheck, B., Neufeld, P., & Dwyer, J. (2000). *Actual innocence*. New York: Doubleday.

Schütz, A. C., Delipetkos, E., Braun, D. I., Kerzel, D., & Gegenfurtner, K. R. (2007). Temporal contrast sensitivity during smooth pursuit eye movements. *Journal of Vision (Charlottesville, Va.), 7*(13), 1–15. doi:10.1167/7.13.3

Seetzen, H., Heidrich, W., Stuerzlinger, W., Ward, G., Whitehead, L., Trentacoste, M., et al. (2004). *High Dynamic Range Display Systems.* Paper presented at the ACM Transactions on Graphics (Siggraph).

Selesnick, I. (2004). The Double-Density Dual-Tree DWT. *IEEE Transactions on Signal Processing, 52*(5), 1304–1314. doi:10.1109/TSP.2004.826174

Shahda, J. (2007). *Paltalk hosts Al Qaeda, Hizballah and Hamas terror chat rooms.*

Shang, Y., Zhang, J., Guan, Y., Zhang, W., Pan, W., & Liu, H. (2009). Design and evaluation of a high-performance charge coupled device camera for astronomical imaging. *Measurement Science & Technology, 20*, 104002–104009. doi:10.1088/0957-0233/20/10/104002

Shannon, C. (1984). *Royal Commission report concerning the conviction of Edward Charles Splatt.* Adelaide, UK: Government Printer.

Shi, Y. Q., Chen, C., & Chen, W. (2007). A natural image model approach to splicing detection. In *Proceedings of the Workshop on Multimedia & Security '07* (pp. 51-62). New York: ACM.

Shi, J., & Malik, J. (2000). Normalized cuts and image segmentation. *IEEE Transactions on Pattern Analysis and Machine Intelligence, 22*(8), 888–905. doi:10.1109/34.868688

Shirali-Shahreza, M. H., & Shirali-Shahreza, M. (2006). A new approach to Persian/Arabic text steganography. In *Proceedings of the 5th IEEE/ACIS international conference on computer and information science and 1st IEEE/ACIS international workshop on component-based software engineering, software architecture and reuse (ICIS-COMSAR'06)*, Honolulu, HI (pp. 310-315). Washington, DC: IEEE Computer Society.

Shirali-Shahreza, M., & Shirali-Shahreza, M. (2007). Text steganography in SMS. In *Proceedings of the International conference on convergence information technology (IC-CIT'07)*, Gyeongju, Korea (pp. 2260-2265). Washington, DC: IEEE Computer Society.

Siegfried, J., Siedsma, C., Countryman, B. J., & Hosmer, C. D. (2004). Examining the encryption threat. *International Journal of Digital Evidence, 2*(3).

Sorell, M. J. (2008). Digital camera source identification through JPEG quantization. In Li, C.-T. (Ed.), *Multimedia Forensics and Security*. Hershey, PA: IGI Global.

Sorell, M. J. (2009). Conditions for Effective Detection and Identification of Primary Quantisation of Re-Quantized JPEG Images. *International Journal of Digital Crime and Forensics, 1*(2), 13–27.

Su, J. K., Hartung, F., & Girod, B. (1998). Digital watermarking of text, image, and video documents. *Computer Graphics, 22*(6), 687–695. doi:10.1016/S0097-8493(98)00089-2

Sun, X., Luo, G., & Huang, H. (2004). Component-based digital watermarking of Chinese texts. In *Proceedings of the 3rd international conference on information security*, Shanghai, China (pp. 76-81). New York: ACM.

Sutcu, Y., Coskun, B., Sencar, H. T., & Memon, N. (2007). Tamper detection based on regularity of wavelet transform coefficients. In *Proceedings of 2007 IEEE International Conference on Image Processing*, San Antonio, TX.

Swaminathan, A., Mao, Y., & Wu, M. (2006). Robust and secure image hashing. *IEEE Transactions on Information Forensics and security, 1*(2), 215-230.

Swaminathan, A., Wu, M., & Liu, K. (2006). *Image tampering identification using blind deconvolution.* Paper presented at the IEEE International Conference on Image Processing, Atlanta.

Swaminathan, A., Wu, M., & Ray Liu, K. J. (2007). Nonintrusive Component Forensics of Visual Sensors Using Output Images. *IEEE Transactions on Information Forensics and Security, 2*(1), 91–106. doi:10.1109/TIFS.2006.890307

Swaminathan, A., Wu, M., & Ray Liu, K. J. (2008). Digital Image Forensics via Intrinsic Fingerprints. *IEEE Transactions on Information Forensics and Security, 3*(1), 101–117. doi:10.1109/TIFS.2007.916010

Tang, X., & Chen, L. (2009). A Color Video Watermarking Algorithm Based on DTCWT and Motion Estimation. In *Proceedings of the 2009 WRI International Conference on Communications and Mobile Computing (CMC '09)* (Vol. 3, pp. 413-417).

Terzija, N., & Geisselhardt, W. (2004). Digital image watermarking using complex wavelet transform. In *Proceedings of the ACM Multimedia and Security Workshop (MMSEC '04),* Magdeburg, Germany (pp. 193-198). New York: ACM.

The Economist (London). (2008). *The long nimbus.* Retrieved December 4, 2008, from http://www.economist.com/specialreports/

The Office of the Privacy Commissioner. (2001). *Guidelines to the national privacy principles.* Retrieved December 8, 2008, from http://www.privacy.gov.au/publications/

Tian-Tsong, N., Shih-Fu, C., Jessie, H., Lexing, X., & Mao-Pei, T. (2005). *Physics-motivated features for distinguishing photographic images and computer graphics.* Paper presented at the 13th Annual ACM International Conference on Multimedia, New York.

Topkara, M., Taskiran, C. M., & Delp, E. J. (2005). Natural language watermarking. In *Proceedings of SPIE-IS & T electronic imaging 2005,* San Jose, CA (pp. 441-452). Washington, DC: SPIE.

Torricelli, G., Argenti, F., & Alparone, L. (2002). Modelling and assessment of signal-dependent noise for image de-noising. In *Proceedings of the EUSIPCO* (pp. 287-290).

Tourancheau, S., Callet, P. L., & Barba, D. (2007). Influence of motion on contrast perception: supra-threshold spatio-velocity measurements. In *Proceedings of SPIE* (Vol. 6492).

van Hateren, J. H. (1992). A theory of maximizing sensory information. *Biological Cybernetics, 68,* 68–70.

van Hateren, J. H., & Snippe, H. P. (2001). Information Theoretical Evaluation of Parametric Models of Gain Control in Blowfly Photoreceptor Cells. *Vision Research, 41,* 1851–1865. doi:10.1016/S0042-6989(01)00052-9

W3C OWL Working Group. (2009, October 27). *OWL 2 Web Ontology Language, Document Overview – W3C Recommendation (W3C).* Retrieved November 16, 2009 from http://www.w3.org/TR/2009/REC-owl2-overview-20091027/

Wang, J., Gao, X., & Zhong, J. (2007). A video watermarking based on 3-D complex wavelet. In *Proceedings of the IEEE International Conference on Image Processing (ICIP '07),* San Antonio, TX (Vol. 5, pp. 493-496). Washington, DC: IEEE.

Watson, A. B. (1993). *DCTune: A technique for visual optimization of DCT quantization matrices for individual images* (pp. 946–949). Soc. Information Display Dig. Tech. Papers XXIV.

Wei, Z., & Ngan, K. N. (2008a). A temporal just-noticeble distortion profile for video in DCT domain. In *Proceedings of the 15th IEEE International Conference on Image Processing* (pp. 1336-1339).

Wei, Z., & Ngan, K. N. (2008b). Spatial Just Noticeable Distortion Profile for Image in DCT Domain. In *Proceedings of IEEE International Conference on Multimedia and Expo* (pp. 925-928).

Wells, G., & Quinlivan, D. (2009). Suggestive eyewitness identification procedures and the Supreme Court's reliability test in light of eyewitness science: 30 years later. *Law and Human Behavior, 33,* 1–24. doi:10.1007/s10979-008-9130-3

Willassen, S. Y. (2003). Forensics and the GSM mobile telephone system. *International Journal of Digital Evidence, 2*(1), 12–24.

Wolfgang, R. B., Podilchuk, C. I., & Delp, E. J. (1999). Perceptual watermarks for digital images and video. In *Proceedings IEEE, Special Issue on Identification and Protection of Multimedia Information* (Vol. 87, pp. 1108-1126).

Woo, C., Du, J., & Pham, B. (2006). Geometric invariant domain for image watermarking. In *Proceedings of the International Workshop on Digital Watermarking (IWDW '06),* South, Korea (LNCS 4283, pp. 294-307). New York: Springer.

Woon, W. L., & Lowe, D. (2001). Nonlinear signal processing for noise reduction of unaveraged single channel MEG data. In *Proceedings of the International Conference on Artificial Neural Networks* (pp. 650-657).

Wu, X., Zhang, D., & Wang, K. (2003). Fisherpalms based palmprint recognition. *Pattern Recognition Letters,* *24*(15), 2829–2838. doi:10.1016/S0167-8655(03)00141-7

Yamada, T. (2006). Image Sensors. In Nakamura, J. (Ed.), *Image Sensors and Signal Processing for Digital Still Cameras* (pp. 95–142). Boca Raton, FL: Taylor & Francis Group.

Yang, C. C., Chen, H., Chau, M., Chang, K., Lang, S.-D., Chen, P. S., et al. (Eds.). (2008). In *Proceedings of the IEEE Intelligence and Security Informatics International Workshops (PAISI, PACCF, and SOCO 2008)* (LNCS 5075). Berlin: Springer-Verlag.

Yu, G. J., Lu, C. S., Liao, H. Y. M., & Sheu, J. P. (2000). Mean quantization blind watermarking for image authentication. In. *Proceedings of the IEEE International Conference on Image Processing, 3,* 706–709.

Yuling, L., Xingming, S., Can, G., & Hong, W. (2007). An efficient linguistic steganography for Chinese text. In *Proceedings of the IEEE international conference on multimedia and expo (ICME'07),* Beijing, China (pp. 2094-2097). Washington, DC: IEEE.

Zarri, G. P. (2005b). An *n*-ary Language for Representing Narrative Information on the Web. In *Proceedings of the Semantic Web Applications and Perspectives (SWAP 2005) the 2nd Italian Semantic Web Workshop* (Vol. 166). Aachen, Germany: Sun SITE Central Europe. Retrieved November 16, 2009 from http://ftp1.de.freebsd.org/Publications/CEUR-WS/Vol-166/63.pdf

Zarri, G. P. (1998). Representation of Temporal Knowledge in Events: The Formalism, and Its Potential for Legal Narratives. *Information & Communications Technology Law – Special Issue on Models of Time. Action, and Situations, 7,* 213–241.

Zarri, G. P. (2003). A Conceptual Model for Representing Narratives. In *Innovations in Knowledge Engineering.* Adelaide, Australia: Advanced Knowledge International.

Zarri, G. P. (2005a). Integrating the Two Main Inference Modes of NKRL, Transformations and Hypotheses. [JoDS]. *Journal on Data Semantics, 4,* 304–340.

Zarri, G. P. (2009). *Representation and Management of Narrative Information – Theoretical Principles and Implementation.* London: Springer. doi:10.1007/978-1-84800-078-0

Zhang, D. (2004). *Polyu palmprint database.* Retrieved from http://www.comp.polyu.edu.hk/ biometrics/

Zhang, W., Zeng, Z., Pu, G., & Zhu, H. (2006). Chinese text watermarking based on occlusive components. In *Proceedings of the 2nd IEEE international conference on information and communication technologies: from theory to applications (ICTTA '06)*, Damascus, Syria (pp. 1850-1854). Washington, DC: IEEE.

Zhang, Z., Kang, J., & Ren, Y. (2008). *An effective algorithm of image splicing detection.* Paper presented at the International Conference on Computer Science and Software Engineering (CSSE 2008), Wuhan, Hubei, China.

Zhang, D., Kong, W.-K., You, J., & Wong, M. (2003). Online palmprint identification. *IEEE Transactions on Pattern Analysis and Machine Intelligence, 25*(9), 1041–1050. doi:10.1109/TPAMI.2003.1227981

Zhang, X. K., Lin, W. S., & Xue, P. (2005). Improved estimation for just-noticeable visual distortion. *Signal Processing, 85*(4), 795–808. doi:10.1016/j.sigpro.2004.12.002

Zhang, Z., Kang, J., & Ren, Y. (2008). An effective algorithm of image splic- ing detection. In. *Proceedings of the International Conference on Computer Science and Software Engineering, 1,* 1035–1039.

Zhao, X., Ho, A. T. S., & Shi, Y. Q. (2009). Image Forensics using Generalized Benford's Law for Accurate Detection of Unknown JPEG Compression in Watermarked Images. In *Proceedings of the 16th International Conference on Digital Signal Processing (DSP2009)* (pp. 1-8).

Zhao, Z.-Q., Huang, D.-S., & Jia, W. (2007). Palmprint recognition with 2DPCA+PCA based on modular neural networks. *Neurocomput.*, *71*(1-3), 448–454. doi:10.1016/j.neucom.2007.07.010

Zhen, Z., Yukun, B., & Xijian, P. (2008). *Image blind forensics using artificial neural network.* Paper presented at the 2008 International Conference on Computer Science and Software Engineering (CSSE 2008), Piscataway, NJ.

Zhu, Y., Li, C. T., & Zhao, H. J. (2007b). Structural digital signature and semi-fragile fingerprinting for image authentication in wavelet domain. *In Proceedings of the Third International Symposium on Information Assurance and Security* (pp. 478-483).

Zhuang, L., & Jiang, M. (2006). Multipurpose digital watermarking algorithm based on dual-tree CWT. In *Proceedings of the 6th International Conference on Intelligent Systems, Design and Applications (ISDA '06)* (Vol. 2, pp. 316-320).

Zhu, X. Z., Ho, A. T. S., & Marziliano, P. (2007a). A new semi-fragile image watermarking with robust tampering restoration using irregular sampling. *Elsevier Signal Processing: Image Communication, 22*(5), 515–528. doi:10.1016/j.image.2007.03.004

Ziou, D., & Tabbone, S. (1998). Edge Detection Techniques-An Overview. *Pattern Recognition & Image Analysis, 8*, 537-559. Retrieved from http://hal.inria.fr/inria-00098446/en/

Zollner, J., Federrath, H., Klimant, H., Pfitzmann, A., Piotraschke, R., Westfeld, A., et al. (1998). Modeling the security of steganographic systems. In *Proceedings of the 2nd international workshop on information hiding,* Portland, OR (LNCS 1525, pp. 344-354). New York: Springer.

Zou, F. h. (2006). *Research of Robust Video Watermarking Algorithms and Related Techniques.* Unpublished doctoral dissertation, Hua zhong University of Science & Technology, China.

Zou, D., Shi, Y. Q., Ni, Z., & Su, W. (2006). A semi-fragile lossless digital watermarking scheme based on Integer Wavelet Transform. *IEEE Trans. Circuits and Systems for Video Technology, 16*(10), 1294–1300. doi:10.1109/TCSVT.2006.881857

About the Contributors

Chang-Tsun Li received the B.S. degree in electrical engineering from Chung-Cheng Institute of Technology (CCIT), National Defense University, Taiwan, in 1987, the M.S. degree in computer science from U. S. Naval Postgraduate School, USA, in 1992, and the Ph.D. degree in computer science from the University of Warwick, UK, in 1998. He was an associate professor of the Department of Electrical Engineering at CCIT during 1999-2002 and a visiting professor of the Department of Computer Science at U.S. Naval Postgraduate School in the second half of 2001. He is currently an associate professor of the Department of Computer Science at the University of Warwick, UK, Editor-in-Chief of the International Journal of Digital Crime and Forensics (IJDCF)and Associate Editor of the International Journal of Applied Systemic Studies (IJASS). He has involved in the organisation of a number of international conferences and workshops and also served as member of the international program committees for several international conferences. His research interests include multimedia forensics and security, bioinformatics, image processing, pattern recognition, computer vision and content-based image retrieval.

Anthony TS Ho joined the Department of Computing, Faculty of Engineering and Physical Sciences at University of Surrey (UK) in 2006. He holds the Personal Chair in multimedia security and is currently Deputy Head of the department. He leads the Watermarking and Multimedia Security Group, one of the largest research groups in the UK specializing in watermarking, steganography/steganalysis, and image forensics. Professor Ho obtained his MSc in applied optics from Imperial College London (1980) and PhD in digital image processing from King's College, University of London (1983). He has published more than 100 articles in international journals and conference proceedings, as well as eight patents granted related to digital watermarking and steganography. He is a Fellow of the Institution of Engineering and Technology (FIET), a Chartered Electrical Engineer (CEng), a Fellow of the Institute of Physics (FInstP), Chartered Physicist (CPhys), and a Senior Member of IEEE. In 2006, he was the recipient of the prestigious IET innovation in Engineering Award for his research and commercialization work on digital watermarking. He has actively participated in numerous IEEE and IET professional and conference activities over the past two decades. Professor Ho was the General Chair for the 8th International Workshop on Digital Watermarking (IWDW09) hosted by the University of Surrey (August 2009). He serves as an Editorial Board member on the International Journal of Multimedia Intelligence and Security and Co-Editor-in-Chief of the International Journal of Digital Crime and Forensics. Professor Ho is also co-Editor of two Springer Proceedings, LNCS 5450 and LNCS 5703 on Digital Watermarking for IWDW'08 and IWDW'09, respectively.

* * *

Irene Amerini received the laurea degree in Computer Engineering from the University of Florence in 2006. Now she's a PhD student at University of Florence and she's working at the Image and Communication Lab at the Media Integration and Communication Center (MICC), University of Florence. Her research interests are mainly focused on Digital and Multimedia Forensics.

Ahmed Bouridane received the "Ingenieur d'Etat" degree in electronics from "Ecole Nationale Polytechnque" of Algiers (ENPA), Algeria, in 1982, the M.Phil. degree in electrical engineering (VLSI design for signal processing) from the University of Newcastle-Upon-Tyne, U.K., in 1988, and the Ph.D. degree in electrical engineering (computer vision) from the University of Nottingham, U.K., in 1992. From 1992 to 1994, he worked as a Research Developer in telesurveillance and access control applications. In 1994, he joined Queen's University Belfast, Belfast, U.K., initially as Lecturer in computer architecture and image processing and later on he was promoted to Reader in Computer Science. He is now a full Professor in Image Engineering and Security at Northumbria University at Newcastle (UK), and his research interests are in imaging for forensics and security, biometrics, homeland security, image/video watermarking and cryptography. He has authored and co-authored more than 200 publications and one research book. Prof. Bouridane is a Senior Member of IEEE.

Roberto Caldelli, graduated cum laude in Electronic Engineering from the University of Florence, in 1997, where he also received the Ph.D degree in Computer Science and Telecommunications Engineering in 2001. He received a 4-years research grant (2001-2005) from the University of Florence to research on digital watermarking techniques for protection of images and videos. He is an Assistant Professor at the Media Integration and Communication Center of the University of Florence. He is a member of CNIT. His main research activities, witnessed by several publications, include digital image sequence processing, image and video digital watermarking, multimedia applications, MPEG-1/2/4, multimedia forensics.

Vito Cappellini obtained the degree in Electronic Engineering from the Politecnico di Torino. After some activity in the industry and research activity at National Research Council Institute in Florence, in 1975 he obtained the Full Professor degree in Electrical Communications at Florence University. He was Dean of the Engineering Faculty (1993-1995). He was also Director of the IFAC CNR Research Centre "Nello Carrara" in Florence. His main research interests are: digital signal-image processing, digital communications, remote sensing, multimedia systems, art-work analysis-restoration and IPR protection (watermarking). He has published over 350 papers in the above fields and contributed to several books. He was Director of the "UFFIZI Project". He is Head of the Laboratory "Image and Communications" at Deparment of Electronics and Telecommunications. He is Vice-Director of the Excellence Centre for Communication and Media Integration. He received in 1984 the "IEEE Centennial Medal". He is "fellow" of the IEEE, member of EURASIP, AEI, and AIT.

Joe Carthy is a Senior Lecturer and Head of School at UCD CSI. He is Co-director of a research group of 18 postgraduate students and has graduated 7 PhD and 18 MSc students. He is the author/co-author of 70 scientific papers and a textbook on Computer Architecture. He is currently supervising 8 PhD students and 3 MSc students in Computer Security and Information Retrieval.

Stephen Cassidy is a student at the University of Ulster studying IT. He is currently working in his placement year for a large software house. His interests include ubiquitous computing and programming.

H.R. Chennamma received her graduate degree in Computer Applications with distinction in the year 2003, Vishwesharaiah Technological University, India. She was a Project Trainee for a year at the National Aerospace Laboratory (NAL), Bangalore, India. She served as a software engineer for a year in a multinational software company, Bangalore, India. Mrs. Chennamma is now a Senior Research Fellow (SRF) in National Computer Forensic Laboratory, Ministry of Home Affairs, Government of India, Hyderabad since 2005. Subsequently, she was awarded Ph.D. program fellowship at the Department of Computer Science, University of Mysore in the year 2006. Mrs. Chennamma is the recipient of "Best Scientific Paper Award" in the All India Forensic Science Conference, Kolkata, India in the year 2007. Her current research interests are Image Forensics, Pattern Recognition and Image Retrieval.

Kevin Curran BSc (Hons), PhD, SMIEEE, FBCS CITP, SMACM, FHEA is a senior lecturer in Computer Science at the University of Ulster and group leader for the Ambient Intelligence Research Group. His achievements include winning and managing UK & European Framework projects and Technology Transfer Schemes. Dr Curran has made significant contributions to advancing the knowledge and understanding of computer networking and systems, evidenced by over 450 published works. He is a regular contributor to BBC radio & TV news in the UK and is currently the recipient of an Engineering and Technology Board Visiting Lectureship for Exceptional Engineers and is an IEEE Technical Expert for Internet/Security matters. He is listed in the Dictionary of International Biography, Marquis Who's Who in Science and Engineering and by Who's Who in the World. He is a fellow of the British Computer Society (FBCS), a senior member of the ACM (SMACM), a senior member of the IEEE (SMIEEE) and a fellow of the higher education academy (FHEA).

Matthew N. Dailey received the B.S. and M.S. in Computer Science from North Carolina State University and the Ph.D. in Computer Science and Cognitive Science from the University of California, San Diego, USA. He spent two years as a Research Scientist with Vision Robotics Corporation of San Diego, CA USA and two years as a Lecturer in the Computer Science and Information Technology programs at Sirindhorn International Institute of Technology (SIIT), Thammasat University, Thailand. His research interests lie in machine learning, machine vision, robotics, and systems security. Dr. Dailey joined the Computer Science and Information Management department at the Asian Institute of Technology (AIT), Thailand, as an Assistant Professor, in 2006.

Michael Davis is a partner of Adelta Legal, a boutique Australian commercial law firm, having practised law in Australia for 35 years. His legal expertise includes technology commercialisation, intellectual property law, contracts and licensing, corporate structuring and finance, regulatory compliance, employment law and risk management. He has wide experience in advising clients in the information and communications technology sector. Michael has a strong interest in the international space industry. He has a Masters Degree from the International Space University in Strasbourg, France and is a part time Faculty member, teaching space policy and law. Michael is an active pro bono contributor to a number of industry and educational organisations and for 14 years was Chair of the Advisory Board to the Institute for Telecommunications Research of the University of South Australia.

Gary Edmond is Associate Professor and Director of the Expertise, Evidence & Law Program, School of Law, at the University of New South Wales. He specialises in the study of expert evidence and the relations between law and science. Originally trained in the history and philosophy of science, he subsequently studied law at the Universities of Sydney and Cambridge. An active commentator on expert evidence in Australia, England, and the United States, he is a member of the Society for the Social Study of Science (US), a reviewer for the National Science Foundation (US), and recently served as an adviser to the Goudge Inquiry into Pediatric Forensic Pathology in Ontario. He is currently involved in a collaborative multidisciplinary project on expert identification evidence with other lawyers, psychologists and forensic scientists, and an empirical study of expert evidence in the courts of New South Wales sponsored by the Australian Research Council. Correspondence to: School of Law, University of New South Wales, Sydney 2052, Australia.

Pavel Gladyshev is a College lecturer at UCD CSI. His research interests are in the area of Information Security and Digital Forensics. Dr. Gladyshev is working on Mathematical Theory of Digital Forensics and its applications to investigations of cybercrimes. Before joining UCD, he worked as a senior consultant in Information Systems Security and Forensics at the Dublin practice of Ernst & Young. Dr. Gladyshev is the programme director for UCD's GDip/MSc programme in Forensic Computing and Cybercrime Investigation.

Sridhar (Sri) Krishnan received the B.E. degree in Electronics and Communication Engineering from Anna University, Madras, India, in 1993, and the M.Sc. and Ph.D. degrees in Electrical and Computer Engineering from the University of Calgary, Calgary, Alberta, Canada, in 1996 and 1999 respectively. He joined the Department of Electrical and Computer Engineering, Ryerson University, Toronto, Ontario, Canada in July 1999, and currently he is a Professor and a Canada Research Chair. Sri Krishnan is also a recipient of the 2007 Young Engineer Achievement Award from Engineers' Canada.

Fatih Kurugollu received the B.Sc., M.Sc., and Ph.D. degrees in computer engineering from Istanbul Technical University, Istanbul, Turkey in 1989, 1994, and 2000, respectively. From 1991 to 2000, he was a Research Fellow in Marmara Research Center, Kocaeli, Turkey. In 2000, he joined the School of Computer Science, Queen's University, Belfast, U.K., as a Postdoctoral Research Assistant. He was appointed Lecturer in the same department in 2003. His research interest includes multimedia security, biometrics, soft computing for image and video segmentation, visual surveillance, and hardware architectures for image and video applications. Dr. Kurugollu is a Senior Member of IEEE.

Roland Kwitt received his Master degree in Computer Sciences from the University of Salzburg (Austria) in March 2007. He further holds a Master degree in Telecommunication Systems Engineering from the University of Applied Sciences in Salzburg. He is currently working on his PhD thesis in the field of medical image classification. His research interests include Image Analysis, Medical Image Processing, Statistical Pattern Recognition, Image Retrieval and Multimedia Security.

Moussadek Laadjel received the "Ingenieur d'Etat" degree in Electronics from the University of Guelma, Algeria in 2003. In September 2006, he joined the Queens University of Belfast, Belfast, UK, as a research student and received the PhD degree from the School of Computer Science in 2009. From

2003 to 2006, he was a research scientist at the Algerian National Centre for Research and Development. He is currently holding a senior research position at the Algerian National Centre for Research and Development, Algeria. His research interests include palmprint, fingerprint and face recognition, image enhancement, image watermarking and information theory.

Raymond Lau received his BSc. degree in computer science from Queen's University Belfast, UK, in 2009. His research interests are secure imaging and digital image recovery.

Qiming Li is a Research Fellow with the Cryptography and Security Department, Institute for Infocomm Research, Singapore. He obtained his Ph.D. in Computer Science and B.Eng. from National University of Singapore in 2006 and 2001 respectively. He was a Research Fellow in the Department of Computer and Information Science, Polytechnic University from 2006 to 2007, and a Research Assistant in Department of Computer Engineering, Chinese University of Hong Kong, in 2005. His research interests include cryptography, multimedia security and forensics and biometrics security.

Hefei Ling received the B.E. and M.S. degree in energy and power engineering from Huazhong University of Science and Technology (HUST), Wuhan, China, in 1999 and 2002 respectively, and the Ph.D. degree in computer science from HUST in 2005. Since 2006, he has been an associate professor with the college of computer science and technology, HUST. From 2008 to 2009, he joined in the department of computer science, University College London (UCL) as a visiting professor. His research interests include digital watermarking and fingerprinting, copy detection, content security and protection. Dr. Ling has co-authored over 50 publications including book chapters, journal and conference papers. He received Excellent Ph.D. dissertation of HUST in 2006 and Foundation Research Contribution Award of HUST in 2005, the best graduate award from HUST, Wuhan, China in 1999.

Jin Liu received the B.E. degree in computer science and M.S. degree in software engineering from Huazhong University of Science and Technology (HUST), Wuhan, Hubei, China, in 2002 and 2006 respectively, and currently pursuing the Ph.D. degree in computer science, HUST. Her research interests include digital image forensics and digital right management.

David Lowe has a background and PhD in theoretical physics, and worked in the UK Defence sector before moving into academia, joining Aston University in 1993 to a Chair in Neural Networks. He has worked in problems of brain state characterisation from EEG and MEG signals, modelling visualisation of temporal sequences of DNA microarrays, financial data analysis, information hiding in digital media, and emergent behaviour in nonlinear coupled MEMS sensor arrays. He is currently investigating Complexity as a guiding principle in a new design philosophy of novel sensor arrays, especially in coupled nonlinear oscillators in microelectromechanical systems (MEMS). He is perhaps best known for being the co-inventor of the Radial Basis Function neural network - one of the most popular artificial neural network architectures in use worldwide, and co-inventor of the NeuroScale architecture for high dimensional topographic data visualisation. He has consulted for various large and small commercial companies in Defence, Finance, Automotive, Biomedical and Paper manufacturing industries. He has been an International Reviewer for the Australian DSTO programme in Data Fusion, and has served on several UK national panels on topics such as "The Future of Computing", "Data Fusion" and academic review panels and is on the Advisory Board of the Leverhulme Trust. He has been a member of the committees of several international conferences at the interface of mathematics, computing, engineering and the medical life sciences.

Zhengding Lu was born in 1944, he is currently a Professor, Ph.D. tutor and Director of the School of Computer Science and Technology at Huazhong University of Science and Technology. His research interests are distributed system and software, and Internet/Intranet. He has published over 160 technical papers and is the author of 9 books.

Milton H. Luoma, Jr. is an Assistant Professor in the Information and Computer Sciences Department and Director of the Computer Forensics program at Metropolitan State University in St. Paul, Minnesota. He holds the degrees of Juris Doctor, M.S. in Computer Science, M.B.A., M.S. in Engineering, and B.S. in Engineering. He has practiced law and worked as a business and legal consultant in Minnesota for over 25 years. He has designed and developed an active learning approach for computer forensics programs. He is a frequent speaker at business and legal conferences including the Computer Security Institute and has been the keynote speaker at several conferences and business organizations. He also holds computer forensics certifications from NTI and Oregon State University.

Vicki Luoma is currently an Associate Professor in the College of Business at Minnesota State University, Mankato. She practiced law and worked as a business and tax consultant for over 25 years while teaching part time. She holds a Juris Doctor degree and is a licensed attorney in Minnesota. She has been a frequent speaker at various conferences including the Computer Security Institute conferences. She is also a business and legal consultant to various organizations and has been a keynote speaker at several conferences. She is a researcher, writer, and published author in the field business law, electronic discovery, and business ethics.

B.R. Matam has received a M.Tech from Mangalore University, India in Digital Electronics and Advanced Communication in 1999. She has worked as a lecturer in one of the leading colleges in Karnataka, India before joining Aston University in 2005 to study towards a PhD. She has recently completed her PhD in Watermarking Biomedical Data under the supervision of Professor David Lowe.

Niall McGrath is a part-time PhD student in UCD and works fulltime in Bank of Ireland. He worked as a senior software developer on many of the Bank's online applications. He recently has joined the IT Security team of which he is a member of the forensic investigations teams.

Peter Meerwald received his Master degree in Computer Sciences from Bowling Green State University (Ohio, USA) in 1999 and University Salzburg in 2001 (Austria). He is currently working on his PhD thesis in the field of image and video watermarking. His research interests include multimedia security, watermarking, and scalable image and video coding.

Ya Qing Niu (Andrea) is lecturer from Communication University of China. Her research area focuses on content based watermarking for video signals. She received the B.E. and M.Sc. degrees in Communication and Information System from Beijing Broadcasting Institute, Beijing, China. She is currently lecturer and Ph.D. candidate in Information Engineering School, Communication University of China, Beijing, China. Ya Qing Niu is awarded the state administration of radio film and television honor for scientific research achievement and teaching courseware in 2005 and honor of outstanding graduate of Beijing in 2000.

Stephen Peacocke is an under-graduate student in Computer Science of the University of Ulster. His research interests include distributed systems, multimedia and Internet Technologies.

Francesco Picchioni received from the University of Florence, Italy , the M.Sc. degree (Laurea) in Telecommunications engineering in 2004. He received a 2-years research grant (2004-2006) from the University of Florence to research on Analysis of Spectral/Spatial characteristics and information extraction from Remote Sensing High-Dimensional Image Data. From January 2007 he is with the Media Integration and Communication Center (MICC), University of Florence as Assistant Researcher. His main research activities includes digital forensic and unmixing of hyperspectral remote sensing images.

Alessandro Piva graduated cum laude in Electronic Engineering from University of Florence on 1995. He obtained the Ph. D. degree in "Computer Science and Telecommunications Engineering" from the University of Florence on 1999. From 2002 until 2004 he was Research Scientist at the National Inter-University Consortium for Telecommunications. He is at present Assistant Professor at the University of Florence. His current research interests are the technologies for Multimedia content security, and image processing techniques for Cultural Heritage field. He is co-author of more than 100 papers published in international journals and conference proceedings. He holds 3 Italian patents and an International one regarding watermarking. He is Person responsible for University of Florence of the European Project SPEED. He is Associate Editor of the IEEE Transactions on Information Forensics and Security.

Lalitha Rangarajan has to her credit two graduate degrees, one in Mathematics from University of Madras, India (1980) and the other in Industrial Engineering (Specialization: Operational Research) from Pardue University, USA during (1988). She has taught Mathematics briefly at graduate level, for 5 years during 1980 to 1985 in India. She joined Department of Computer Science, University of Mysore, to teach graduate students of the Department, in 1988, where she is currently working as a Reader. She completed Ph.D. in Computer Science in the area of pattern recognition in 2004. She is presently working in the areas of Feature Reduction, Image Retrieval and Bioinformatics.

Andrew Robinson is an under-graduate student in Computer Science of the University of Ulster. He is presently working in the Northern Ireland Telecommunications industry on placement and his research interests include security and Internet Technologies.

Sujoy Roy is a research fellow in the Computer Vision and Image Understanding (CVIU) department of the Institute for Infocomm Research, Singapore. He completed his PhD in computer science from the National University of Singapore and his MS from the Indian Institute of Technology, Delhi in the year 2006 and 2001 respectively. His research interests are in the field of multimedia security and forensics, media understanding and knowledge discovery in large multimedia archives.

Natthawut Samphaiboon received the B.E. in Computer Engineering and M.E. in Science and Engineering on Mathematics and Computer Science from The National Defense Academy (NDA), Japan. Currently, he is a Ph.D. student at Asian Institute of Technology (AIT), Thailand. His research interests are information security, steganography, cryptography, and pattern recognition. Sqn.Ldr. Samphaiboon is an officer and a researcher of The Royal Thai Air Force, and a member of The Institute of Electronics, Information and Communication Engineers (IEICE), JAPAN.

Alice Sedsman originally studied journalism before turning to law in 2005. She graduated from Flinders University with an Honours Degree in Laws and Legal Practice in mid 2009. She is also a graduate of the Mobile Enterprise Growth Alliance incubator program. Alice is the most recent solicitor to join Adelta Legal. She provides support and assistance to the four partners and the senior associate of the firm. Alice provides services to clients in a broad range of matters including contracts and licensing, corporations and telecommunications law. Alice has a particular interest in technology commercialisation and is a member of the South Australian chapter of the Australian Interactive Media Industry Association.

Yun Qing Shi has joined the Department of Electrical and Computer Engineering at the New Jersey Institute of Technology (NJIT), Newark, NJ since 1987, and is currently a professor there. He obtained his B.S.degree and M.S.degree from the Shanghai Jiao Tong University, Shanghai, China; his M.S. and Ph.D. degrees from the University of Pittsburgh, PA. His research interests include visual signal processing and communications (motion analysis, video compression and transmission), multimedia data hiding and security (robust watermarking, fragile- and semi-fragile lossless data hiding, authentication, steganalysis, and data forensics), applications of digital image processing, computer vision and pattern recognition to industrial automation and biomedical engineering, theory of multidimensional systems and signal processing (robust stability of linear systems, 2-D spectral factorization, 2-D/3-D interleaving). He is the chairman of Signal Processing Chapter of IEEE North Jersey Section; the founding editor-in-chief of *LNCS Transactions on Data Hiding and Multimedia Security* (Springer), an editorial board member of *International Journal of Image and Graphics* (World Scientific) and Journal on *Multidimensional Systems and Signal Processing* (Springer), a member of IEEE Circuits and Systems Society (CASS)'s Technical Committee of Visual Signal Processing and Communications, Technical Committee of Multimedia Systems and Applications, and Technical Committee of Life Science, Systems and Applications; a member of IEEE Signal Processing Society's Technical Committee of Multimedia Signal Processing; the chair of Technical Program Committee of IEEE International Conference on Multimedia and Expo 2007 (ICME07), the chair of Technical Program Committee of International Workshop on Digital Watermarking 2007 (IWDW07), a fellow of IEEE. He also served as an Associate Editor of IEEE Transactions on Signal Processing, IEEE Transactions on Circuits and Systems Part II.

Matthew Sorell is Senior Lecturer in telecommunications and multimedia engineering in the School of Electrical and Electronic Engineering at the University of Adelaide, South Australia. He is general chair of e-Forensics - the International Conference on Forensic Applications and Techniques in Telecommunications, Information and Multimedia; an Associate Editor of the International Journal on Digital Crime and Forensics, and a recent Short-Term Visiting Fellow at the University of Warwick. His research interests include a range of commercially relevant telecommunications topics, public policy relating to regulation of multimedia entertainment, and forensic investigative techniques in multimedia. He holds a BSc in Physics, a BE in Computer Systems (with first class honours) and a Graduate Certificate in Management from the University of Adelaide, and a PhD in Information Technology from George Mason University (Virginia, USA).

Andreas Uhl is an associate professor at the Department of Computer Sciences (University of Salzburg, Austria) where he leads the Multimedia Processing and Security Lab. His research interests include image and video processing and compression, wavelets, media security, medical imaging, biometrics, and number-theoretical numerics.

Jonathan Weir received his BSc. degree in computer science from Queen's University Belfast, UK, in 2008. He is currently pursuing his Ph.D. degree in computer science at Queen's University Belfast, UK. His research interests are visual cryptography, digital imagery and image processing.

WeiQi Yan received his Ph.D. degree in computer engineering from Academia Sinica, China, in 2001. He has been a lecturer at Queen's University Belfast, UK since September 2007. His current research interests are multimedia security and forensics. Dr. Yan has co-authored nearly 80 publications. He is serving as an associate editor of the Journal of Multimedia, associate editor of International Journal of Digital Crime Forensics and is also a guest editor of the Springer transactions on data hiding and multimedia security. Dr. Yan is a Senior Member of IEEE.

Qin Zhang was born in Beijing, China in 1957. He received the Bachelor degree from the Tianjin University, Tianjin, China, the master degree from Beijing Broadcasting Institute, Beijing and the Ph.D from the University of British Columbia, Canada, all in electrical engineering. His research interests lie in real-time digital image processing, digital signal processing and their applications in CATV system.

Xi Zhao received a BSc and a MSc in information systems from the University of Greenwich and the University of Surrey in 2002 and 2003, respectively. He is currently studying toward a PhD in the Department of Computing, Faculty of Engineering and Physical Sciences, University of Surrey. His research interests include digital watermarking, data hiding and digital forensics.

Fuhao Zou received B.S. in computer science from Huazhong Normal University, Wuhan, China in 1998, and the Ph.D. in computer science from Huazhong University of Science and Technology (HUST), Wuhan, China, in 2006. Currently, he is a Lecture with the college of computer science and technology, HUST. His research interests include digital watermarking, digital right management and copy detection.

Index